Drawing to See

Nathan Goldstein
Harriet J. Fishman

*The Art Institute of Boston
at Lesley University*

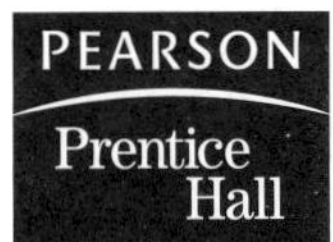

Upper Saddle River, New Jersey 07458

Library of Congress Cataloging-in-Publication Data

Goldstein, Nathan
Drawing to see/Nathan Goldstein, Harriet J. Fishman.—1st ed.
p. cm.
Includes index.
ISBN 0-13-098178-8
1. Drawing—Technique. 2. Visual perception. I. Title.
NC730.G61723 2005
741.2—dc22

2004044714

Editor-in-Chief: Sarah Touborg
Publisher: Bud Therien
Acquisitions Editor: Amber Mackey
Editorial Assistant: Keri Molinari
Production Editor: Jean Lapidus
Copy Editor: Stephen C. Hopkins
Prepress & Manufacturing Buyer: Sherry Lewis
Photo Researcher: Francelle Carapetyan
Image Permission Coordinator: LaShonda Morris
Electronic Artist: Maria Piper
Marketing Manager: Sheryl Adams
Marketing Assistant: Cherron Gardner
Cover Design: Kiwi Design
Cover Art: Jean Antoine Watteau (French, 1684-1721), *Two Shells*.
Drawing, 28.2 × 22 cm. Photographer: Michele Bellot. Louvre, Paris, France.
Art Resource/Reunion des Musées Nationaux.
Composition: Preparé, Inc.
Printer/Binder: Courier Companies, Inc./Stoughton
Color Insert Printer: Lehigh Press
Cover Printer: Lehigh Press

Pearson Education LTD.
Pearson Education Singapore, Pte, Ltd
Pearson Education, Canada, Ltd
Pearson Education—Japan
Pearson Education Australia PTY, Limited
Pearson Education North Asia Ltd
Pearson Education de Mexico, S.A. the C.V.
Pearson Education Malaysia, Pte, Ltd

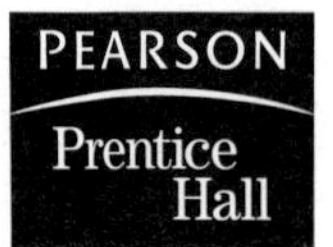

10 9 8 7 6 5 4 3 2 1
0-13-098178-8

For Barbara, Mark, and Renee

Contents

Preface

Among the earliest traces of our common ancestry are cave drawings and paintings of plants, birds, hands, people, animals, and even hunting scenes. Although we can't really know what motivated these remarkable images (magic? score-keeping? amusement?), it seems that making visual images has been necessary to humankind, almost from the start, for many kinds of clarifying, recording, and expressive reasons.

As you embark on the study of drawing, it is important to recognize that, to this day, drawing is still a direct (and enchanting) way to clarify, to record, and to express. Indeed, drawing well is mostly about doing these three things in a resolute and appealing way. No matter what your ultimate goal for drawing may be, you will always be trying to communicate your ideas and experiences clearly.

There are many reasons and ways to draw. A drawing may be motivated by a wish to study a form's appearance, or to plan a creative work in another medium. A drawing may serve to show a client what you intend to create, or to explore the images of your imagination in order to see what they may look like and where they may take you. Many drawings are motivated by a wish to experience the visual and expressive character of something that is seen or recalled—the places, things, and people in the world around you.

But whatever stimulates you to draw, the "ticket of admission" into the great realm of drawing is the ability to see a subject's parts *in a relational way*, that is, to see the similarities and differences among a subject's many features and conditions. For example, if your subject is your own hand, opened before you, palm side up, with your extended fingers spread, the middle finger is longest, but by how much when compared to the ring finger? to the little finger? And is the little finger shorter or longer than the thumb? Looking at the spaces separating the fingers, which space is the widest and which, the narrowest? And, although the four fingers are similar in their shape, what differences do you see in their contours? Where are the lightest tones on your hand, and where are the darkest ones? Among the hand's many folds and creases, which are the most pronounced?

These are only some of the questions you need to answer in order to draw the unique nature of your hand in an objectively truthful way. Learning how to draw begins with, and is nourished by, learning how to see, and learning how to see begins with recognizing that inquiries about relationships of size, shape, value, position, and more, must lead the way. It is the inability to see such relationships that stands squarely in the way of learning to draw. Although your eventual creative expressions may take you far from drawing in an objective mode, reaching these goals cannot benefit from a functional blindness to the relational matters fundamental to drawing.

The authors of this book, having taught drawing for many years, have repeatedly seen the often rapid development in drawing skills among those student-artists who approach the learning of drawing in an inquiring, and not in an arbitrary or declarative, way. Such students soon realize that sensitively relating a subject's parts and its underlying patterns, when comparing, measuring, and choosing, is a vital key to creating drawings, in any mode, that ring true and come alive.

With that in mind, the authors felt that starting this study of drawing with an introduction to a wide range of relational matters (Chapter One) will alert you to more of them than you would otherwise be likely to see and consider. The advantage of beginning in this way is important because seeing more of what is there to compare and relate means you have more control of what you draw at every stage of your studies—the more we see the better we draw. For example, reading Chapter One's discussion on seeing directions—the tilts and turnings of a subject's parts—in alerting you to where and how these directions show themselves—will help you to better draw the main topic of Chapter Two: a subject's *gesture.*

The authors further felt that, just as a drawing is invariably created by a process which moves from the general to the specific, the teaching of drawing can also begin (more or less) with a concentration on the most encompassing matters of drawing before turning to more particular ones. That is why, once you have been alerted to what measurable matters to look for in a subject, we have presented the concept of gesture as the most pervasive feature of anything you set out to draw. This is so because everything has gesture, has some enveloping pattern of action and energy that underlies its form, be it the human figure, an eyelid, a staircase, or a sparrow.

And, just as Chapter Two ends with an approach to the visual element of *line,* (for the underlying matter of gesture soon rises to the surface where lines are a direct and efficient means of proceeding further), Chapter Three begins with line, exploring its several guises and functions, and ends by approaching the next logical matter: *shape.* Proceeding on our journey from the general to the specific, Chapter Four examines the several roles of the element of shape in drawing, especially shape's role in forming a volume's surface facets, or planes. And planes, when they get together, produce a form's *surface structure,* a major focus of Chapter Five, which then goes on to explore two more visual elements: *value* and *volume.*

Chapter Six examines some issues in drawings that use the element of *color*, perhaps the most mysterious of the visual elements, and the most powerful too, as it modifies all the other elements. Chapter Seven and Chapter Eight depart from our general approach and move toward to specific approaches, as each chapter concentrates on ever-present matters fundamental to drawing. Chapter Seven takes on the illusive but crucial matter of *composition*, and shows that the successful communication of your creative meanings owes much to the underlying dynamic forces alive in the things you draw. Up to this point the book has concentrated on how to better draw the things you actually see. Chapter Eight considers how to respond to subjects that you don't actually see: those of *recall* and *imagination*. All of the preceding chapters will have prepared you for encountering and capturing these more personal and often fleeting visions. Chapter Nine concerns the materials and tools of drawing, an important subject because of their influence on the images you will make. Lastly, we have included a glossary of terms as used in this book, to help you get the most out of each discussion.

Put simply, learning to draw means doing a lot of it as you take on the many challenges of relational seeing. One of the most useful tools for enabling you to draw anywhere and at any time is the sketchbook, an invaluable learning device that students and artists have used for several hundred years. There are many kinds and sizes of sketchbook. The authors suggest selecting one that can be easily carried around. A sketchbook that measures approximately $8\frac{1}{2}$ by 11 inches is just about right.

In the relative privacy of a sketchbook you are more likely to "take chances," to more bravely risk losing a drawing that tries to reach for an idea, a procedure, or a subject that, earlier on, was too difficult to manage. Think of your sketchbook as a private journal or sanctuary, not available for others to browse without your permission. It also helps to think of it as a kind of gym, a place where you go to visually "work out." And, as in a gym environment, where a failed attempt is simply dismissed and tried again (and again), a sketchbook drawing that doesn't succeed should likewise be dismissed and tried again, and not be seen as an unmovable limit of your ability to draw.

To continue the analogy, as with your physical limits in the gym, where you can jump only so far or lift only so much, learning *how* to jump farther or *how* to lift more will, in time, get results. It is the same with drawing. Learning *how* to see more will, in time, result in drawings that succeed in saying better what you mean them to say. The sketchbook helps to speed up the process of seeing, because many sketchbook drawings are likely to be of short duration—a condition that encourages artists to see in a more selective and relational way—the better to recall the subject, which may have moved on. This practice makes for better observation and more resolute results.

The advantages of the sketchbook for practice, investigation, planning, and the recording of subjects you would otherwise not encounter are too important to bypass. Browsing this book's reproductions of old and contemporary master drawings will show how many of these works are, if not actually sketchbook drawings, in the investigative spirit of sketchbook drawings.

A word about the drawings that appear in the book is in order here. The authors felt that showing you the most outstanding examples of matters referred to in the text far outweighed all other considerations. The idea of insisting on a policy that would all but exclude either contemporary artists or old masters in making our selections seemed unnecessarily restricting as extraordinary drawings are to be had from each era. Instead, we searched for works that most clearly demonstrated the various points in each chapter with little regard for when or where a work was created.

Another matter to think about as you embark on the study of drawing is the evaluation of your efforts by others. Art students, like professional artists, will have their works judged now and then. The famous art school "critique" of student work is one example of this, the opinions of friends and family, are another. Although such evaluations can be valuable to the development of your drawing skills, it is usually difficult to hear that your judgments or manner of drawing are regarded as faulty in some way. It may be of some help to recognize that there are, broadly speaking, two categories of criticism: those having to do with provable fact, and those with opinion. Teachers of basic drawing will generally emphasize the former: "the legs are too short for the rest of the body," or "the perspective of the table is off," or "the volume of this form isn't clear to me." Such criticisms, being plainly factual, can be readily accepted. Criticisms having to do with opinion may also be valuable, but these often have as their basis certain artistic beliefs or other values of importance to the critic that he or she hopes you will consider. When, in the opinion of an art teacher, your drawing is regarded as "too tight," "too carelessly observed," "too concerned with surface effects," or "unbalanced on the page," you are probably getting good advice. But when a relative or a friend suggests your drawings should be "prettier," "less messy," or "not so sad," you can safely disregard the criticism, however well meant it may be. Criticism is best sorted out by having in mind the goals you hold for yourself.

As you read (and draw!) your way through this book (ideally while enrolled in a drawing course), remember that you are probably a good judge of your progress in developing your drawing skills, in the light of where you wish to go. But so too, are the artist-teachers who are helping you by alerting you to possibilities, problems, and challenges you need to confront to reach your goals. They can help you work through obstacles and achieve results. The authors hope this book will also help you in that important way.

ACKNOWLEDGMENTS

As part of their lives as artists and educators, the authors have participated in or conducted drawing workshops and seminars around the country, from Rhode Island to Hawaii. In comparing experiences, we found the primary interest of virtually all beginning art students is to acquire the empowering (and some would say, magical) ability to create drawings that objectively reflect what they see. For, no matter what their varying artistic goals, they intuitively know what their art teachers will confirm: that bypassing the basic visual skill of seeing and drawing will significantly limit their creative understanding and ability.

We have each even had the experience of encountering advanced students who are uneasy about their grasp of fundamental drawing skills and eager to discuss and reexamine perceptual matters of the most elementary kind. This logical necessity of first learning how to see, reflected in the views of our many colleagues near and far, led us to consider a concise and straightforward text designed for the student embarking on an exploration of the magnificent realm of drawing.

This book is our attempt to organize and clarify those basic perceptual and organizational matters necessary to create drawings that interpret an observed subject in an objective and sensitive way. Although the book concentrates on the options and challenges of drawing a subject that is physically present, it shows how those matters can be applied to subjects of our imaginative and more subjective "inner eye."

We wish to express our deep appreciation to the many students, artists, and friends who have helped in various ways to bring this book into being. We wish also to thank the many museums, galleries, and collectors for granting permission to reproduce drawings in their collections.

We wish especially to thank Bud Therien of Prentice Hall for his initiative and considerable assistance and Jean Lapidus, our outstanding production editor, for their finely honed skills and deep involvement in helping to give this book its present form. The authors also thank the following reviewers for their helpful suggestions: Andrew Murad of McLennan Community College, TX; Angela C. Curreri of Barry University, FL; Drake Gomez of Keystone College, PA; Ken Burchett of University of Central Arkansas, Arkansas; Adrienne La Vallee of Saint Anselm College, NH; Ruth Trotter of University of La Verne, CA; Kevin Sparks of Asbury College, KY; Stephen LeWinter of University of Tennessee at Chattanooga, TN; and Ann M. Beiersdorfer of Xavier University, OH.

Finally, the authors wish to thank Sarah and Jessica for their inspiration, affection, and sense of wonder, which have always nourished us.

Nathan Goldstein
Harriet J. Fishman
The Art Institute of Boston at Lesley University

1

Matters of Measurement

The central theme of this book is focused on expanding your ability to see and relate qualities and conditions in an observed subject so that you can draw it in an objectively truthful and sensitive way. Although it is likely that the subjects you draw will be physically present, enabling you to check what you are drawing against what is positioned before you, the information in this book should also help you to better draw something you have recently seen or even imagined. The rationale for this approach is the same as for dealing with ourselves and with the life around us: it is necessary to see things as they really are before trying to make them better. For artists, "better" has to do with more personal satisfaction in a drawing's power to capture and express what was intended. It seemed logical to the authors that starting with a chapter that shows you the many ways to capture and convert the forms you see around you onto the flat page, in an objective way, will enable you to better apply the book's information and guidance as you progress in your studies. It will also bring you sooner to the point where your more personal ideas and needs will find expression in ways that others can understand and enjoy.

Developing the skills for objectively drawing what we see begins with the recognition that seeing relationships of size, shape, placement, and tone among the parts of the subject in front of us plays the crucial role. Other important relationships that are more or less "under the surface" of the subject have to do with how the parts are arranged and constructed. Learning how to find such connections and to "see" a subject's subterranean aspects is similar to learning about grammar and syntax. Just as finding the right words and getting them in the right order produces sentences we can understand, so does finding the right lines and tones in the right order produce drawings we can understand. Although acquiring such drawing skills is far more exciting than tedious, it does require both practice and patience and is, in any case, a necessary prerequisite to any form of visual expression. Learning about gesture, perspective, and structure; seeing how line, shape, and value create volume and space; and discovering how the tensions and energies that animate our drawings come about are some of the important "under the surface" factors we will examine in depth. But running through them all is the matter of comparison, of measurement—of allotting to each part of a drawing its needed direction, scale, shape, and value. Good representational drawing always depends on such measurements, and such measurements depend on relational seeing, that is, on comparing one part to another to see the similarities or differences between them.

A FORM'S DIRECTION

Seeing the actual tilt or angle of a form is, of course, necessary to drawing it on the page. Consider the hammering together of a crate. To construct a crate each board needs to be measured and cut to the right *size* and *shape*, and placed in the right *location* and *direction* before nailing it to the rest. That is not unlike the kinds of measurement that go into the making of an objectively conceived drawing. In such drawings, the "boards" are the marks we make to represent the things we see.

> ***All drawings consist of a variety of marks made on a blank surface. They may be lines, smudges, or stains ... together they form groupings that can objectively simulate a subject's parts.***

All drawings consist of a variety of marks made on a blank surface. They may be lines, dots, smudges, or stains, or some combination of such marks. Together they form groupings that can objectively simulate a subject's parts. To succeed in doing so these groupings of marks, representing the various forms of the people, places, and things we draw, in addition to being the right size and shape, need to be positioned in the *right place* and in the *right direction* on the page.

Vertical and Horizontal Rightness

To establish a form's rightness of direction, or tilt, you must be mindful of the vertical and horizontal boundaries of the page you are drawing on. Holding in mind the two "given" directions of the page helps you to better judge whether a specific part in your drawing is tilted in the same direction as the same part in the subject, thereby helping you to avoid drawing a house or a horse at some impossible angle. If, for example, you see a tree trunk that is almost, but not quite, vertical, the degree of its departure from a true vertical is easier to judge when you compare the trunk's tilt to the vertical direction of the edge of your page. Another aid in determining a true vertical or horizontal direction is "hard wired" in our brain, and has to do with gravitational force and our sense of balance. It's what makes it possible to hang a picture on a wall and know with certainty when its position is no longer at an angle, however subtle, but is "straight." Calling on this built-in sense as you draw also helps you to judge a part's angle by comparing it to your intuitive feel for vertical and horizontal rightness.

Seeing the angle of a form you wish to draw requires you to see the centerline or *long axis* of that form *before* regarding its contours because a form's contours seldom match the direction of a form's long axis (Figure 1.1). Bypassing a search for a part's actual tilt to get at its contours first often shows the contours to be drawn at wrong angles.

Figure 1.1

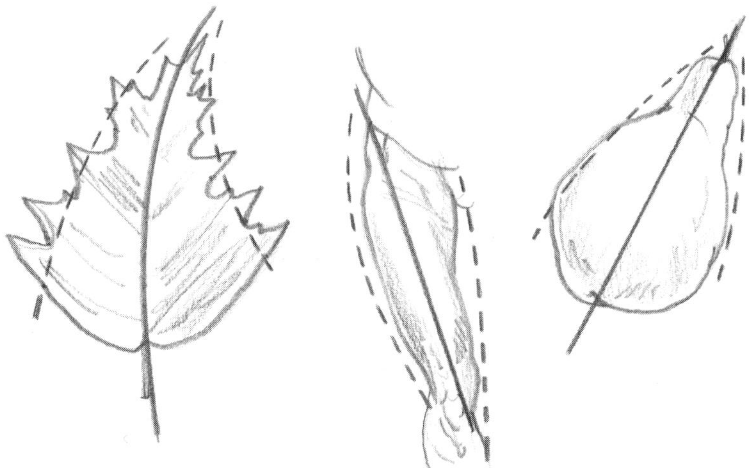

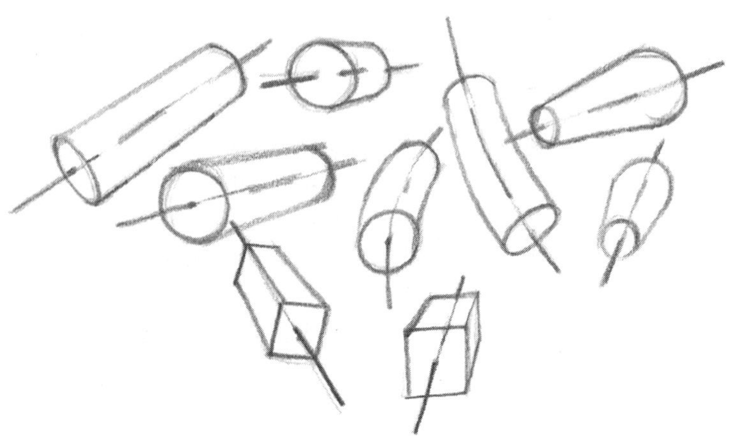

Figure 1.2

The main difficulty in drawing a subject's parts at the angles they actually offer to your view is that many of the parts you see do not face you frontally, but are turned away from your view to some degree. They are not parallel to your eyes, but are seen at an oblique angle, moving back into a spatial field of depth. Such more or less "end on" or *foreshortened* views are confusing at first because we cannot easily disentangle a form's two-dimensional state from its three-dimensional one. But remember that the marks you make on the two-dimensional page, as well as the forms they represent, must first be seen as two-dimensional—as tilted to some degree *on the page* (Figure 1.2). Drawing forms to suggest they go back into a spatial field of depth will be of much interest to us later in this text, but here it is a form's orientation on the page that must be seen.

The Clock's Long Hand. In Figure 1.3, the variously angled, often foreshortened forms convey an appearance of "rightness." We accept the many tilts and lengths of the figure's parts as necessary to the depiction of this pose. But Abeles had to first locate these forms on the flat surface of the page. For example, he had to see that the figure's left upper leg was positioned vertically and that the lower portion of the woman's hair was oriented horizontally. If you imagine a clock face to surround each of a subject's forms, with the clock's long hand running through the form's longest dimension you can locate the tilt of parts with some precision. For example, in Figure 1.3, the figure's right upper leg is turned to two (and eight) o'clock, her lower right arm to five (and eleven) o'clock, and so on, as in Figure 1.4. Artists

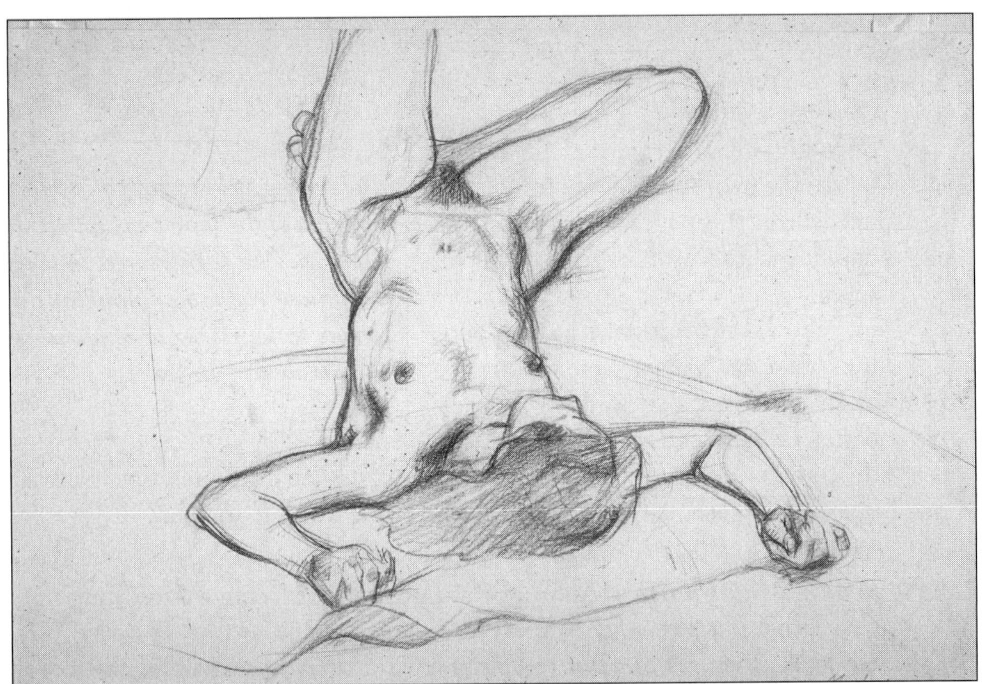

Figure 1.3 Sigmund Abeles (1934–), *Bridging from Bed to Floor*. Charcoal pencil, 16 × 20 inches. Courtesy of the artist.

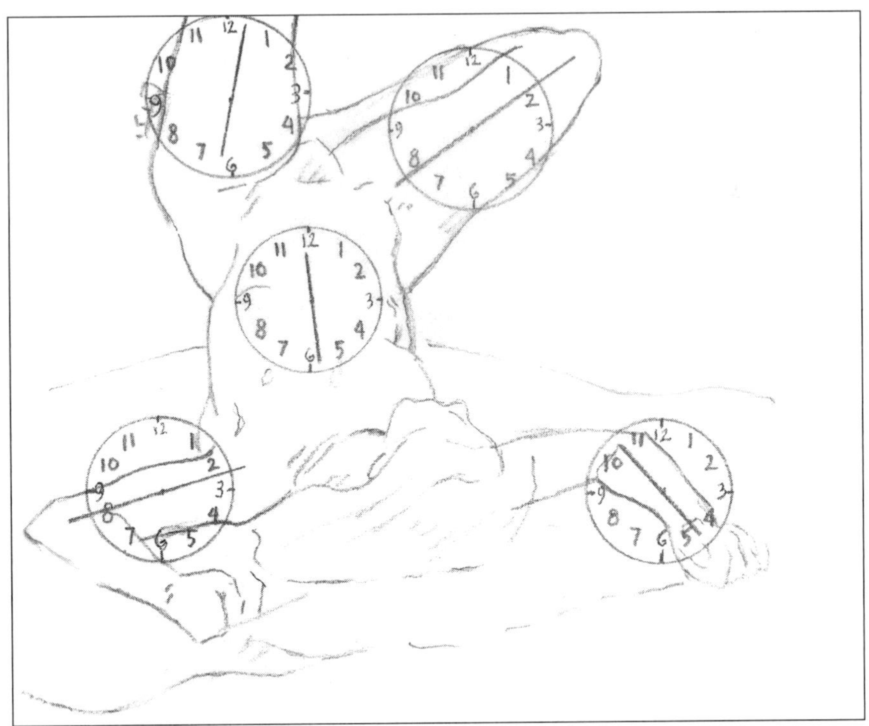

Figure 1.4

often use this convenient tactic to better see the two-dimensional directions needed on the page that are used to depict a three-dimensional form in space.

To aid in seeing the angle a part must take on the page, many artists close one eye when looking at that part, a tactic which somewhat reduces the sense of depth perception. With the form's "in and out" aspects now reduced, it is easier to see its two-dimensional direction. Try it and see.

> ***Learning to see that solid masses have a flat shape configuration that can be transferred to the page is one of the most important concepts in learning to objectively draw what you see ...***

Seeing Alignments. An important offshoot of seeing a part's long axis is seeing what other parts or edges of parts are in alignment with it. For example, in a still life setup, the base of a bottle on the left side may be aligned with the top edge of an apple on the right side. Or, as in Figure 1.5A, shapes of differing kinds, drawn at different angles are aligned in forming a horizontally oriented S-shaped pattern. Not only are such alignments necessary in objectively establishing certain observable facts about your subject, but they serve to "weave" a drawing together, by showing relationships of position and tilt that might otherwise be missed.

Seeing "Flat." Learning to see that solid masses have a flat shape configuration that can be transferred to the page is one of the most important concepts in learning to draw objectively what you see, and is an important feature of Chapters Three, Four, and Five. Almost all beginners find it easier to make a more accurate drawing when their subject is seen in a photograph, because they are then recording the edges, alignments, and tones of one flat surface onto another flat surface. But when the same subject shown in the photograph is actually placed before them and seen from the same view, the beginner cannot "see" that the two-dimensional properties of direction and shape, so easily seen in the photograph, are still present in the subject now before them. To better see the two-dimensional actualities of a subject in front of you, it helps if you imagine it to be a photograph of the subject—as having only shapes and tones on a flat surface. Again, closing one eye helps to see the subject in this way. It converts what you see to a flatter, monocular image, and not a binocular one. Then, too, with the subject seen somewhat "flatter, it is easier to judge the various lengths and widths of its parts. Similarly, squinting at your subject, because it reduces your ability to see details, helps you to see and evaluate a subject's important generalities of shape, direction, and tones.

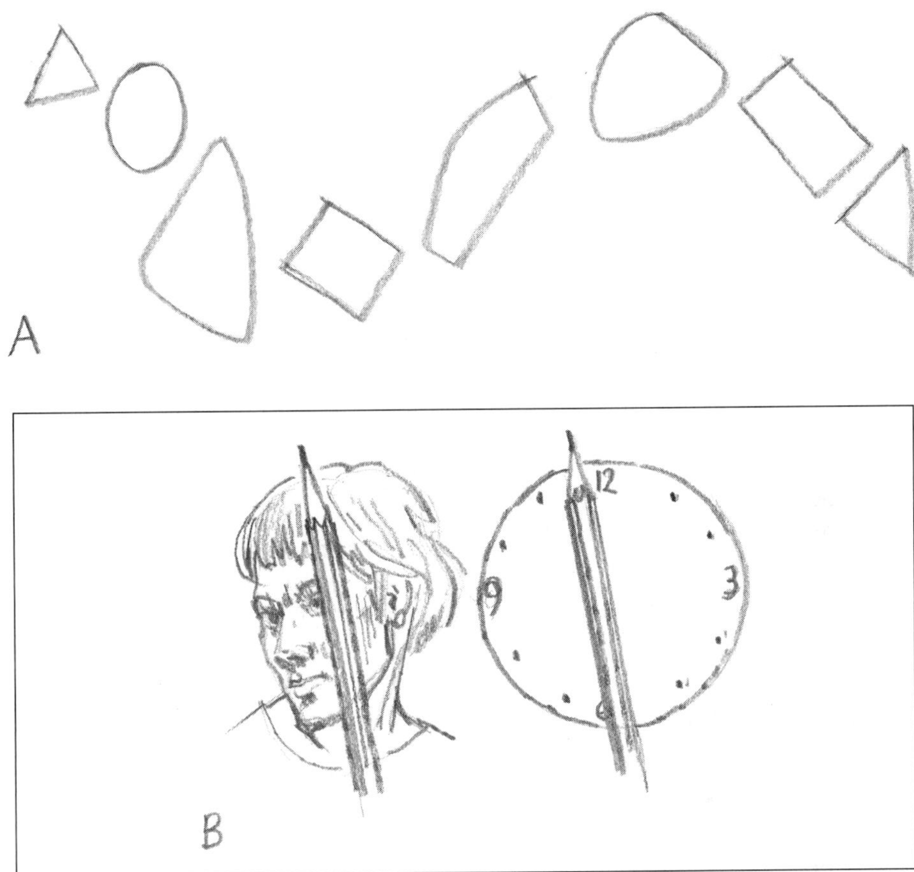

Figure 1.5

Judging Tilts. Another useful way to judge the various directions of a subject's parts is to hold a pencil (or any straight-edged object) at arm's length and turn it in the direction of a part's long axis, or centerline. Similar to the device of imagining the long hand on a clock face as a guide, your pencil, aligned with the part's long axis, now shows the angle needed in your drawing of the part, as in Figure 1.5B. This way of judging a long axis is also useful in seeing the alignment of parts.

Still another important way of measuring the direction of an observed form is to see it in relation to the direction of other forms in the subject. If, for example, we set out to draw a wagon wheel, we know that each spoke emerges from the wheel's hub and aims for the rim in a direction slightly different from that of its neighbors. But will the spokes in our drawing be equally spaced apart at the rim?

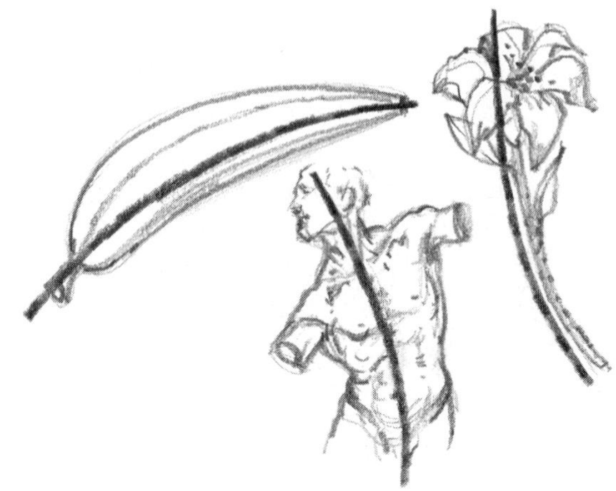

Figure 1.6

They will be if we accurately see the direction of each spoke in relation to the others. It is necessary, therefore, in developing your drawing to constantly judge the angle of one form in relation to the angle of another.

A long axis is often seen to be straight, but, depending on the form, it can be curved. A banana, a bent torso, or a flower stem are a few of the many forms that may better conform to a simple C-shaped centerline (Figure 1.6). As with seeing the relationship between the angles of forms, judging the degree of curvature of a form's long axis is best done by comparing its curve to any other curve in your subject.

In drawing, the spaces between forms are as important to see objectively as are the forms themselves (see Figures 3.7 and 3.8). If the centerlines and shapes of such interspaces are wrong, the encircling or adjacent forms will also be wrong in some way. Seeing the direction (as well as the shape and scale) of such *negative* spaces in your subject is basic to observational drawing, as we will see in Chapter Three.

DIRECTION AND CONTOUR

> ***... no two artists will interpret the same contours in the same way.***

Just as a solid form (or part of a form) has a single straight or curved axial direction, so do its contours show segments of edge turned in various directions. Once we have drawn the tilt of a form we can turn our attention to seeing the differing directions of these large and small contour segments.

Straights and Curves

Measuring the length as well as the angle of each segment of a form's edges is necessary when drawing contour turnings. For example, as Figure 1.7 shows, line B was drawn by seeing that its subject, line A, could be analyzed as consisting of seven segments, each with its own angle and length. To help you clarify what you see as you follow the contour's turnings, it is useful to interpret each turn as being either a straight line or a simple C-shaped curved line, with its apex at one of the three places shown in Figure 1.8. This slight simplification of each segment defines contours in a more incisive way, and makes it easier to draw even complicated contours. This straight or curved manner of analysis results in contours that are both accurate and resolute; we feel that such contours have an authoritative character. Rubens, Rembrandt, Degas, and Picasso are some of the many artists whose drawings show something of this clarifying tactic (Figure 1.9). It is important to point out that no two artists will interpret the same contours in the same way. Some artists will favor straight lines, some curved lines, and some will show a more balanced use of these two options. This is so because each artist has his or her own way of looking at form. It is a procedure that allows for more personal notions of how to see and draw contours. What these variations of response have in common is purposeful judgments about the ever-changing directions of a contour.

As with the difficulty of seeing the direction and length of a foreshortened form's long axis, so, too, is it challenging to see the actual tilt and length of a

Figure 1.7

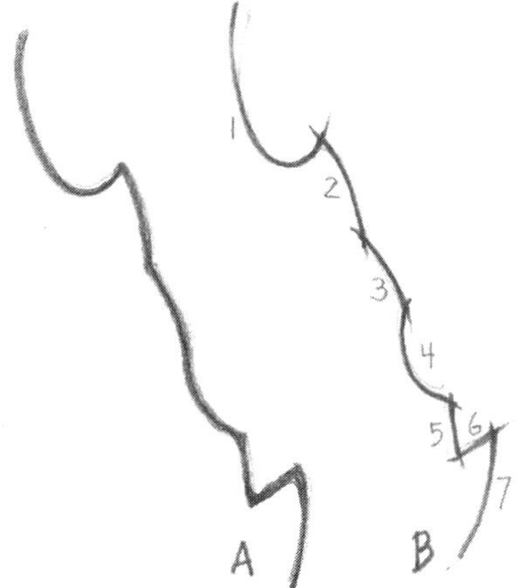

Figure 1.8 Apex of line 1 is in curve's center. Apex of line 2 is near top of curve. Apex of line 3 is near bottom of curve.

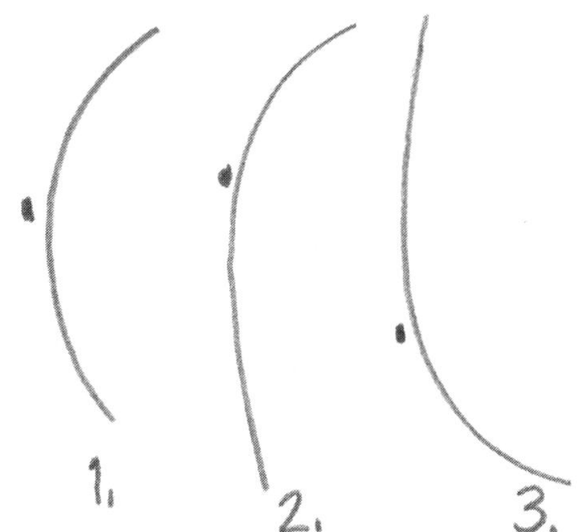

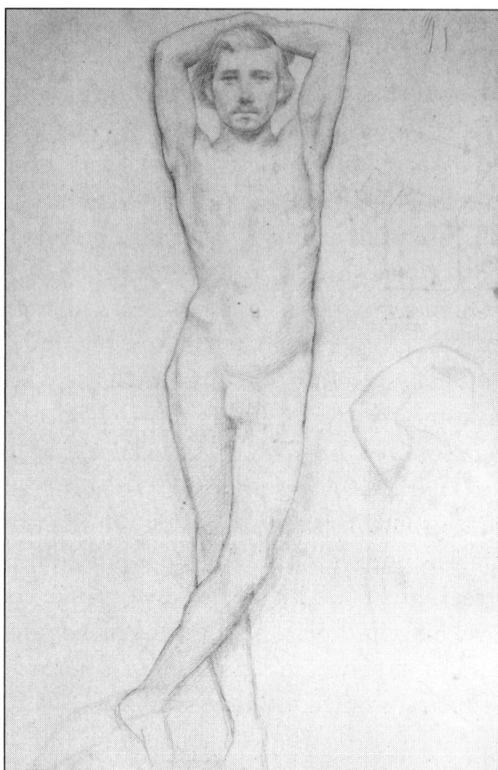

Figure 1.9 Edgar Degas (French,1834–1917), *Standing Male Nude (recto)*, 19th century. Red chalk on paper, 18 × 12 in. (45.72 × 30.48 cm). *Source:* The Nelson-Atkins Museum of Art, Kansas City, Missouri. Gift of Mr. and Mrs. Milton McGreevy, through the Westport Fund (F56–66).

foreshortened segment of a form's edge. The solution is the same in either case: seeing the form or any segment of that form's contour as "flat," that is, as *two-dimensional,* tells you how to show its direction and length on the flat page, as Figure 1.2 demonstrates.

SCALE RELATIONSHIPS

One of the most important (if sometimes vexing) challenges in drawing objectively is getting all the subject's parts in proportion. Getting them right can be made to sound simple and easy: just be sure that all the parts of your drawing are the right size according to each of their positions in the spatial field. Of course, that's just what you want to do, but the question is how. The answer consists of several measuring methods that work together in establishing the right size and location for the parts of a drawing.

One method, already discussed, determines the long axis of an object's angle according to an imagined long hand of a clock face. If, in addition, the line

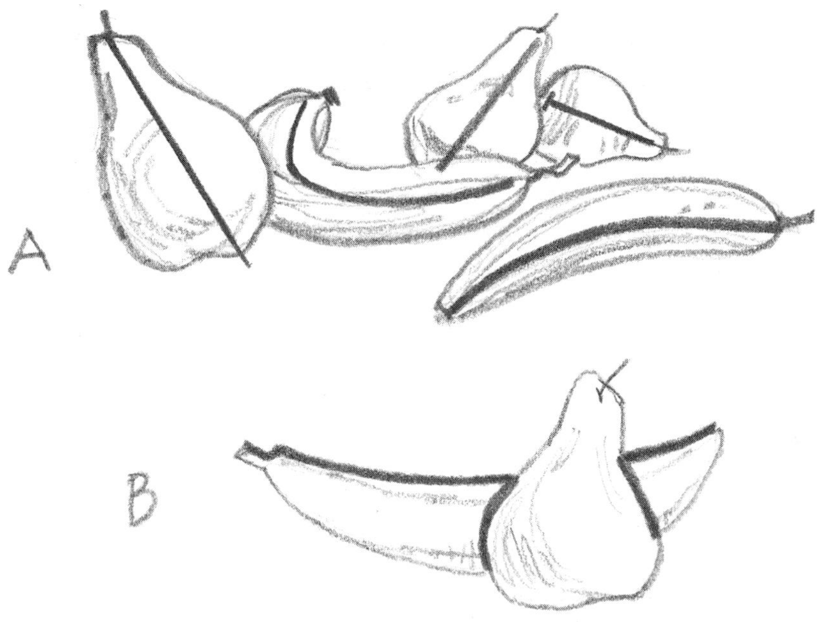

Figure 1.10

representing the long axis also measures that object's length in relation to the lengths of other forms in the subject, it strongly benefits a drawing's overall scale relationships. For example, the three pears and two bananas in Figure 1.10A, each shows a different angle and length of its long axis. Judging wrongly on either the tilt or the length of these centerlines would adversely influence location, scale, or both.

Another important way of helping you to draw a subject in correct proportions has to do with the distance between you and your drawing. Major errors in proportions are sure to occur when we "crowd" our drawings, keeping our head only a few inches away from the page. The fact is we just cannot judge scale relationships well when we are very close to our drawing. Stepping back a few feet will reveal even subtle size discrepancies. Stepping back often in a drawing's early stage is critical as *almost all* of the proportion and direction errors occur in the first few minutes of a drawing.

Intersections

Another helpful measuring tactic that will alert you to the length of a line is noticing the point where it meets (or intersects) another line. Even though you may be sensitive to the various turnings of a contour, you need also to notice the places along its route where it intersects with other lines, as in Figure 1.10B, where the upper edge of the banana visible to the right of the pear is shorter than it is to the left of the pear. Conversely, note the length of the pear's contours "inside" the banana when compared to the length of the rest of the pear's contour. Such length judgments of contour segments based on points at which they meet other contours provide important information about the location and sizes of a subject's parts.

Convergence

The principles of perspective are more fully discussed in Chapter Four, but it will be useful here to note one of perspective's basic propositions. Linear perspective holds that parallel lines or edges, such as the rails of railroad tracks or the edges of corridors, appear to converge as they move back into a spatial field to meet at a point (called the *vanishing point*) on the *horizon line*, which, it is important to remember, is always at your eye-level. This means that anything placed far back in the spatial field (such as the ties of the railroad tracks) will also appear smaller than it would if placed far forward in the field (Figure 1.11).

Although we are all aware that things looks smaller when they are farther away, knowing how much smaller is something we can discover by applying the

Figure 1.11

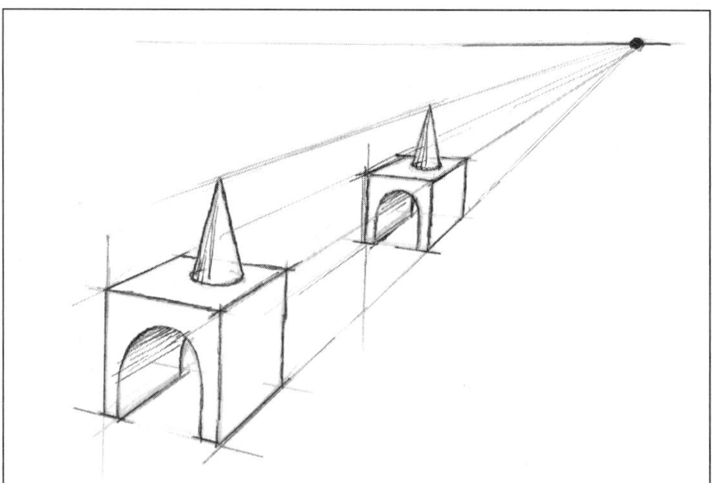

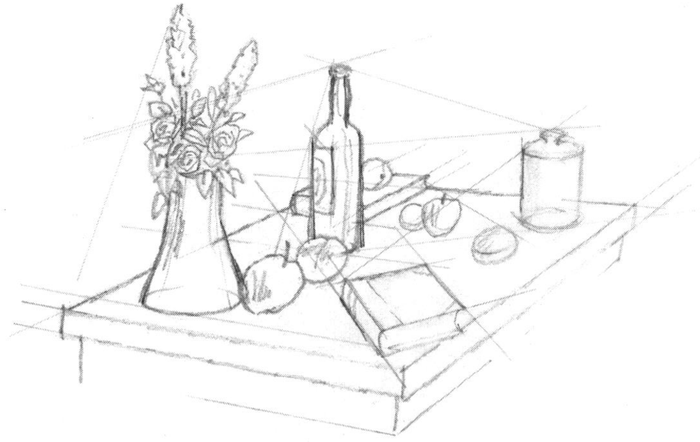

Figure 1.12

convergence principle of perspective, as Figures 1.11 and 1.12 demonstrate. Note that in both illustrations, lines have been extended from the near objects to those farther back to show the scale limits of the far forms. The correct scale of some complex forms (especially of an organic kind such as those of the figure, or forms of a rounded and curvilinear nature) is easier to find if you enclose those forms in transparent "blocks" (see "Blocking," in Chapter Four). Doing so helps to more easily apply the convergence principle, as in Figure 1.13. Note, also, how the views of these objects change when they are below, at, or above the horizon line.

Figure 1.13

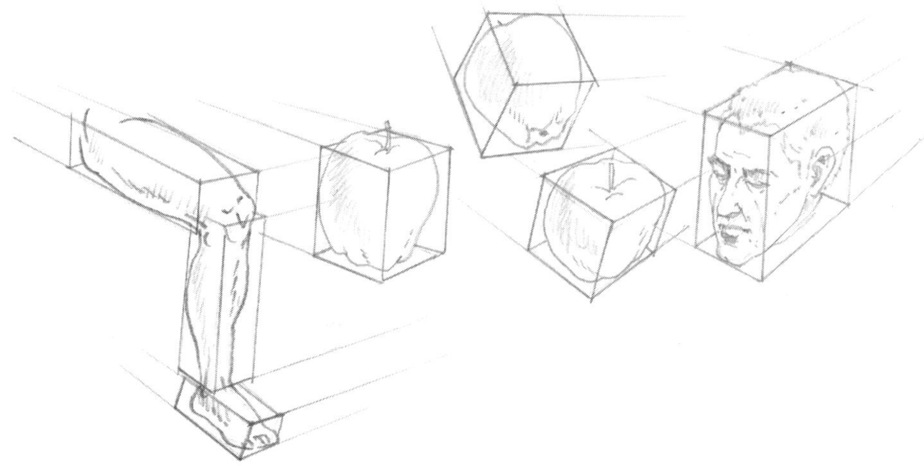

AIDS IN SEEING

L-Frames. A simple device you can easily cut from any stiff cardboard consists of two L-shaped pieces that are used to help compose a drawing or to verify relationships of direction or scale, as in Figure 1.14. These L-shaped tools needn't be large. Each "leg" of an L-shape can be some 4 or 5 inches long, and about $1\frac{1}{2}$ inches wide. Note that this device easily shows the height to width proportions of the foreshortened circle representing the end plane of the cylinder in Figure 1.14. Only one L-frame is needed to clarify the tilt of a form or segment of edge, or to search for vertically and horizontally positioned forms or edge segments (Figure 1.15). A useful variation of the L-frame results from connecting two rectangular strips of cardboard by a fastener, as shown in Figure 1.16. This is one more way to judge the exact angle of a diagonal edge in relation to a vertical or horizontal one.

The Measuring Tool. Any straight edged object such as your pencil, a small ruler, a dowel, or a thin strip of wood or metal can function as a measuring device. Whichever tool is used, hold it at arm's length ("locking" your elbow to keep the arm straight insures that all your measurements will be consistent) and sight any part whose size you wish to determine. By moving your thumb up or down along the length of the tool you can measure the correct length of a part or an edge. This is done by lining up the tip of the tool with one end of whatever is being measured and moving your thumb up or down on the tool until it lines up with the other end, as in Figure 1.17. Once a measurement has been made, bend and move your arm to the drawing surface without changing the thumb's position on the tool, and then compare the measurement just made to any other part or edge you wish to measure.

Figure 1.14

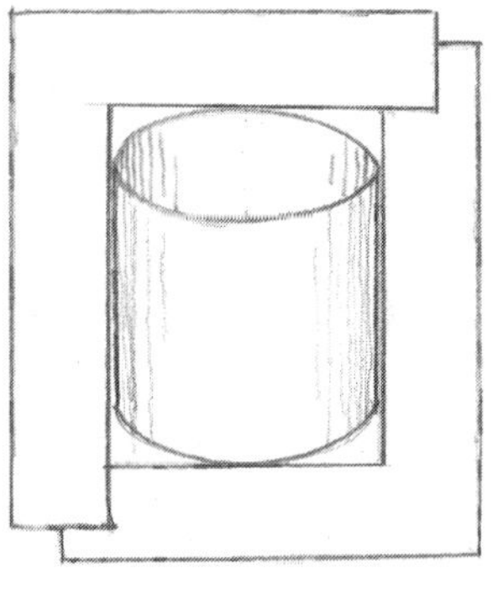

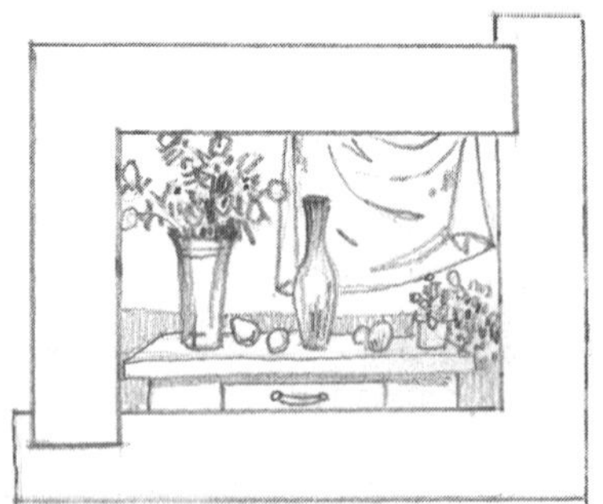

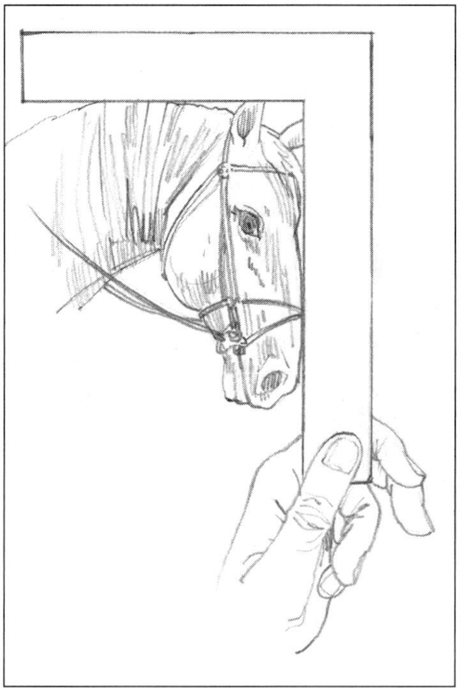

Figure 1.15

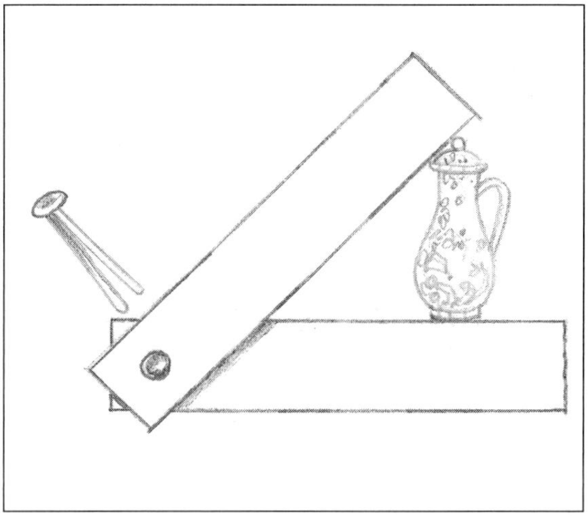

Figure 1.16

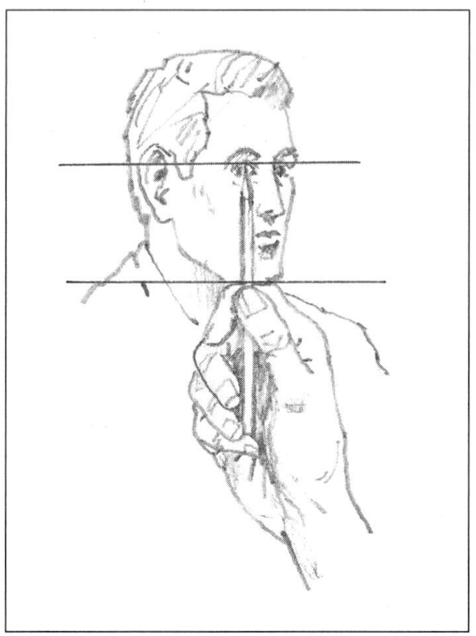

Figure 1.17

Finding Grid Lines. Some artists lightly sketch lines that extend beyond the edges of the forms in their drawings to check on the placement and angle of one part to another, or to confirm the alignments of parts. But certain media such as pen and ink or oil-based crayon, because they cannot be erased, do not allow for drawing preliminary measurement lines that are not to be part of the finished work. Drawings made with such media can benefit from the use of a prepared grid. (See "Making a Grid," below.)

Other media, such as the graphite (the common "lead") pencil and vine charcoal, do permit you to make lightly drawn, schematic lines that measure the distance, size, and location of one part of your subject in relation to another. Because of your "built in" ability to recognize true vertical or horizontal directions, these are the easiest measurement lines to draw from one point to another. Each of these measurements is made by choosing a point in your drawing that may represent a form's centerline, corner, or edge, and then lightly drawing a line straight down or straight across from that point to see what neighboring parts in the drawing the line strikes, as in Figures 1.18, 1.19, and 1.20. If, say, you lightly place a vertical line in your drawing that strikes in the same place as seen when you hold your drawing tool up to the subject, then the measurement line confirms your judgment. If the line does not strike the same point in the drawing as it does in the seen subject, it tells you what to relocate, to adjust the scale of, or otherwise to change in your drawing.

The more of these searching, diagrammatic lines you draw, the more relational discoveries you will make, and each of these findings provides you with information you need to make your drawing more accurately represent your subject. Measuring from one point to another that requires you to draw lines at an angle also provides useful information. Seeing the angle in the subject and transferring that angle accurately to the drawing is best done by recalling the clock face tactic, or by holding your drawing instrument at that angle, as shown in Figures 1.18 and 1.19.

Making a Grid. A variant of this procedure makes it possible to use grid lines when making a pen and ink drawing or a work done in any other nonerasable medium. To do this, draw a grid of $\frac{3}{4}$-inch squares on clear acetate (designed to receive ink), using a ballpoint pen and a ruler. For increased stability the sheet of acetate should be mounted on a mat (Figure 1.21). Hold the grid up to your subject to observe what the vertical and horizontal grid lines strike and then examine your drawing to see if the same alignments hold true. If they do then the scale, location, and shape of the parts are correct. Because of the nonerasable nature of the medium, the earlier you do this in the drawing's progress, the better. Of course, the acetate grid can also be used for drawings in an erasable medium.

Another method uses grid lines lightly drawn in graphite on the page itself. By holding the acetate grid up to the subject you can then see which parts of the

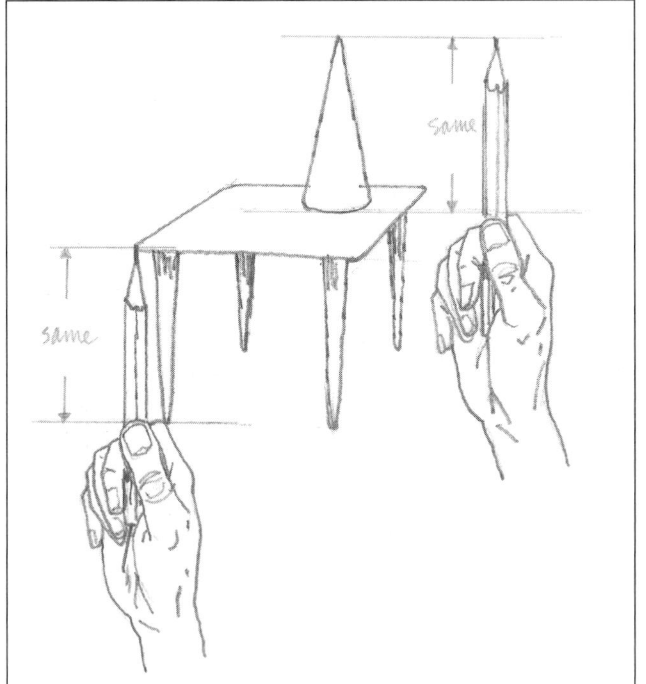

Figure 1.18

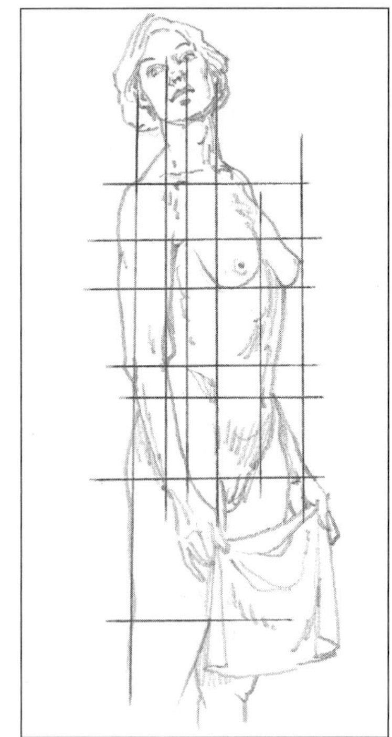

Figure 1.19

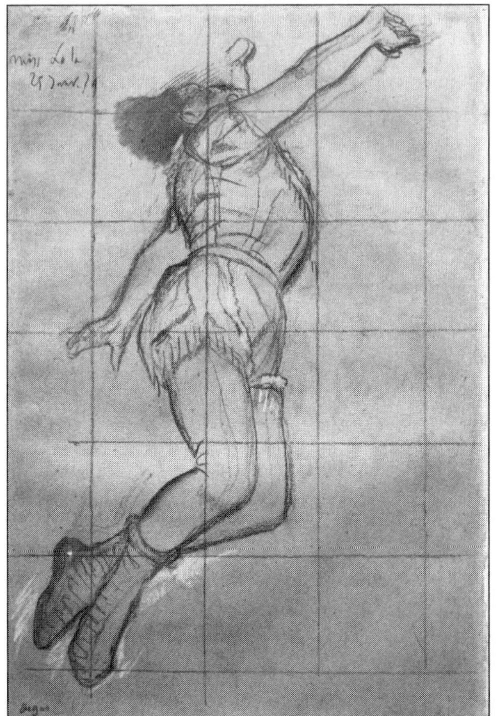

Figure 1.20 Edgar Degas (1834–1917), *Miss Lala at the Cirque Fernando*, 1879. Black chalk and pastel on paper. *Source:* The Barber Institute of Fine Arts, University of Birmingham/Bridgeman Art Library.

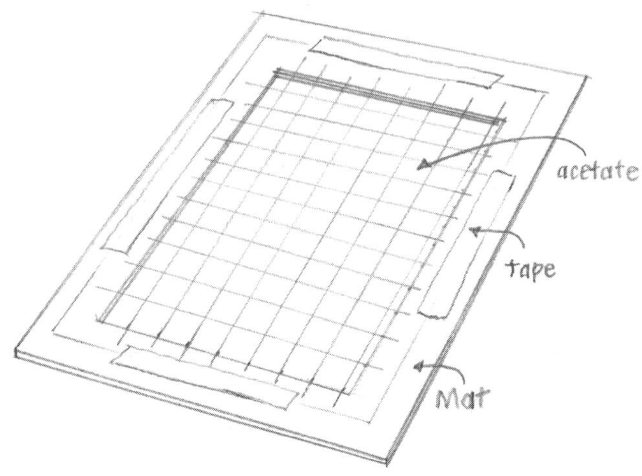

Figure 1.21

subject fall within each part of the grid, and draw these parts in the corresponding squares of the grid on your page.

Of course, such a procedure may result in a stilted looking drawing. This can be avoided by first drawing *lightly* in graphite pencil, with a view to locating the parts of your subject on the page in a simple and schematic way. These preliminary lines should be few and general; just enough to serve as guides to make it easier for you to use ink or some other nonerasable medium in a free and inquiring manner. When the drawing is completed, the graphite lines of the drawing's grid as well as the preliminary guidelines can be erased. By changing the size of the squares in the drawing's grid, you can enlarge or reduce the drawing's size (Figure 1.22).

Point to Point. Another tactic that helps establish the location and shape of a subject's parts once a drawing is underway uses key points as a means of relating and measuring the distances and position of these parts. To do this, select several places along your subject's edges or on some of its inner features such as corners or any other prominent features, and mark these places by lightly drawing these points in your drawing, as in Figure 1.23A. Using your pencil, the cardboard L-shape, or other measuring tool to judge the angle and distance between any two points helps to locate them more accurately. Next, lightly draw straight or C-shaped lines that "connect the dots," as in Figure 1.23B. Invariably, some of these points will have been drawn "off the mark," but these misjudgments are easier to see once the drawing is underway. They can then be adjusted.

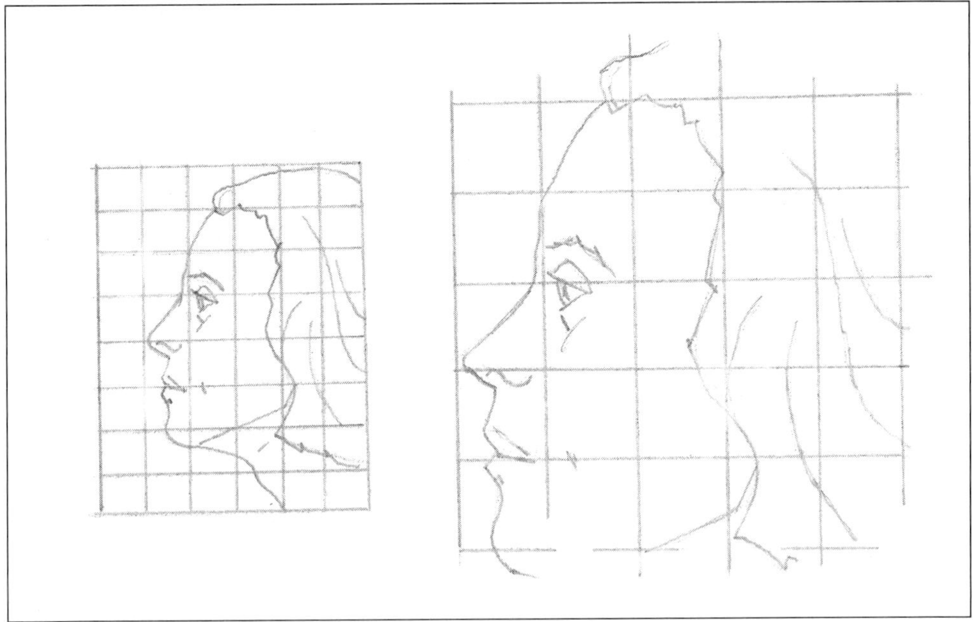

Figure 1.22

Figure 1.23

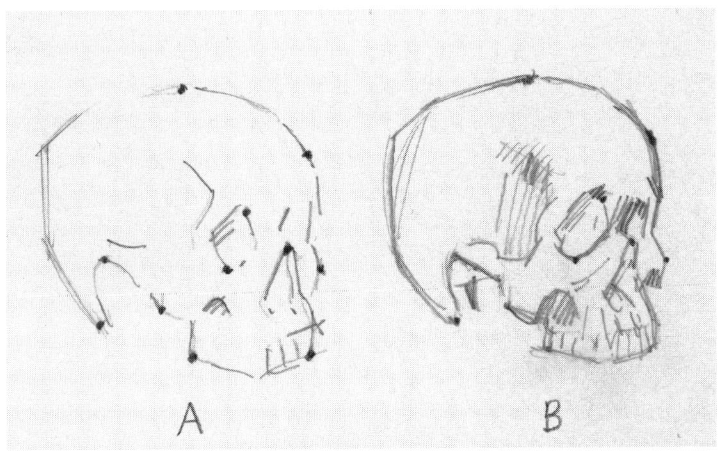

MEASURING VALUE

The methods of measurement described so far are all aids in seeing the angle, length, location, and scale differences among the parts of a subject, so that you can more accurately establish a subject's shapes. They are, then, ways of relating that have to do mainly with seeing line, alignment, or edge. In a way, we have been learning how to objectively see the "geography" of a subject's parts. Now we turn to measuring the tones that help to explain the "topography" of the parts—the hills and valleys that make up its surface character, and the light and dark areas resulting from the way light falls on this surface.

For artists, a *value* is the degree of lightness or darkness on any part of the surface of any form or space. Values are the result of two conditions: *local-tone*, the inherent tone of a form or space; and the *illuminating source*, the incidental nature and direction of light falling on a form or space. For example, a lemon is inherently light; a plum, dark. Their local-tones are very different. When both objects are illuminated from the same side, the value of the illuminated sides will be lighter than the objects' local-tone, while the surfaces turned away from the light source will be darker than their local-tone. However, under most lighting conditions, the lightest value to be seen on the plum will be darker than the darkest value on the lemon. Therefore, when judging a subject's values bear in mind the inherent local-tone of its various parts and try to see these tones in a relational way (Figure 1.24).

Figure 1.24

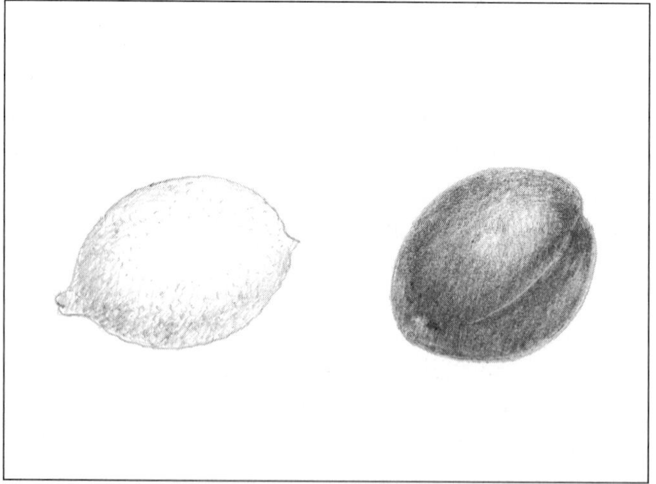

One of the difficulties of measuring values accurately is that we see the things around us in color. We live in a world made of colored forms and spaces, and "extracting" the value from any part of what we see means developing the skill to disregard an observed color in order to concentrate on its value instead. We have to "see" in black and white. When we do, we need a way to measure the many gray tones between black and white that exist in the colors we see around us.

Seeing in Black and White. One of the best ways of measuring the lightness or darkness of any form's color is to imagine seeing the form as it would appear in a black and white photograph. You are then more likely to "see" the light gray of a pink flower and the darker gray of a red apple. The more intense the color, the greater effort it takes to see its value. Judging the values of dull colored objects is somewhat easier, because their colors possess a degree of grayness anyway. A useful practice is to get some eight or nine sample color chips from a paint supply store, or to cut from a magazine an equal number of 1-inch squares of different colors and paste them in a row onto a sheet of paper. These colors should not vary in hue or value, but should each be one consistent color. Next, using graphite pencils, draw in below each of these color swatches the particular gray tone you judge to best match each color. For example, a yellow hue would translate to a light gray value, an orange one, to a darker gray, and a deep blue, to a very dark gray. If a color is darker than the darkest tone you can get with graphite, switch to charcoal pencils. If correctly done, your eye will seem to move smoothly through the gray tone and into the color swatch because of their common grayness. If incorrect, the boundary between the color chip and the gray tone will appear to be a strong barrier.

The Window. Comparing the values in your drawing to those in your subject, to better match their degrees of lightness or darkness is aided by an isolating window that enables you to judge values more objectively. Such a window can be made by cutting a $\frac{1}{2}$-inch square window from the center of a light or middle gray-toned stiff paper or cardboard sheet measuring approximately 5 by 5 inches. By holding the paper at arm's length and looking through the window at the part in question in the subject, and then using the window to look at the same part in your drawing, you will be better able to judge and compare the two values. The gray tone of the paper through which you look also serves a purpose. If the paper were white, all the values seen through the window would seem darker than they actually are. Of course, seen through the window of a black paper or board, values would seem lighter than they are.

The window serves another purpose, too. Whether a subject is strongly or weakly illuminated, various parts will be light and other parts dark. But are all the light areas alike in value? Are all the dark areas alike in value? And are the middle-toned values all alike in value? Using your window to move from one light area to another may reveal that some parts are lighter than others. Likewise, there are likely to be different degrees of dark-toned and middle-toned areas. In addition, when drawing in color, the window makes it easier to judge a part's color and intensity, as well as its value.

Seeing a Value's Shape and Scale. As we go about the matter of daily living we tend to see the shadowed and lighted areas of the things around us collectively indicating their surface form, and we are less aware of the sizes and shapes of these light and dark areas, be they cast shadows, interspaces, or *planes*. Planes can be thought of as a form's surface facets. For example, the six sides of a block are planes, as are the risers and treads of a staircase, or the five curved facets of a banana. But to draw the things around us tonally we need first to accurately see the shapes and sizes of these planes, interspaces, and shadows, whatever their value. As noted earlier, seeing forms and their interspaces as flat, as having silhouettes, helps you to draw the shape and size of these parts because you are then less concerned with what they represent than with objectively assessing their two-dimensional configurations. It is the same with shapes of tone. The fact that part of a form's surface is illuminated and another part is in shadow does not exempt us from analyzing their differing shapes, sizes, and values. In tonal drawing, the important measurements, then, have to do with judging *and* comparing the size, the shape, and the value of all areas, planes, or parts.

Three-Value Analysis

Another method for estimating the subject's values and for establishing a drawing's overall distribution of values is based on separating all the values you see in the subject into three general groups. If we think of a value scale where white is zero and black is one hundred, then the first group would consist of white plus some few slightly darker tones, up to, say, approximately thirty degrees of value as in Figure 1.25A. The second group would comprise darker values, from just over thirty degrees of tone to about sixty degrees, as in Figure 1.25B and the third, darkest, group would contain all the values darker than sixty degrees, running all the way to black, at one hundred degrees (Figure 1.25C).

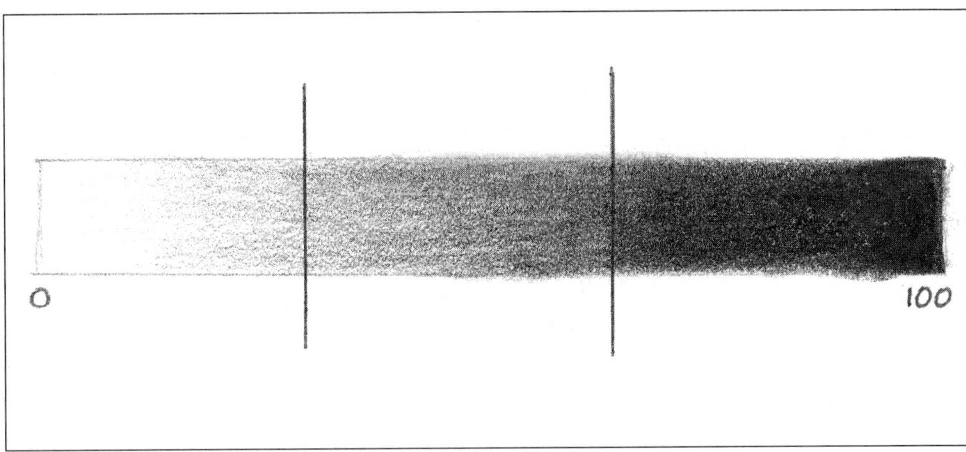

Figure 1.25

Seeing your subject in this way promotes a search for value similarities among its most far-flung parts as well as among nearby ones. This helps to develop all of a drawing together, instead of approaching it in a piecemeal way, which is almost always detrimental to a drawing's accuracy and unity.

Starting with a search for the subject's lightest values means that although you see a number of light, but differing tones, you will temporarily show them in your drawing as just one tone—the tone of the paper. But, because these values will be represented by the (usually) white tone of the paper, the first value you actually draw is the one representing those in the middle group. In doing so, the lightest toned areas appear "automatically" when you draw the locations and shapes of the middle value, as in Figure 1.26A. This middle tone also covers a range of tones, the aforementioned thirty to sixty degrees on our value scale, and can be represented by a tone of about forty degrees. The third group is often (but not necessarily) drawn last, and represents the various dark values you see in the subject. It can be shown as a tone of about seventy degrees. When the darkest group of values *is* drawn last, it is often the case that artists will not only use the middle value to represent all the observed middle tones, but all the darkest tones as well. This, of course, results in a two-value drawing, as in Figure 1.26A. The darkest values are then introduced, becoming subdivisions of the general middle value, as in Figure 1.26B. Some artists find this procedure helps them to organize the three value groupings better. Once the drawing is developed to this stage you can more easily subdivide these three large value groupings into the various degrees of tone you actually see (Figure 1.26C).

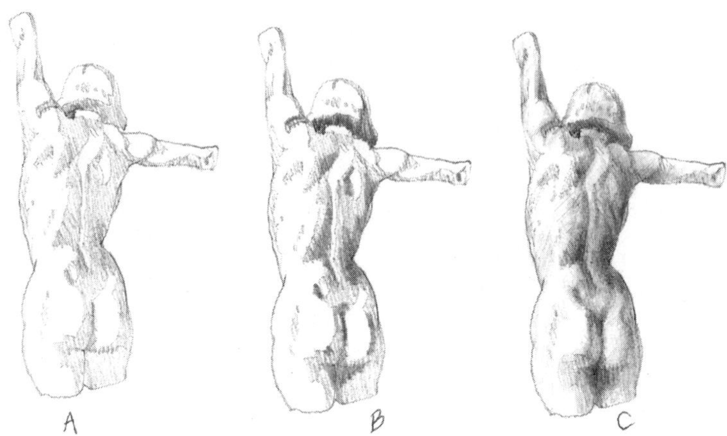

Figure 1.26

This three-value system for organizing the tones you actually see will reappear in Chapter Five, as an aid in creating volumes in a spatial field more clearly. (See, "Planes and Light," Chapter Five.)

As you continue your study of drawing, you will find other features and conditions in the subject *and* in your drawing that warrant comparison—which will benefit by measurement and by relating one part to another. But the matters of measurement discussed in this chapter will give you the principal means needed to make the judgments and connections that perform the magic of turning a blank page into an objective representation of what you have seen.

Things to Think About:

1. Judging the size relationships of a subject's parts is an important measurement when drawing. What are some other kinds of relationships to look for in your observed subject that will help you to objectively draw what you see?
2. How are the terms *long axis* and *alignment* alike? How are they different?
3. What role do negative shapes and interspaces play in more accurately establishing the shapes of a subject's forms? Why is it important to see the shapes of forms and interspaces in the first place?
4. How does correctly seeing intersections help in establishing the proportions of a subject's parts?
5. How does judging the angle of a form's long axis help you to draw the form's contours?

Critique Considerations:

A. Do your drawings show some of your subject's parts to be correctly tilted on the page (and in space) while other parts are not? Do you know why this occurs?

B. Are some of your drawings "out of proportion?" There are several reasons why this occurs.

1. Do you "crowd" your drawing? Stepping back frequently, especially at the drawing's outset, will enable you to better estimate the relative sizes of various parts.
2. Do you start at the top of the page, drawing from top to bottom?
3. Do you start and finish one form at a time?
4. Do you forget to relate the sizes of parts as the drawing progresses?

All of the above difficulties are often due to drawing in a sequential, rather than a relational, way.

C. Are some of the forms in your drawings "out of perspective?" Review the section "Convergence," in this chapter, and see "Perspective Fundamentals," Chapter Four.

D. Do your tonal drawings appear light in value, with few, if any dark tones? This sometimes has to do with a reluctance to draw dark tones, especially over large areas. Sometimes the problem can be traced to the use of the harder graphite pencils, especially when used on newsprint paper. Using the three-value analysis will help you to establish a greater range of values in your drawings.

2

Gesture to Line

GESTURE DEFINED

Almost all nonartists, when asked to make a drawing of anything placed before them, do two things. First, they will select one part of the subject, draw it to the best of their ability, and then move on to complete a second part, a third, and so on until each part has been dealt with. If the subject is the human figure, the trip usually begins with the head and ends at the feet. If it is a forest landscape, the drawing is made tree by tree. They draw in a sequential, piecemeal manner, carefully finishing one part at a time. Second, they will merge the particular features of what is in front of them with memories—with stored notions of what such features are *supposed* to look like. As a result, in drawings of the head, for example, the eyes will often be found near the top of the face, the nose may be quite long or reduced to two dots representing the nostrils. And even though the head before them is tilted and turned to a three-quarter view, it will invariably be drawn as upright and facing forward. Tree trunks will likewise stand straight, each tree showing a ball-like arrangement of leaves in summer and groups of Y-shaped branches in winter.

Both "symptoms" reveal a kind of functional blindness to qualities visible in any subject. In the first instance, the nonartist fails to note alignments and the sense of movement and energy that these alignments generate. Looking at the forms, parts, and interspaces that compose a subject, they do not see how a subject's parts "belong" to each other through similarities and variations in position, shape, scale, and value—how these visual conditions unite to energize and animate the subject. In the second instance, the non artist has an inability to acknowledge—to "take on"—a subject's particular, measurable, characteristics of shape, size, and so on, and instead the nonartist turns to remembered notions of what the subject ought to look like. Although they certainly see these characteristics, nonartists are seldom consciously aware of them until they are pointed out. They do not examine the actual visual nature of the forms they look at. Instead, they identify them as belonging to certain categories of similar forms stored in their memory, and call on their recollections to help in drawing the forms before them. In this way the unique characteristics of a particular tree or of an individual's features are largely disregarded in favor of remembered, generic solutions. But for artists, these qualities of a form's particular characteristics are vital and fundamental to drawing what they see. Most beginners it seems rely more on their concepts than on their perceptions.

Artists usually begin a drawing with a search for what the entire subject is *doing*, that is, with the actions and energies that seem to be moving within it, and not by seeing its parts separately. Some subjects are difficult to see any other way. For example, it is not possible to see a necklace or a shark without responding to their graceful, curving sweep before we can examine their particular parts. Most subjects, however, do require that the artist consciously bypass specifics to first see the subject's overall arrangement of forms and moving actions. This tactic also helps the artist decide where to place the subject on the page and what size it will be. Although artists are mindful of a subject's particular characteristics and may even make a few notations about them, their concentration is fixed on swiftly responding to the rhythms and energies that animate the entire subject. Drawing in a free and resolute manner they try first to extract these vital actions. To do this they must identify with these actions—must experience the easygoing or forceful movements coursing through the subject's parts while simultaneously noting at least the general nature of the subject's forms. This identification with the subject's actions—with "becoming" the subject, calls on our kinesthetic sensibility, that is, on our ability to experience the movement in the things we see. Watching a circus performer maintain balance on a high wire, or a dancer leaping across the stage, stirs feelings in us as our bodies experience these actions. But we can also respond kinesthetically to inanimate forms, can feel as well as see the graceful turnings of a wicker chair or a racing car, and can feel the suspense in the imminent fall of a dew drop. The ability to identify with a subject in this way is, to some extent, always present for artists at any stage of a drawing, but is a strong presence at a drawing's outset.

The kind of swift drawing we have been describing, whether intended as a final state or as an underdrawing—that is, as a kind of armature to build upon—is called *gesture drawing*. Typically, a gesture drawing takes anywhere from thirty seconds to two minutes. The brevity of the time itself makes the artist concentrate on what the subject is doing, rather than what it looks like. Toulouse-Lautrec's animated drawing of a rearing horse (Figure 2.1) shows just how much of a subject's spirit and substance can be conveyed in a brief time by a gestural approach to what is seen.

Although the graceful forms of the horse ring true, they say even more about the animal's energy and motion than they do about precision of observation. Note that the artist's lines move inside and even outside the forms. They are not restricted to contours only. Drawing contours with some accuracy will come sooner and better by first establishing their general and more rhythmic state. Sometimes gesture drawings show even less concern with contour, as Figures 2.2 and 2.3 demonstrate. Such more "scribbled" drawings often seem to concentrate more on a subject's three-dimensional nature—seem to be experiencing the way its volumes move in a spatial field of depth.

For all artists, there is always a subject, always something to be "seen."

Gesture drawing supports a basic strategy common to all creative expression, which is to develop a work, in whatever medium, by moving from the general to the specific. This enables poets, musical composers, and architects to experience the essential character of a work before refining it. The poet may jot down a few words or phrases that seize the spirit of a concept, as does the composer with a few musical notations, and the architect, with a few lines and shapes. They each benefit from capturing the vital generalities that will guide them to a work's final realization.

Gesture drawing (as you will see in Chapter Eight) is equally important when drawing something you saw in the past or even imagined. For all artists, there is always a subject, always something to be "seen." Although the subject may not be actually present, it can be seen on the screen of your imagination. This screen is notoriously murky and unsteady, and it's not an easy matter to fix your subject in place, even for a brief time. All the more reason to capture these fleeting images by an approach that quickly establishes the subject's essential arrangement and form character.

Gesture Drawing Exercises

Starting a drawing in a gestural way may seem to be taking you away from your interest in creating drawings of an objective kind. In fact, it is the most efficient (and fastest) way of *extracting* the most important qualities from the "raw material" of

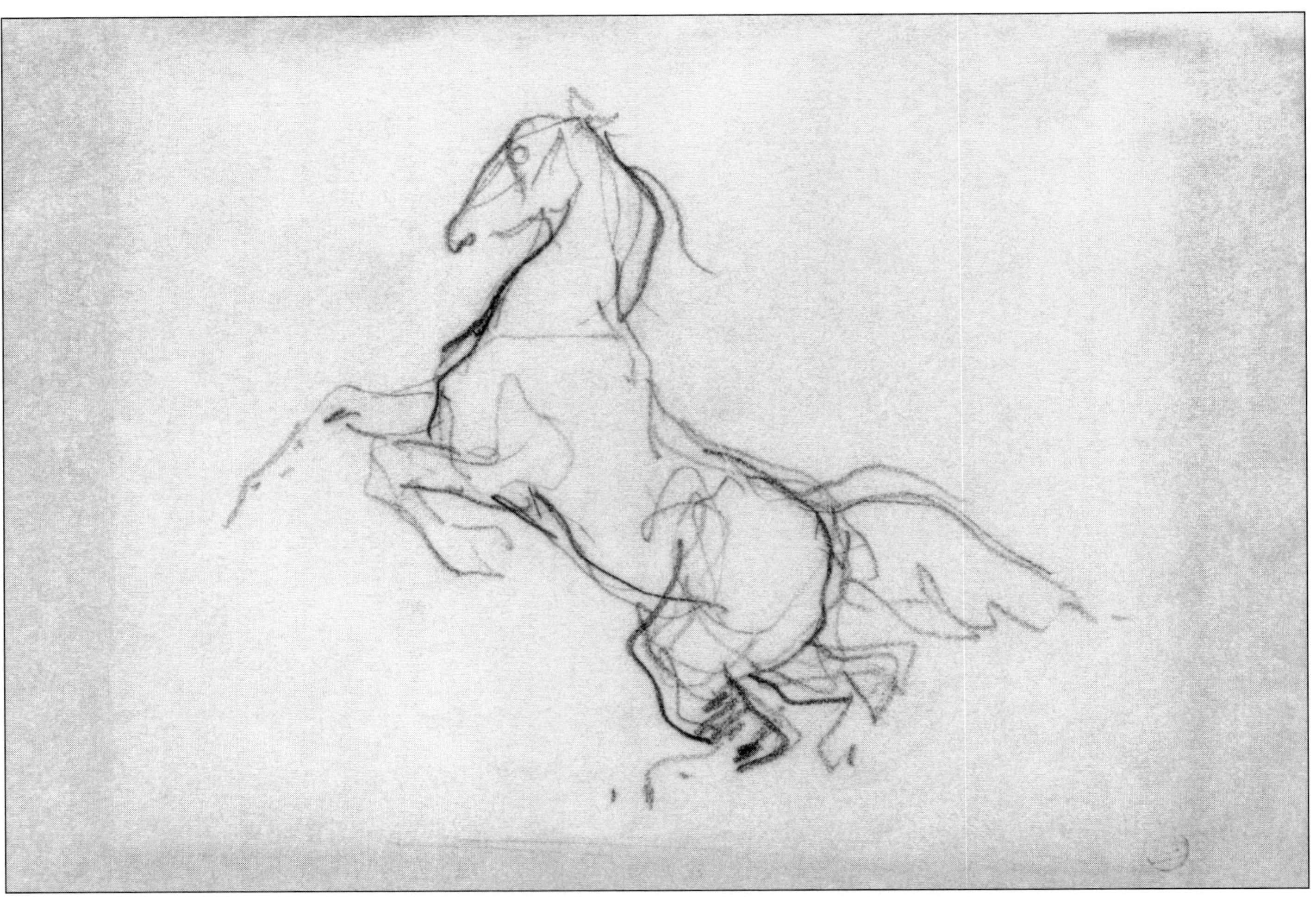

Figure 2.1 H. Toulouse-Lautrec (1864–1901), *Sketch of a Rearing Horse*. 11.5 × 14.5 cm. *Source:* Museum of Czech Literature, Karasek Gallery, Prague.

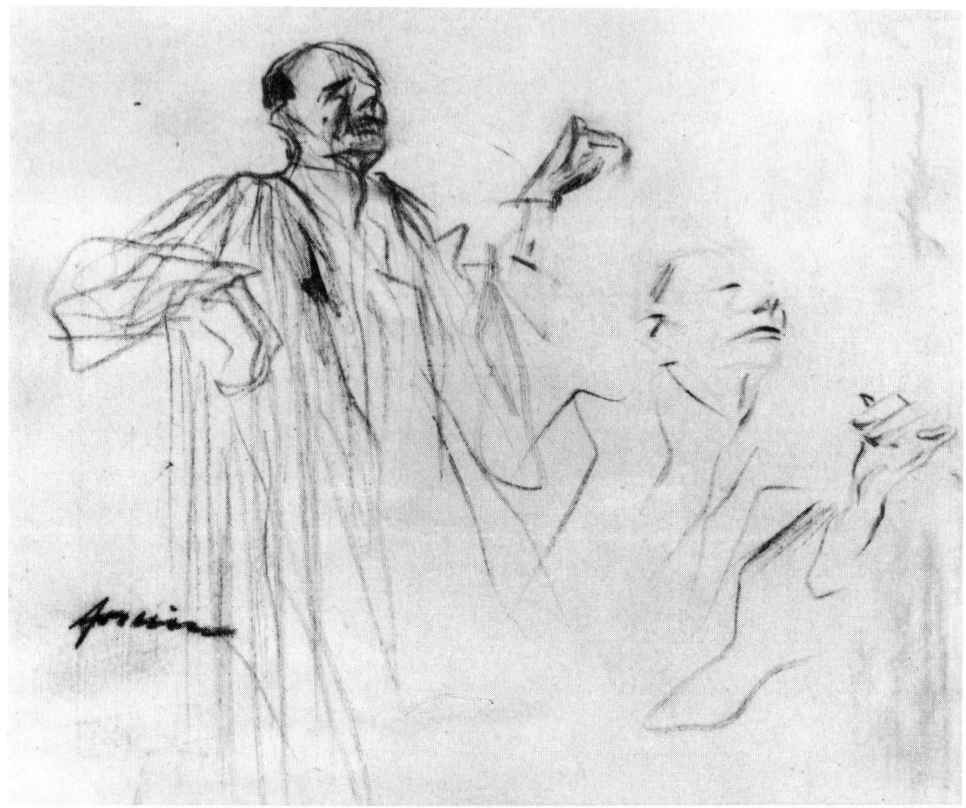

Figure 2.2 Jean-Louis Forain (French, 1852–1931), *The Orator*. Coloured chalks, 20.6 × 21.5 cm. (K-33819). Photograph © National Gallery in Prague 2004.

your subject—its unique arrangement of forms, their essential character, and the moving energies that unite and enliven them. It enables you to break through old, step-by-step drawing habits because with only a minute or two in which to draw, your pencil or chalk must race everywhere almost at once, to experience the action as well as the basic character of the forms. This speed of execution is also an aid in seeing proportions more accurately because again, in visiting every part almost at once, you are made more aware of the relative lengths and sizes.

Gesture drawings are best made in groups of fifteen to twenty. It may take a few drawings just to relax and to summon up the daring needed to push aside all tendencies to go after surface or contour details, and to concentrate on searching for and *feeling* the strongest movements, and on drawing only the briefest of form notations. Using a timer helps to keep your drawings to the brief time allotted. Start with some five or six two-minute drawings; reduce the time to one-minute for the next five or six, then return to two-minute drawings for the remainder.

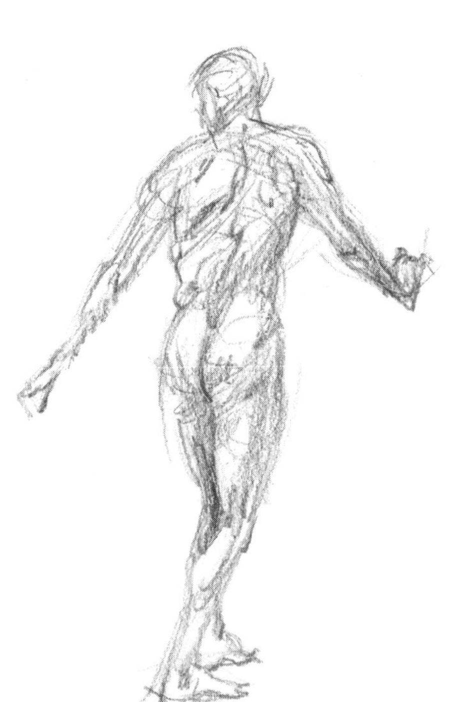

Figure 2.3

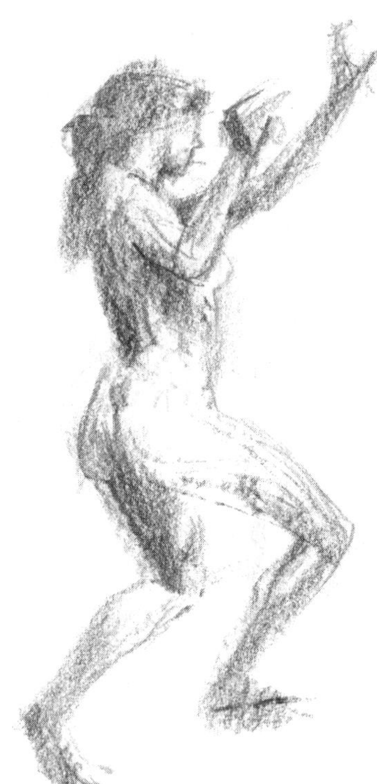

Figure 2.4

Your subject can be the human figure, draped or nude, a still life arrangement, a single object, or even your own unoccupied hand. Most things made of leather such as jackets, gloves, or boots are useful. In a pinch, use photographs of figures or landscapes.

Although the softer graphite drawing pencils work well, consider using a small (1-inch) piece of conte crayon, or any kind of black or dark-toned chalk. Such broader media discourage going after details, and by using the side of the chalk, at least at a drawing's outset, you are more able to lightly draw the broad path of a part's movement rather than its contour (Figure 2.4). Gesture drawings can be of any size but here you should use a drawing pad that measures approximately 18 by 24 inches.

Begin to draw by regarding your subject as alive with large moving actions that race through every part. The key word in the previous sentence is "through," because only some of these actions are conveyed by contours. In these one- and two-minute drawings, you should be looking at your subject more than at your drawing—you may find that you can actually draw for a few seconds *while* looking at the subject.

Your goal here is to extract the major moving actions and general form characteristics. Contours are seductive and seem to promise answers to questions about the location and the angle of parts, their various sizes, and the energies coursing through them. But concentrating on contours will only divert your attention from these matters. Then, too, in the early stages of a drawing it is not possible to know with any precision just where the contours will be. In such quick drawings contours can't contribute as much as a more forceful and broader search for a subject's essential rhythms and form characteristics, a search that moves on, in, and even outside the forms. As we saw in Figure 2.1, Toulous-Lautrec's lines move freely through, on, and beyond the animal's forms.

At first, the two-minute drawings may seem too brief a time in which to get anything underway, but after doing a few their very brevity teaches you that there is time only for the most evident actions and the most outstanding form characteristics. And once you've adapted to this time frame you'll find that the one-minute drawings demand even bolder summaries of the subject's basic visual conditions. Returning to the second set of two-minute drawings, you will probably find that you can see more and do more than you did in the first set.

A useful exercise in experiencing gesture is done by placing tracing paper over photographs of people, places, and things, and extracting the gestural qualities discussed above. This is in no way "cheating." In fact, being able to see the subject at all times, and having your drawing actually superimposed on it provides insights and experience that can then be utilized in drawing observed subjects. As in the gesture drawing exercise discussed earlier, restrict these drawings to one and two minutes each.

The best representational drawings reveal the artist's recognition of the energies that underlie everything we see. The graceful spiral of a winding staircase or a bit of string, the eruptive spread of a flower arrangement or your own extended fingers, the roller coaster ride of a gnarled branch or a garden hose—everything is imbued with motion. Even forms like a book or an apple that seem to be without it still show some moving action, if only in the thrust of the book's long axis or in the circular action of the apple's form.

So much is this the case that artists of all persuasions regard seeing implications of movement in (and between) things that are not actually in motion to be a given condition of creative perception. We might even presume the act of drawing to be as much about the governing of energies as about the depicting of a subject's particularities. After all, good observational drawing is about more than sound measurement, it is about making the things we choose to draw come alive on the page.

> ***... good observational drawing is about more than sound measurement, it is about making the things we choose to draw come alive on the page.***

ENERGY AND ALIGNMENT

For artists, only some of the underlying energies that animate their drawings are found in the observed subject. In addition to the earlier noted energies emerging from the actual alignments and rhythms among a subject's parts are several other factors artists call on to bring their drawings to life.

The first of these is to *slightly* exaggerate the alignment of a subject's parts, for the more nearly edges, shapes, angles, or interspaces align, the more forceful is the moving energy between them (Figure 2.5A). This is especially useful if you find your gesture drawings to be somewhat timid or tight. If they are, these subtle overstatements may actually help you to draw what is nearer to the truth of what you are seeing because the cautious drawing tends to understate rhythmic turns, angles, and alignments. However, bringing edges and parts into stronger alignments should be done with discretion. Extreme exaggerations will give a gesture drawing an overbearingly streamlined look. When that happens the relationships of alignment and the energies they create are more burlesqued than clarified (Figure 2.5B).

A second means by which artists enliven and unify a gesture drawing comes from the use of the drawing material itself. No matter which medium you use, you will, with practice, come to see which turnings of the pencil, brush, or chalk are best suited to get at what you are trying to draw. Each of us has a unique way of making marks.

Figure 2.5A

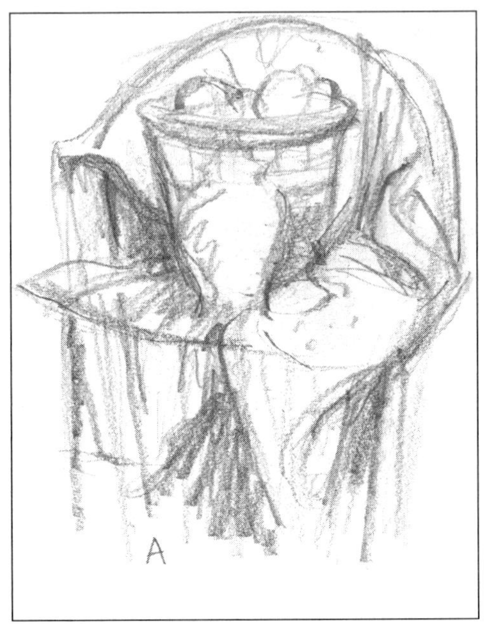

Figure 2.5B

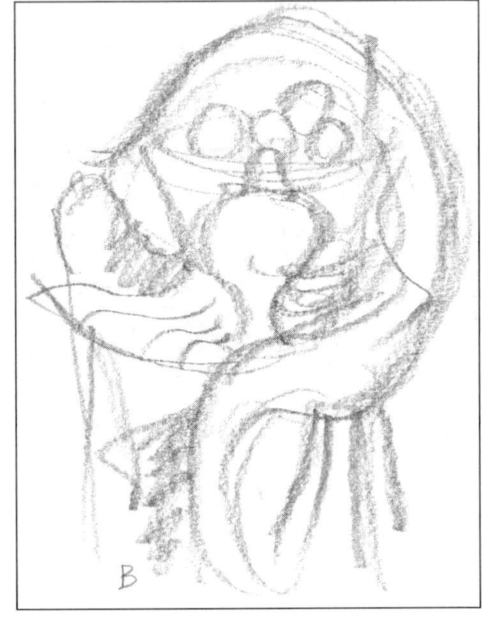

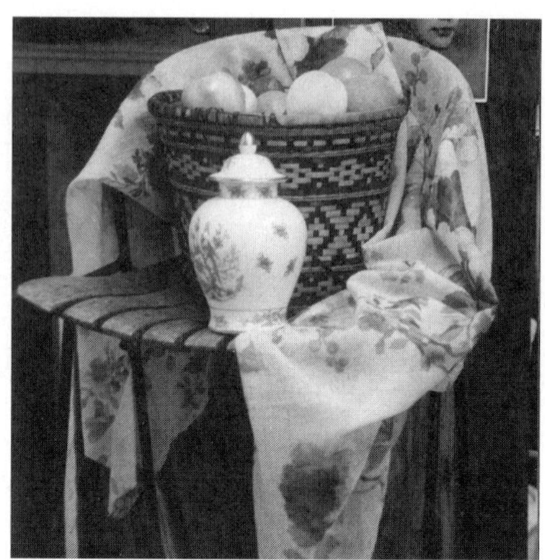

Figure 2.5C

It is ingrained in our particular way of processing what we see and is a part of what is called our *style*. Before long, your particular way of mark-making will take on a certain ease and rhythm. It is not unlike your first stilted-looking alphabet letters when you first learned to write in script, which, with time, took on the particular flow and character of your handwriting today. Similarly, the flow of the lines and tones of your drawings will also generate the energy that familiarity and practice provide, giving your drawings added force and a sense of the parts belonging together (see "Handling," Chapter Seven). The energy and unifying effects of an assured handling of a medium can be seen in Corot's charcoal drawing (Figure 2.6). Compare his drawing with another use of charcoal in Figure 2.7. The use of the medium is different, but both drawings show the benefits of a familiarity with charcoal.

An important dividend in acquiring a skill for seeing the broad underlying movements that sweep and twist through your subject, and even in strengthening them in your gesture drawings, is that you are more likely in time to see such actions in and among all forms. You may come to search for the gestural activity in everything, large and small. And because it exists in everything, it will be there. This will give your extended, more ambitious drawings, and even your paintings and sculptures, a stronger feeling of animation and unity.

Gesture Drawing as a Goal

When artists wish to make an energetic and spirited drawing, or when their subject is available for only a brief time, they will draw in a more gestural manner. Such drawings, as Figures 2.6 and 2.7 show, can have an order and realization that

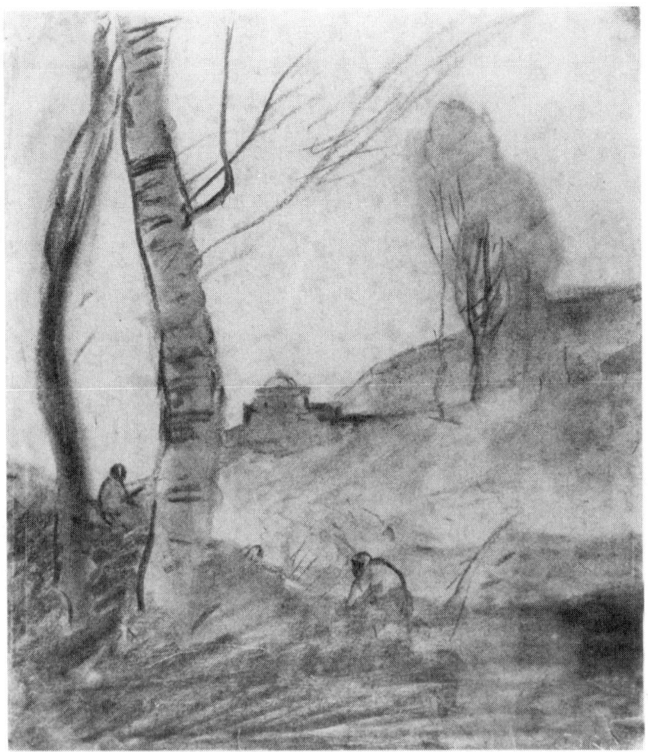

Figure 2.6 Jean-Baptiste Camille Corot (French, 1796–1895), *The Great Birch: Souvenir of Ariccia*. Charcoal, 27.1 × 23.3 cm. *Source:* Princeton University Art Museum. Gift of Frank Jewett Mather, Jr. © 1980 Photo: Trustees of Princeton University. May not be reproduced without permission in writing from Princeton University Art Museum, Princeton, NJ 08544.

makes them complete visual statements. That such drawings can have charm and completeness is demonstrated by Rembrandt's *Cottage Beside a Canal* (Figure 2.8). A complex scene, Rembrandt is able to show the character of these forms by extracting their essential shape and mass with animated contours aligned in ways that send undulating motions throughout the drawing. Notice that the pen lines used to suggest the shaded parts of the trees and roofs are themselves fast moving and gestural in character. Again, in Lebrun's *Seated Clown* (Figure 2.9), although it shows a head that is carried beyond the gestural stage, the clown's burly figure is defined by bold, sweeping lines of a strongly gestural nature. Lebrun's drawing is a good example of just how powerful a gestural approach to drawing can be. As these four examples indicate, drawings in a gestural mode can stand as final works, and can convey a variety of moods and meanings.

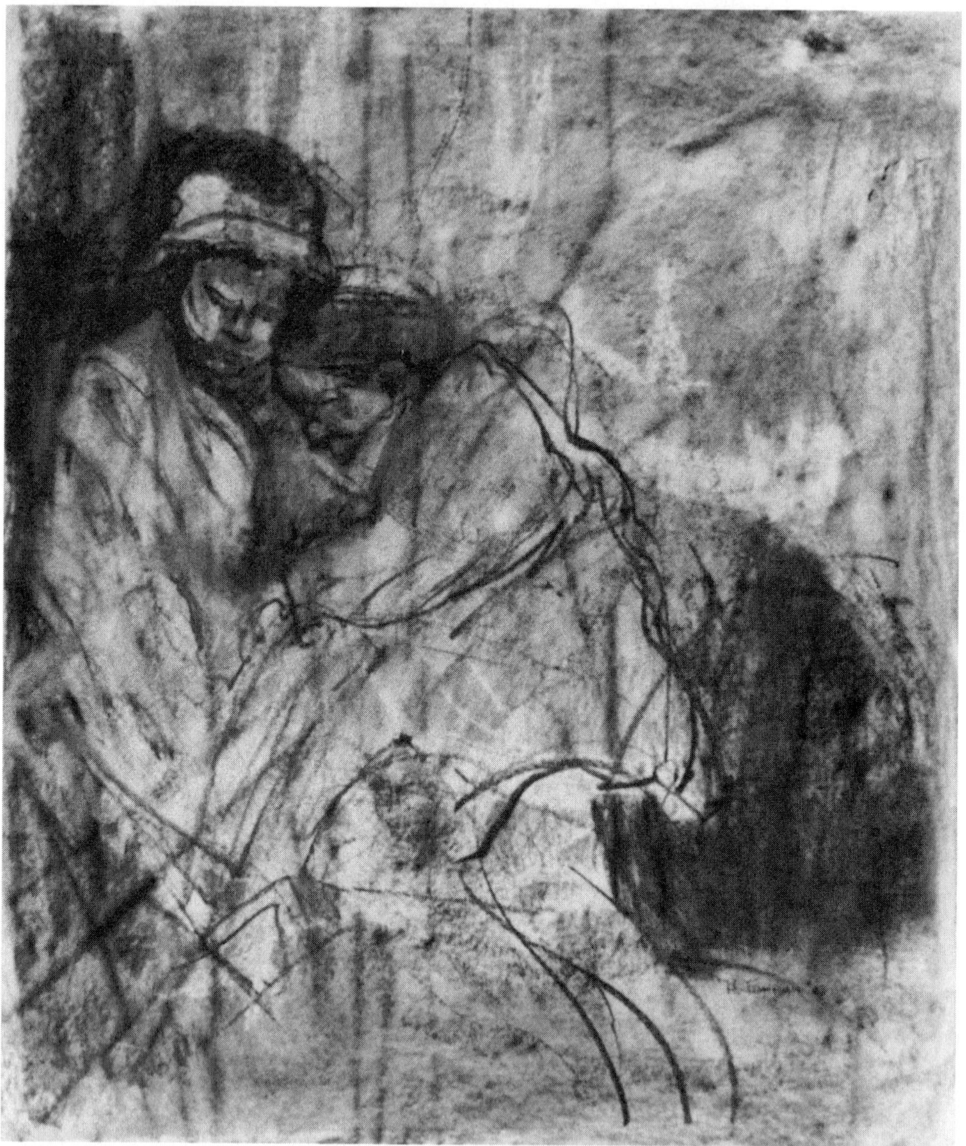

Figure 2.7 Harriet Fishman, *Mother and Child.* Charcoal, 31 × 21 in. *Source:* Collection of Sarah Hannah.

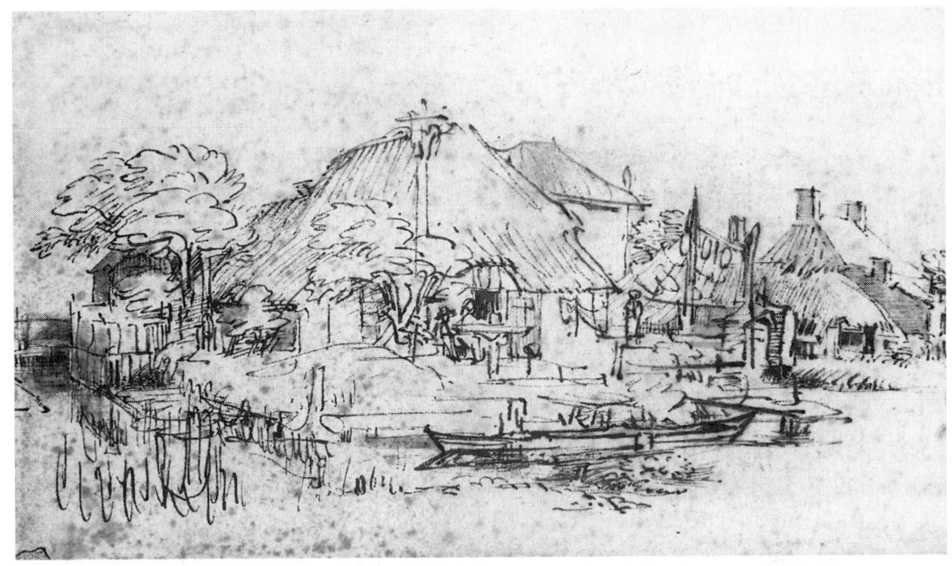

Figure 2.8 Rembramdt Harmenszoon van Rijn (Dutch, 1606–1669), *Farmstead Beside a Canal* (c. 1650–53). Pen and brown ink, with touches of brush and brown wash, on cream laid paper (discolored to tan), 14.9 × 24.8 cm. Clarence Buckingham Collection, (1953.37). *Source:* Reproduction, The Art Institute of Chicago.

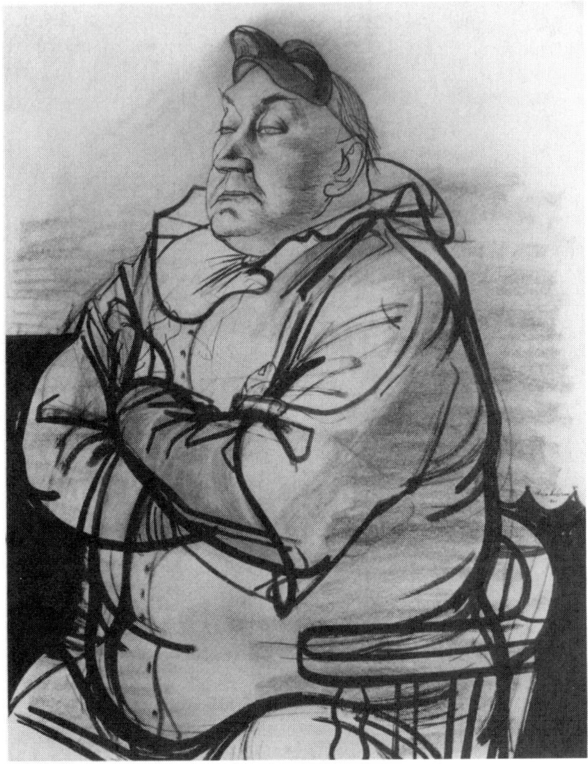

Figure 2.9 Rico Lebrun (1906–1964), *Seated Clown*, 1941. Ink and wash, $39\frac{1}{2} \times 29$ inches. *Source:* The Koplin Del Rio Gallery. Santa Barbara Museum of Art, Gift of Mr. and Mrs. Arthur B. Sachs.

Gesture as Underdrawing

Most artists begin their drawings with some manner of gesture drawing. It may be extensive and boldly drawn, with the subsequent drawing being bolder still, as in Bischoff's *Model Resting* (Figure 2.10), or it can be as delicate, sparse, and searching as the light, ghostlike lines that flit about on the outskirts of the forms in Doyle's *War Belt* (Figure 2.11). Sometimes a drawing retains much of its gestural origins, especially when an overall feeling of animation or atmosphere is intended, as in Baudry's *Study of Sleeping Children* (Figure 2.12), where only the serving cart and the French doors are brought into clearer focus.

Usually, however, the gesture drawing that underlies works of a more extended and fully realized kind is intentionally kept sparse and lightly drawn. Such lines and tones are intended only as a means of faintly setting down the subject's placement on the page and the main "routes" of movement. These lines may be used to rough in general shape notations, to mark key points or turnings in the forms, and to broadly suggest a drawing's compositional strategy. If this rough "armature" of notations is carried too far, there is the danger it may interfere with the lines and tones of the

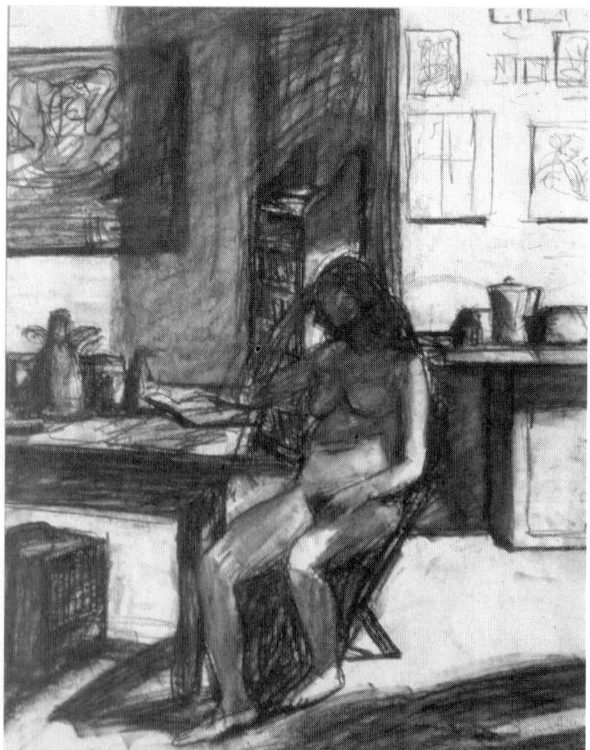

Figure 2.10 Elmer Bischoff (American, 1916–1991), *Model Resting*, 1973. Charcoal on paper, 26 × 20 inches. Courtesy Elmer Bischoff Estate/John Berggruen Gallery, San Francisco. Private Collection.

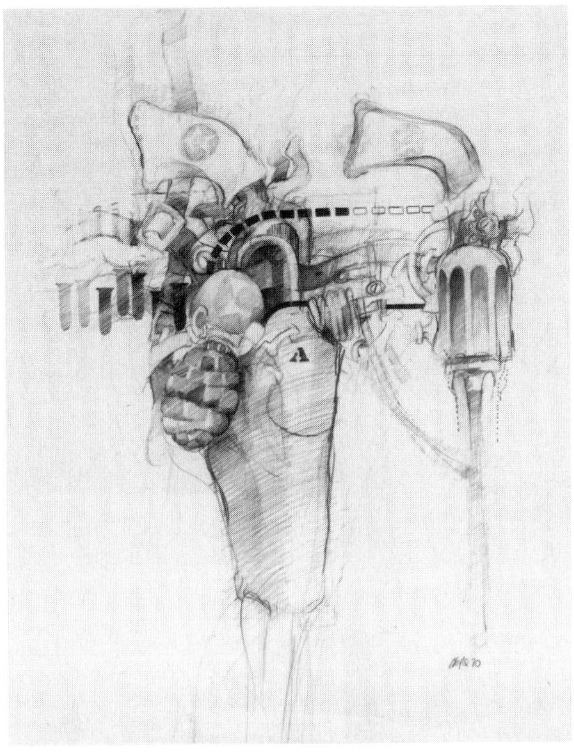

Figure 2.11 John L. Doyle (American, b. 1939), *War Belt*, 1970. Graphite on paper, $36 \times 25\frac{1}{2}$ inches. *Source:* Chrysler Museum of Art, Norfolk, VA. Gift of the Irene Leache Memorial. Museum reference number: 71.10.1.

drawing's later stages unless you intend a bold image, as in Figure 2.10. Because this kind of gesture drawing is almost always absorbed by the drawing's later stages, it is seldom visible in the completed work (Figure 2.12). Some drawings however, especially preparatory sketches, where artists have realized their intentions with some of the initial gesture drawing still evident, let us see this process at work (Figure 2.14).

Because gesture drawing concentrates mainly on large moving actions, seeing in a gestural way is, as noted earlier, often a matter of running through forms rather than moving along their contours. This can be seen in Bishop's *Nude Bending* (Figure 2.15), where still discernible ink washes move through the forms from the ankle to the head. When artists do roughly indicated edges, as in Figure 2.13, the preliminary lines are generalized and light, as in the lower, ghostlike version of the violin and in the musician's legs.

But whichever way a gestural drawing is begun (and artists often combine both methods), it can be sustained only for a short time. After a few minutes, with the main moving actions and a few indications of the subject's outlines roughed in,

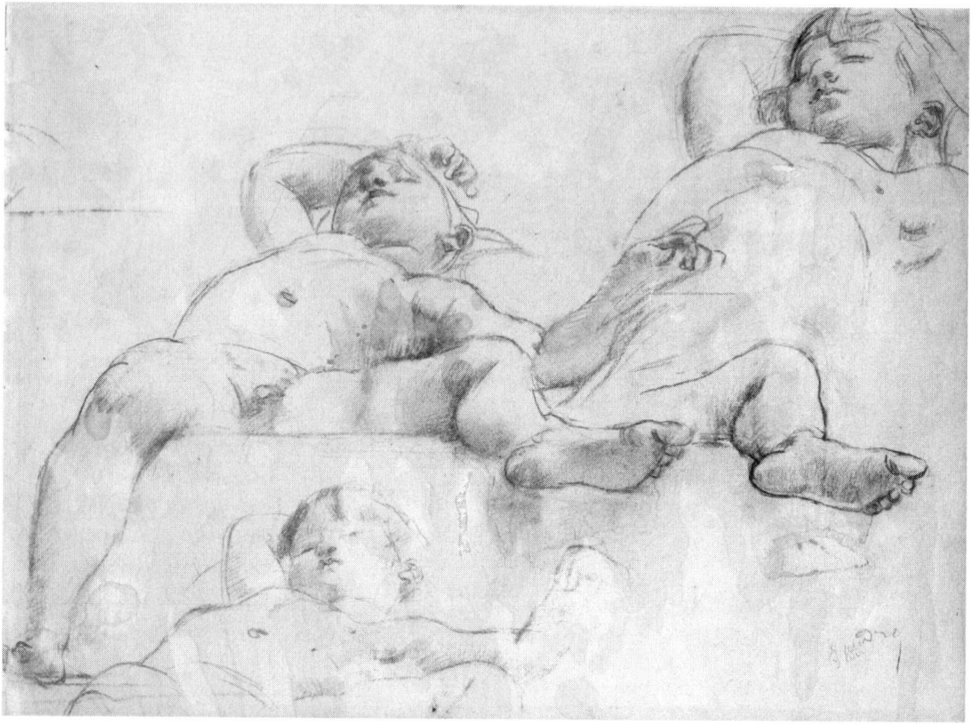

Figure 2.12 Paul Baudry (French, 1828–1886), *Study of Sleeping Children.* Charcoal on tan wove paper, 29.9 cm × 40.4 cm. Courtesy of the Fogg Art Museum, Harvard University Art Museums. Bequest of Grenville L. Winthrop. Photo Credit: Allan Macintyre. © 2004 President and Fellows of Harvard College.

there is nowhere else for a representational drawing to go but toward a more deliberate examination of edges, with a view to developing the general shape character of the things we see in some more objective way.

All forms, from the needle to the haystack, have a silhouette, or shape.

GENERAL SHAPE CHARACTER

Although the element of shape is one of the main subjects of the next two chapters, here it will be useful to mention something of its importance in drawing objectively. All forms, from the needle to the haystack, have some kind of two-dimensional state, have a silhouette, or shape. Once the gestural phase of a drawing is established you will, as noted above, find yourself beginning to examine the edges of the forms you have up to now only loosely suggested. At this stage

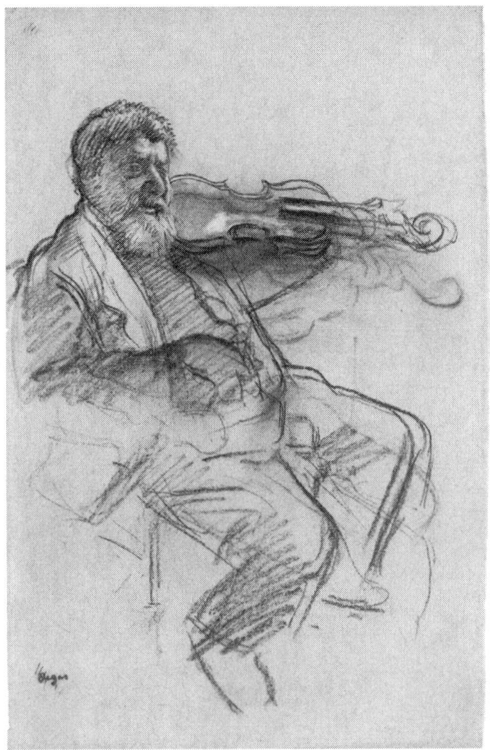

Figure 2.13 Edgar Degas (French, 1834–1917), *The Violinist*, about 1879. Charcoal heightened with white on blue-gray paper. Sight: 47 × 30 cm ($18\frac{1}{2} \times 11\frac{13}{16}$ inches). Frame: 63.5 × 48.5 cm ($25 \times 19\frac{1}{8}$ inches).
Source: Photograph © 2004 Museum of Fine Arts, Boston. William Francis Warden Fund, (58.1263).

it becomes necessary to make some judgments about the general shapes of your subject's larger forms because a form's shape is the "field of play" within which the form's planes, textures, and values are found. And these too create shapes. Seeing a form's general shape is a necessary prelude to seeing its specific one. The most common means of establishing a shape's general *and* specific configuration is by using line to track its variously turned edges. But line can do much more, as we will see in the next chapter.

Things to Think About

1. What problems may arise if you start a drawing with an exclusive concentration on the subject's contours?
2. What are some of the benefits of a gestural approach to drawing?
3. If a gesture drawing is to serve as an underdrawing in an extended tonal study, where it will be covered over by values and textures anyway, why draw it at all?
4. Name a few forms or subjects that cause you to respond kinesthetically.

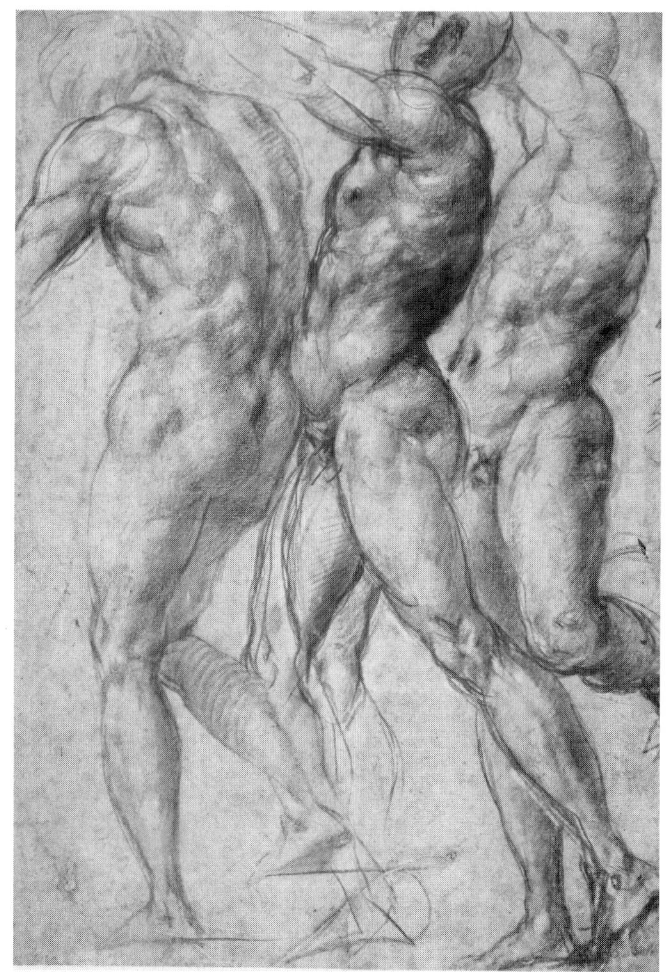

Figure 2.14 Jacopo Pontormo (1494–1557), *Study of Standing Male Nudes. Source:* Inv. Pl. 162. Photograph © Reunion des Musees Nationaux/Art Resource, NY.

Critique Considerations

1. Do your gesture drawings continue to emphasize contours? Sometimes this is partly the result of using a pointed instrument like the graphite or charcoal pencil. Try drawing with the side, as well as the tip of a one-inch piece of conte crayon, compressed charcoal, or pastel. The resulting tones will help to move through forms, and also encourages a search for larger rhythmic movements. Remember that a gesture drawing is *not* a very fast contour drawing.
2. When making gesture drawings do you note the various angles of your subject's parts? Searching for a part's long axis (whether you actually draw it or not) should precede drawing the part.

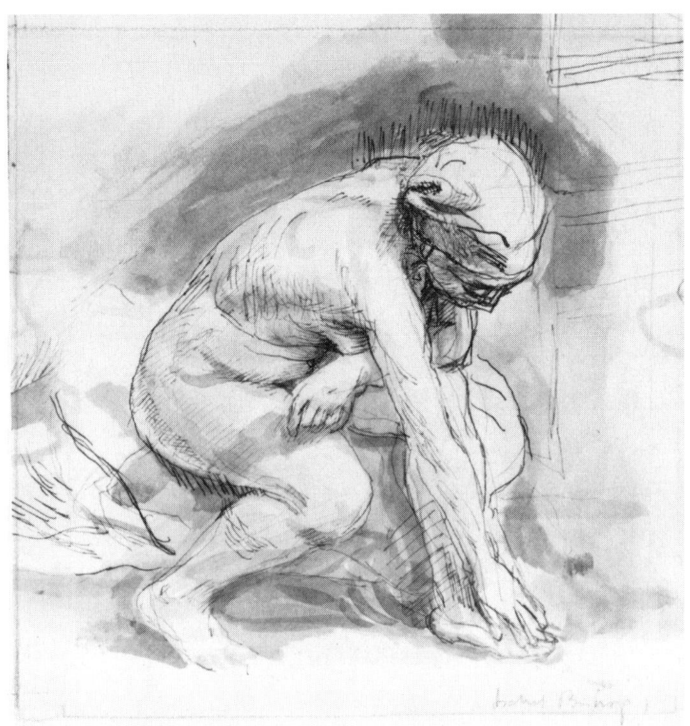

Figure 2.15 Isabel Bishop, *Nude Bending*, 1949. Ink and inkwash on paper, $5\frac{3}{4} \times 5\frac{1}{2}$ inches. Private Collection, Courtesy DC Moore Gallery, NYC.

3. In a one- or two-minute gesture drawing, do you try to include details of edge, textures, folds, or other small facts? This may have to do with an inability to accept the gesture drawing's brief time frame. Think of a gesture drawing as a visual report that must account for the major characteristics of what you see, but you are allotted only one or two minutes to do it. There will be time only for the most inclusive and basic truths about your subject.

4. Are your gesture drawings small-scale, lightly drawn, somewhat "shy" or "wooden?" If so, it may be that you are drawing one form at a time, instead of boldly drawing your subject's essential characteristics. It may also mean that you find safety in edges, in being cautious, and in avoiding a subject's large, sweeping actions and energies. Try drawing larger, darker, and with an eye on the subject's strongest features and movements. Don't be concerned about "making a mess." All good artists do so from time to time. Gesture drawings require sensitive observation *and* some courage. If you succeed in getting three or four out of ten gesture drawings to capture a subject's essential action and character, you're doing well.

3

Line to Shape

LINES OF MEASUREMENT

Diagrammatic Line

As we have seen, objectively drawing anything you see usually begins with an animated gesture drawing that captures the overall pattern of the subject's parts and at least some general observations about the character of these parts. As your drawing proceeds beyond the gestural stage, it is important to reexamine the various tilts or angles you have given to the subject's parts. Often, in the excitement of extracting a subject's gestural energies, a part may be shown as tilted too much or not enough, and it is important to make such adjustments as early as possible in a drawing's development. Investing time and effort in the drawing of, say, an arm, a spoon, or a church spire, only to find that the form, however well you've drawn it, is headed in the wrong direction is a frustration easily avoided by noting the imaginary line of its long axis. Whether you actually draw such a centerline or only notice its tilt is up to you, but consciously searching for it is the important thing.

Once the angles of your subject's parts are noted, your attention should turn to developing the correct size and general shape character of each part. Doing this doesn't mean you need to avoid noting major planes or divisions within a shape, or even occasionally showing something of the major light and dark values within it. It means the emphasis should be on objectively seeing a part's size and general shape-state. Just as failing to see a part's angle will create a major problem later in the drawing's development, so will failing to see a part's scale and actual shape configuration—its "silhouette"—do the same. No matter how much you go on to develop that part's inner conditions of planes, values, textures, and details, none of that will outweigh the damage to the objectively oriented drawing as does a form's distorted size and shape. And diagrammatic lines are ideal for starting the process of seeing a form's shape-actualities, and then, using shorter diagrammatic lines, to "close in" on a shape's silhouette.

The scale, angle, and shape of a part are usually indicated by lightly drawn, schematic lines, often called diagrammatic lines. In fact, such lines often play a part in a drawing's gestural stage (Figure 3.1). But whether or not they do,

Figure 3.1

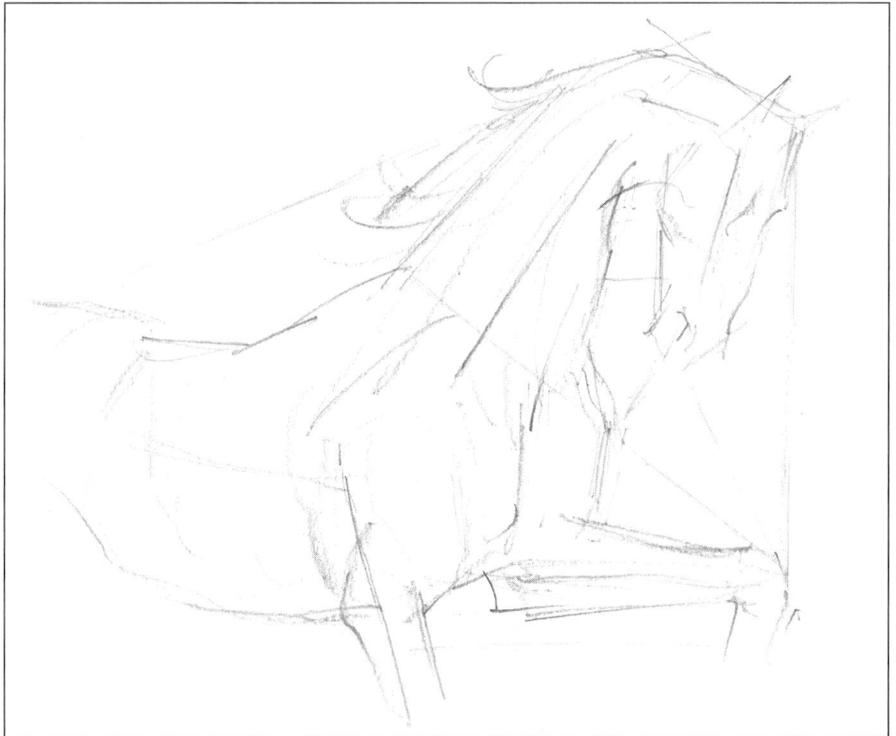

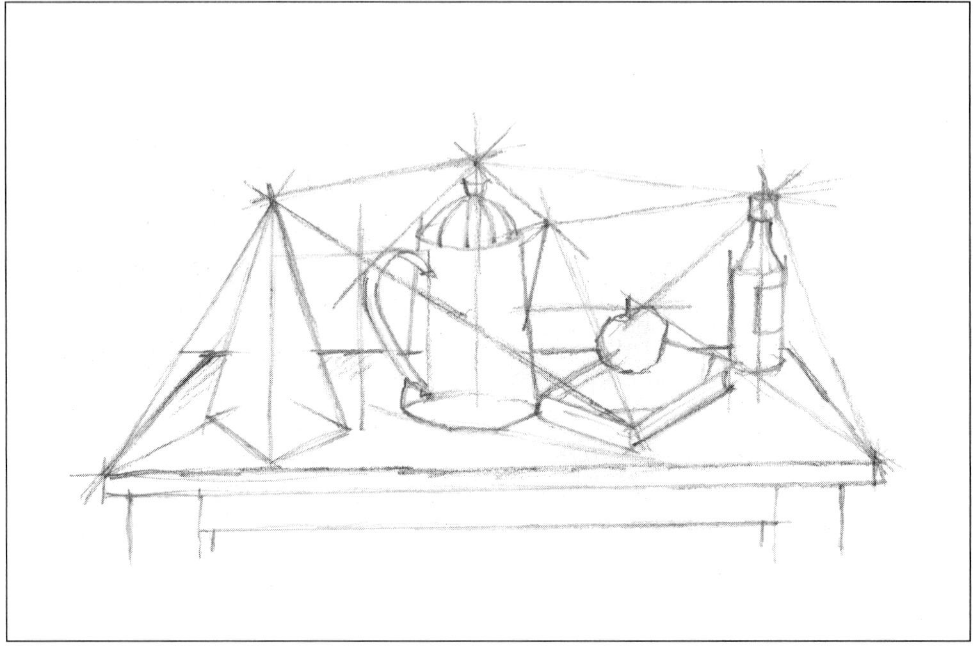

Figure 3.2

diagrammatic lines often lead the way out of the gesture drawing toward more deliberate measurements and judgments of the subject's parts. Diagrammatic lines can find the relative height among parts, can determine the distance separating one part from another, and can determine the location, scale and, of course, the shape of parts (Figure 3.2).

> ***In objective drawing the shapes of the spaces separating parts ... must be seen with the same degree of inquiry we give to seeing the shape of the parts themselves.***

Practicing what diagrammatic lines can help you find is very useful in sharpening your observational skills. In Duchamp-Villon's study (Figure 3.3), you can see diagrammatic lines measuring height, location, and proportion. Notice that the artist uses thicker lines to rough in the general shape character of the figure's forms. These heavier lines are partly the result of repeatedly going over a shape's boundaries, making subtle adjustments that get at the shape's main turnings, and partly as a result of emphasizing and distinguishing the figure's forms from the web of encircling, lighter diagrammatic lines. Note, too, that most of these heavier lines are straight. In Chapter One, we saw that analyzing edges by using straight and curved lines clarifies what segments of edge really

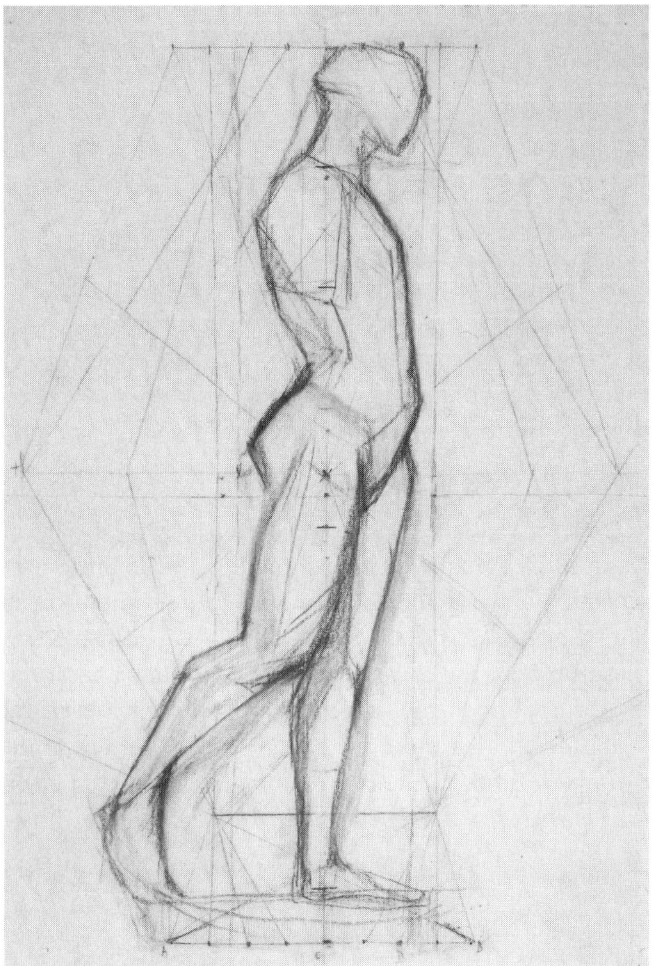

Figure 3.3 Raymond Duchamp-Villon (1876–1918), *Nude man, Proportions Study*. Charcoal on paper. AM 2053 D. *Source:* Photograph © CNAC/MNAM/Dist. Reunion des Musees Nationaux/Art Resource, NY.

look like (see Figure 1.7). However, when doing so, many artists favor using more straight than curved lines for this analyzing process. They do so for two reasons. First, because all curves can be broken down to the several straight lines of which they are composed, artists have more control when using straight lines in determining the subtleties of a curve. By submitting a curve to the "test" of first drawing it as a series of straight lines at subtly changing angles, the resulting lines will, of course, more accurately suggest the particular path of the curve, which can then be drawn over by lines that are actually curved (Figure 3.4).

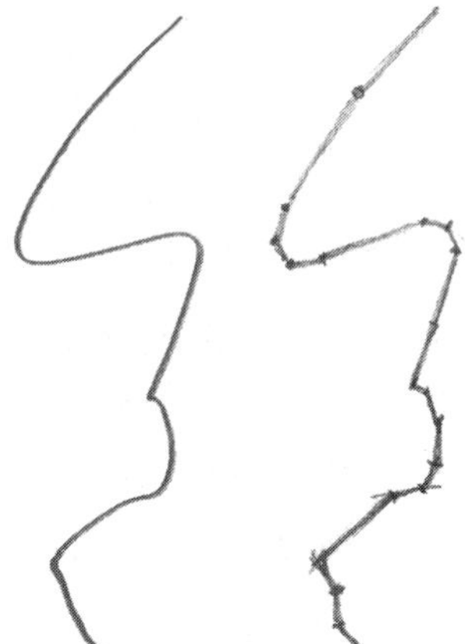

Figure 3.4

Second, because this kind of analytical seeing takes a little more time and effort than a general, "sketchy" approach, the drawing's subsequent development strongly benefits from what the artist has found. This is so because once the subject's "scaffolding" is established, the artist can more accurately and authoritatively draw the rhythms and actions of the subject than can be achieved by the less demanding, sketchy manner. This can be seen in Figure 3.5 where some parts of the figure still show the drawing's earlier, more analytical approach, while other parts, having been carried further, have benefited from the straight-line inquiries

Figure 3.5

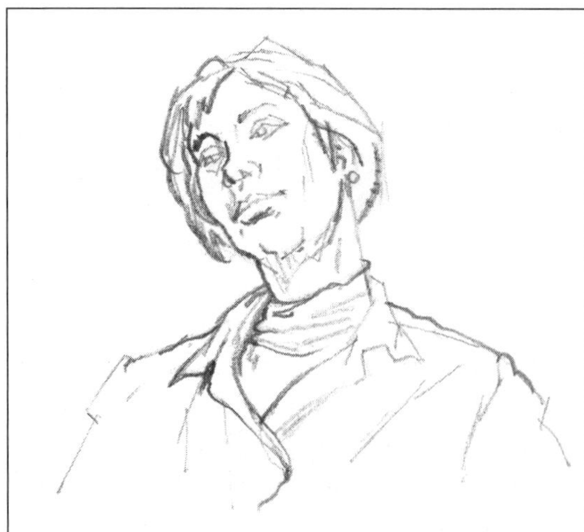

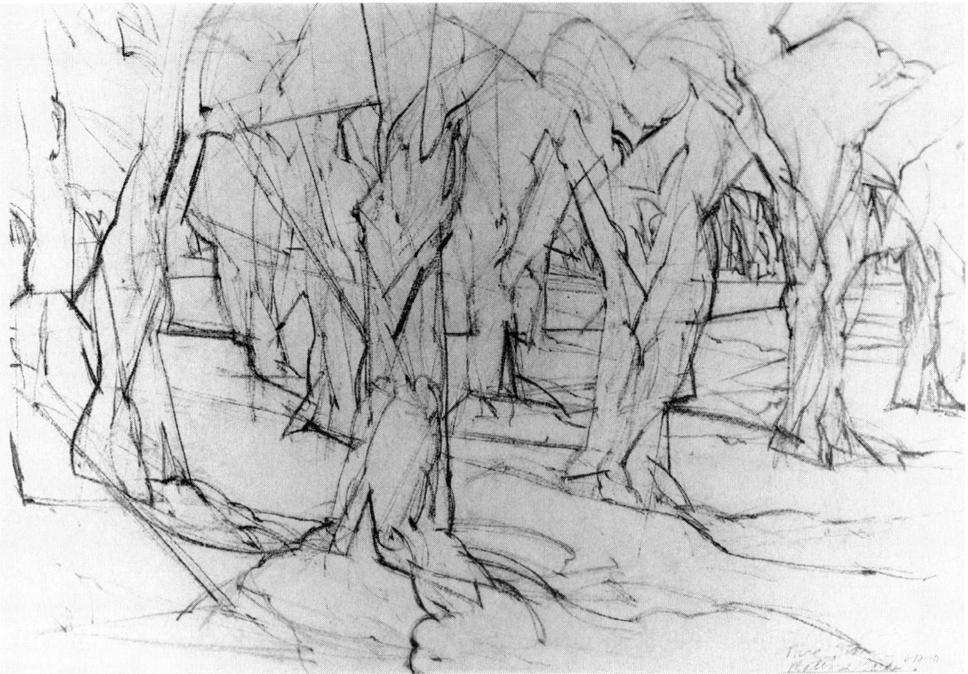

Figure 3.6 Conley Harris, *Matisse Garden, Nice, France*. Charcoal, 1970. Reproduced courtesy of the Boston Public Library, Print Department. By permission of the artist.

that underlie them. Although diagrammatic lines are generally used in a work's underdrawing stage where they establish vital information about location, proportion, and shape, some artists use this kind of line as their sole means of graphic expression. As Figure 3.6 shows, diagrammatic lines can convey strong energies and a resolute manner.

What this drawing also shows is the artist's awareness of the interspaces between the trees. In objective drawing the shapes of the spaces separating parts, or *negative shapes*, must be seen with the same degree of inquiry we give to seeing the shape of the parts themselves (the *positive shapes*). Here again, diagrammatic lines can play an important role in seeing the shape-actualities of interspaces, as in Figure 3.7. Note that only some of the negative shapes are entirely enclosed by positive ones. Others, encircling the outer boundaries of positive shapes, are shown here as being completely enclosed themselves, in order to make them more readable as shapes. In fact, when drawing a form's shape, it is as important to see these outer, surrounding negative areas as those fully enclosed ones. If you can imagine (or even temporarily draw lightly) an enclosing outer boundary to these otherwise open-ended shapes you will more easily be able to see them as shapes, as Figure 3.7 shows.

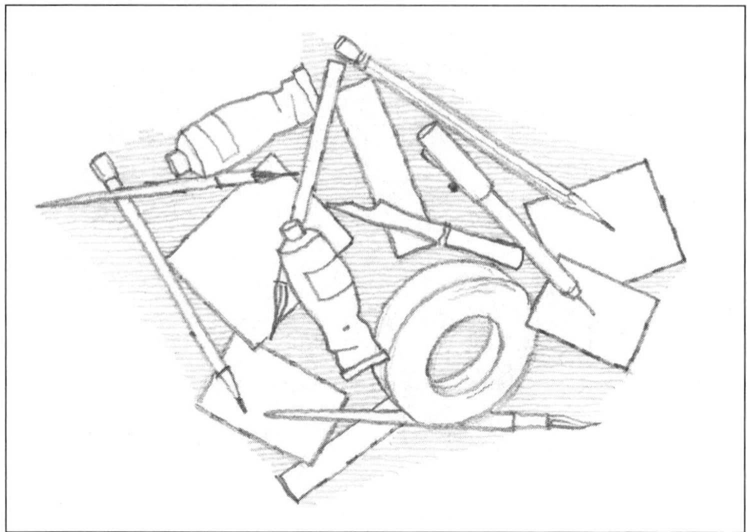

Figure 3.7

And seeing the configuration of these adjacent, negative shapes is necessary to accurately seeing the shapes of the subject's forms because *they share a common boundary*. As Figure 3.8 illustrates, distorting the spaces between the fingers makes the fingers distorted, too.

Another benefit of concentrating on the boundaries of negative shapes has to do with our tendency to often draw convex turnings more accurately than concave ones. But when a concave passage of a form's contour is seen "from the other side,"

Figure 3.8

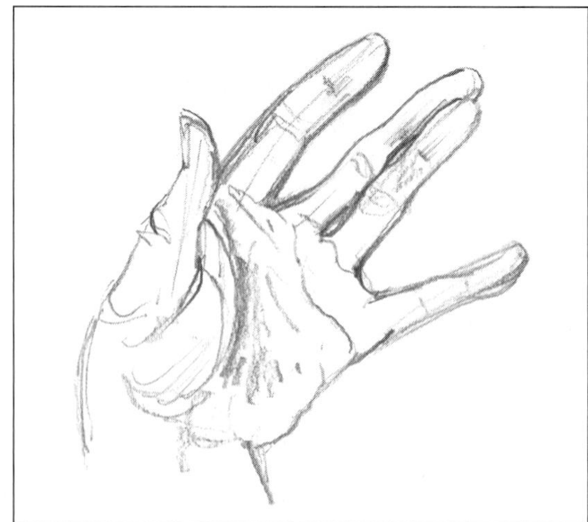

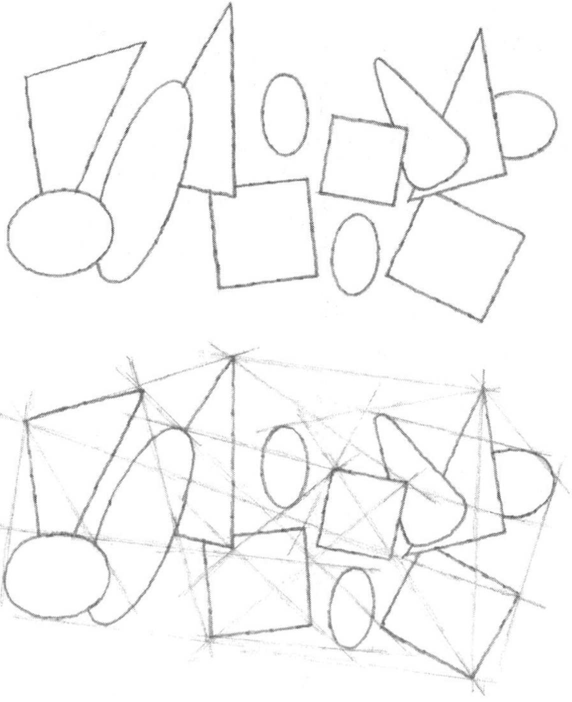

Figure 3.9

that is, as the convex passage of an abutting negative shape, we are more likely to make the subtle adjustments that make that passage more true to our subject's shape-actualities.

An additional function of diagrammatic line has to do with the sometime overlooked "line": the alignment of a subject's parts. Lightly drawn, sweeping diagrammatic lines that run from one part to another are ideally suited to quickly find the angle, size, location, and height relationships of parts. Although seeing how parts are aligned plays an important role in a drawing's gestural stage, it is still necessary to "fine tune" your judgments about these measurable matters, as Figure 3.9 shows.

Structural Line

Related to diagrammatic lines are those versatile lines that explain the volumetric and even tonal condition of surfaces: *structural lines.* We will meet these lines in Chapters Four and Five and see how convincingly they can convert shapes into solid masses. But here it is useful to note that these two kinds of line, often working together, although they can convey strong expressive character, are mainly the more inquiring, "finding" kinds of line. They measure and explain (Figure 3.10). Other kinds of line, although they do their share of finding and explaining, are more driven by the artist's feelings about and experiences with a subject's spirit and substance.

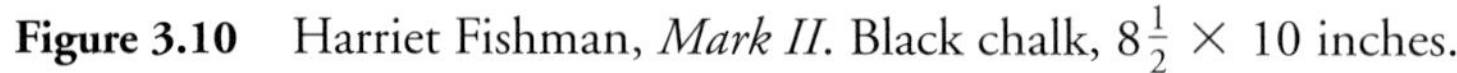

Figure 3.10 Harriet Fishman, *Mark II*. Black chalk, $8\frac{1}{2} \times 10$ inches.

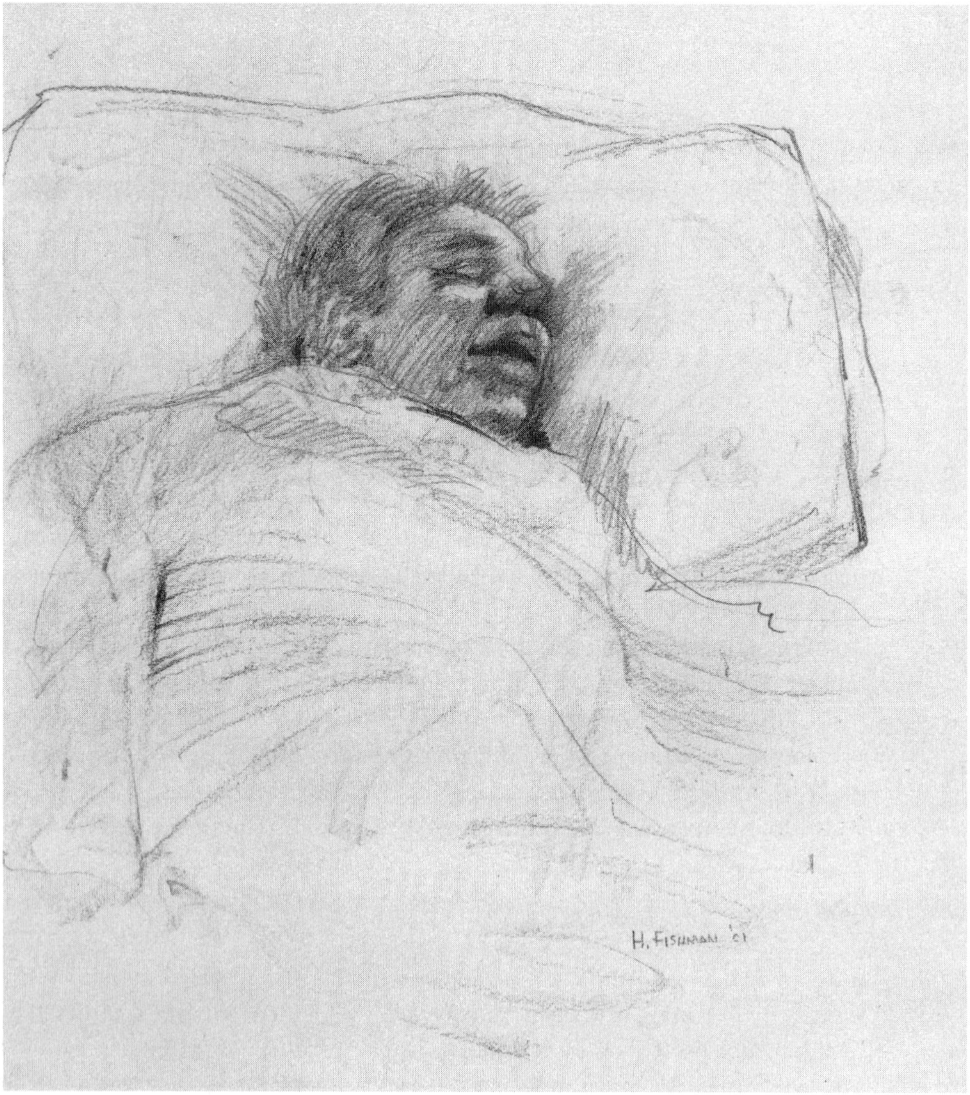

EXPERIENTIAL LINES

We have seen how a form's shape can be objectively drawn by first noting its general shape and then closing in on its more particular turnings by mainly straight-line segments. Another way of becoming sensitized to the various, and often subtle turnings of a shape's configuration is to practice what is commonly referred to as the *blind contour drawing*. Once you have made several such drawings you should go on to make several *controlled contour drawings*. These two exercises will strongly contribute to your ability to see what contours really look like.

Contour Exercises

Blind Contour. Select for your subject a figure, either draped or nude, your own unoccupied hand, almost anything made of leather (a jacket, glove, boot, or the like), a houseplant, a doll, or other objects of an organic nature. For blind contour drawing, start by placing your pencil on the page at a place that represents any point you choose on the subject's outer contour. Next, look up to find that point on the subject's contour and begin to *slowly* draw that edge as your eye *simultaneously* moves along the form's contour. Your eye and hand are doing the same thing at the same time. Do not look at your drawing or lift your pencil at any time during this exercise.

As you do this try to feel that your pencil tip is actually touching the subject's edges at the instant that your eye is "touching" the same edges, and that you just can't move one without moving the other. There are four unbreakable rules in this exercise: do not look at your page until the drawing is ended, do not lift your pencil until the drawing is ended, do not speed up the line, and do not begin to draw until you are able to feel that your eye and your hand are *one* and can only move *together*. If you break the first rule you will be amused (or alarmed) by the drawing's often outrageous distortions. If you break the second rule you are likely to lose your way. If you break the third rule you will miss most of the form's subtle turnings. And breaking the fourth rule loses the entire point of making a blind contour drawing in the first place. Breaking one or more of the first three rules will break your concentration on the fourth rule: to convince yourself that your eye and hand are locked together and can only move as one unit.

Once you have experienced the rather pleasant sensation of the eye and hand doing the same thing at the same time you will begin to more fully understand the eye as inquirer and the hand as servant. There is no strict time limit on such a drawing, but it is difficult to keep up this kind of intense concentration for more than fifteen minutes.

The key to getting the most from this exercise is drawing *slowly*. The more you are determined to see and draw every slight change in the contour's turnings, the slower your eye and hand will move. Again, the best way to do this is by imagining that your pencil is actually touching the form's edges.

But working against this is our natural desire to "get on" with any task. Often, before you are aware of it, your line has begun to speed up and the drawing has become more generalized. It takes some discipline to stay concentrated on finding every nuance of change in the subject's edges, and in holding on to the notion that your eye and hand can only move together.

The completed drawing will look very strange! Although the line will probably suggest a caring and sensitive quality and will be free of mannerisms, it will appear to waver (especially if you have been sensitive to noting the smallest changes in the contour); it may cross over itself now and then, and even intrude on another part of the contour. The positions and proportions of parts may vary wildly. That's normal. In fact, the more your drawing shows these characteristics, the more likely it is that you've fully experienced the sensation of the eye and hand moving as one. And that is important because once you have felt this simultaneity of movement you can better understand how the eye gives commands to the hand.

As you go on with the study of drawing what you see, making observations *before* you draw them, the marks you will then make will reveal a sensitivity to what your eye has experienced. And that is what the next exercise is all about.

Controlled Contour. Of course, it isn't possible to control a drawing if we cannot look at the page to see if what we have seen has been accurately set down. However, the experience of the eye and hand doing the same thing at the same time is the essential prerequisite to having them do it in sequence. Once your hand has "learned" to record what your eyes are seeing, your hand can wait until your eyes have seen a few contour turnings before it draws them, with your eyes now on the page, to see that your hand is doing what it has been told to do. But just as it is nearly impossible to hear nine or ten numbers or sounds and correctly repeat them, so is it as unlikely to see that many turnings in a contour and then draw them accurately. In fact, drawing even four or five changes along an edge from memory is seldom possible. In a controlled contour drawing, noting two or three turnings at a time is about all one can observe and then accurately draw.

Begin by selecting a new view of the subject used for the previous drawing. Lightly rough in a rather spare gesture drawing, that is, one reduced to only what is necessary to establish the tilt of parts, their proportions, and a few faintly drawn generalities about shapes, as in Figure 3.11A. Using this rough sketch as a guide, place your pencil on the page, at a point where you wish to begin the contour drawing. But keep your hand stationary as your eye first examines only the first two or three contour turnings. Then, with your eyes turned back to the page, draw only

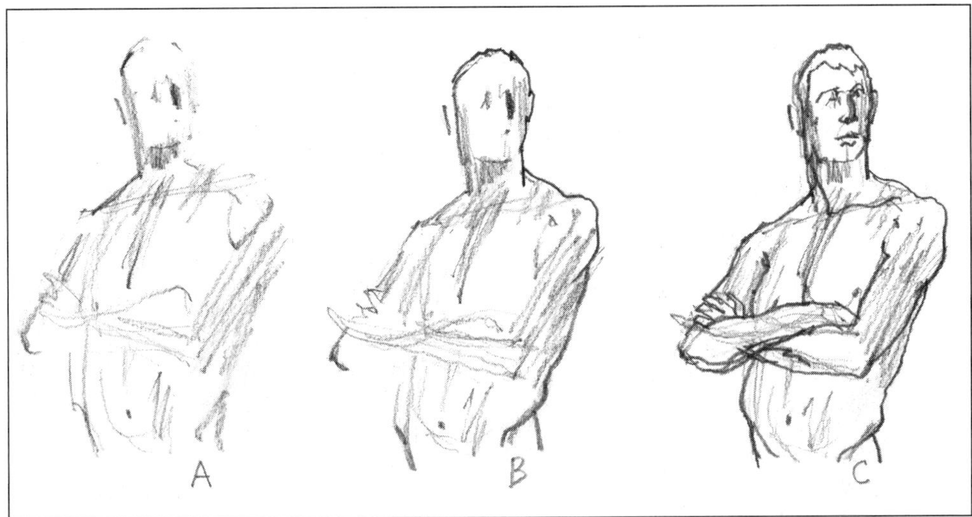

Figure 3.11

those few turnings (3.11B). Keeping your pencil on the page where the last contour segment ended, look up at the subject to see the next few contour turnings, draw them, and keep repeating the process until the contour drawing is completed (3.11C). In this kind of drawing you can lift your pencil on occasion, but try to keep the pencil on the page as much as possible.

Here, too, you should occasionally assess the drawing's proportions, the angle of parts, and the shape of forms, making any changes you deem necessary as the drawing progresses. During such drawings you may be surprised to find that you are occasionally drawing *while* looking at the subject. The more familiar you become with drawing the more often this may happen. With some practice this manner of line drawing can be done with little or no gestural underdrawing (Figure 3.12). Some artists employ this approach for more subjective purposes. Even though Porter's drawing (Figure 3.13) shows some obvious exaggerations, it is evident that he is sensitively attuned to the subject's contours and the distortions are nevertheless respectful of the actual form character.

Cross-contour Line

Related to both blind and controlled contour drawing is the kind of line that leaves a form's edge to move "overland," slowly feeling its way over the form's

> ***Drawn lines ... are never passive; they are carriers of energy.***

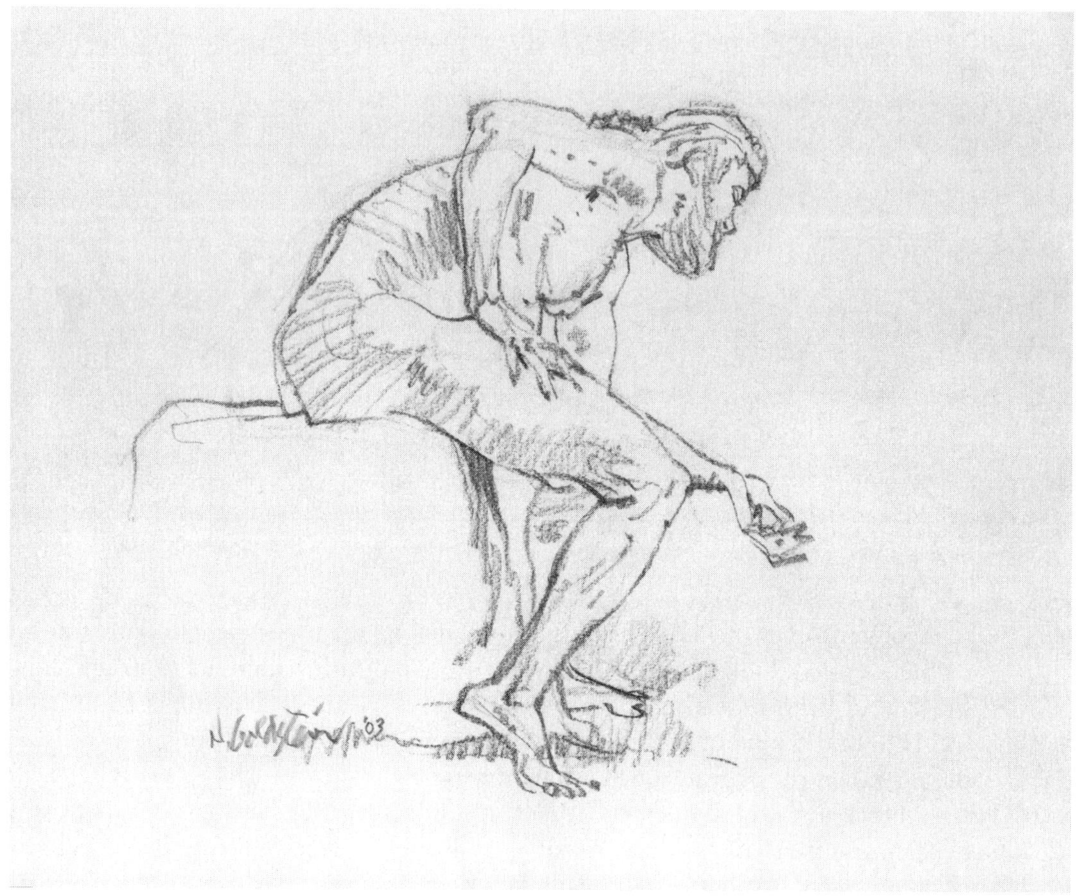

Figure 3.12 Nathan Goldstein, *Seated Male Figure.* Black chalk, $8\frac{1}{2} \times 10$ inches. Courtesy of the artist.

surface terrain. Such "cage" or "cross-contour lines" can be thought of as coming from a bug dipped in ink, slowly leaving a trail that marks its path upon the hills and valleys of a form's changing surface, as in Figure 3.14A. Cross-contour line drawing demands that you strongly identify with every subtle rise and fall in the form's surface. If we imagine our subject to be a snow-covered landscape, then cross-contour lines can represent a skier's trail, like the long lines in Figure 3.14B. And, if we imagine a skier so deft as to touch down on the snow only in the valleys, we can see the transition from cross-contour lines to hatching lines, like the many short lines in the same illustration. Cross-contour lines yield the most information about a form's terrain when they move slowly over the surface, whereas

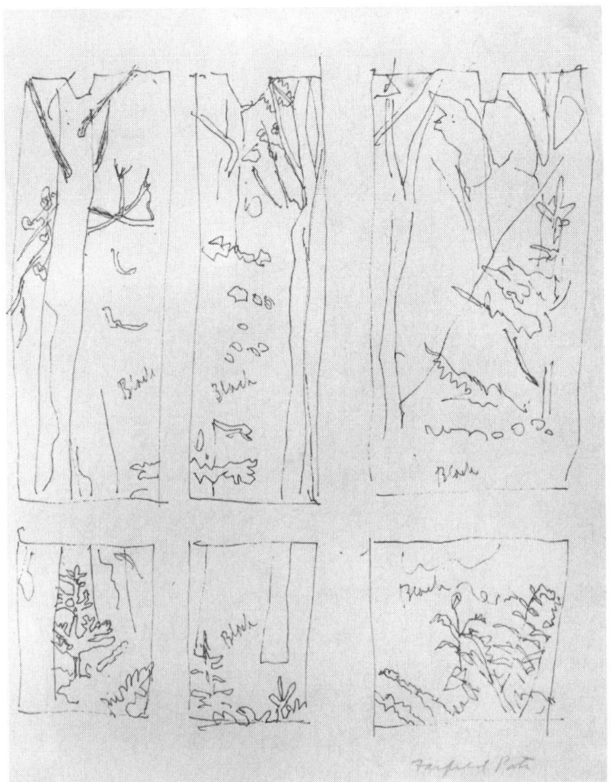

Figure 3.13 Fairfield Porter (1907–1975), *Study for the Door to the Woods*, ca. 1972. Ink on paper, $13\frac{1}{2} \times 10\frac{1}{4}$ inches (34.29 × 26.04 cm.) *Source:* Collection of Whitney Museum of American Art, New York. Gift of Alex Katz (77.63).

the shorter, hatched lines (establishing planes, indents, and shaded areas) tend to move faster (Figure 3.14C). Notice that often the hatched lines are running in the same direction as the cross-contour lines among them. Raphael's preparatory sketch (Figure 3.15) shows cross-contour lines on the figure's upper back, lower abdomen, and along the neck and arm—and also hatchings establishing indents and planes here and there on the torso.

Cross-contour Exercises

1. Using a 2B graphite pencil and working from a photograph of a nude or draped figure, or of a close-up of a part of a figure, place a sheet of tracing paper over the photograph and *slowly* draw lines that move around forms as in Figure 3.14A and 3.14B. These lines can run vertically, horizontally, or diagonally on

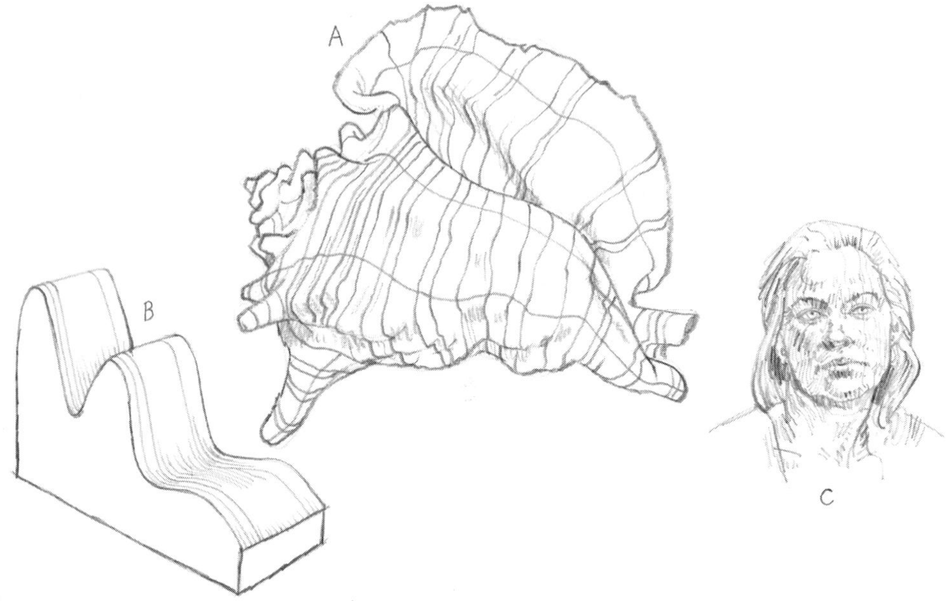

Figure 3.14

a form, riding the surface terrain as if the line were actually leaving a trail on the form.

2. Using as your model a green pepper, a sneaker, or any object with similarly undulating surfaces, draw the subject by first establishing its gesture. Then, analyze the subject's shape by using segments of straight and C-shaped curved lines. Next, rework the contour in the controlled contour manner. Finally, slowly draw cross-contour lines on the form that move in a variety of directions.
3. Using as your model a small stone or rock, preferably one that is not too rounded, but shows a few abutments of planes, make a large drawing of it (approximately ten times the size of the stone), using the procedure described in the previous exercise, and then slowly draw cross-contour lines in a variety of directions.

Calligraphy of Line

Every drawn line, no matter what its descriptive duties, shows its own tactile, schematic, or other expressive character. Although the term *calligraphic* is commonly used to describe lines of an animated, curvasive nature, we can regard every kind of line as suggesting movement, as having some manner of carrying

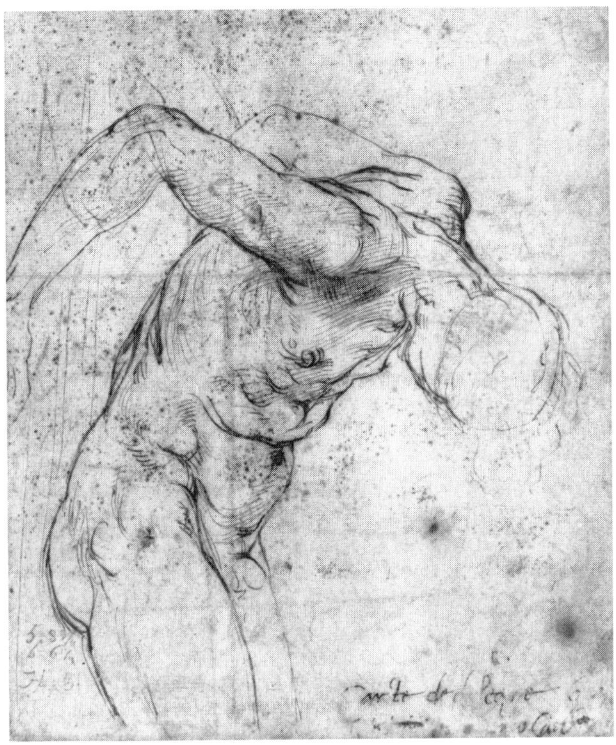

Figure 3.15 Raphael (Raffaello Sanzio or Santi) (1483–1520), *Study of a Nude Male Figure.* Pen and brown ink, h. $8\frac{13}{16}$ × w. $6\frac{1}{4}$ inches. *Source:* Metropolitan Museum of Art, Rogers Fund, 1964 (64.47 verso).

energy. Whether they are long, short, straight, curved, thick, thin, or varied in width, all lines allude to movement. They may be impulsive or deliberate, bold or shy. They may be more given to measurement or to emotion, but whatever their particular characteristics, their actions, in working together to create and animate the drawing, collectively reveal the artist's understanding of, and feelings about the subject. And they form the drawing's active, calligraphic nature: a kind of graphic "handwriting." And like your handwriting, which formed over time, your drawings too, as you continue to draw, will show certain linear characteristics that result from your creative purposes, your drawing experiences, your kinesthetic sensibilities, and even your motor control. This merging of what you want to draw and how you need to draw it will become your style. Whether line will play a major or minor role in your drawings will depend on how you go on to experience and communicate the things around you. Style, though, is not something you can consciously work at; it is the natural result of analytical understanding and expressive necessity.

Often, when artists want the subject to be shown by linear means, values, either of broad washes, strokes, or hatched lines, are kept to a minimum or omitted altogether. Even a gestural underdrawing may be largely absent. The more evident it is that line is to be a drawing's main or only "voice," the more aware are we of the drawing's calligraphic character. This is evident in Schiele's *Portrait of Artist's Wife* (Figure 3.16), where the fullness and flow of the subject's forms emerge from slow, undulating lines of a strongly tactile nature. Usually, as here, the greater the search for subtle contour changes, the slower the line moves, and the drawing's calligraphy shows this. A faster reading of the form will result in bolder simplifications and a more animated calligraphy (Figure 3.17). Sometimes an artist's intense excitement for the subject generates a linear "handwriting" that matches such feelings, as in Van Gogh's reed pen drawing (Figure 3.18), where the lines go well beyond depiction to suggest the artist's reaction to the scene as a system of animated forms and patterns of motion. As Schiele's and Van Gogh's drawings demonstrate, a drawing's calligraphy is often the key to the work's expressive intent. Note, for example, the gentle caress of Ingres's lines (Figure 3.19) and the frenzied animation of Daumier's (3.20). The Daumier drawing also shows lines producing a characteristic sometimes seen in a drawing's shapes, namely the open shape, that is, shapes that do not show clear enclosing boundaries. This can also be seen in Figures 3.6 and 3.17. As these three drawings demonstrate, open shapes provide a feeling of airiness, a flow of movement and energy between parts, and of the lines seeming to stay as much on the page as in a field of spatial depth.

Because, as noted earlier, all lines have some manner of calligraphic and expressive role, even the aforementioned diagrammatic and structural lines are endowed with such functions. Diagrammatic lines do so through their sweeping search for connections; and structural lines, "traveling in packs," do so by their moving over forms to produce planes and values, as we saw in Figures 3.14 and 3.15. More examples of this can be seen in Figures 3.21, 3.22, and 3.23. Of course, these groups of lines are better known as hatchings and cross-hatchings, which we will explore further when we meet them again in Chapters Four and Five.

In drawing, line is the most available and versatile of the visual elements, the element we most associate with drawing. We have seen that line can establish the location and angle of parts, can measure their proportions, can explore edges, can have their own calligraphic play, can express the artist's feelings about the subject, and can construct its surface terrain. But one of line's more evident functions remains the setting up of a drawing's shapes. In doing so it transfers the flat "puzzle-piece" configurations of the subject's parts onto the flat surface of the page, and sets the stage for converting contours into edges and shapes into planes.

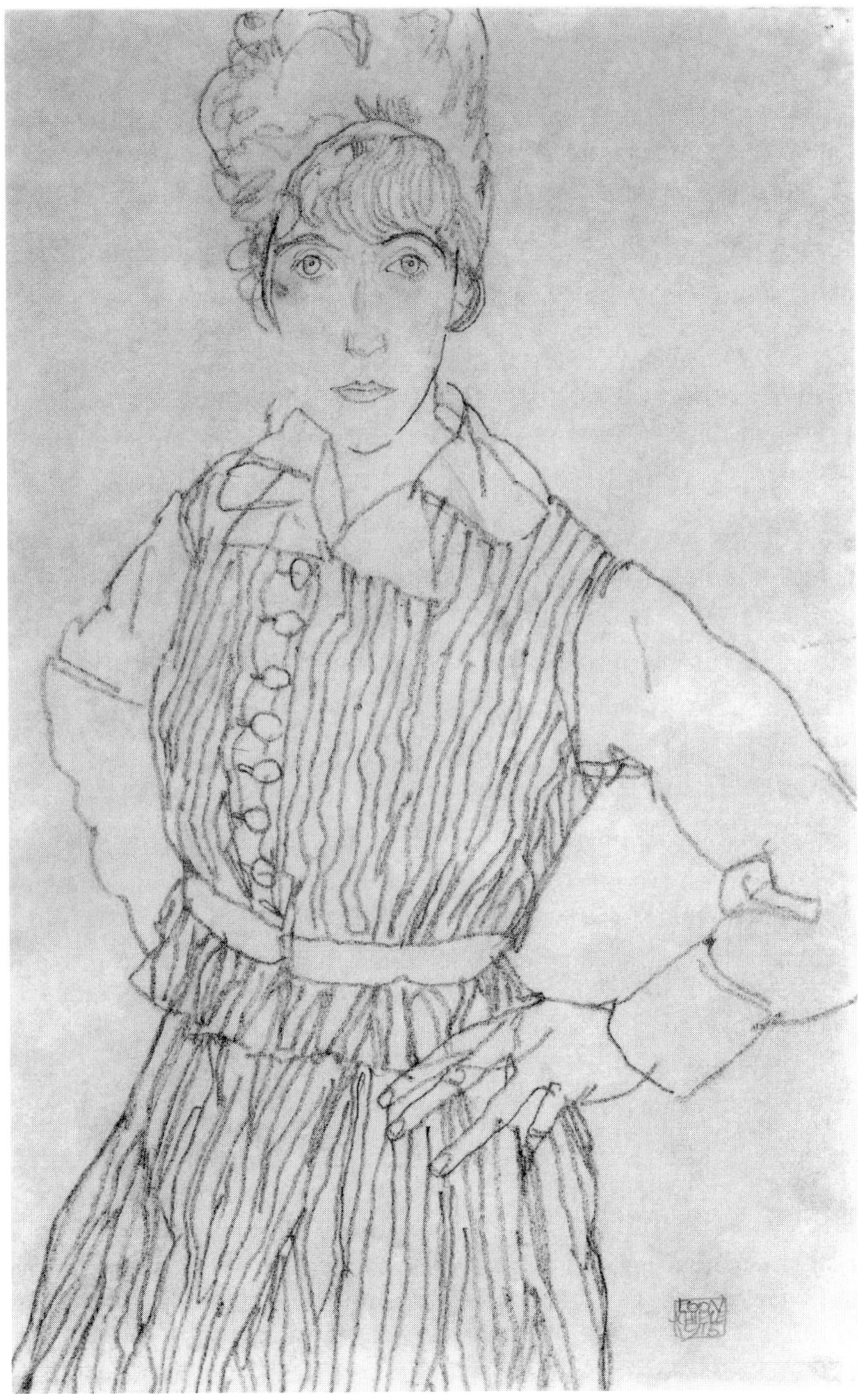

Figure 3.16 Egon Schiele. *Portrait of Artist's Wife, Standing, with Hands on Hips*, 1915. Black crayon. 18 × 11$\frac{1}{4}$ inches. Private collection. Courtesy Galerie St. Etienne, New York.

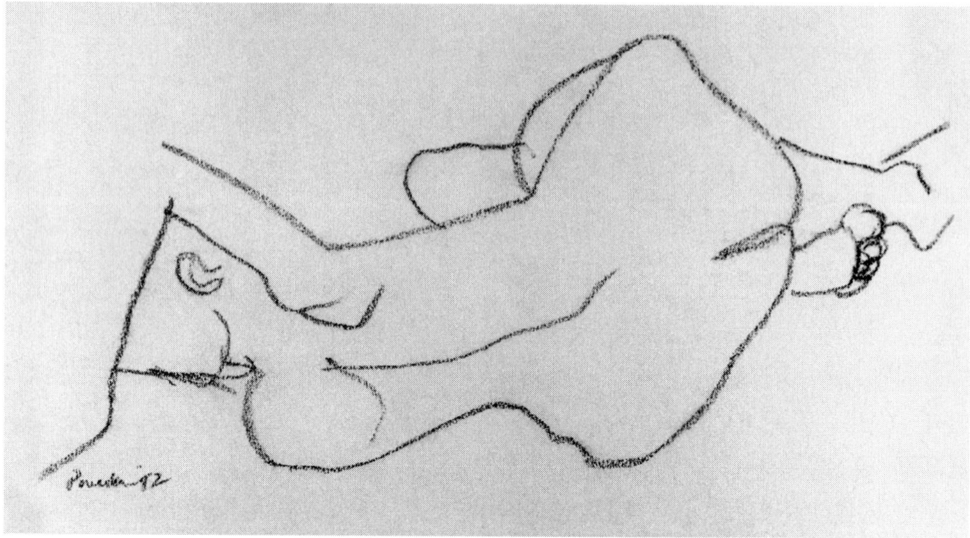

Figure 3.17 Marianna Pineda, *Reclining Nude, Rear View*, charcoal, 1982. Reproduced courtesy of the Boston Public library, Print Department. By permission of the heirs of the artist.

Things to Think About

1. How are diagrammatic and structural lines alike? How are they different?
2. Why is it important to experience the eye and hand moving simultaneously if that can happen only when you look at your subject and not at your drawing?
3. Blind and controlled contour drawings provide experiences and information through the use of line. Can you devise similar exercises for seeing a subject's planes or values?
4. Is there any similarity between cross-contour drawing and clay sculpture?
5. Drawn lines are carriers of energy. Are shapes?

Critique Considerations

1. If your drawings show parts to be wrongly positioned or out of proportion, you need to see the subject in a more relational way. It is helpful to lightly draw diagrammatic lines that measure the relative height and tilt of parts, as described in Chapter One. (See Chapter One: "Vertical and Horizontal Rightness," "Seeing Alignments," and "Intersections.")

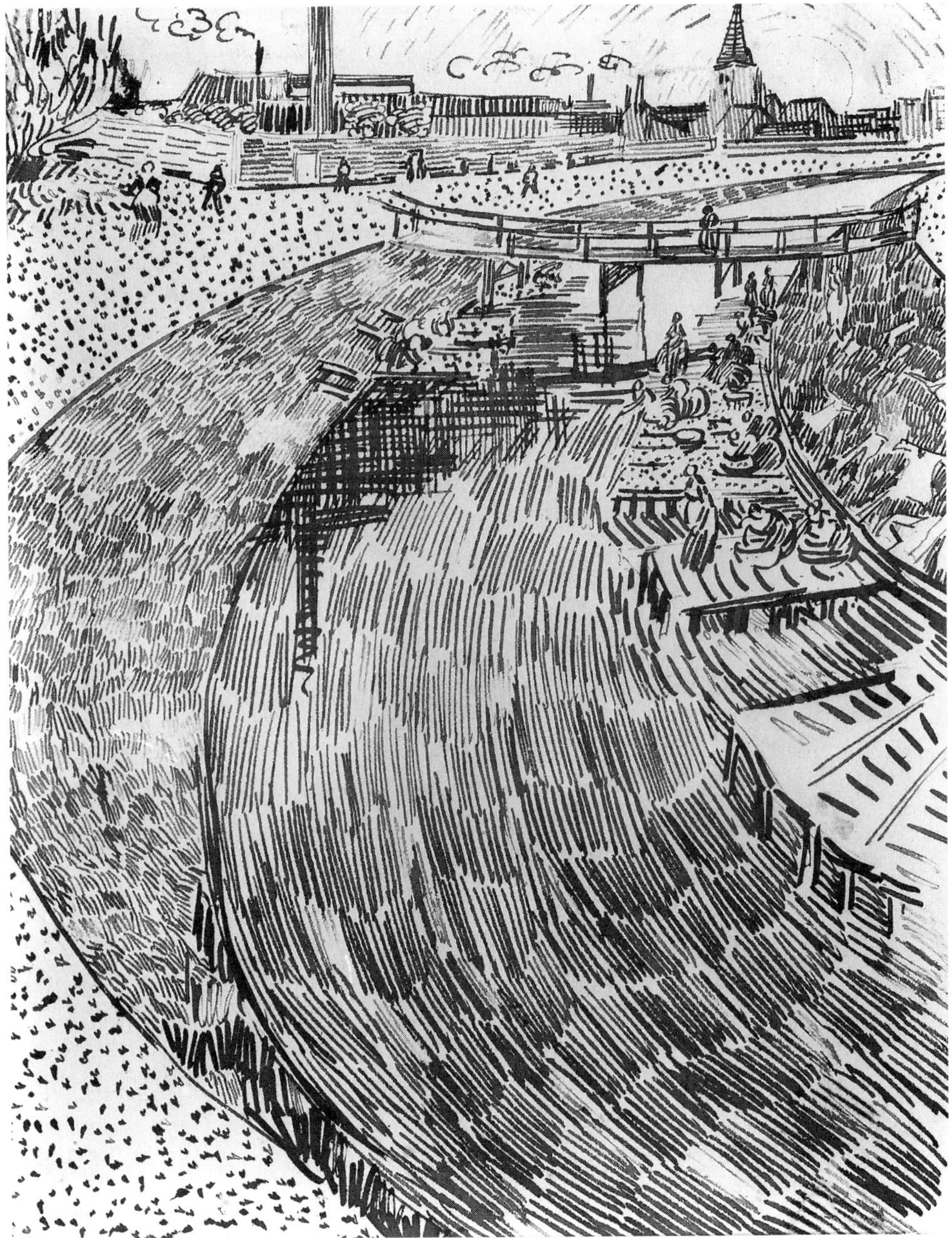

Figure 3.18 Vincent Van Gogh (1853–1890), *The Washerwoman*, drawing, 1888. *Source:* Photograph © Foto Marburg/Art Resource, NY.

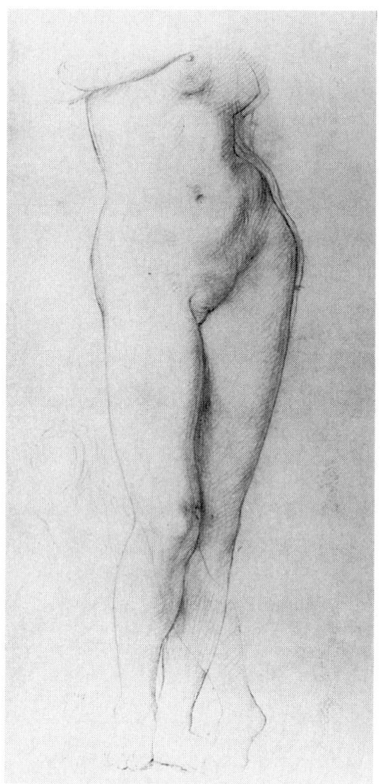

Figure 3.19 Jean-Auguste-Dominique Ingres (French, 1780–1867), *Study for "La Source"*. 355 × 171 mm. *Source:* Museum Boijmans Van Beuningen, Rotterdam.

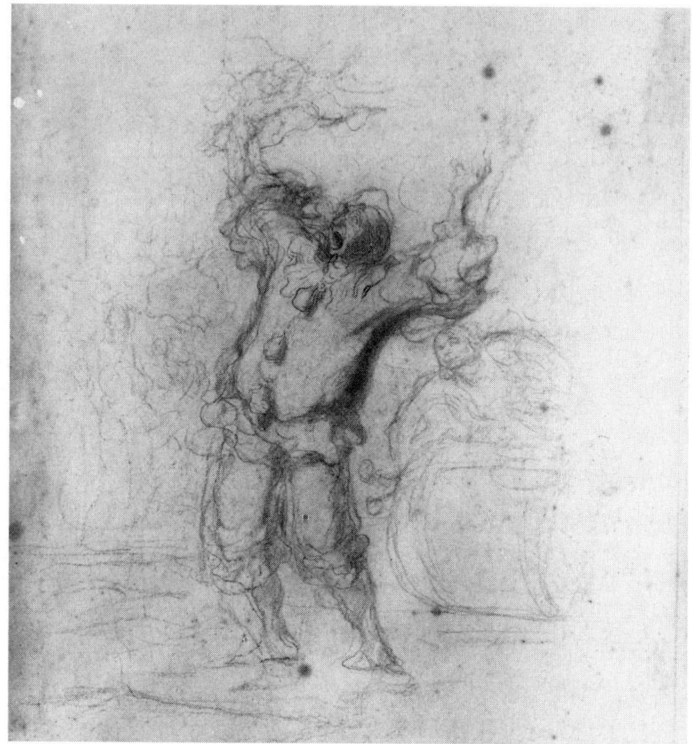

Figure 3.20 Honoré Daumier (French, 1808–1879), *The Clown*. 406 × 360 mm. *Source:* Museum Boijmans Van Beuningen, Rotterdam.

2. Are the shapes of the forms in your drawings markedly unlike those in the observed subject? It may have to do with your concentrating on a form's volume in space—on its three-dimensional condition—to the exclusion of first seeing it as a flat, enclosed area, as a two-dimensional configuration.

An exercise that reveals the *shapes* of volumes requires a china marker pencil or a water-based marker pen, and a sheet of Plexiglas. Simply hold the Plexiglas sheet in front of the subject and trace the outlines of its forms onto the glass. In doing this, you will have disregarded the subject's "near and far" aspects, its values, and the foreshortened state of some of its parts. The resulting shapes will accurately show the subject's two-dimensional configurations. It is this kind of

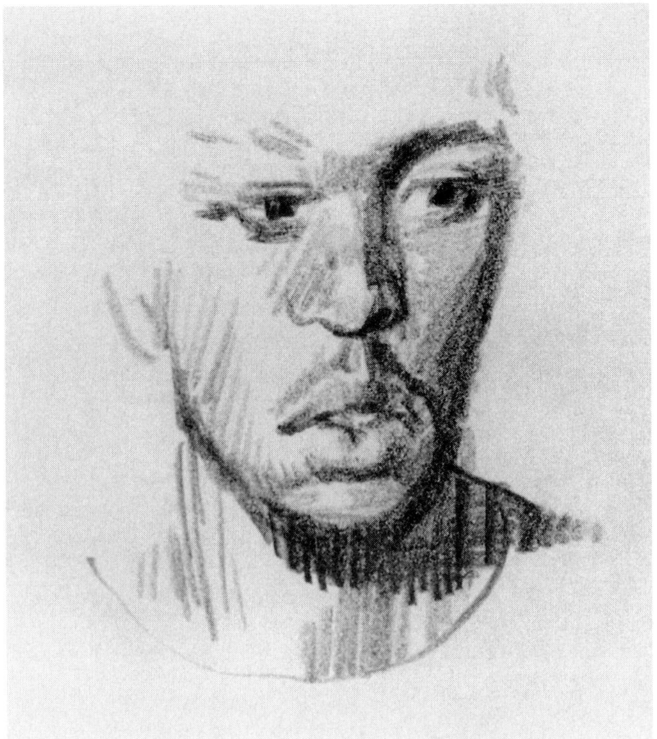

Figure 3.21 Arthur Polonsky (1925–), *Head of a Young Black Man*, graphite, n.d. *Source:* Reproduced courtesy of the Boston Public Library, Print Department. By permission of the artist.

shape extraction you need to consider in the early stages of a drawing. (See Chapter One: "Seeing 'Flat'," and "Straights and Curves.")

3. Do some of the lines in your drawings appear to leave the forms and spaces they were meant to define and rise to the surface of the page? This occurs when lines are not "employed" in depictive roles but are gratuitously added for whatever reason. This is not the same as the (often) many lines used to search out a shape or to adjust an earlier judgment, or to measure a distance or a direction. Such lines *are* employed in the struggle to get at the truth of what is seen or wanted. Avoid drawing lines that have no particular purpose, or that merely create a kind of allover texture for purposes of style. Draw as many lines as needed to find and communicate what is important to you about the subject, but every line should have something to do. Avoid unnecessary lines.

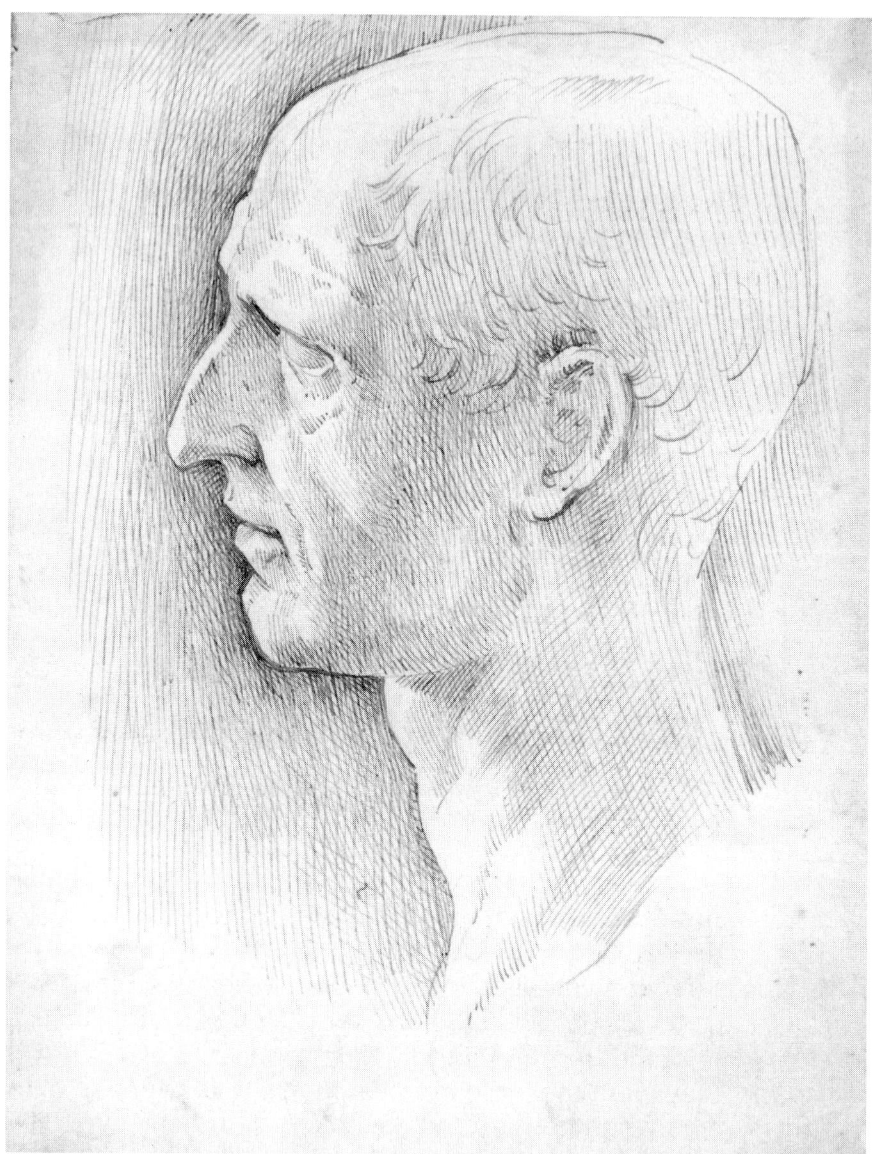

Figure 3.22 Parmigianino (Francesco Mazzola, 1503–1540). *Head of a Man in profile to right*, from the Antique, *Julius Caesar*. *Source:* The Royal Collection © 2004, Her Majesty Queen Elizabeth II.

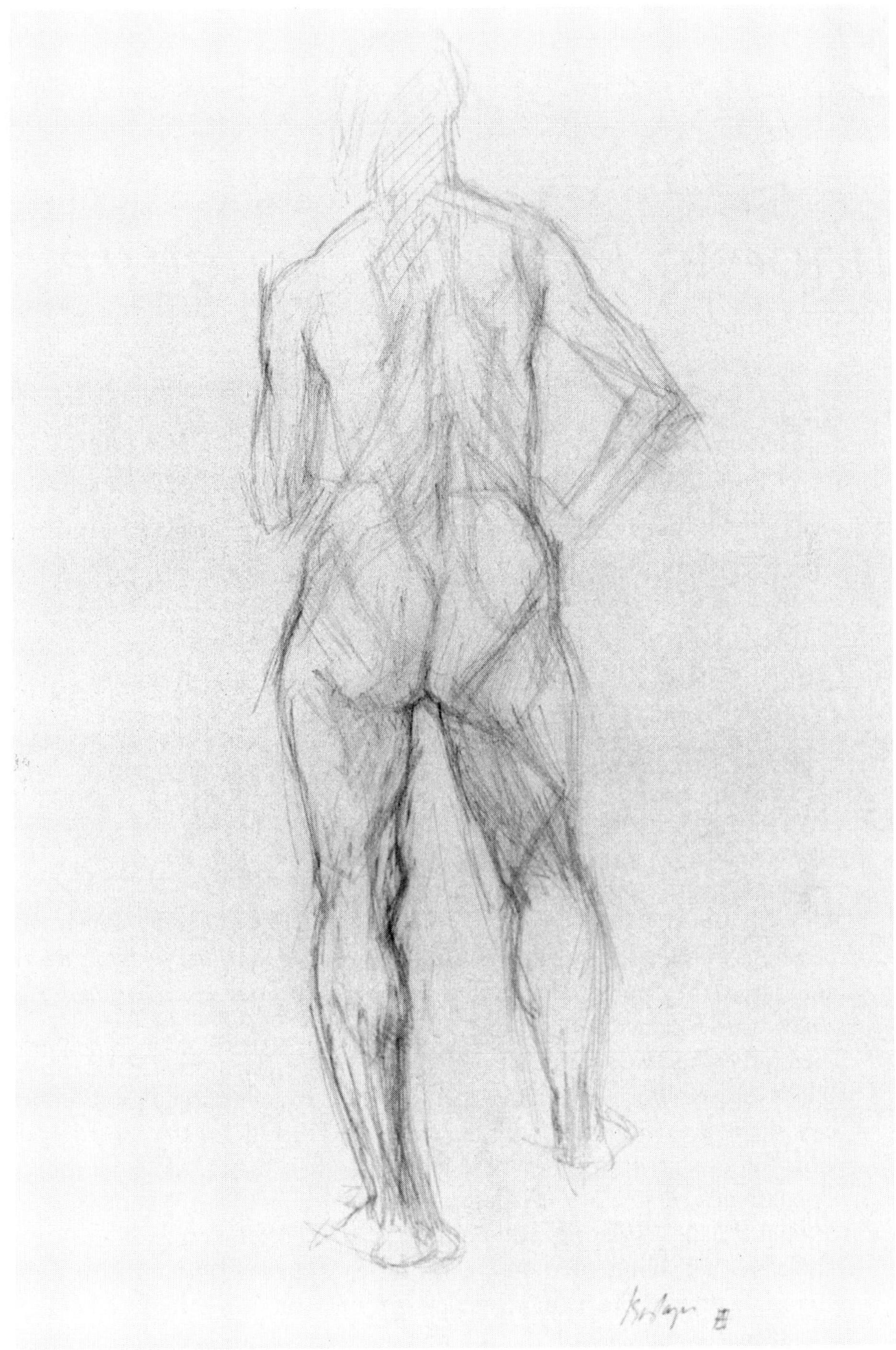

Figure 3.23 Iso Papo (1925–), *Standing Figure, Back View.* Graphite, 15 × 20 inches. Courtesy of the artist/Collection of Nathan Goldstein.

4

Shape to Plane to Structure

EDGE TO PLANE

> ***... if a plane's shape is wrongly drawn, the form on which it resides can never look right.***

Planes are the surface facets of forms, representing the structural nature of the things we see. But, because planes have boundaries, they can also be understood as shapes, as two-dimensional configurations. Therefore, when we see foreshortened surfaces, as in the forms in Figure 4.1A, we need to make a conscious effort to note their shape-actualities, as shown in Figure 4.1B. One of the most important insights for anyone drawing in an objective mode is to see the shape configurations of planes located at various angles in space. Holding on to the concept that no matter what a plane's foreshortened position is, it still offers you its silhouette, will help you to see that silhouette more clearly. It's vital to remember that if a plane's shape is wrongly drawn, the form on which it resides can never look right (Figure 4.2).

Planes, being the stuff that a form's surface structure is made of, are everywhere. In fact, when you think about it, some of the edges of the things we draw are made up of planes seen "on end." A playing card seen on end will appear as a thin line.

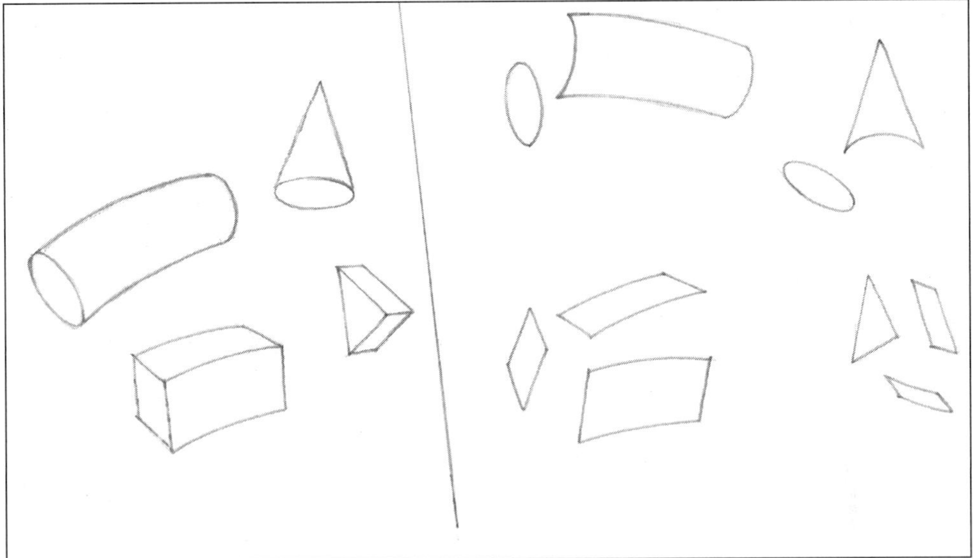

Figure 4.1

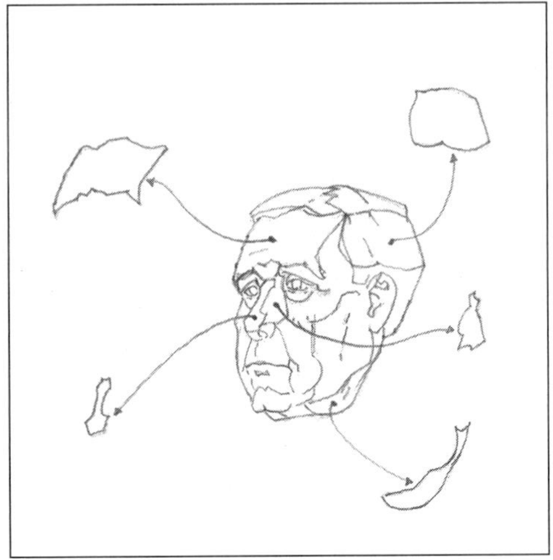

Figure 4.2

Such segments of a form's contour can be understood as totally foreshortened planes (Figure 4.3A). Sometimes a segment of contour turns inward, away from the edge, and "opens up" to become a plane (Figure 4.3B). Such a plane is sometimes suggested by some hatched lines, or, in the case of a fluid medium, by washes of tone. Such hatchings or washes establish the general shape of the plane (Figures 4.4 and 4.5).

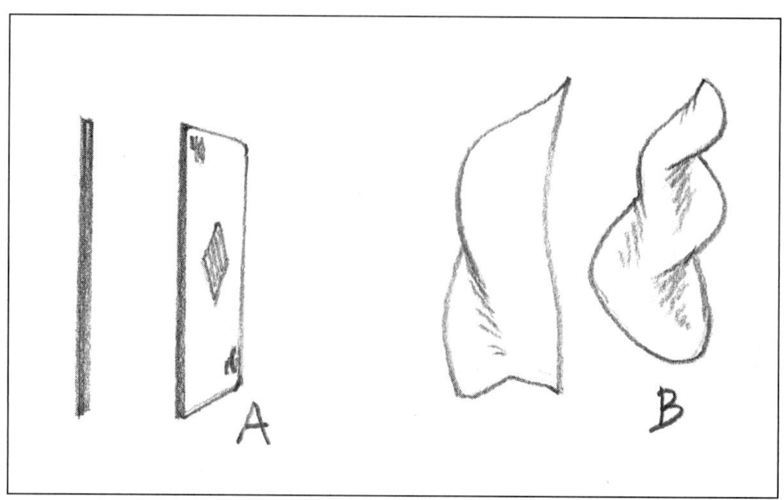

Figure 4.3

Figure 4.4 Jean-Francois Millet (French, 1814–1875). *Man Leaning over a Bale of Grain II (studies for Harvesters Resting)*, 1851–1853. Black conte crayon on white wove paper. Catalogue Raisonne: Murphy 38. Sheet 29.3 × 20 cm ($11\frac{9}{16} \times 7\frac{7}{8}$ inches).
Source: Photograph © 2004 Museum of Fine Arts, Boston. Edwin E. Jack Fund (61.627).

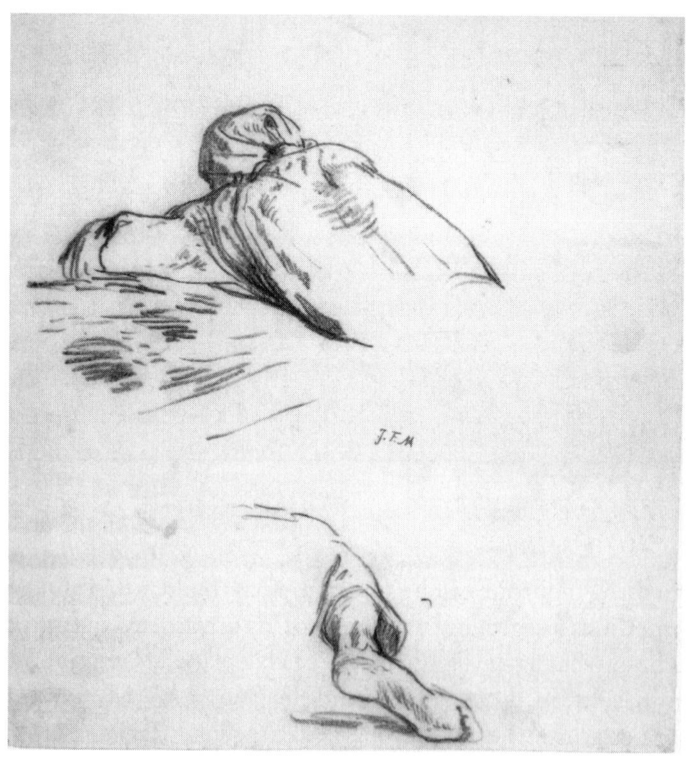

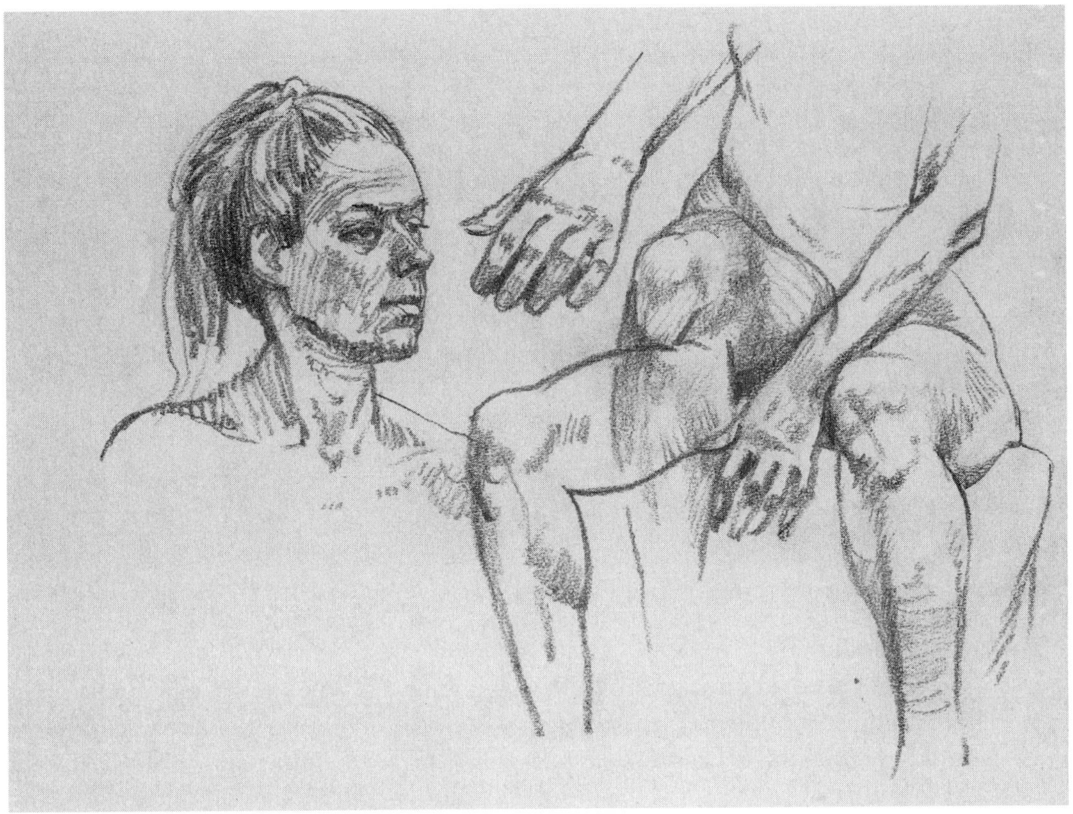

Figure 4.5 Nathan Goldstein, *Page of Sketches.* Red chalk, $8\frac{1}{2} \times 10$ inches.

Note how, in Millet's drawing, the contour of the figure's left side turns inward where it fans out to show some hatchings that represent a plane made up of several folds in the shirt. Again, in the man's headress, note the contour turning in to show, by several short hatchings, the side plane of a fold. Likewise, in Figure 4.5, notice how often hatchings of tone establish planes on the figure where segments of contour turn inward to become a plane.

PUTTING PLANES TOGETHER

Chapters Two and Three, in concentrating on line and shape, emphasized important "geographical" or two-dimensional aspects of objective drawing. We were looking for the "flat" aspects of things that are "round." In doing this we came to see that certain inquiries had to be made: what were the scale, tilt, location, and configuration of a form's overall shape *on the page*? Without this information it would not be

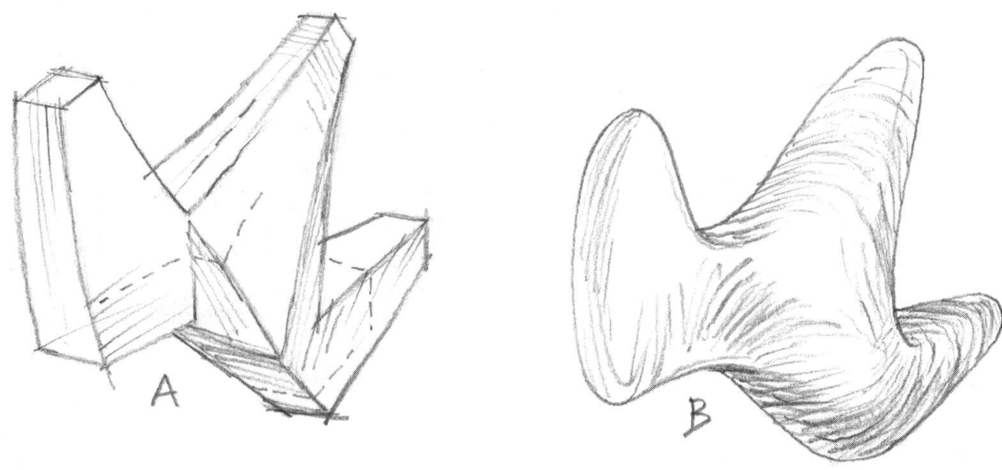

Figure 4.6

possible to proceed further with a drawing intended as an objective representation of something encountered. Here, though, we leave off charting the shoreline of forms and move overland to explore their terrain, where new inquiries and challenges await.

Earlier you were asked to consider line for its more analytical functions before turning to its more experiential possibilities. Here, too, we will examine planes in more analytical, structural terms (Figure 4.6A) before going on to experience the "roller-coaster ride" of the surfaces of many forms (Figure 4.6B).

On the page, some shapes seem not to lie flat but to be positioned at various angles in space, giving them the appearance of planes. But a minimum of two planes is necessary to give a clear impression of a form in space (Figure 4.7). As you begin to examine the surface structure of the things around you, you'll see that many forms show quite complex surface conditions. Plainly, you need some means for understanding and organizing these conditions in order to draw whatever interests you in a convincing way.

Once again, the best means for doing so have to do with seeing your subject's general features before turning to its specific ones. Just as gesture drawing depends on seeing a subject's essential actions and essential form characteristics, so does modelling a form's surfaces begin with seeing its essential structural nature. Seeing the wedge that underlies a foot, the disk that underlies a daisy, and the cone that underlies a Christmas tree are useful concepts that start us on the right road to showing those forms in convincing volumetric terms (see Figure 4.14).

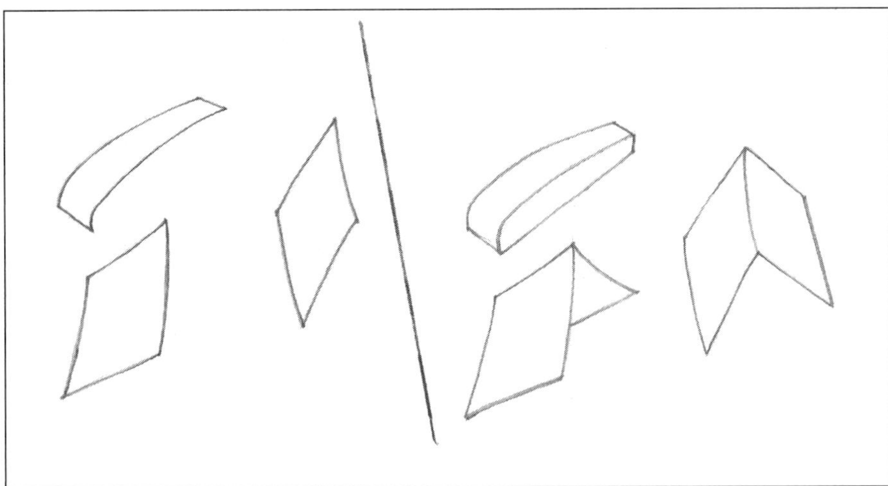

Figure 4.7

All forms fall into one or the other of two categories. The wedge, cylinder, and cone, along with the block, pyramid, cylinder, and sphere, as well as forms made by combining or modifying these simple structures, are called *geometric forms* (Figure 4.8). Other forms, more often found in nature, such as human and animal forms, rocks, clouds, clothing, foliage, fruits and the like, are called *organic* forms. Almost always, organic forms are more complex than the more "pure" geometric forms, made up as they are of many smaller, often subtle turnings and textures.

Figure 4.8

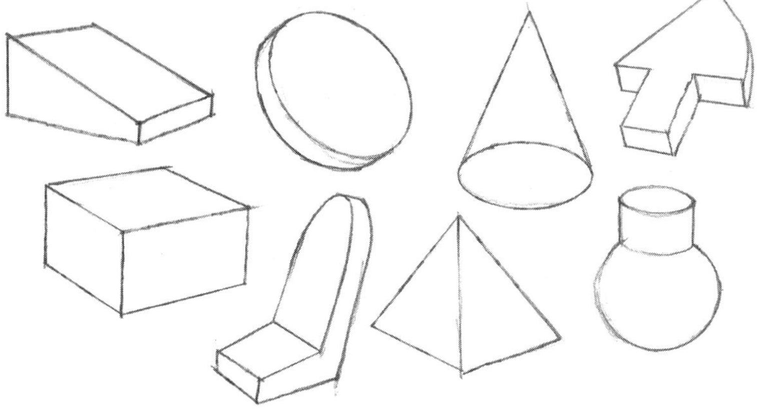

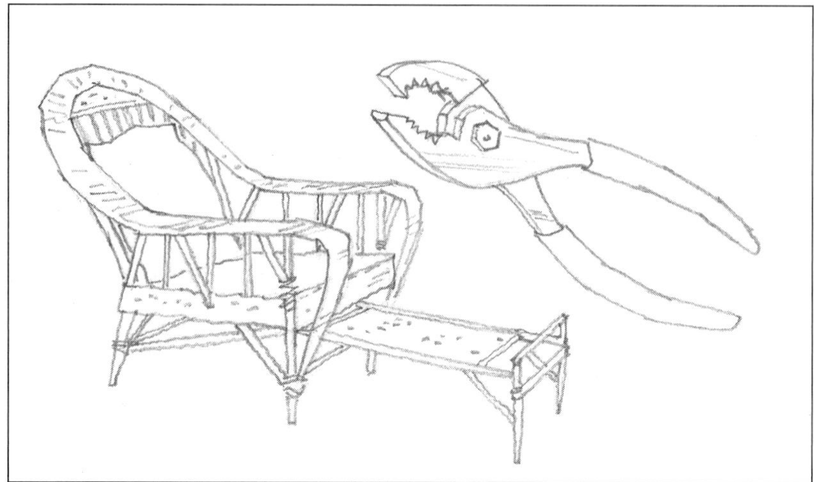

Figure 4.9

However, the combining of various geometric forms can produce quite intricate subjects (Figure 4.9). Notice that some of the curved planes have been restated as made up of several flat planes that collectively produce the curved surface of a part. It is sometimes helpful to clarify a curved surface in this way and many artists use this device in a drawing's early stages to better understand a part's essential structure. This can be seen in Sargent's *Draped Figure* (Figure 4.10). Here, the preliminary drawing of the folds in the drapery on the man's right arm are more simplified and given harsher abutments, thereby showing their structure more clearly, whereas the folds of the shirt, having been developed further, are given gentler turnings.

BLOCKING

A useful way of finding the structural order of any complex subject is to analyze its major planes (general) before exploring its minor ones (specific). For example, seeing the tilt and shape of the major plane of a staircase before drawing the minor planes of the steps, helps you to get the tilt and shape of each step more accurately drawn (Figure 4.11). The more complex the subject, the more enveloping and daring should be the search for major planes. Although it's impossible to know if Cambiaso drew his *Group of Figures* (Figure 4.12) by observing a model taking each of the poses or by imagining this group of animated people, his drawing (probably a preliminary sketch for a painting) is instructive in showing how extreme the stripping away of smaller planes can be, to get at the major ones.

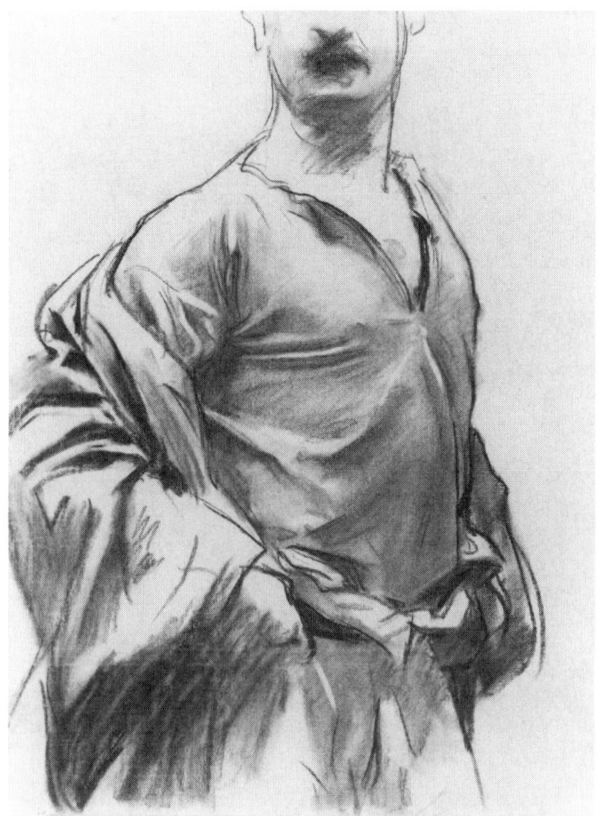

Figure 4.10 John Singer Sargent (American, 1856–1925), *Draped Figure*. Charcoal. 29.135. *Source:* Museum of Art, Rhode Island School of Design. Gift of Miss Emily Sargent and Mrs. Francis Ormond, through Thomas A. Fox. Photo by Del Gogart.

Figure 4.11

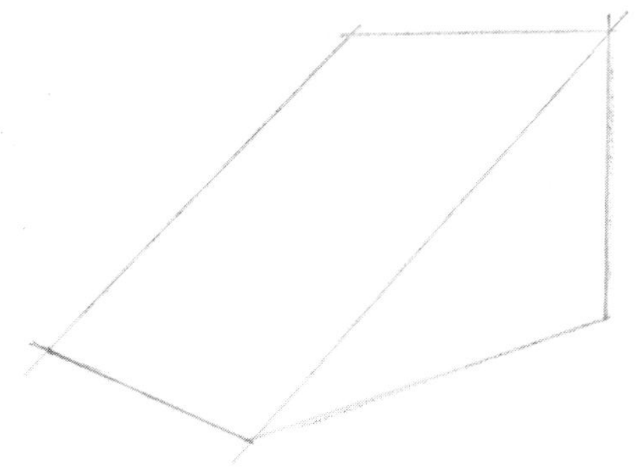

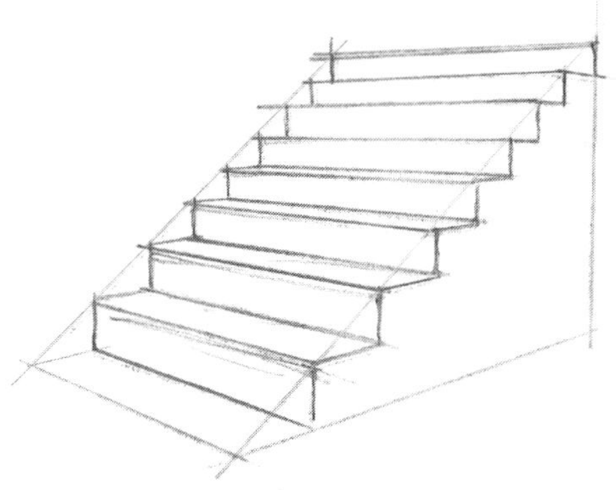

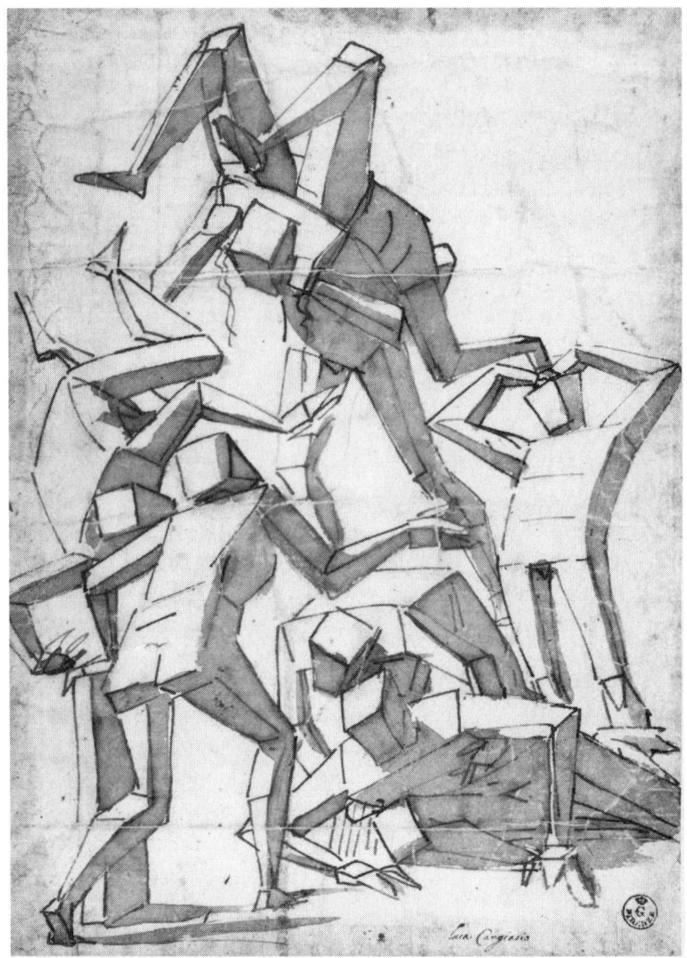

Figure 4.12 Luca Cambiaso (1527–1585), *Group of Cubic Figures.*
Source: Photograph © Scala/Art Resource, NY.

Such a stripping away of lesser surface turnings to find a part's basic structure is often referred to as blocking, and is a more common practice than you might suppose. This can be seen in a drawing by Pontormo, an artist given to forms of a sensual and tactile kind (Figure 4.13; see also Plate 10). Although the drawing seems very nearly completed, the figure's two hands are drawn in a much more schematic and generalized way. Did the artist intend to leave the hands this way? We'll never know for sure, but it is reasonable to assume that he would not have switched styles in such an abrupt and arbitrary manner. A more likely explanation is that Pontormo wanted to more fully understand the structure of these foreshortened and complicated parts before he went on to fully realize their form, but for whatever reason, did not do so.

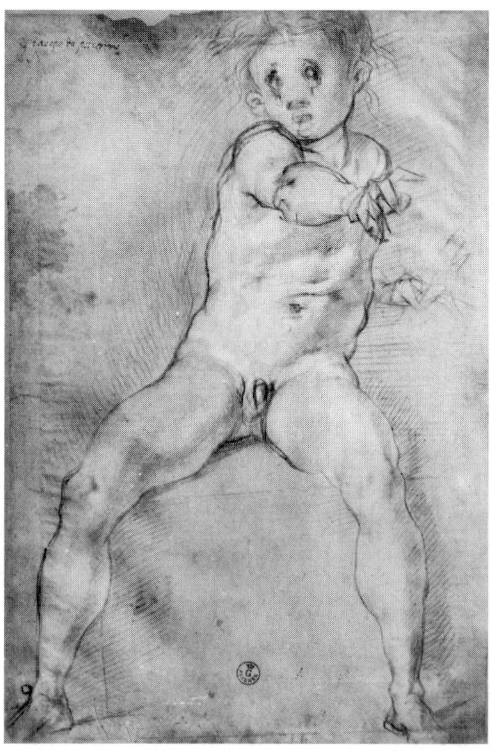

Figure 4.13 Jacopo Pontormo (1494–1557), *Study of a Male Nude or a Seated Young Man Pointing to Something*. *Source:* Photograph © Alinari/Art Resource, NY.

Blocking, then, as the term implies, has to do with envisioning the simplest, often blocklike "container" that can enclose a form, as Figure 4.14 demonstrates. Note that some forms can be better contained in other basic structures such as the wedge, the cylinder, the cone, or some other simple structure of your own devising. Note, too, that sometimes a form is reducible to more than one container solution, as in the drawing of the legs. Whichever enclosing structure you use (and the block *is* often the visually most logical one because, in the end, anything can be placed in a box), blocking will be best understood if we now examine a few basic perspective principles to guide your perceptual understanding in general and your grasp of structural analysis in particular.

Perspective Fundamentals

As noted in Chapter One (See "Convergence"), for artists the fundamental linear perspective principle declares that lines (or edges) known to be parallel appear to converge as they move back in the spatial field to meet at a point on the horizon line (Figure 4.15). To see this phenomenon more clearly some artists will temporarily

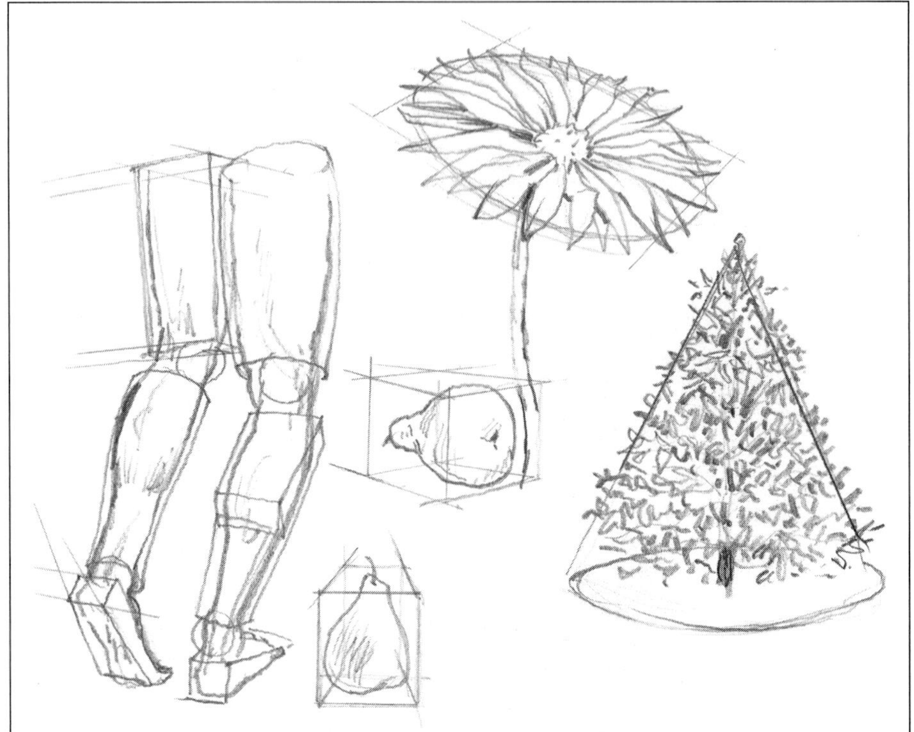

Figure 4.14

Figure 4.15

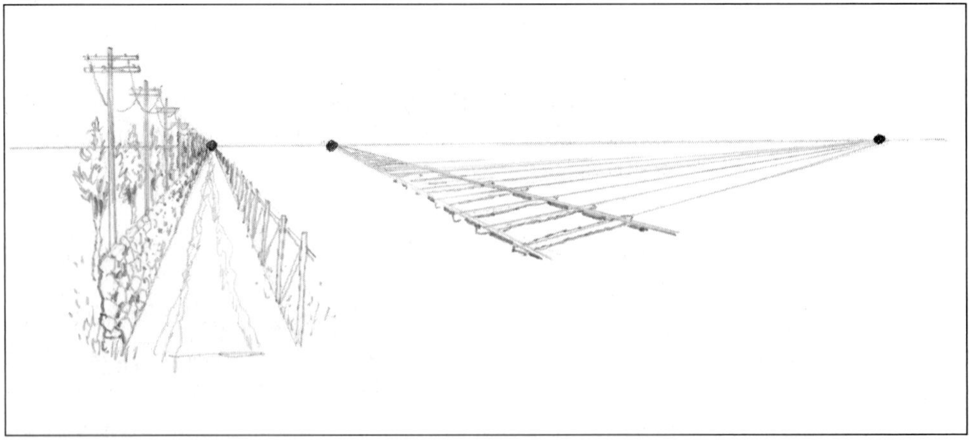

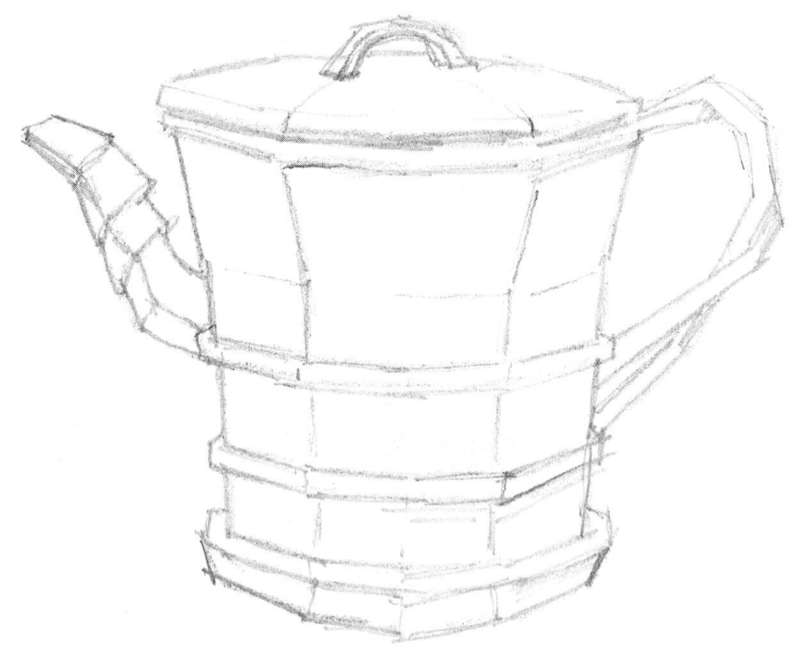

Figure 4.16

convert all or most of a subject's curved planes to straight ones, as we saw in Sargent's, Cambiaso's, and Pontormo's drawings, and as Figure 4.16 illustrates.

Matters pertaining to perspective are clarified by recognizing that, as noted above, any form we wish to draw, no matter how large, small, or complex can be envisioned as contained in a blocklike cage. As Figure 4.14 shows, some of the "caged" forms show only one set of converging lines, while others show two sets. In the first instance the forms are drawn in *one-point perspective*, and in the second, in *two-point perspective* (see Figure 4.15). To understand these differing views better, we'll start by using the block itself as our subject.

A block (and, of course, the form it may contain) is in one-point perspective when, as in Figure 4.17A, one of its sides faces us directly, that is, when this surface is at a right angle to our line of sight, as in Figure 4.17B. In this position the block shows only one set of converging lines going

Knowing whether a form is above or below your eye-level is basic to knowing how to correctly place it in space.

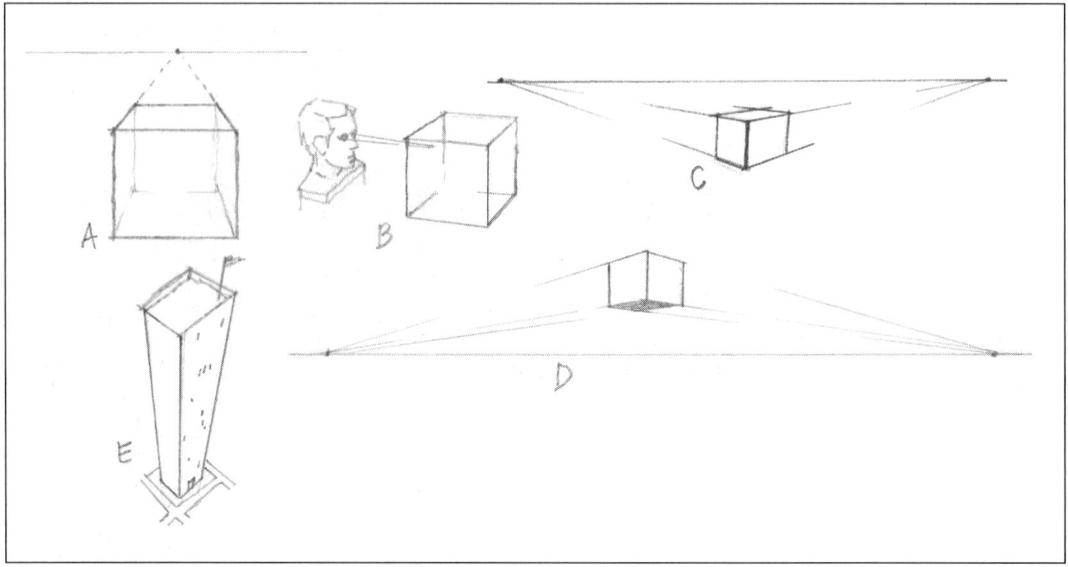

Figure 4.17

back in the spatial field to meet at a point on the horizon line. This point, reasonably enough, is called the vanishing point. However, when the block is turned so that we see one of its corners, as in Figure 4.17C, we view the block in two-point perspective. In this position the block shows two sets of converging lines going back to meet at separate vanishing points on the same horizon line. As for the horizon line itself, it is determined by, and equivalent to your eye-level, when you are looking straight ahead. The low horizon line you see when you look out at a large body of water becomes much higher when the same scene is viewed from atop a high building. Indoors, forms can still be located as being above or below the horizon line by noting whether a form is above or below your eye-level. Knowing whether a form is above or below your eye-level is basic to knowing how to correctly place it in space.

When you look down upon a block placed on any horizontal surface such as a table, or floor, the horizon line will be located above the block, as in Figures 4.17A and 4.17C. If you see a block oriented parallel to the horizontal surface, but hovering above it high enough to reveal its underside, that is, its bottom plane, the horizon line will be located below the block, as in Figure 4.17D. Normally, the vertical lines representing the abutments of the block's four side planes are drawn as true parallels—they show no convergence. This still holds true when a block is not viewed in an upright position, but at some angle. An exception to this principle occurs when looking up at a tall building or down a deep shaft. When this is

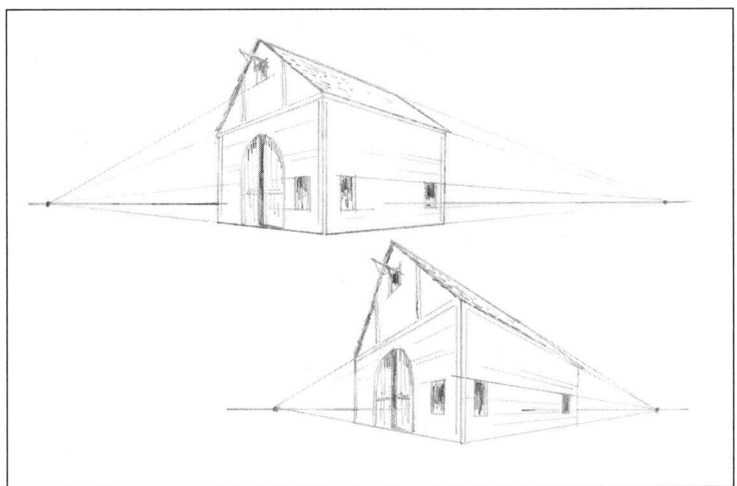

Figure 4.18

the case, the vertical lines *do* appear to converge, as Figure 4.17E shows. Such forms are then seen in *three-point perspective.*

When drawing a form in two-point perspective, be sure to place the two vanishing points quite far apart, as locating them near each other produces a diamond rather than a block form. Getting the points too close together when roughing in a blocklike cage to better draw the form within it, will result in distortions such as those in Figure 4.18.

Once these few simple principles having to do with convergence are understood, you can more easily draw (or check the accuracy of) the forms that make up your drawing. The forms in Figures 4.19 and 4.20 show how even complex subjects can be realized by applying these principles. In Menzel's study for his painting *The Iron Rolling Mill,* we understand the horizon line to be low because he has us looking up at the factory's many beams and girders, and he places us in a spot where we view this large interior in one-point perspective. Note that despite the rough nature of this preparatory sketch (rough to the degree of making the worker appear skewered by a supporting beam), the lines denoting the roof, walls, and some of the beams, because they move back into the spatial field, do aim at a single vanishing point. Note also, that the roof planks and vertical girders grow thinner and closer together as they go back in space even though we know these planks would all be alike in thickness and spacing and that the vertical supports are likely to be the same in heft. Like the ties and rails of a train track, these boards and girders are drawn in conformity to another perspective principle: that evenly spaced forms known to be similar in size appear to grow smaller and closer together as they recede in the spatial field (Figure 4.21).

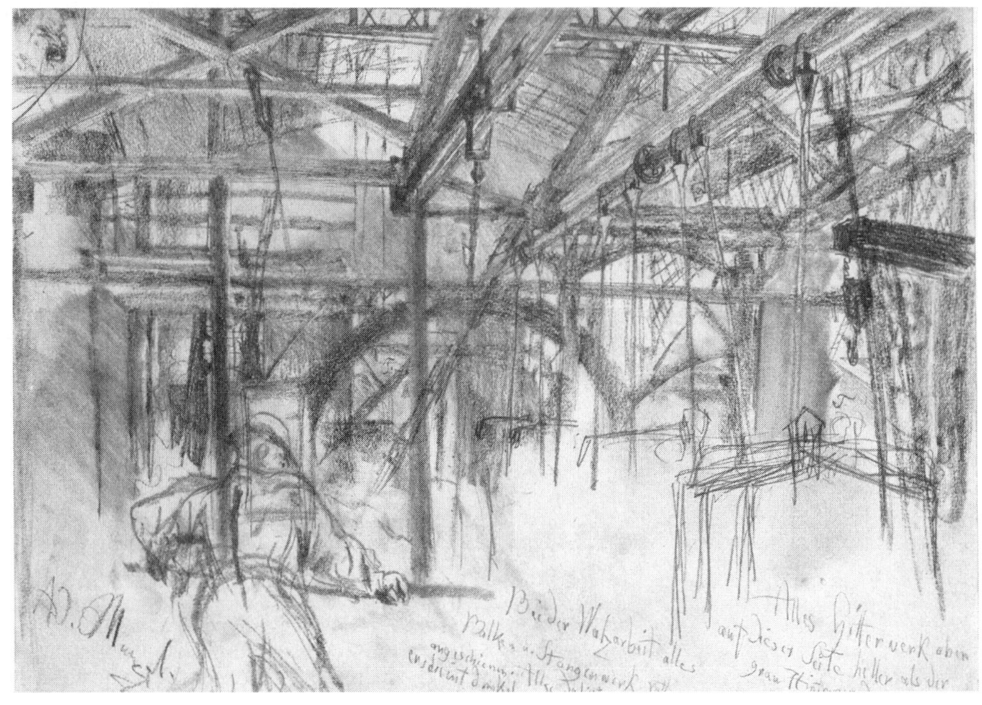

Figure 4.19 Adolph von Menzel (German, 1815–1905), *Hall in the Iron Rolling Mill Koenigshuette*, (1872–1874). Graphite on paper, 23.8 × 32.9 cm (Inv. SZ *N 155).* *Source:* Photograph © Bildarchiv Preussicher Kulturbesitz/Art Resource, NY.

Figure 4.20 Peter Paul Rubens (Flemish, 1577–1640), *Two Farm Wagons*, undated. Black and red chalk on paper, 23.5 × 14 cm (Inv. KdZ 3237). *Source:* Photo: Joerg P. Anders. Photograph © Bildarchiv Preussicher Kulturbesitz/Art Resource, NY.

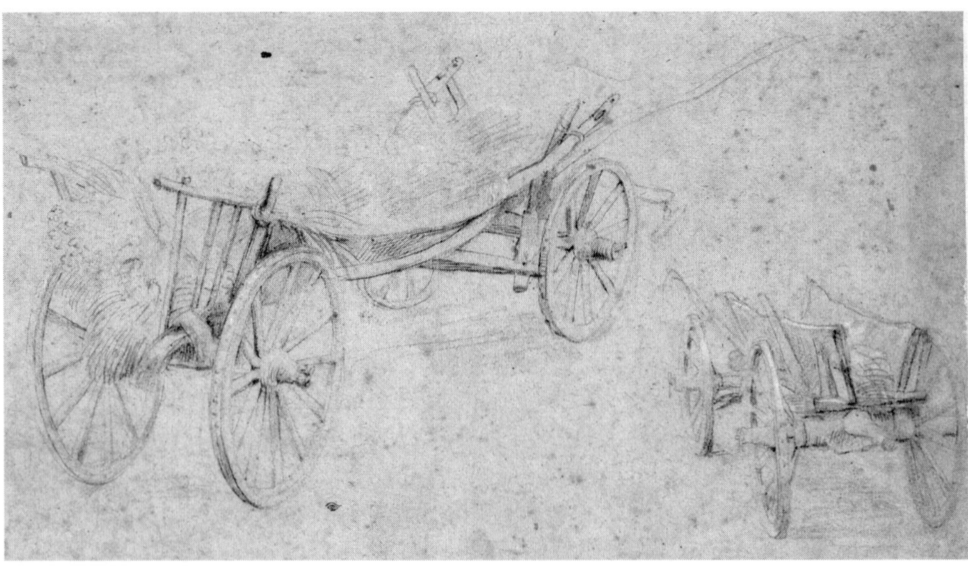

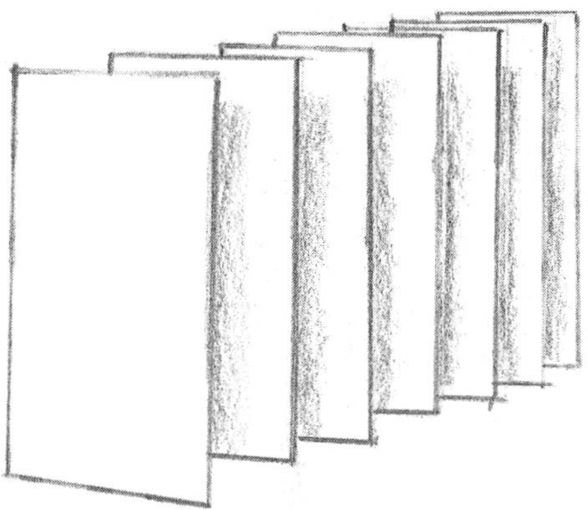

Figure 4.21

The two wagons in Rubens' sketch are drawn in two-point perspective; he places us behind and to one side of each wagon. And, unlike the Menzel drawing, here we look down on the subject. Interestingly, although there isn't a single vertical or horizontal pole in these wagons, we know the wagons are upright and in correct perspective because the wheels are (more or less) vertical and the axles are parallel to the horizontal ground plane.

The drawing of wheels brings up another perspective matter. How are circular or curved forms drawn in correct perspective? Again, the principle of converging lines aids in the drawing of rounded forms because any form can be "boxed." Viewed from any oblique angle a circular shape may appear as an ellipse, growing narrower in width as it approaches total foreshortening, at which point it is seen as a line (Figure 4.22A). But a foreshortened circle is not an ellipse. Bisecting an ellipse on its long axis produces two equal halves. But bisecting a foreshortened circle in this way produces a slightly fuller curve in the near half, as in Figure 4.22B.

The angle of a foreshortened circle is determined by its long axis. When a foreshortened circle is vertical, its axis will be vertical. When it lies upon a horizontal surface and is centered on the viewer (a one-point perspective view), its long axis will be horizontal. All other positions will show the long axis inclined to some degree, as in Figure 4.23A.

Drawing a foreshortened circle, cylinder, or any other round-bodied form in correct perspective is made easier if you first draw its square, rectangular, or block-like container at the desired angle, as in Figure 4.24. Next, lightly draw diagonal lines from corner to corner. Where they cross is the perspective center of the shape.

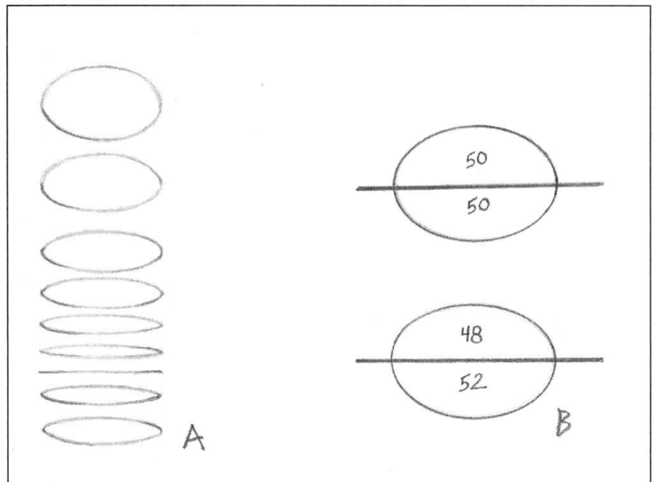

Figure 4.22

Figure 4.23

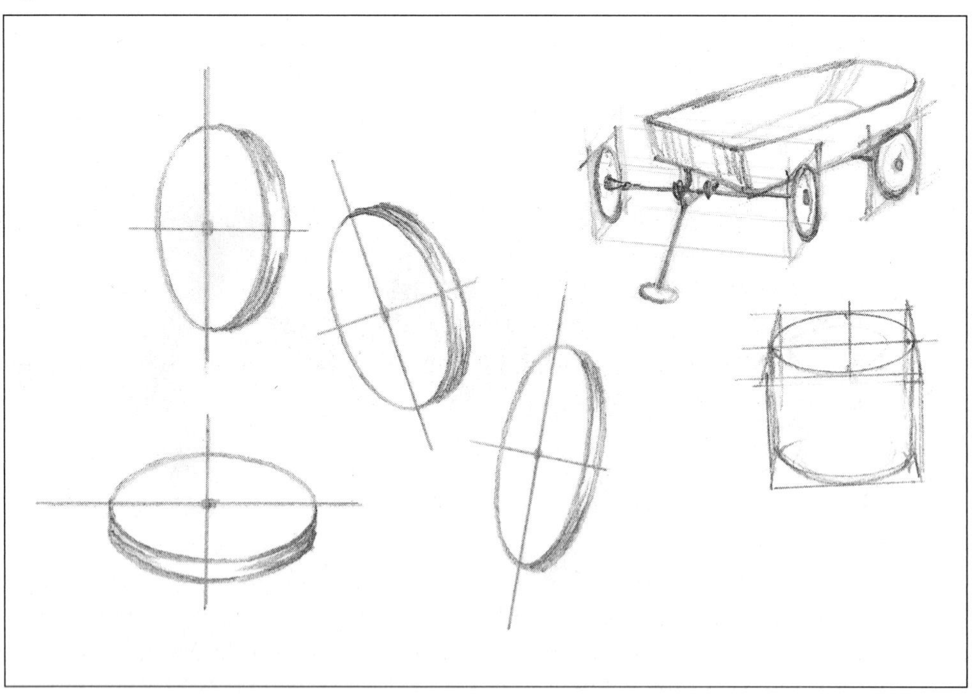

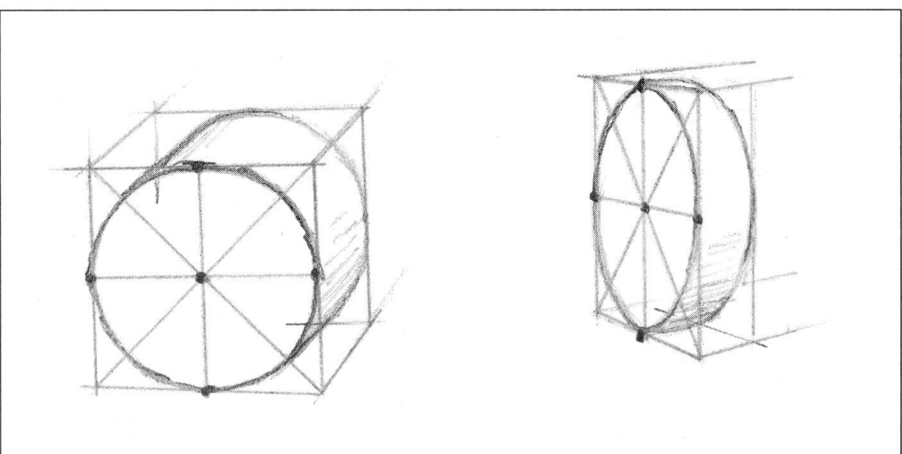

Figure 4.24

Now lightly draw a vertical and a horizontal line that both run through the perspective center. Placing a dot at the point where each line strikes the container's edge will help you rough in the drawing of a curvilinear shape, as in Figure 4.24.

Cast Shadows

The principle of convergence also affects the shape and size of cast shadows, which always "flee" in the direction opposite the light source. When forms are illuminated by a nearby source of light such as a candle, a street light, or a lamp, their cast shadows will radiate from the point of the light source, as Figure 4.25 illustrates. Here both the light source and its base determine the direction, size, and length of the shadows cast by the encircling forms.

When forms are illuminated by sunlight, the radiating effect is far less evident because of the sun's great distance. Figure 4.26 shows how the sun and its "base" (the point on the horizon line directly below the sun) determine the direction, shape, and length of cast shadows. Note that the cast shadow is affected by three vanishing points.

Although harsh cast shadows sometimes intrude on the spatial and structural clarity of a subject, and should be modified or even omitted in your drawing when they do, they are often useful in explaining space, mass, and atmosphere, as Figures 4.27 and 4.28 show. In each drawing, a light source, playing over the subject, generates shadows that help make clear the distance separating one part from another, adds to the clarity of each form's surface structure, and imparts a sense of quietude and time.

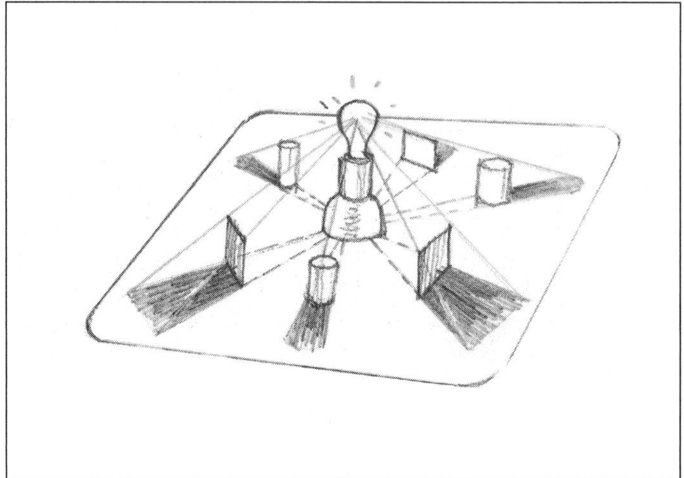

Figure 4.25

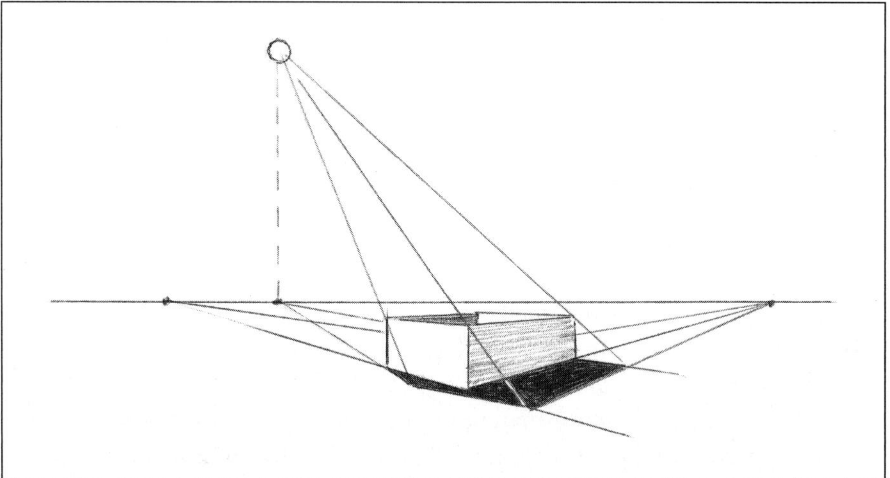

Figure 4.26

Some Perspective Exercises

With some practice, a knowledge of the few and simple perspective principles discussed in this section is easily acquired and as easily put into practice, making it possible for you to draw subjects that might have seemed too complex or unusual to confront before. A few basic exercises that will speed up your understanding and control of perspective are listed here.

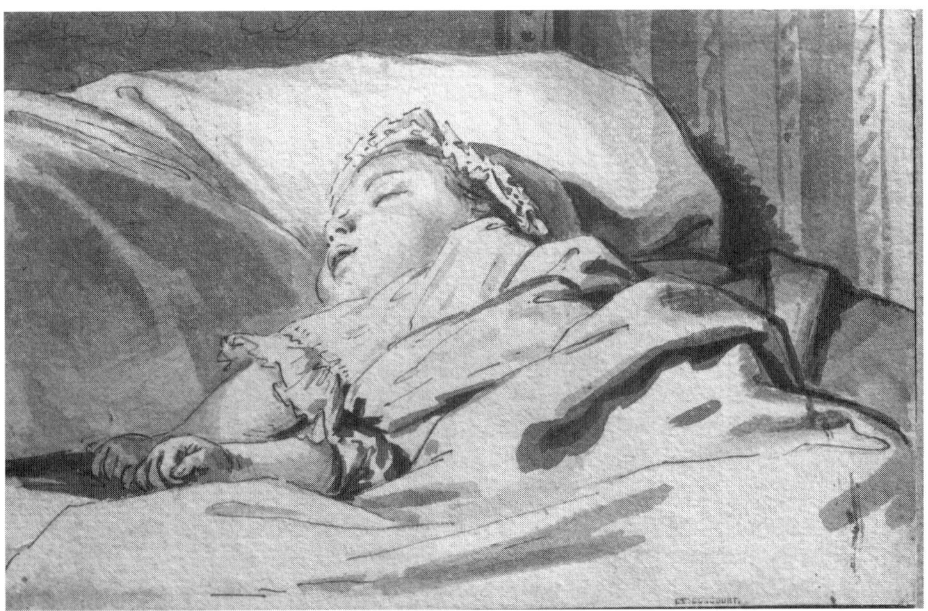

Figure 4.27 Jean-Michel Moreau (French, 1741–1814), *The Artist's Daughter Asleep (facing left)*, about 1770. Pen and black ink and black wash over charcoal. Overall: 10.2 × 15.1 cm (4 × 5$\frac{15}{16}$ inches) *Source:* Photograph © 2004 Museum of Fine Arts, Boston. Bequest of Forsyth Wickes. The Forsyth Wickes Collection (65.2593).

Figure 4.28 Conger Metcalf, *Still Life with Pipe.* Pencil with wash., n.d. Courtesy of the Boston Public Library, Print Department.

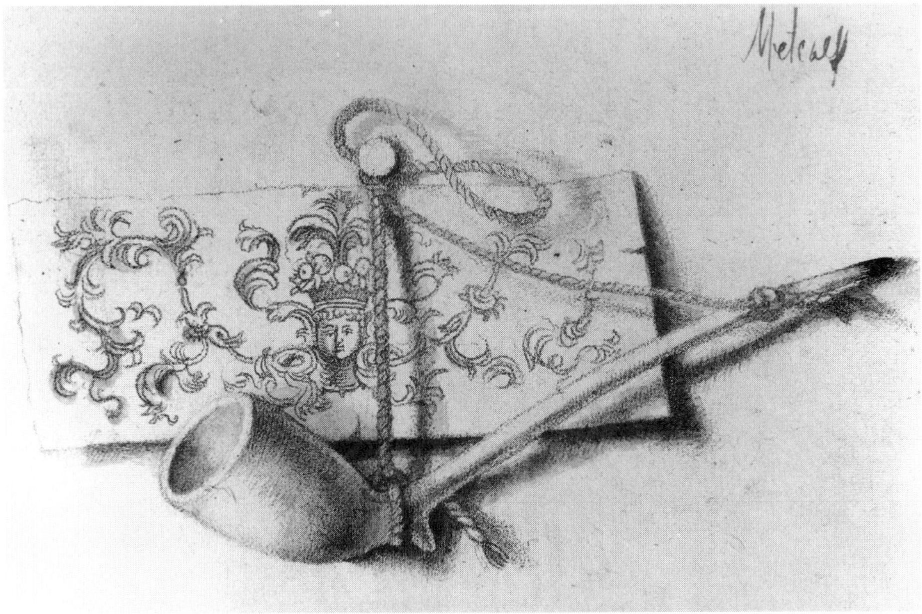

1. Place tracing paper over photographs of landscapes, cityscapes, still lifes, and interiors; and also over objects such as furniture, machinery, vehicles, and tools. Locate and draw in line on the tracing paper the horizon line, the vanishing points of at least some of the forms, and the perspective centers of foreshortened surfaces. Search for any three-point perspective conditions that may be present (tall structures or shafts) and draw the converging lines of such forms to see where they meet.
2. Arrange on a tabletop several simple forms, such as differently sized blocks of wood, books, cylinders, and cones, and draw them using line only, beginning with the tabletop itself. Positioning yourself squarely in front of the table, draw lines leading from the tabletop's side edges back to where they meet, as this will locate the horizon line. Draw the one- or two-point perspective lines of all forms placed flat upon the tabletop; they should meet at various vanishing points on the same horizon line. Forms that are tilted in some degree away from the horizontal plane of the tabletop will show vanishing points above or below the horizon line. Foreshortened surfaces such as the end planes of cylinders or arches should be drawn by first establishing the perspective center of their "container shapes" (Figure 4.29).
3. Draw from your imagination some twelve to fifteen (or more) geometric forms. These can be blocklike letter or number forms, or forms similar to those in Figure 4.30A. Draw these forms in a more or less transparent way, as this illustration shows. Select several of these forms and draw them in different positions, as in Figure 4.30B. Draw some

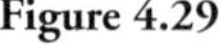

Figure 4.29

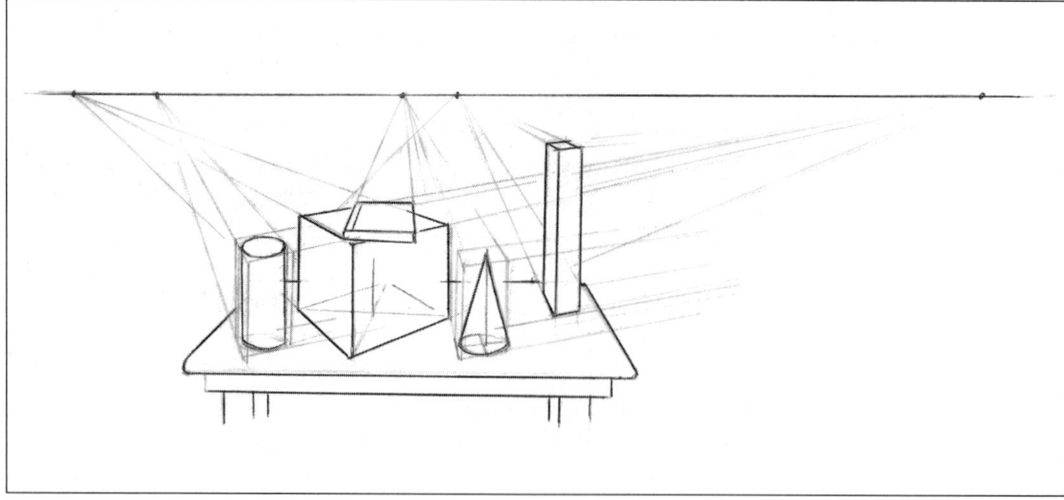

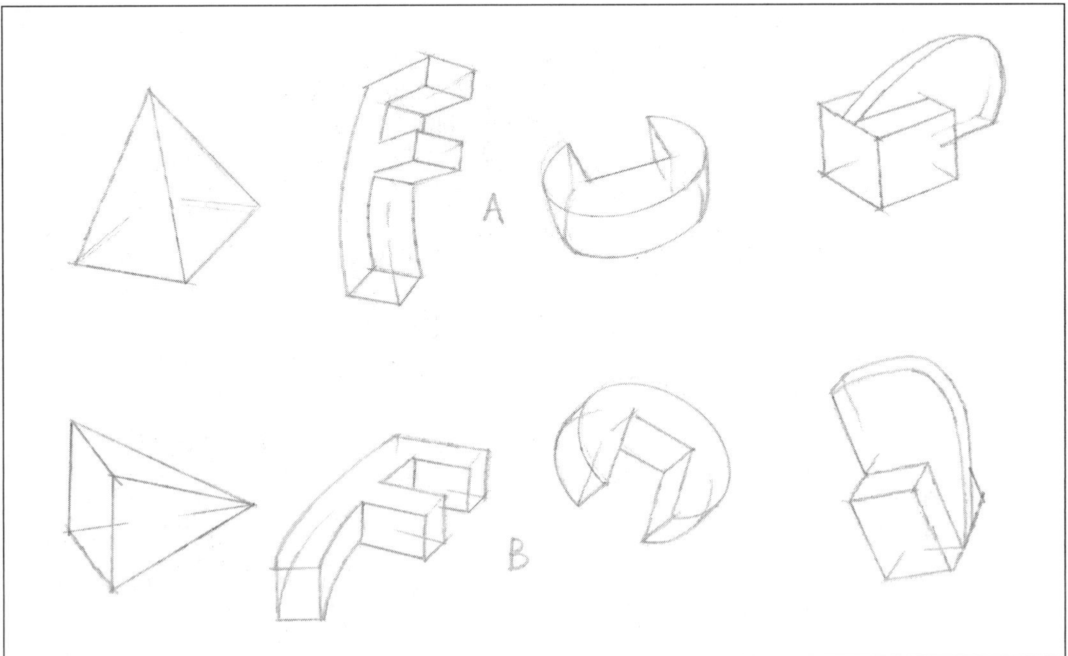

Figure 4.30

three or four pages of such sketchbook doodles every week for a few months. Some artists continue to do so for years; often creating very complex arrangements of forms. The better you can envision forms in various combinations and positions the better you can analyze those you see. (See also Chapter Eight.)

4. Examine a familiar object and draw it as it might appear if it were floating in the air, as in Figure 4.31. With the object before you as you draw, it is easier to imagine it in another position. When the drawing is completed you can hold the object up in the same position as the one in your drawing, to see where you got it right and where you didn't.
5. Make a drawing from your imagination, of some twelve to fifteen geometric shapes floating in deep space. Some of these shapes may overlap. Make the near shapes larger, and fill them with various dark tones, using bold hatchings. Make the farther ones smaller, their edges less focused, and the tones less textured, as in Figure 4.32.
6. Using a nearby lamp as your strong light source for a simple still life drawing, arrange the still life objects in a way that creates interesting cast shadows. Although the drawing of objects may be in line only,

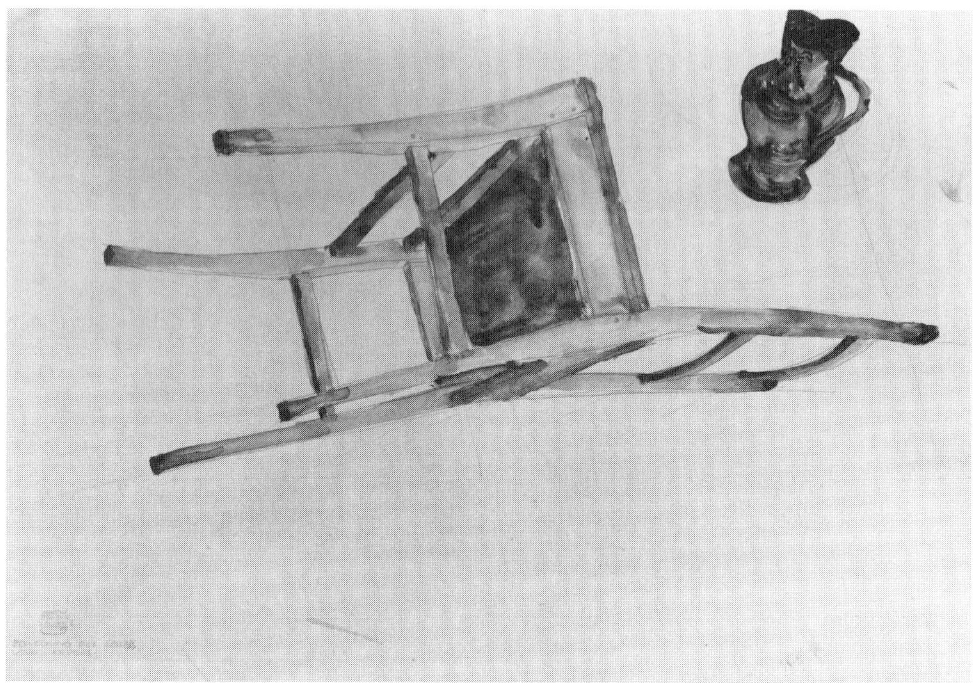

Figure 4.31 Egon Schiele (Austrian, 1890–1918), *Organic Movement of Chair and Pitcher,* 1912. Watercolor and pencil on paper. Albertina, Wien.

draw the cast shadows as toned. Do not show the boundaries of cast shadows where they run into each other, but treat them as joined to make a larger cast shadow, as in Figure 4.33.

STRUCTURAL ANALYSIS

In examining the perspective principles above, it may seem we've drifted from our earlier concepts and procedures having to do with gesture, shape, and the rest. But we have only paused to more fully concentrate on these principles of perspective because of their important influence on perception. Knowing that edges appear to converge, that horizon lines and vanishing points are at work among the things around us, your examination of a subject is informed in ways that help you to analyze the position and structure of a subject's parts.

Here we return to making drawings that respond to a subject's gesture, to the shapes and scale of parts and planes, and to blocking (now reinforced by linear perspective), with a concentration on planar analysis. All this will help us to understand and show a subject's surface structure.

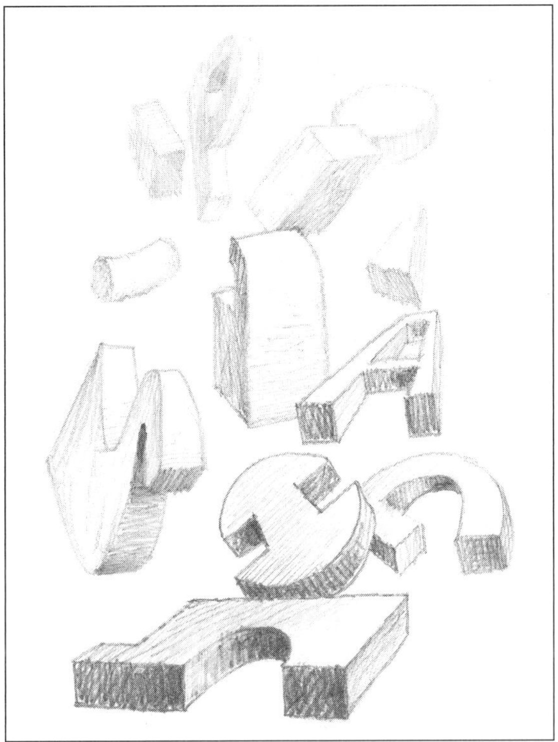

Figure 4.32

Some Structural Analysis Exercises

1. Let's begin by drawing objects whose planar structure is incisive, clear, and not too complex. Place before you a manufactured object such as a wrench, a pair of pliers, a can opener, or any other tool or utensil that has clearly abutting planes and is not overly complicated in its parts or design. Make your drawing somewhat larger than the object you've selected because it's easier to construct the drawing's smaller planes in this enlarged scale. Using a soft graphite pencil begin with a light gesture drawing that sets up the directions and general shapes of the subject's parts. Give special attention to the object's main axis (or axes). Next, using only straight lines, establish the major turnings that make up its shapes. Search out edge intersections, that is, where edges meet (see "Intersections," Chapter One), and note the shape-actualities of any negative shapes. Avoid tones, keeping the drawing in a linear, schematic, and transparent mode.

   Once you have formed a rough sketch of the object's general features you may wish to enclose some parts of the subject in whatever

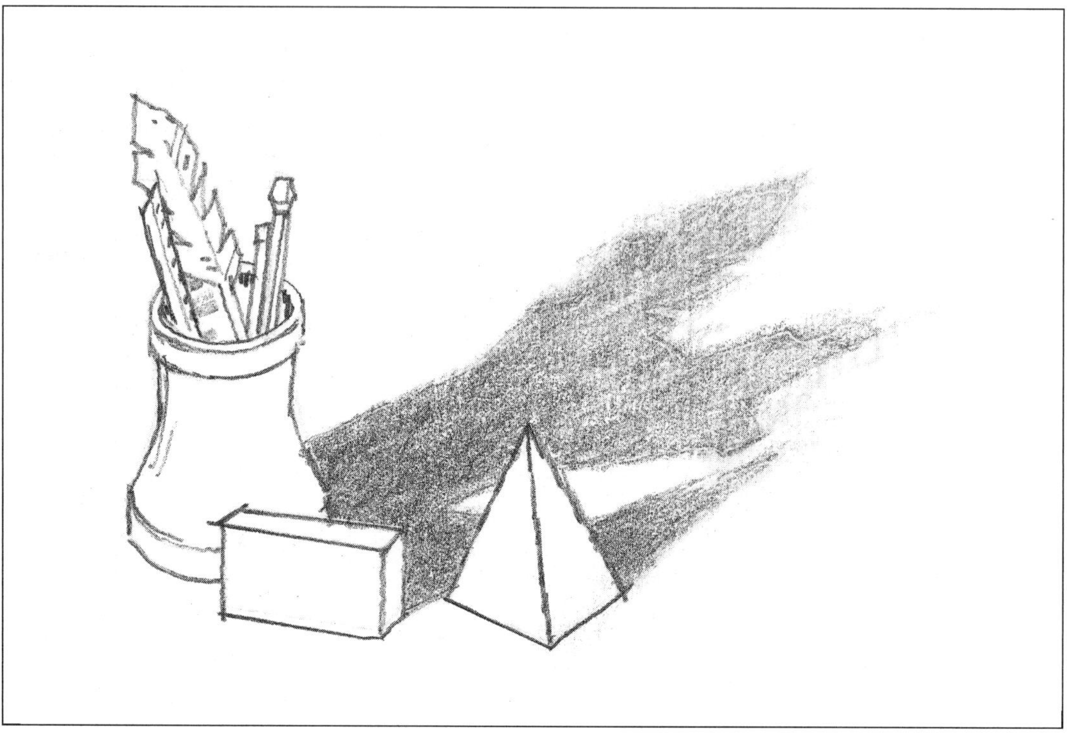

Figure 4.33

blocklike containers would best suit each part, in order to better examine the drawing's perspective. This is the time to check on where a judgment of axis or edge may have gone wrong, and to more firmly "lock" the drawing into an overall system of converging sets of lines (Figure 4.34A).

Continue to locate smaller edges and planes, and to establish the first curved edges by "filing off" the corners where straight lines meet by using some hatched lines, as in Figure 4.34B. Once you feel confident that the drawing's masses and interspaces reflect the directions, shapes, proportions, and the perspective of those in the object, you can erase many of the earlier, more schematic lines. To make the subject's parts appear more substantial you can add a light tone to those planes turned well away from the light, as in Figure 4.34C.

There is a clear and orderly appearance to such machine-tooled objects. The flat planes abut sharply, the curved ones do not waver, and their unseen planes are easier to envision. This is generally true of most manufactured things, from a steam kettle to a skyscraper. But it

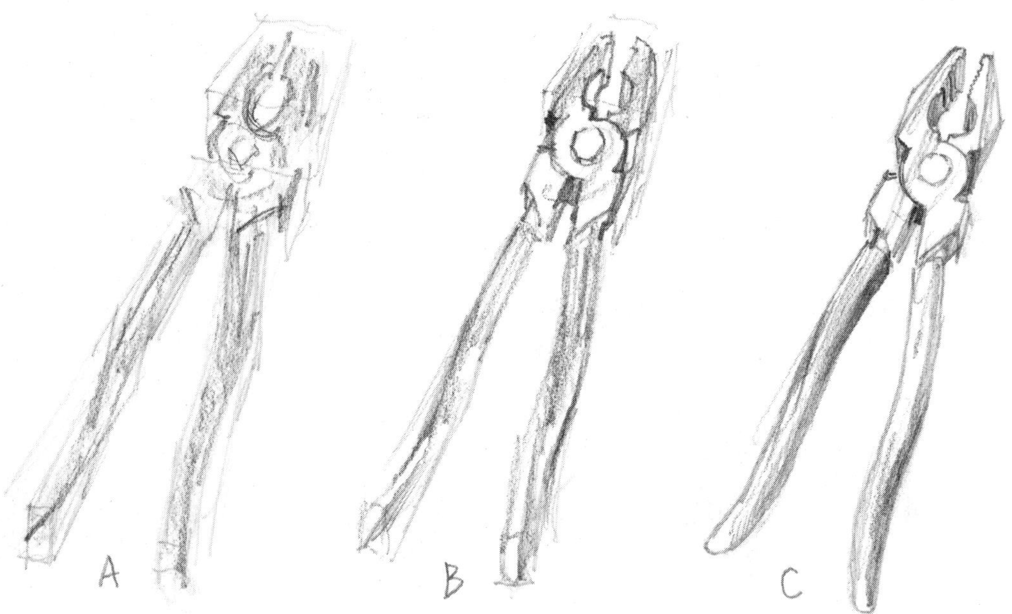

Figure 4.34

is far less the case in subjects of a more organic nature, whether a tree branch, a human figure, or a pillow. These require not only your most concentrated analytical skills, but also your ability to "feel" the rhythms, the weight, and the energy of your subject.

2. For your second drawing, select any object made of leather. Hats, shoes, jackets, boots, handbags, or gloves all serve as useful intermediate kinds of subjects—they retain some of the features of more purely geometric forms and possess many of the features of organic ones.

Again, plan your drawing to be somewhat larger than the object. After searching out its gestural character and its main axial directions, continue to draw by establishing the subject's shapes and major planes, using mainly straight lines. Now your use of blocky containers and transparent passages should be more selective, being restricted to larger parts of the object, or where you are having difficulty seeing the exact tilt or basic geometric basis of a part. It helps to walk around your subject to see parts hidden from your view of it, because this often shows why the planes you do see are arranged as they are.

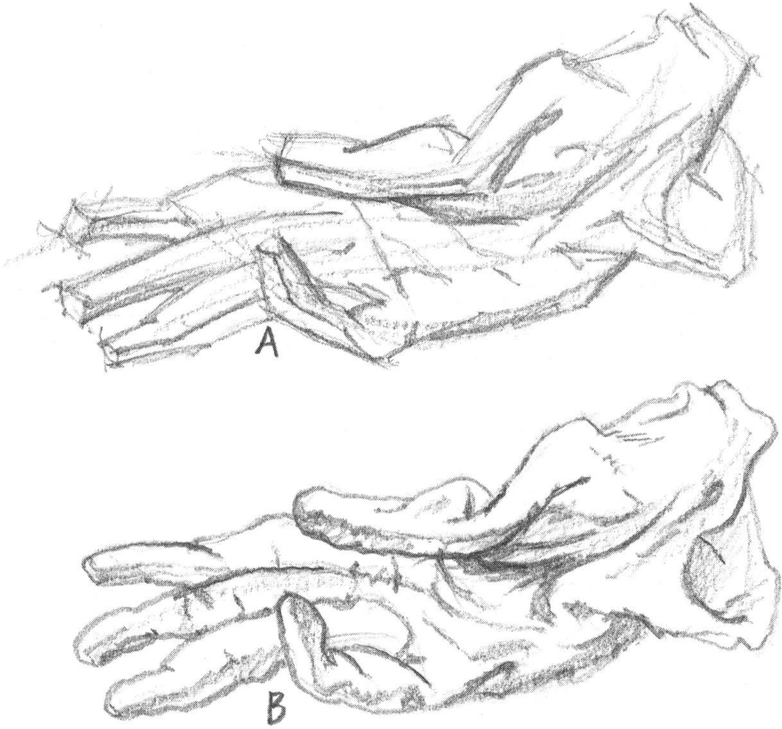

Figure 4.35

Resist the temptation to draw small surface details having to do with textures, decorative patterns, or the effects of light. Instead, try to "break through" the object's surface to see the basic planar structure that a more analytical treatment of it would show, as in Figure 4.35A.

Because you have been using more straight than curved lines and have been concentrating on seeing planar shapes and abutments, the drawing is likely to seem schematic and angular, even harsh. It is, after all, a drawing of the subject's structural conditions rather than its surface details. As such, you should now consider it to be a kind of armature or scaffold that will support a more tactile and experiential use of line. If your drawing has darkened with the application of many lines, erase any that are not important in their armature role. Using a kneaded eraser is best for this operation, as it will not roughen the paper's surface. You may even wish to lightly erase the lines you do wish to keep, setting the stage better for the last phase of this drawing exercise.

To shift from the more analytical underdrawing to a more experiential mode of seeing, examine the edges of the drawing's planar abutments and "turn" them with curved lines that round off the corners. These lines, unlike the more schematic and faster lines that first establish a plane's shape and tilt, should move in a more deliberate and caring way because now you are experiencing the rise and fall of an edge, its undulations telling of tensions, movement, and the mass it contains. Where a contour's edge moves "inland" to open into a plane, use a few hatched lines to suggest the plane (see "Edge to Plane," this chapter). In general, these lines should be lightly drawn, making them darker or heavier when they overlap another line representing an edge further back in the spatial field. Your goal here is to experience every hill and valley as revealing the nature of form, of movement, and of weight.

In turning from the valuable but more schematic search for a form's shape to the experiencing of a form's mass, your line is shifting from a search for outline to a search for contour, which is a volume-revealing line. It is no longer a line that treats the boundaries of shape with a kind of sameness, as outline do, but a line that may vary in density and even in some adjustments of shape, resulting from your understanding of the volume that the contour line contains. Lastly, add a few light tones on planes and parts located further back in space or which are overlapped by other parts, as in Figure 4.35B.

Both of these drawing exercises ended by adding some values to give forms a more substantial and structurally clear appearance. At this stage of your studies, it seems value is knocking at the door. In the next chapter we'll let it in and see just how much value can contribute to a drawing's structural clarity, and to drawing what you see in a compelling and sensitive way.

Things to Think About

1. How do the shapes of planes create the impression of volumes in space?
2. Why is it important to see a subject's major planes before its minor ones, if it is the minor planes that convey a subject's specific structural nature?
3. How does blocking help a form to be in correct perspective?
4. When you look down on a block positioned in one-point perspective before you, its top plane is visible, and the horizon line will be a little above the top of the block. What plane comes into view if the block rises to a height that places it a little above your eye-level?
5. When you look down a road with a row of many trees on either side, why do the trees diminish in size, and appear to be placed closer together, the farther away they are from you? Why, at the horizon line, do the two rows of trees seem almost to touch?
6. Under what circumstances will you see three-point perspective?
7. How would drawing a circle be helped by first drawing a square?
8. How can a cast shadow help to explain the form it strikes? How can a cast shadow deny or "camouflage" the form it strikes?
9. How are the terms *outline* and *shape* different?

Critique Considerations

1. Do the more organic forms in your drawings, such as human forms, fruits and vegetables, drapery, clothing, and the like, seem less structurally clear than the more geometric ones, such as books, boxes, cups, chairs, and tables? One can better see organic forms by envisioning their underlying, more geometric basis. For example, when drawing an orange or a tomato, hold in mind their underlying spherical form, or try to "see" the more angular basis of a drape's folds, and the cylinders and blocks that can contain human forms.
2. If your drawings continue to show forms "out of perspective," as when a book appears to stand or float over a table instead of lying on its surface, it is probably because the converging lines of the book meet at one horizon line, while those of the table meet at another horizon line.
3. Do the cast shadows in your drawings seem to rise to the surface of the page? Do they seem unconnected with the surfaces they fall on? Do they appear harsh and too dark or isolated from the rest of the drawing? These faults can arise if cast shadows, by their shape, fail to conform to the terrain of the surfaces they fall on, or if the cast shadows are too sharply focused and/or dark. Remember that cast shadows are simply areas of less light on the surfaces they strike.
4. In your more fully developed drawings, do the contours of organic forms seem to suggest something of the volumes they contain? If not, try to think of such lines as taking their shape from the forms and forces inside. This is especially useful when contours define forms that are bounded by "container" surfaces, as, for example, in the case of human and animal forms, upholstered furniture, or bags of groceries.

5

Structure to Value and Volume

PLANES AND LIGHT

Although line is the predominant means by which most drawings are formed, we know that there are no lines in nature, however thin, that encircle or separate one thing from another. We often use line as a convenient means to mark off the boundaries between a subject's shapes, planes, colors, values, and masses. But when we see these conditions in our subjects, we see them engaged in all manner of abutments, overlappings, and fusions, without the benefit of line to sort it all out. Here, we will examine how values define planes and edges, separate one form from another, convey the effects of light playing across forms, substitute for color, and help to create volume and space.

Line and value are the two most important visual elements in drawing because it is with one and/or the other that shape, texture, mass, light, and space are produced. In Chapter One we discussed the several ways of seeing and estimating value differences (see "Measuring Value," Chapter One). It would be useful now to review those passages as we explore value's structural role.

Put simply, a value is the quality of lightness or darkness of the tones we see on the things around us. In drawing, values are produced by deposits of a dry medium

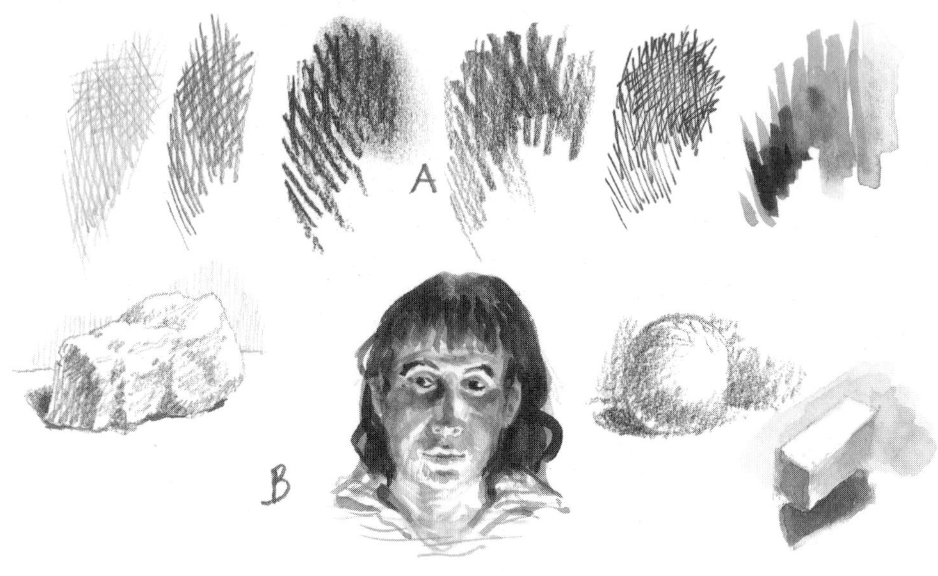

Figure 5.1 In A, HB graphite, 2B graphite, compressed charcoal, crayon, pen and ink, brush and ink.

such as graphite, chalk, or crayon, or by a wet medium such as ink or paint. A particular light or dark tone is determined by the light or dense application of a dry medium, or by the mixture of a wet medium with its appropriate thinner. Values are also produced by closely placed hatchings in these or any other medium to create the optical effect of a tone (Figure 5.1A).

In nature, light reveals values; in drawing, values reveal light. Changes in value are the only means for showing how a form's surface structure is affected and revealed by light. Value, as noted in Chapter One, can also show the local tone of objects, that is, the inherent lightness or darkness of a form or a surface. An object's local tone is of course affected by the light falling on its surfaces, but it is separate from it. No matter what degree of light may illuminate them, an egg's local tone remains lighter than a plum's. Only the use of value in drawing can sort out such facts.

Unless color is actually used (see "Color in Drawing," Chapter Six), values "stand in" for colors by representing their various light and dark tones. We therefore translate the dark gray tone of the lips in a drawing of a woman's head to be lipstick and the light gray tone in the upper part of a landscape drawing to represent a cloudless blue sky. Or, in a tonal drawing of the American flag, a nearly black tone will stand in for the stars' blue field, and a middle-gray tone will translate to the flag's red stripes.

Generally, areas of tone create shapes. When these variously toned shapes suggest that an object's planes are revealed by a light source, the impression of volume is enhanced (Figure 5.1B). And when these toned shapes are made of structural lines, that is the hatchings that move around or across a surface, changing direction as the planes change their angle or tilt, the structural clarity of volume surfaces is further increased, as in Van Gogh's *Peasant Woman Gleaning* (Figure 5.2). This is not to suggest that modelling forms by structural lines is *the* way to draw. There are, after all, the tones in countless wash drawings, the tones in drawings made by rubbed-on dry media, or the sparse use of tones in some line drawings that are all very clear in showing the solidity of forms. But using hatchings to model forms, because it *is* a demanding (and very informing) way of experiencing surface structure, is an important step in learning to draw. And while many artists from Raphael to Cezanne to some contemporary artist *do* "carve" forms by hatchings, such structural modelling should be understood as one of several ways of looking at form: as a process rather than a technique.

The form of a ball of yarn is easy to understand because of the yarn "crosshatchings" that curve around the sphere in all directions.

The rationale for suggesting the use here of hatched tones instead of those produced by broader applications or by blending is to help you to think of a plane's direction, that is, its tilt on a form's surface. Applying "clouds" of smudged tones evades this challenge (and often destroys a drawing's freshness and spontaneity). Usually, such structural hatchings are drawn in the direction of a flat or curved plane's *short* axis, especially upon foreshortened planes, as in Figure 5.3.

Van Gogh's drawing, done in the early years of his brief career, is a vigorous examination of his subject's major and secondary planes. He does not pause to record many smaller surface facets but shows the hat's structure to consist mainly of two planes, the woman's back, of one plane, and so on. Notice how, in the voluminous skirt, hatchings change direction according to the changing directions of its many flat or curved planes, and how curved hatchings encircle the arms and hands. Note, too, that in the woman's sleeve and skirt there are places where structural lines move over the same plane in *two* directions. This is called cross-hatching and is a common tactic for darkening or strengthening the clarity of an area. The form of a ball of yarn is easy to understand because of the yarn "cross-hatchings" that curve around the sphere in all directions. In drawing, too, structural lines can move in any direction that *acknowledges* a form's surface turnings (Figure 5.3).

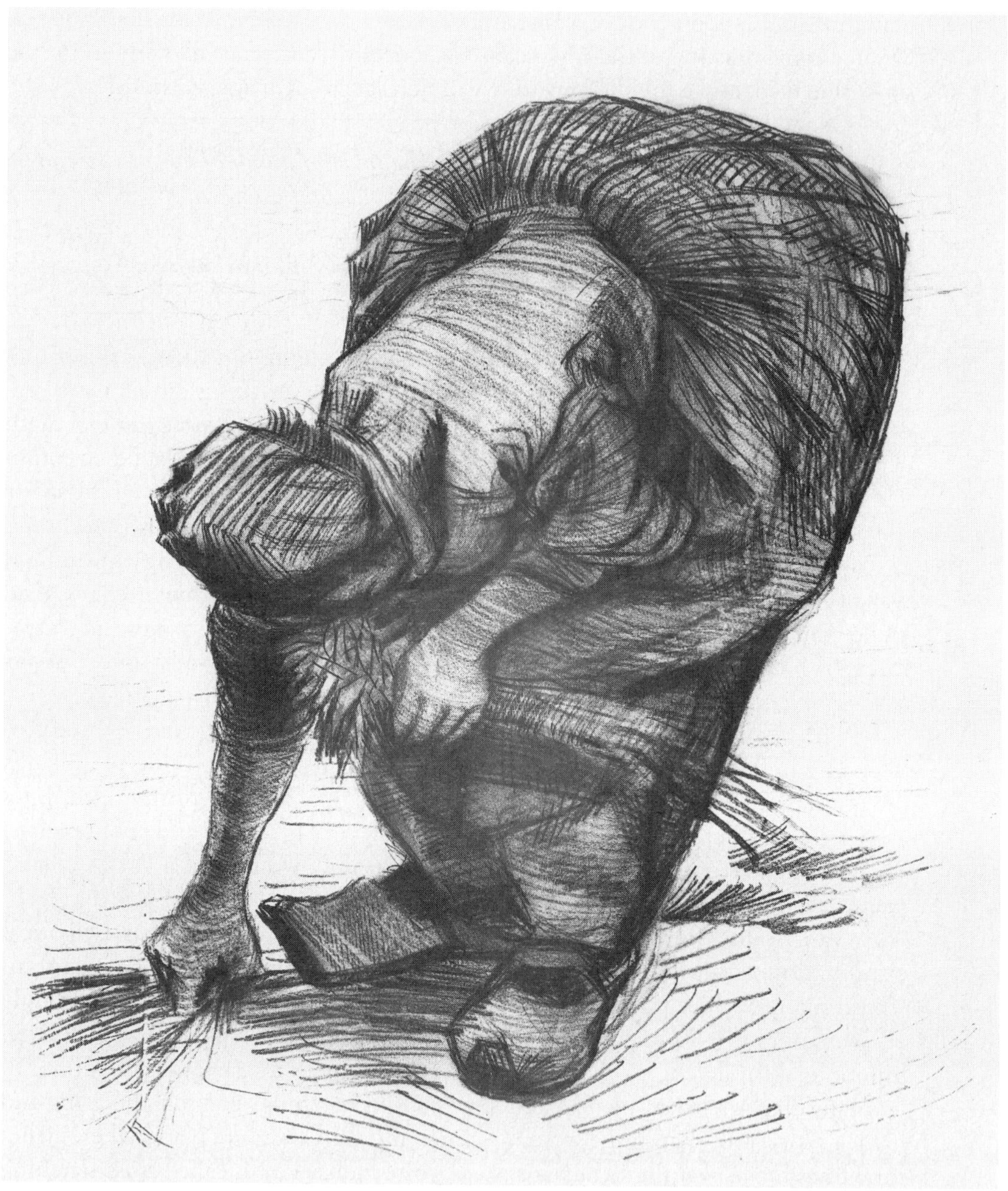

Figure 5.2 Vincent Van Gogh (Dutch, 1853–1890), *Peasant Woman Gleaning*, 1885.
Source: Museum Folkwang, Essen, Germany.

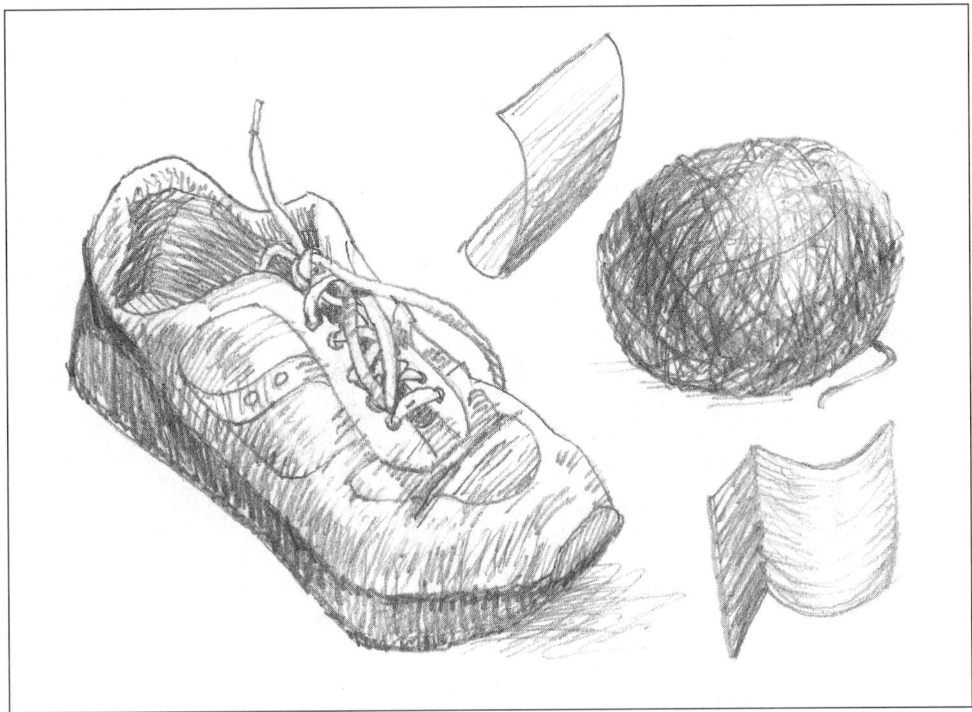

Figure 5.3

The three-value analysis discussed in Chapter One was offered as a convenient means for evaluating the relative lightness and darkness of a subject's parts (see "Three-value Analysis," Chapter One). But seeing your subject's values as divided into three groupings also aids structural matters. The distribution of values in Van Gogh's drawing, because it suggests a light source falling on the figure from directly overhead, helps us to decipher the variously turned planes. If Van Gogh had drawn the woman's blouse as dark and her right sleeve as light, and had given the many planes of her skirt a variety of light and dark tones, our understanding of the subject's structure would be lessened, and so too would our sense of light falling on the forms.

This union of structural modelling and of light-bathed form goes together nicely. It can make for simplified and strong extractions of a subject's actual appearance (Figure 5.4), or for more precise and delicate ones (Figure 5.5). In Harris's landscape drawing, the boulders' top and side surfaces are expressed by lighter and darker hatchings that suggest their various tilts. Additionally, he makes the near forms dark and the far ones lighter, and the interspaces among them lightest of all, giving the scene its illuminated and brooding atmosphere, as well as an organized spatial arrangement.

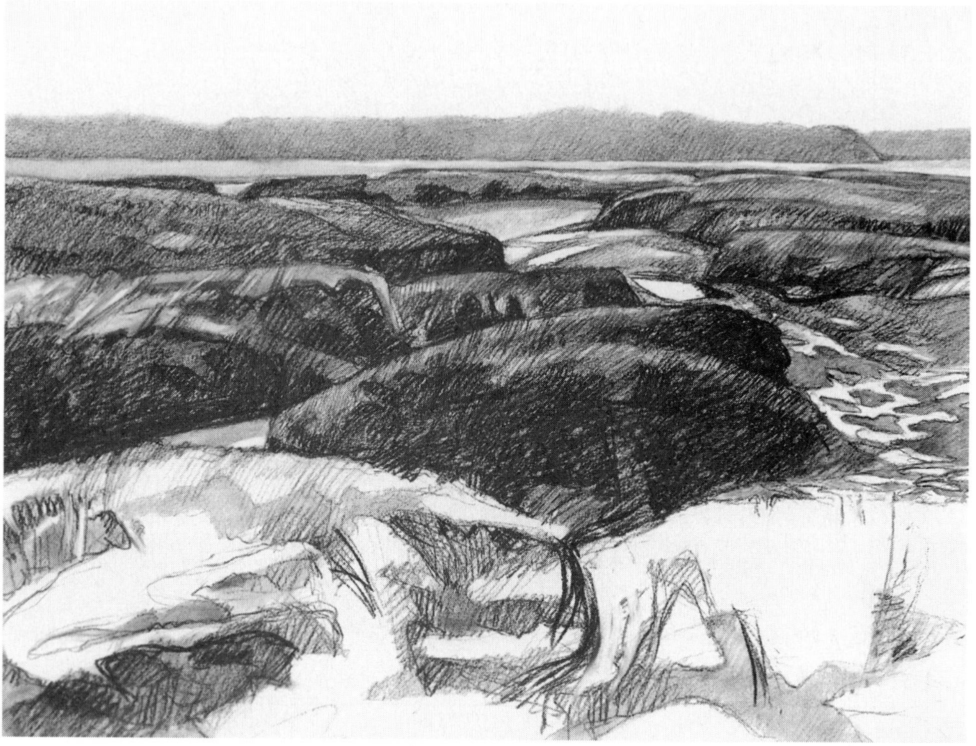

Figure 5.4 Conley Harris, *Rocks and Water,* 1970s. Sheet: 22 × 30 inches (approximate). Reproduced courtesy of the Boston Public Library, Print Department, by permission of the artist.

By contrast, Boccioni's portrait sketch is less dramatically lit, and some details of the subject's planar condition more fully explained. Here, too, a three-value system is used: eye pupils and small shadowed areas are dark, most of the hair and the planes of the face are lighter, and the remainder uses the white of the page. Boccioni added a few additional values to suggest how light affects the hair and some of the variously tilted planes of the face, but the drawing suggests that essentially the artist thought in terms of three tonal divisions.

The more an artist wants to explore a subject's surface changes the darker the drawing is likely to become. Compare Boccioni's willingness to assign much of the woman's head to the white page with Kollwitz's more "sculptural" treatment of a similar subject (Figure 5.6). Note, too, the artist's more extensive use of cross-hatching in the larger head, and the underlying three-value analysis of the subject's planes.

Squinting at your subject at the outset of a drawing, because it temporarily reduces your ability to see a subject's details, helps you to see its important generalities. Just as good drawing requires you to see a subject's main directional thrusts

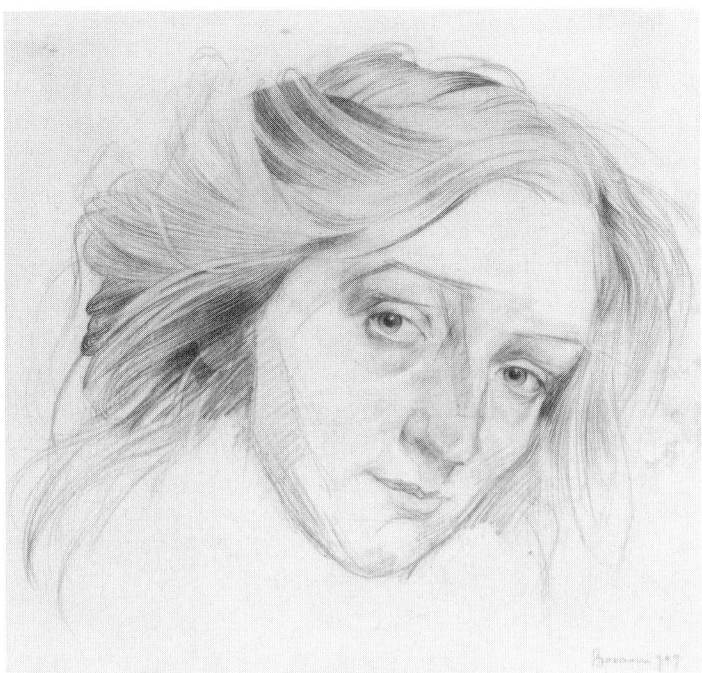

Figure 5.5 Umberto Boccioni (Italian, 1882–1916), *Woman's Head*, 1909. Graphite, on buff wove paper, 38.2 × 39.4 cm. Margaret Day Blake Collection, 1967.(244R recto)
Source: Reproduction, The Art Institute of Chicago.

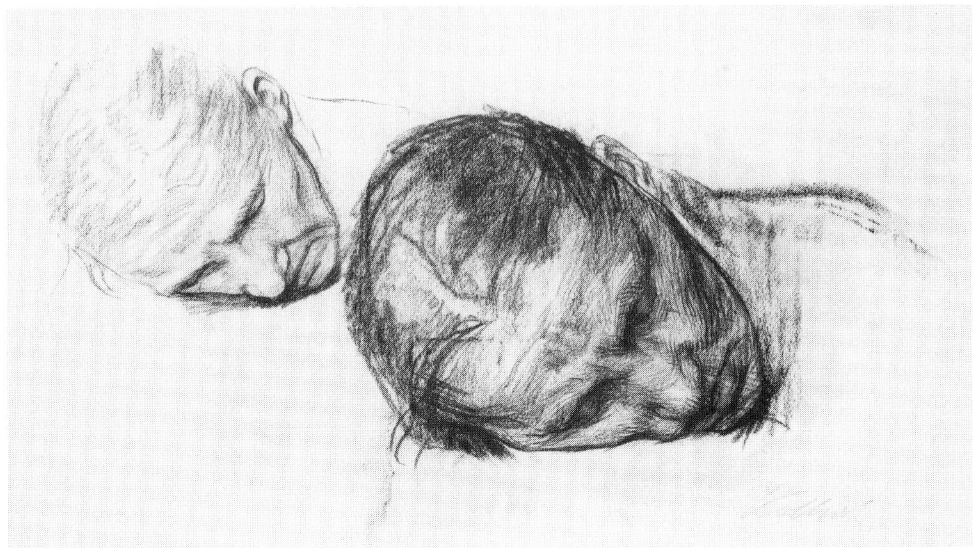

Figure 5.6 Kathe Kollwitz (German, 1867–1945), *Two Studies of a Woman's Head.* Drawing, c. 1903, black chalk on tan wove paper, 19 × 24$\frac{3}{4}$ inches (48.26 × 62.87 cm.). *Source:* The Minneapolis Institute of Arts. Gift of David M. Daniels. © 2005 Artists Rights Society (ARS), New York/VG Bild-Kundt, Bonn.

and basic form character, that is, its gestural condition, before finding its smaller ones, so must you see a subject's general distribution of values before searching out its subtler tonal variations.

Holding in mind the three-value system of analysis helps to rough in a subject's essential value condition (there *are* subjects and creative purposes that justify seeing a subject in two or in four values, but more of that, later). It is important to recognize that in establishing these lighter and darker tones you are also noting the general *shapes*, *sizes*, and *locations* of the subject's values. And while these observations have mainly to do with two-dimensional matters, that is, with the size, location, and shape of values are on the page, these values already suggest a little of the subject's surface structure as Figure 5.7B demonstrates. Notice that squinting at Figure 5.7A simplifies the values you now see and "justifies" the broad laying in of the values in 5.7B.

Figure 5.7A

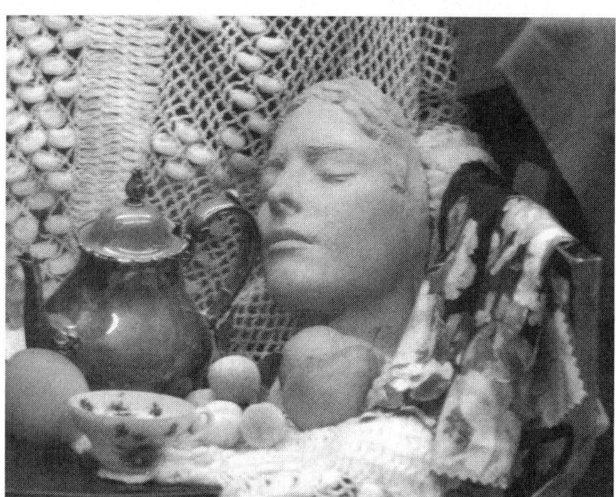

Figure 5.7B

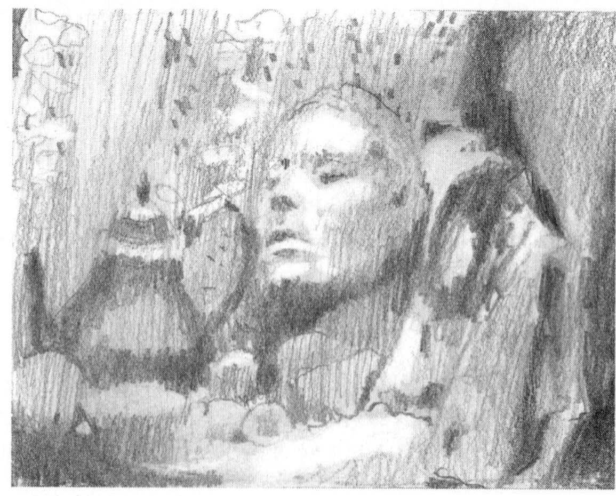

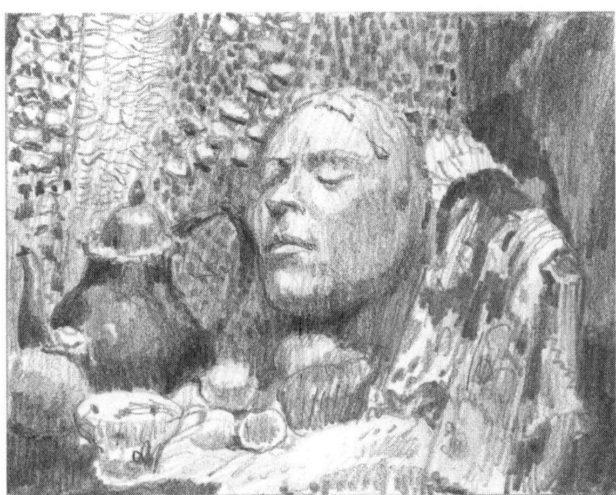

Figure 5.7C

Note, too, that squinting at a later stage of the drawing (Figure 5.7C) again produces the general value distribution in both 5.7A and 5.7B.

Because light rays do not bend, we understand the subject's lighter and darker areas of illumination to be revealing changes of direction in the form's surface, and not in the direction of the light rays. When a surface faces parallel to the path of the light, it receives only some illumination, usually represented by a light value. This raking light, moving in the same direction as the surface, is often referred to as a *half-tone*.

Knowing that every value change indicates a change in surface terrain alerts you to the importance of these changes in modelling convincing volumes. Abrupt value changes on a form suggest the abutting or overlapping of flat planes. Gradual value changes suggest rounded planes (Figure 5.8).

THE SUBJECT ILLUMINATED

For most artists there are four main ways in which they like to see light strike solid masses: from one side (by either a high or low source on that side), from directly above, from two sides, and frontally. Forms lit from below are unusual and sometimes appear rather theatrical, although some artists are attracted to this kind of illumination; and forms lit by several light sources often tend to obscure, rather than explain the forms.

1. Light coming from one side will rake over a form, striking any plane aimed in its direction. If the light is located high on the side, it will also strike planes tilted upward to some degree. If the light is low on that side, it will strike planes tilted downward to some degree (Figure 5.9A).

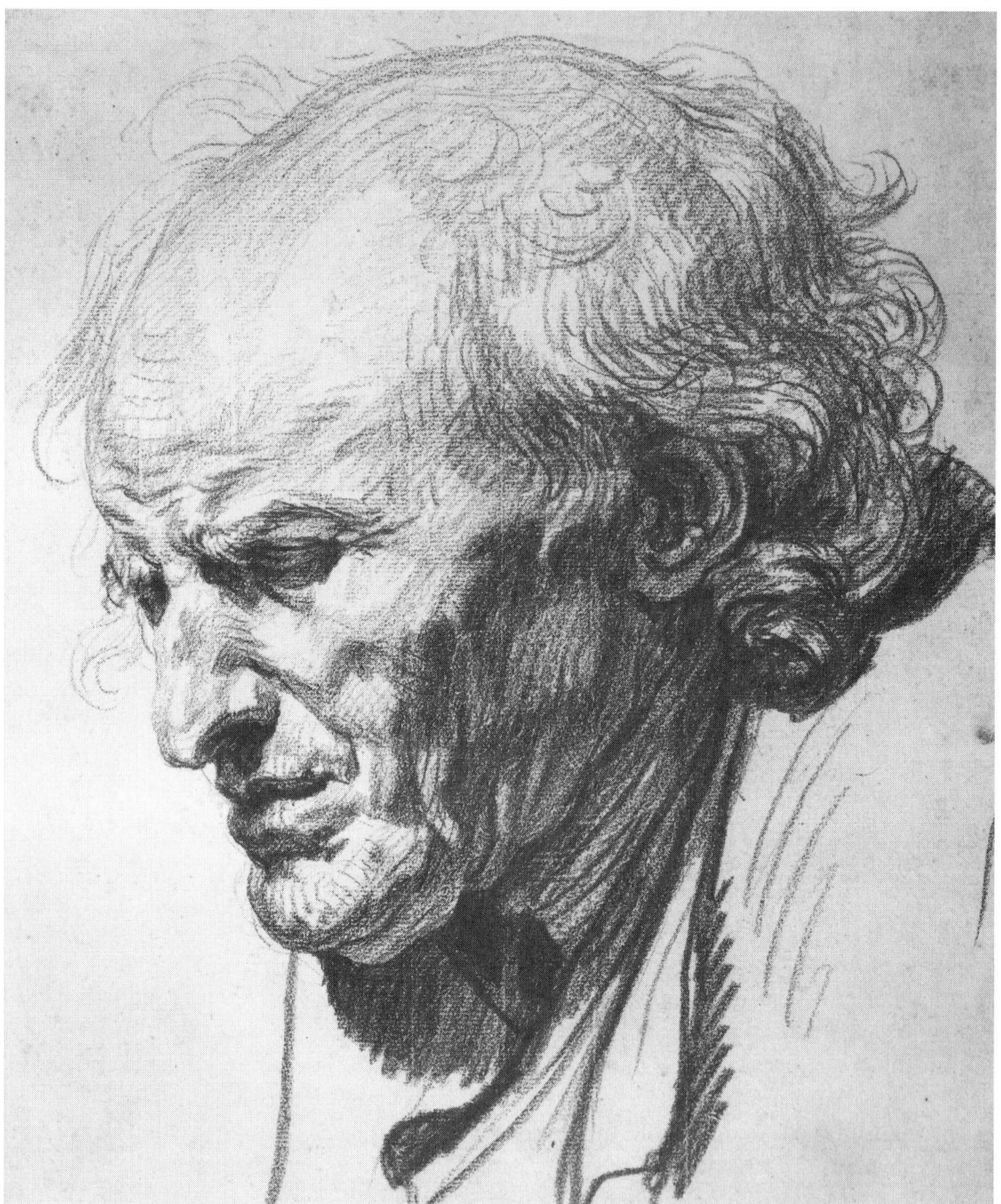

Figure 5.8 Jean-Baptiste Greuze (French, 1725–1805), *Study of the Head of an Old Man*, about 1755. Red chalk, 39.7 × 32.1 cm ($15\frac{5}{8} \times 12\frac{5}{8}$ inches). Courtesy of the J. Paul Getty Museum, Los Angeles, CA.

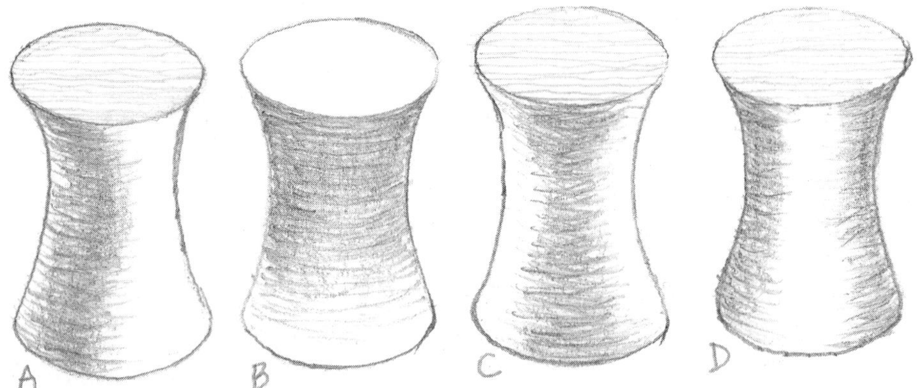

Figure 5.9

2. Light falling from above will strike upward facing planes or projections (Figure 5.2 and Figure 5.9B).
3. Light striking both the left and right sides of a form illuminates planes aimed in either direction, leaving the planes facing the artist somewhat darker (Figure 5.9C).
4. Light striking a form straight on, strikes the planes facing the artist, and leaves both sides of the form somewhat darker. Such a light source can be thought of as coming from a direction just behind the artist (Figure 5.9D).

In practice it is seldom that light strikes forms *only* from the side or *only* from above. True side lighting would only come from a lamp or other source placed off to one side, more or less at your eye-level, as you would view the subject, also placed at eye-level. True overhead lighting would exist out-of-doors only at noon, and indoors, by placing the subject directly beneath a ceiling light source.

Usually a form, indoors or out-of-doors, is lit by *two* light sources. Indoors, because ligh falls from the ceiling, from a floor lamp, from a window, or from a table lamp, there is light from above and from the side. The forms then receive light from two sources, as illustrated in Figure 5.9A. Outdoors, the sun, except at noon, falls from one side in the morning and from the other side in the afternoom, as well as from above. Although Figure 5.10 may have been drawn indoors or outdoors, the light plainly falls on the puppet from above *and* on the (puppet's) right side. Notice the strong cross-hatching on the head, and that the artist uses a very light middle tone and a very strong dark tone. Doing this implies a strong light source.

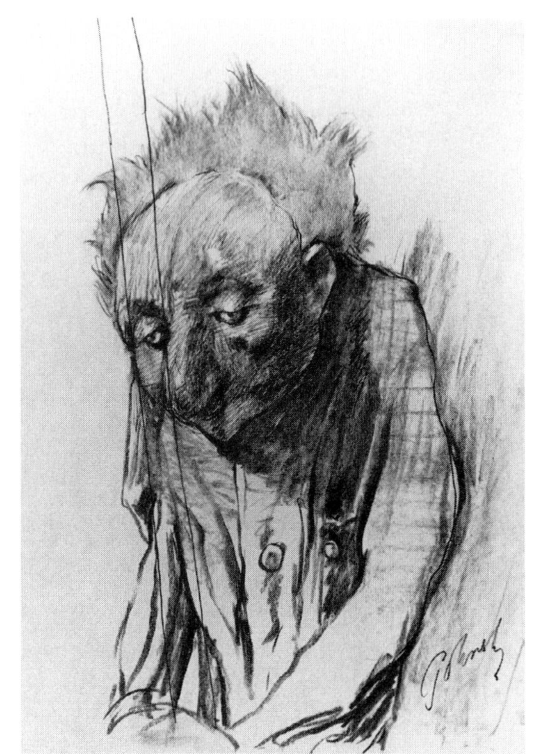

Figure 5.10 Arthur Polonsky (1925–), *Puppet Portraits IV,* charcoal, 1993. Reproduced courtesy of the Boston Public Library, Print Department, by permission of the artist.

Compare this drawing with Figure 5.6, where the light source is less intense because the middle tones are given a much greater role to play.

Another feature in Polonsky's drawing has to do with the differing degrees of completion among the parts of the subject. He makes much of the puppet's head, but only broadly suggests the shirt. Even the puppet's hair is left as one light value. As many of the drawings in this book attest to, it is only occasionally that the artist brings every part of the drawing to the same level of completion. Sometimes it has to do with compositional matters, as we will see in Chapter Seven; sometimes, with preparatory or expressive purposes; and sometimes with the wish to stop when the artist feels that his or her goal has been reached.

From the six planes of a block to the countless number of planes in the human head, every form has its unique structure. Changing the light source on a form changes how the light explains (and sometimes obscures) the form, but the form's structure, of course, remains the same. Because tonal modelling can explain both the form's structure and how the form is lit, these two considerations often work well together.

Ideally, the value changes observed in your subject reveal both changes in its surface terrain and in the direction of the light falling on those surfaces. But when existing light conditions do not show important planes and turnings, or when the light obscures or "denies" a form's structure, either because of weak or multiple light sources, or by cast shadows that camouflage or fail to show surface changes, you should consider introducing tones that do explain the form's turnings. After all, light falls upon matter in an incidental and uncaring way. It is up to the artist to clarify the volume and space conditions of the subject. The nature of a subject's form in space is its first truth.

> ***... it is often the case that the darkest tone on a form will not be at the form's edge but nearest to the strongets light on the form.***

Sometimes a form can be further clarified by using reflected light, that is, light that bounces off nearby surfaces to strike those planes of a form that are turned away from the initial light source. Light waves *do* travel in straight directions, but only until they strike some obstacle, when they are deflected back in the general direction of the light source, as Figure 5.11 shows. Note the reflected light on the heads in Figures 5.6 and 5.10. As these two drawings demonstrate, reflected lights are almost always weak and usually shown as no lighter than half-tones.

Because the light striking a subject often reflects from one part to another, or from a nearby surface, reflected lights are a fairly common occurrence. As a result it is often the case that the darkest tone on a form will not be at the form's edge but nearest to the strongest light on the form. Rounded forms show this effect most clearly. This occurs because the reflected light, weak as it may be, is illuminating the far (dark) side of the form, as in Figure 5.12 and 5.13. In the Millet drawing, notice how reflected light illuminates the bottom part of the hay on the wagon, placing the darkest value on the hay nearest to the topmost plane illuminated by sunlight.

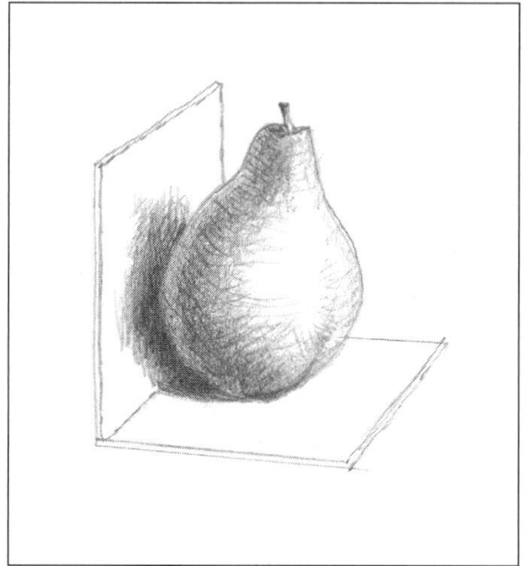

Figure 5.11

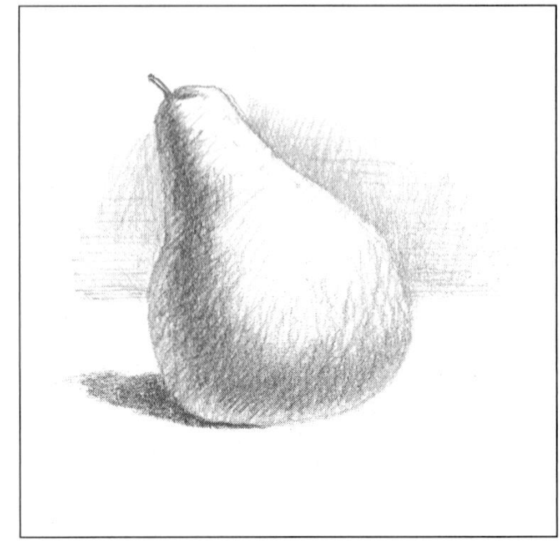

Figure 5.12

Figure 5.13 Jean-François Millet (French, 1814–1875), *The Gleaners*. $11\frac{1}{4} \times 9$ inches.
Source: © Copyright The British Museum, London.

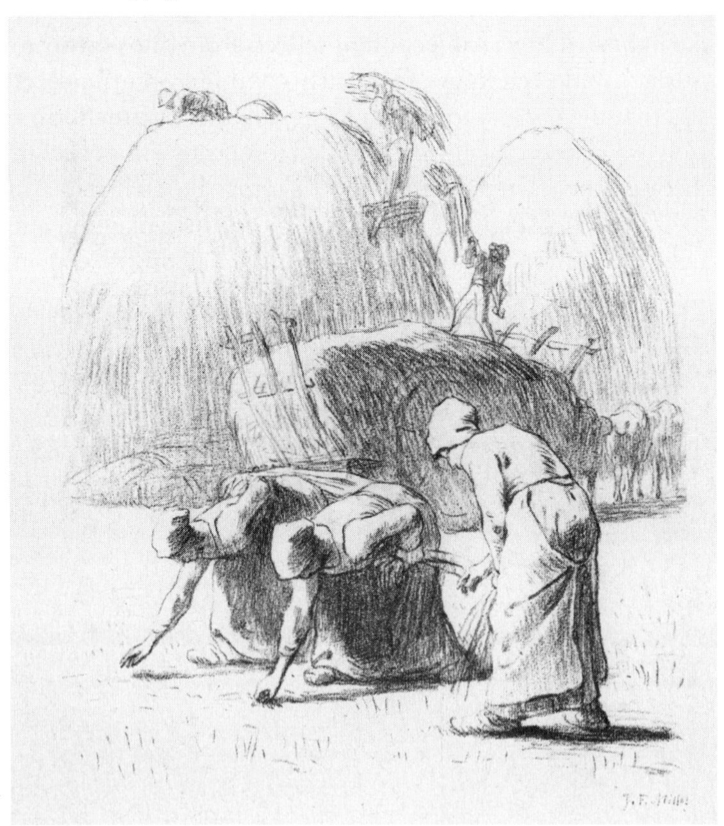

This phenomenon can be seen again, on the left sleeve and on the skirt of the central figure.

Millet's drawing demonstrates another characteristic of drawings that rely heavily on value to make their point: the lessened use of contour line as the means for establishing shapes and planes. In this drawing, Millet frequently explains an edge by placing a dark tone up against a light one. The dark skirts of the three figures are shaped much less by line than by meeting up with the light value of the field. Note how, in the central figure, contours almost disappear as she is shaped by the encircling dark tones, and how the dark side of the wagon's hay load meets the illuminated side and top planes without the benefit of defining contour lines.

Even though most subjects readily take to a three-value analysis, some artists, especially those intending a less tonal drawing, will begin by seeing their subjects as divided into two value categories (Figure 5.14), or, if intending a more fully toned drawing, into four (Figure 5.15). In Korman's drawing, the light and dark grays of the blanket, which reappear on the wall and pillows are important tonal (and

Figure 5.14 Calvin Burnett, *Baby's Head.* Gouache and opaque color on darkened surface. Reproduced courtesy of the Boston Public Library, Print Department, by permission of the artist.

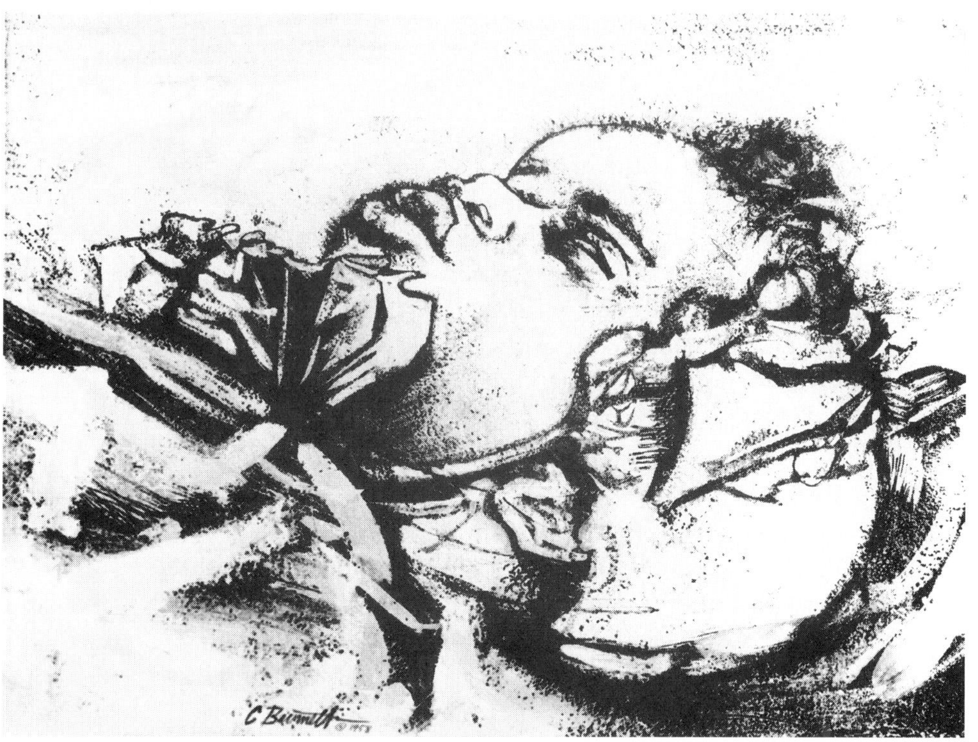

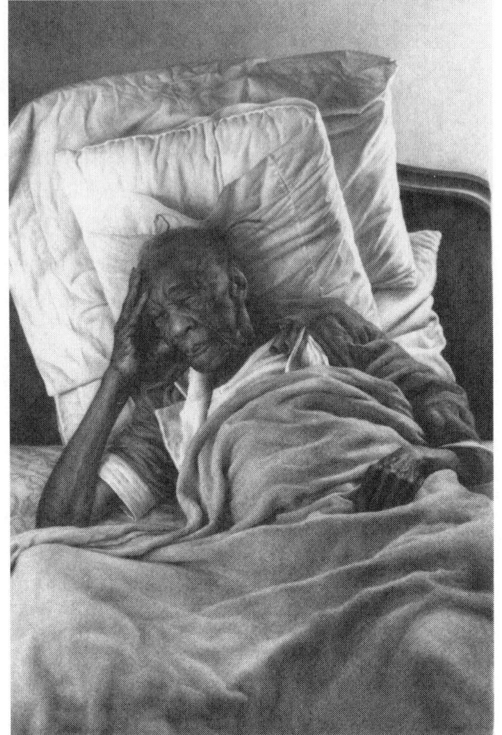

Figure 5.15 Ira M. Korman, (American, New York, 1962–) *Sweet Virginia*, 1994. Charcoal on paper, $47\frac{1}{4} \times 28\frac{3}{4}$ inches. *Source:* Arkansas Arts Center Foundation Purchase: 1994–95, Collectors Group Fund. (1994.044) Courtesy of the Koplin Del Rio Gallery, Los Angeles, CA.

expressive) facts of the image and set the stage for the drawing's near white and near black tones. In this fully tonal drawing, notice that line, as contour, is entirely absent, with edges being established by contrasting values. Again, note the reflected light on the dark side of the woman's head.

Always relate the value of one plane or area to another, not only when they are close together in the drawing but when they are located far apart on the page.

AERIAL PERSPECTIVE

In tonal drawing, subject matter seen at a considerable distance will be somewhat changed by water and dust particles in the air. Aerial perspective refers to the things we see far away in the spatial field, such as hills, buildings, and trees, usually located near the horizon line. Such forms will do more than diminish in scale. They will undergo three additional changes. The most evident change has to do with their clarity. Distant forms lose detail and edges appear less distinct. Next, distant forms will show less value contrast, often appearing lighter than we know them to be. Thus, a mountain at the horizon may show only a few closely related light-toned values. Lastly, distant forms show little or no texture; a stand of pine trees appearing as a soft-edged light-toned shape.

When drawing tonally, it is useful to "bracket" your subject's tonal range by noting its lightest and darkest passages early in the drawing's progress. Doing this helps you to estimate better the degrees of value to follow, because no subsequent value can be lighter or darker than the tonal extremes already drawn. Always relate the value of one plane or area to another, not only when they are close together in the drawing but also when the are located far apart on the page. Seeing each form or interspace in an isolated way risks overmodelling them by running the gamut from white to black in each one. Yet, a white couch drawn in a far corner of a darkened room would be, in its lightest parts, only a middle-gray tone at most. Making it actually white (which can happen if you are not relating it to its tonal environment) would make it appear to be strongly illuminated, or lit from within. Maintaining the consistency of a subject's tonal environment means that the values you draw are those you actually see *in relation to each other*, as the light reveals them.

As a number of the drawings in this book show, values can model forms in either of two ways. They can model them in the context of their inherent lightness or darkness, as in Figures 5.15 and 5.16, or in the context of seeing every part as having the same local tone, that is, with no regard for the lightness of some parts and the darkness of others, as in Figure 4.13 and Figure 5.17. In the first, fully tonal mode, Thiebaud tells us the woman's hair and the chair seat are dark; the chrome, the floor, and the skin are light. This doesn't exempt the artist from modelling either the dark or the light parts; he notes the inherent values of these parts in addition to his modelling of them. Thiebaud's drawing is another example of how effectively reflected light can help explain volume. Note the reflected lights in the cheek, lower arm, and legs, and that the darkest tones in these places are nearest to the lightest ones on each of these forms.

In the second mode, Ingres doesn't distinguish between the values of the hair, the chair, or the man's garments; it is as if everything was the same in value: white. Such an approach clears the way for more fully concentrating on every part of a subject's volumetric character because no attention need be paid to the local tone of its parts. This approach is often used for preparatory drawings, when artists want to study a subject's gestural stance, general form characteristics, and surface structure, which is what Ingres is concentrating on in this drawing.

As Figure 5.7 demonstrates, beginning a fully tonal drawing starts as a search for the sizes, location, and shapes of tones, and tries to group these observed values into some three (or four) categories. Sometimes, two or more adjacent forms will share the same value. When this is the case many artists will merely hint at or even temporarily

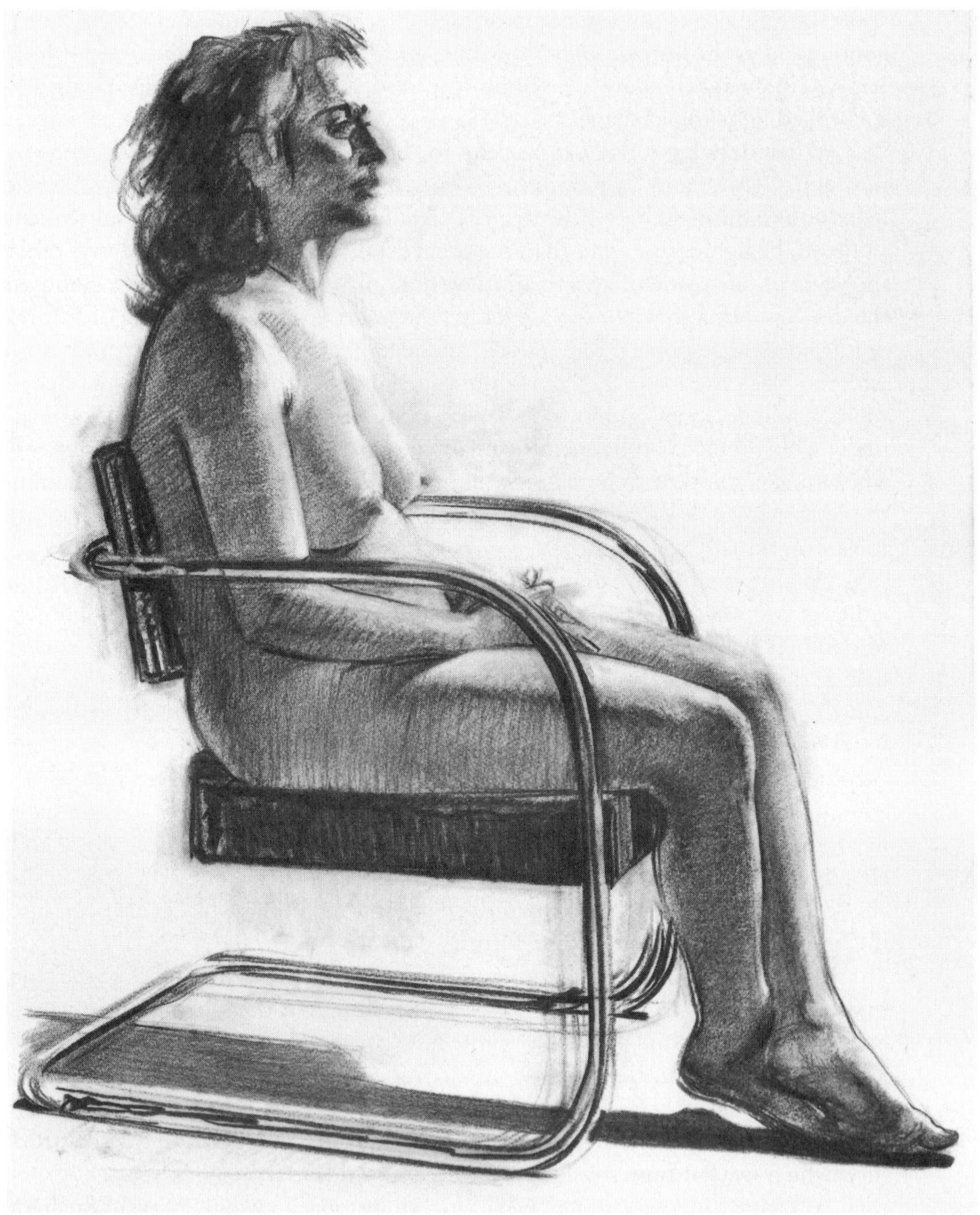

Figure 5.16 Wayne Thiebaud, *Nude in Chrome Chair*, 1976. Charcoal on paper, $30\frac{1}{8} \times 22\frac{3}{8}$ inches (76.5 × 57.8 cm.). *Source:* San Francisco Museum of Modern Art. Private Collection. © Wayne Thiebaud/Licensed by VAGA, New York, NY.

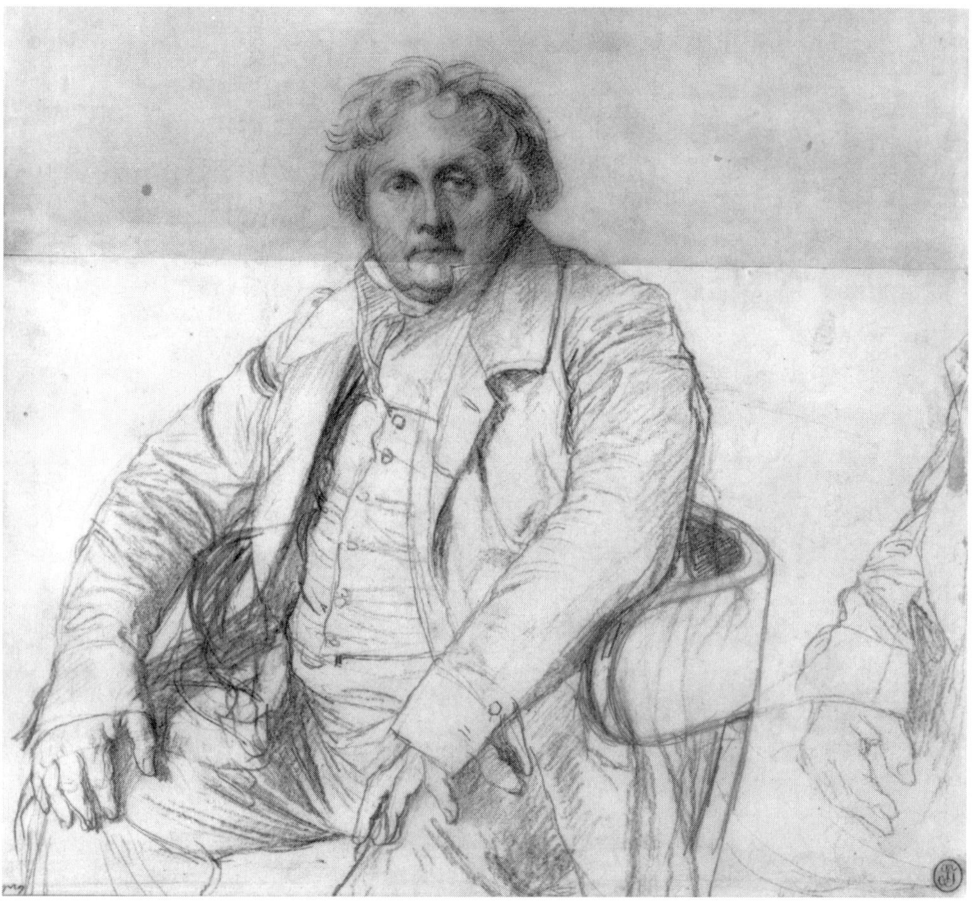

Figure 5.17 Jean-Auguste-Dominique Ingres (1780–1867), *Study for the Portrait of Louis-François Bertin* (1766-1841). Black chalk and graphite, $13\frac{3}{4} \times 13\frac{9}{16}$ inches (34.9 × 34.5 cm).
Source: The Metropolitan Museum of Art, Bequest of Grace Rainey Rogers, 1943 (43.85.4).

omit the border that separates them, as in Figure 5.18A. This is done to establish the subject's tonal environment *before* using values to model the forms. Doing this makes it far more likely that light-toned forms will remain light and dark ones dark, after their volume has been modelled. As Figure 5.18B shows, once the forms are modelled, the edges separating like-toned areas reappear. The "mapping out" of shapes of tone also allows you to see how a drawing's values are arranged compositionally, that is, how their pattern on the page may contribute to the movements and balance of the drawing's design. As noted earlier, the modelling of forms *does* introduce additional values, as Figure 5.18B demonstrates, but establishing a subject's overall value distribution early in a drawing's development assures maintaining both its tonal order and design.

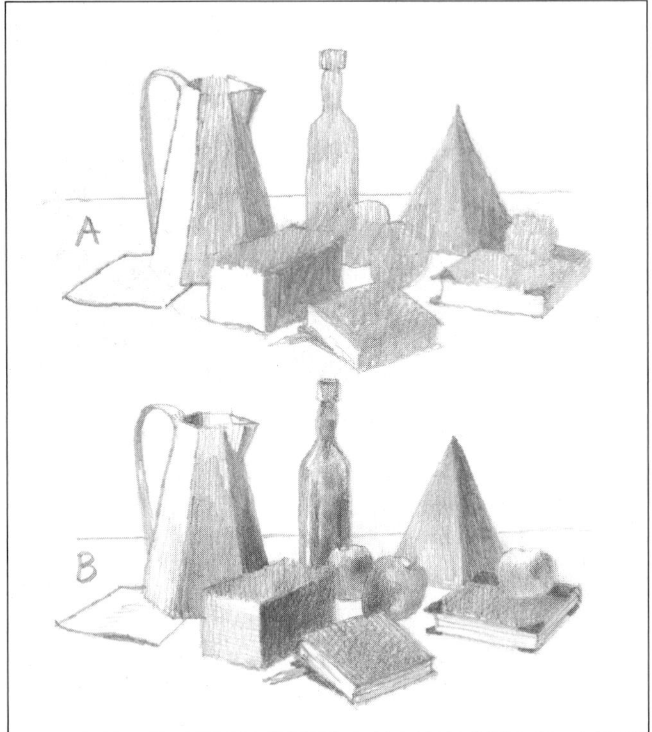

Figure 5.18

Tonal Drawing Exercises

Making a Fully Toned Drawing Select some three or four simple objects, such as fruits, books, cups, and the like, and set them on a plain tabletop against a middle-gray, plain background, and light this still life from a source that is high and to one side.

Using any erasable medium, begin with a light gesture drawing as in Figure 5.19A. Adjust the drawing to show some general characteristics of each object's shape, and the differing lengths and tilts of these objects, as well as their distance from one another. This is a good time to check on the drawing's perspective (Figure 5.19B).

On this gestural "armature," broadly divide into three categories the values of the objects, their shadows, and the one or more tones of the tabletop and background. Remember that the three values include the (usually) white tone of the page, a light gray, and a darker one, as in Figure 5.19C. Where objects show pronounced value

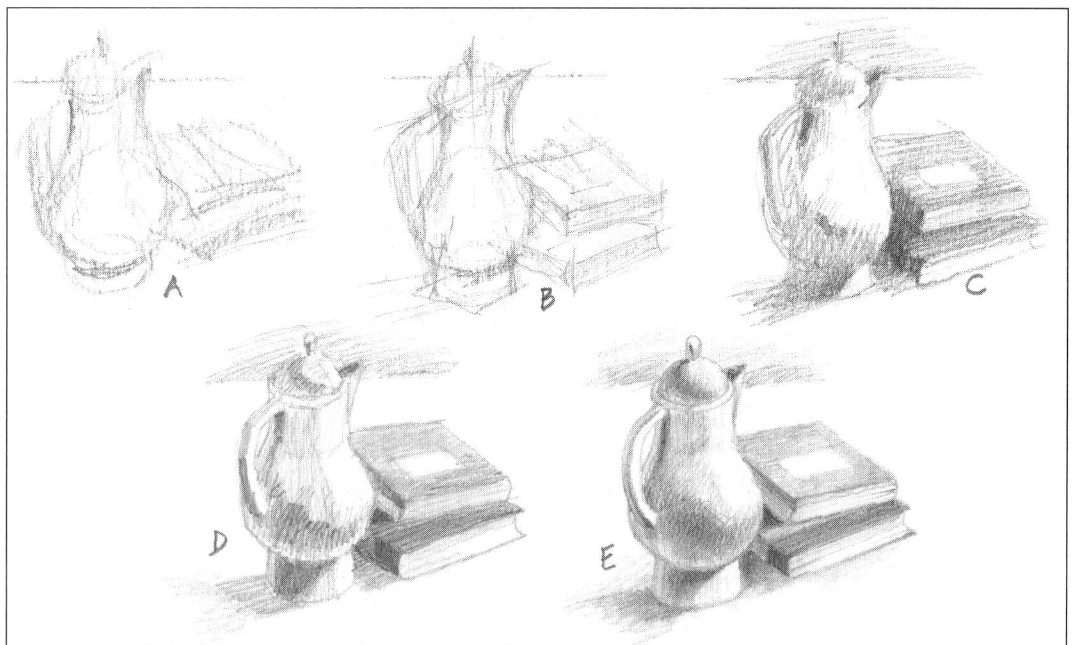

Figure 5.19

differences, as in the books, note these differences at this stage in your drawing. Where the value changes are subtle, as in the vase, use whichever of the three values is closest to the tone of the object, applying it over the entire form. Of course, the lightest tones in your drawing are represented by the tone of the page, so the first values you actually draw are the light gray ones. Notice that Figure 5.19C shows some values running from one part into another with little or no lines marking the boundaries where this occurs.

Up to this point the values you've drawn represent the shapes of planes and areas. The next stage brings us to the modelling of the forms. This begins by taking into account how the light strikes the entire set up. If the light falls, say, from the left side, you will, of course, see the right sides of objects to be somewhat darker. Where planes change abruptly, as in a book, the value changes are easy to see. Where value changes are gradual, as in any rounded form, it helps to squint at the object, to see the "margin" where the light can no longer strike the form's surface, as in Figure 5.19D. As with the analytical, "plane finding" lines that precede hatching, this may have the effect of (temporarily) giving each form a more angular and faceted appearance. This more angular treatment of rounded forms is a necessary prelude to modelling them because it more clearly shows the margins where the "filing off" modelling process produces the impression of rounded surfaces, as in Figure 5.19E.

Again, note that sometimes the darkest value on a rounded form is nearest to the lightest value, as we saw in Figures 5.12, 5.13, 5.15, and 5.16. Additional, transitional values will start to appear once you begin to round off the more abrupt abutments of tone. Now, too, is the time to search out subtle tonal differences that, earlier, you combined to produce the simpler, three-value analysis. All the foregoing is designed to more quickly and effectively bring your tonal drawing to the point where you can now further clarify the forms' solidity and the spatial field they occupy, as light can reveal them.

The first laying in of a drawing's light or dark gray values, as in Figure 5.19C, can be made with hatched lines (Figure 5.20A), or by a (more or less) even tone, applied by the side of the drawing lead or charcoal (Figure 5.20B). Note that when preliminary hatchings are used to establish a toned area, it is wise to avoid pronounced textures or strong directions because they may conflict with the lines and/or tones, of the later, modelling stage of your drawing.

Some artists prefer to establish both the underlying values as well as the modelling values by a more rubbed application of tone, as in Korman's drawing (Figure 5.15). This technique requires a drawing paper with at least a moderate "tooth" or surface grain, to file off the pigment particles of graphite, chalk, or charcoal. A rubbed-on tone still shows a little of the white of the paper within it and gives this manner of application a fresh look. When integrated with some hatched lines the result can be both informing and spirited, as in Figure 5.21. But rubbing is not the same thing as smudging, which is a process of repeatedly moving the medium around on the page, driving the pigment particles into the paper with the fingertips or with a paper stump. While a little smudging in a drawing's early stage may simplify or unite a passage, using it as the main manner of application almost always gives an overworked, smoky, and fussy result.

Figure 5.20

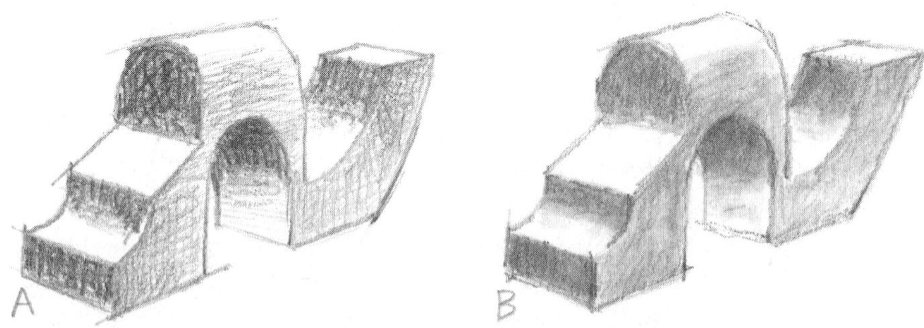

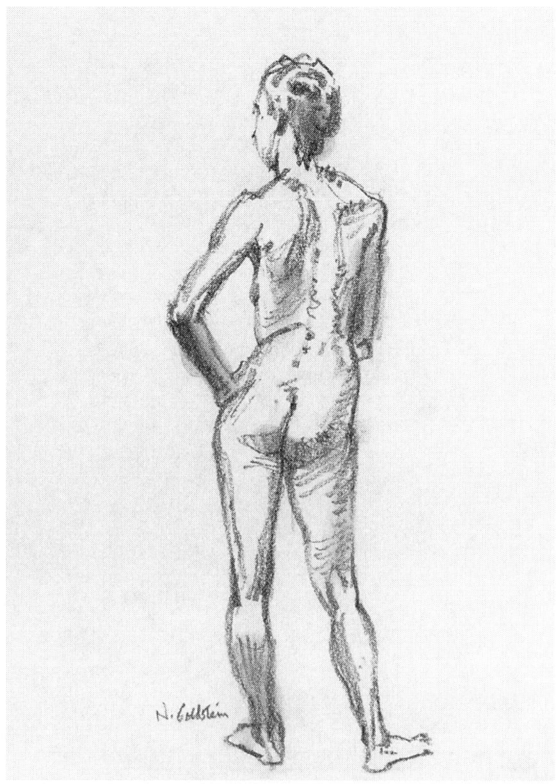

Figure 5.21 Nathan Goldstein, *Standing Female Figure*, Back View. Red chalk, 7 × 10 inches. *Source:* Collection of the artist.

Other artists prefer to establish only the underlying values by rubbing on tone, and use hatching as the modelling technique, as is somewhat the case in Pontormo's drawing, and even more so in Thiebaud's drawing (Figure 5.16). Whichever method is used, to successfully model a form requires that you understand the "hills and valleys" of its surface terrain, as we saw in Chapter Four and earlier in this chapter. Modelling forms that give a strong impression of solidity and illumination calls on your ability to feel you are touching your way around each form's surface without faltering, and seeing that the inherent value of each form conforms to the tonal order of the whole subject.

Making a Tonal Drawing of White Forms If you disregard the inherent value of objects, for example, the dark hair, the light sweater, and so on, you can more directly confront the structural nature of the things you draw. Now nothing is lost in shadows or so brilliantly lit as to intrude on modelling the form. Although drawing subjects as if all their parts were the same in value can still suggest strong light and deep shadows, many artists who choose to model forms in this way feel less bound by matters of illumination and more free to explore matters of surface structure.

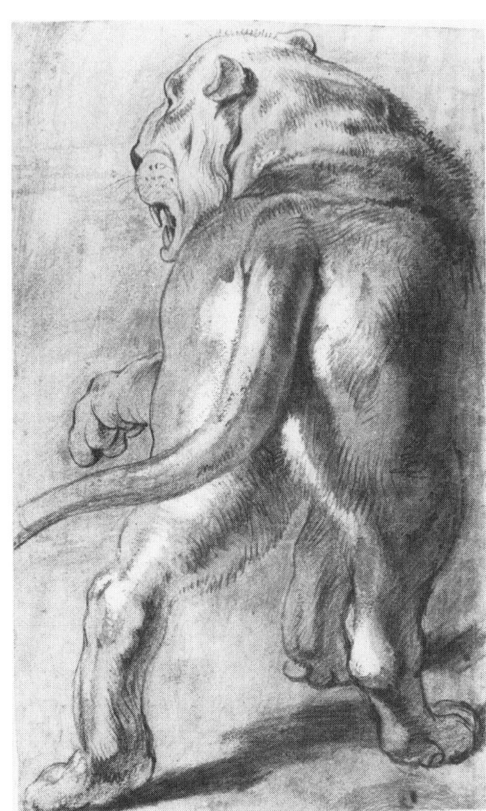

Figure 5.22 Peter Paul Rubens (Flemish, 1577–1640), *The Lioness.* $15\frac{9}{16} \times 9\frac{1}{4}$ inches.
Source: © Copyright the British Museum, London.

As noted earlier, sometimes this more analytical way of looking at form is selected for purposes of study. And often such drawings show some passages that rely on line more than value, as in Rubens's *The Lioness* (Figure 5.22), where the animal's head and upraised paw are almost entirely in line, and where line is used to establish many of its contours.

Although some light and dark tones are rubbed on to suggest light falling from the left and somewhat behind the artist, and white highlights add emphasis to the source of light, Rubens does not distinguish between value changes inherent on the animal's parts, or between it and the background. The hatched lines, moving around the forms at various angles, are primarily concerned with experiencing the turnings of the animal's parts and secondarily, with showing the texture of the fur. Note the several cross-contour lines near the root of the tail.

The drawing's emphasis on volumetric solidity suggests that Rubens is trying to experience the surface structure and weight of the animal's forms, as well as its grace and power. This combination of line and tone promotes a more direct and spontaneous handling, where the spirited nature of the calligraphy, the shape character, and the modelling convey the artist's purposes more clearly than do some fully toned drawings.

This manner of drawing almost always begins with a lightly drawn search for the subject's gesture and general shape character, which can still be seen in a few barely discernible lines in the animal's hind legs. Many artists will then turn to developing the contours, adding values when and where structural clarification requires it as the drawing progresses. In this case, Rubens may have left the head and upraised paw mostly in line because these forms are farthest away, and then concentrated his search for solidity on the nearer forms, giving them an almost sculptural weightiness.

Another example of treating forms as white is Van Dyck's *A Seated Man, Leaning Backwards* (Figure 5.23). Here, too, we can see traces of some preliminary gesture and shape drawing, especially in the figure's right leg and arm. As this preparatory drawing plainly shows, Van Dyck's main focus, like Rubens's, is in experiencing

Figure 5.23 Sir Anthony Van Dyck (Flemish,1599–1641), *A Seated Man, Leaning Backwards.* Black chalk with white chalk highlights. *Source:* Museum Boijmans Van Beuningen, Rotterdam.

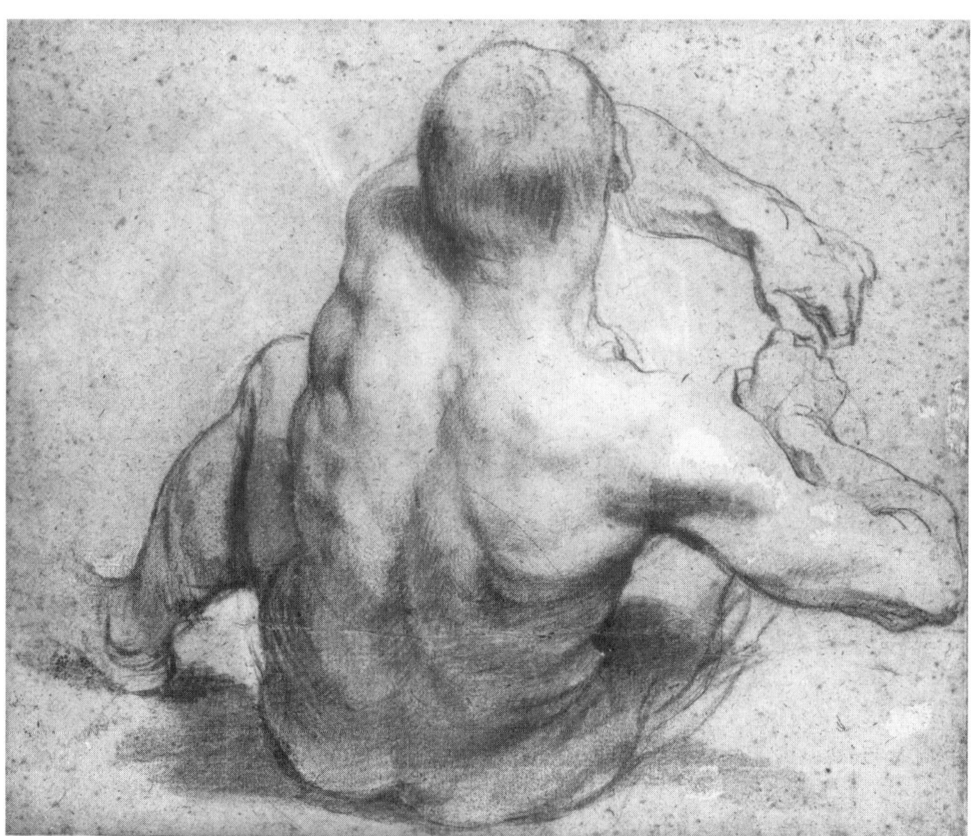

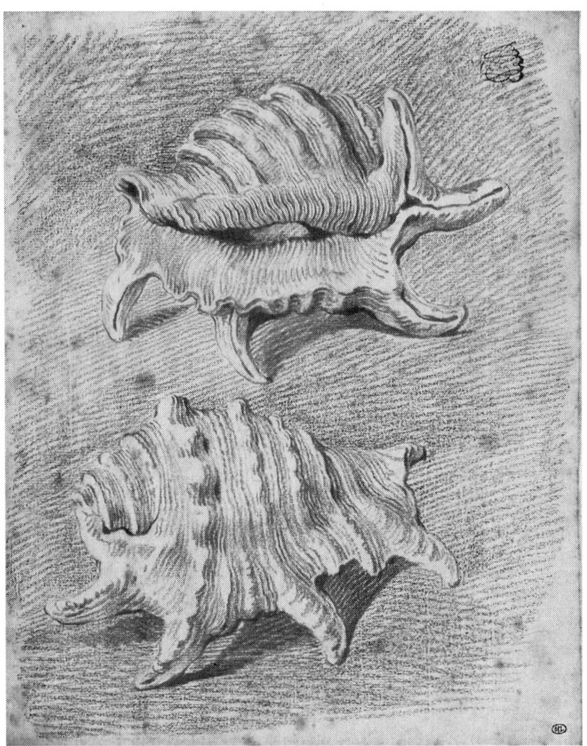

Figure 5.24 Jean Antoine Watteau (French, 1684–1721). *Two Shells*, drawing, 28.2 × 22 cm. Photographer: Michele Bellot. *Sources* Location: Louvre, Paris, France. Art Resources/Reunion des Musees Nationaux.

the subject's structural and spatial character; in this case, the weight, and the solidity of a back view of the figure's torso. The inherently differing tones in various parts of the subject hold little interest for Van Dyck. Here, tones mainly serve structure. While line drawing suffices for the limbs, the torso is seen in variously toned planes, its surface structure advantageously revealed by the light, which falls from above and somewhat to our right. Again, surface turnings are expressed by hatchings laid over some broadly rubbed light and dark tones. Note how, in the lower back, cross-contour lines trace the larger surface undulations.

Sometimes, as in Figure 5.24, the nature of the subject allows cross-contour lines to be the main means for explaining the terrain. Like the undulating lines in Figure 3.14, Watteau's wavelike cross-contour lines are punctuated by darker hatched lines marking more pronounced surface changes. Notice that these hatchings move in the *same* direction on the seashell. Again in Figure 5.25, broken cross-contour lines draw the texture of the hair. While both of these drawings suggest a strong light source, neither one alludes much to differences in the local tone of the parts.

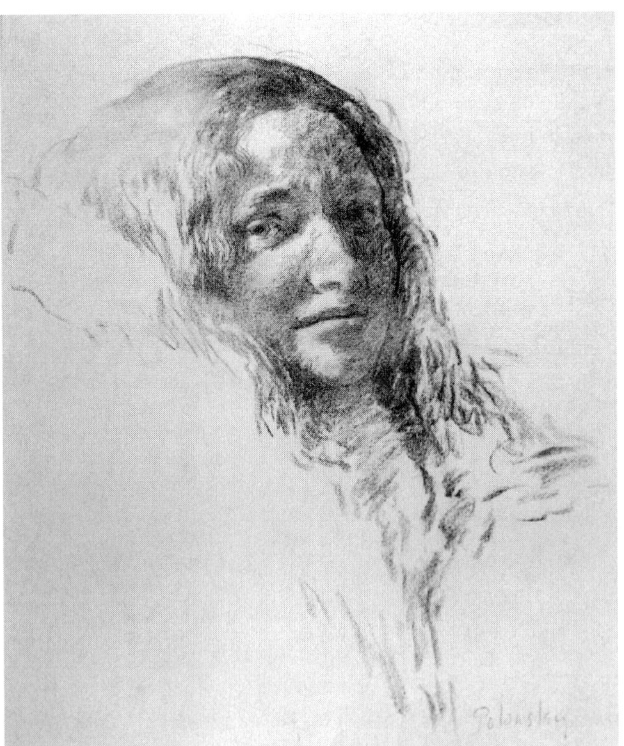

Figure 5.25 Arthur Polonsky (1925–), *Before Leaving*, charcoal, 1973. Sheet: $25\frac{1}{8} \times 19$ inches. Reproduced courtesy of the Boston Public Library, Print Department, by permission of the artist.

Such "white form" drawings are often more linear than tonal. Degas's sketch of mounted jockeys relies mainly on contour lines that flow with the grace and rhythm of the animals' forms themselves, and contains only some broad masses of rubbed and hatched light tones to help suggest the surface character and solidity of these forms (Figure 5.26). Sometimes, too, such drawings show a more balanced interest in the linear and tonal means for expressing form and light (Figure 5.27).

As we have seen, more fully toned drawings usually allow for less calligraphic play of line, while drawings made by some combination of line and value cannot go as far in explaining mass, light, and local tone as do fully toned drawings. It seems we can't have it all, and that drawing requires us to make decisions about the raw material of our subjects. What do we include and what do we omit? Our choices will vary according to what it is we see and want from our subjects in order to satisfy our individual sense of order, invention, and expressive need. And it is by the nature of the choices made that we know the nature of the artist.

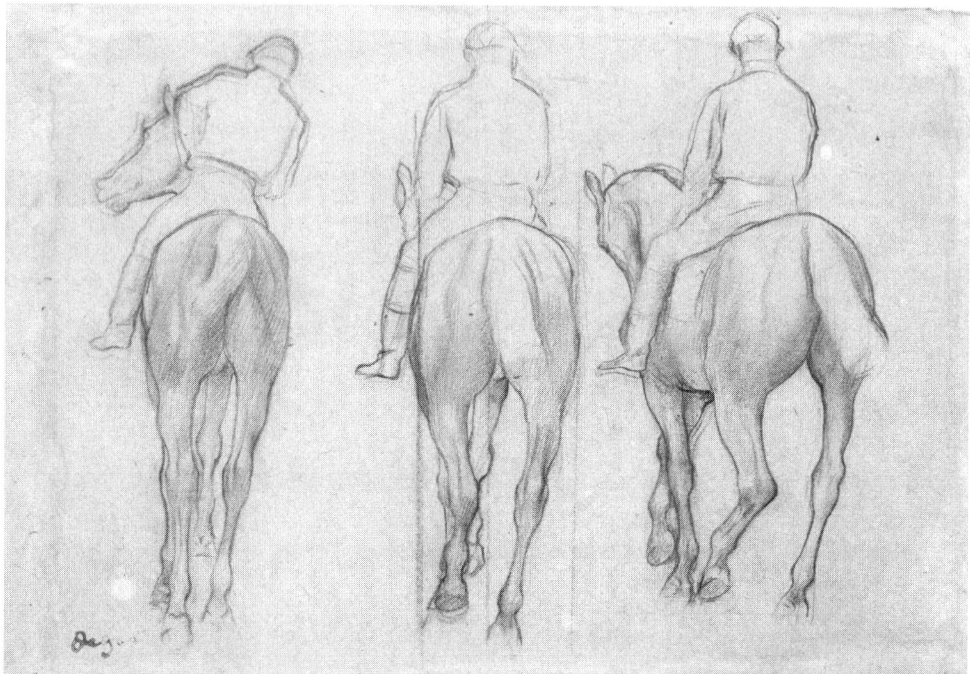

Figure 5.26 Hillaire-Germain-Edgar Degas (Paris, France, 1834–1917). *Three Studies of a Mounted Jockey*, c. 1868–1870, graphite and charcoal on tan wove paper, 19.8 × 27.5 cm. (1943.809) Courtesy of the Fogg art Museum, Harvard University Art Museums. Bequest of Grenville L. Winthrop. Photo credit: Allan Macintyre. © 2004 President and Fellows of Harvard College.

Sometimes the choices may include color. Although color lives on the outskirts of drawing, all the things we see around us are, of course, colored forms in colored settings. What happens when we add color to our list of things to consider when drawing is the subject of the next step in learning to objectively draw what we see.

Things to Think About

1. Light reveals the structure of forms. What else does light reveal about forms?
2. What is the advantage to the artist of seeing a subject illuminated by two sources?
3. Why, when we see a half-moon, is there often no reflected light to be seen on the unlit part of this large sphere?
4. When might skyscrapers and mountains be seen as light-toned and somewhat indistinct forms, and what causes this to happen?
5. What does *tonal order*, or *tonal environment* mean, and how would it apply to white curtains in a darkened room? To a white house seen against the setting sun?

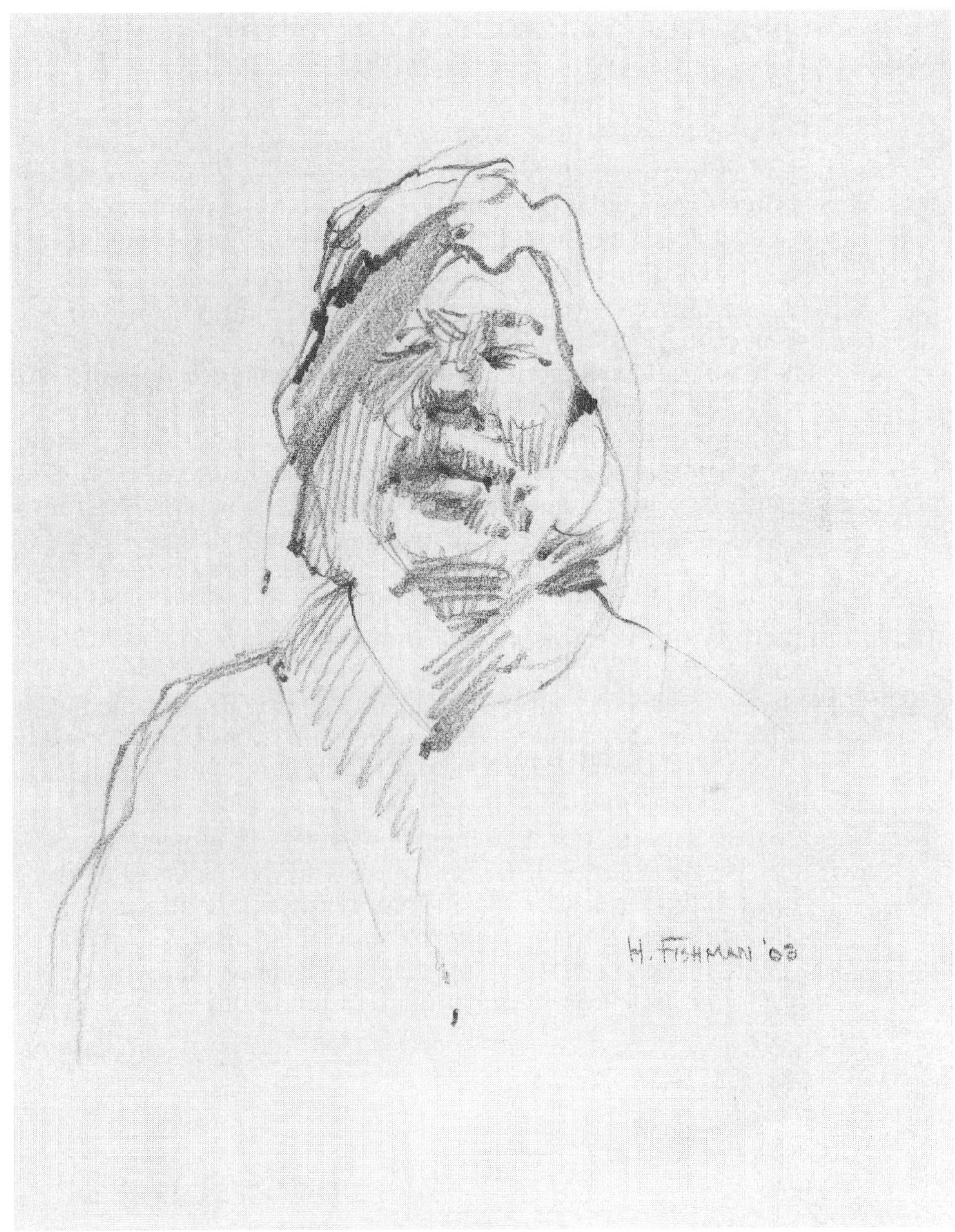

Figure 5.27 Harriet Fishman, *Head of a Woman*. 2003. Black chalk, $8\frac{1}{2} \times 10$ inches. Courtesy of the artist.

Critique Considerations

1. Do your tonal drawings suggest, even subtly, that the forms are illuminated in one of the several ways described in "The Subject Illuminated" section of this chapter? Or does light seem to strike forms in a random manner? If the latter, locate (or decide on) the subject's light source *before* you begin to draw, and, as the drawing progresses, check to see if you have modelled the forms according to the direction of the light's rays.
2. Do the forms in your drawings show the values and shadows of your subject just because they were there? That is, did you merely copy them without considering whether they explained the form or not? This is an easy trap to fall into because you are trying to draw what you actually see. But remember that light falling on a subject is indifferent; it doesn't mean to explain anything. It's up to the artist first to understand each form's surface structure and to experience their turnings and abutments, and second, to select and even alter the accidental effects of light on the forms, in order to more fully express their volume and the space they exist in.
3. Do most of the forms in your drawings seem to show values that run from white to black? This often results from the earnest wish to show each form as three-dimensionally convincing. The problem is that modelling your subject in this way provides no overall, enveloping light, and no way to show the local tone of various parts. It also separates the drawing's component parts, making for a disunited image.
4. Do the forms in your drawings seem more illuminated than structurally and spatially clarified? A fascination with the effects of light can sometimes lead to a lessening of volumetric and spatial clarity among a drawing's parts. Remember that a form's surface structure, whether fully realized or broadly suggested, is a more vital and informing aspect of graphic communication than the light falling on it.

6

Color in Drawing

COLOR DEFINED

Learning to draw what you actually see includes learning to objectively analyze the colors of the things around you. Once you do, you'll be more sensitive to the ways in which color can expand your options of response to what you see, and to the ways that color can add dimensions and meanings to your work.

Webster's dictionary defines color as a perceived phenomenon ". . . that enables one to differentiate otherwise identical objects." There are three ways in which color enables you to make these differentiations: hue, value, and saturation. A color's *hue* is simply the name it is known by. When we refer to the red hat or the blue house we are naming the observable hue of those things. This is true even when naming the object's hue isn't so easy: "Not the brownish-gray tree trunk, but that greenish-golden, sort of tan, one!" When we refer to a color's value we are, as discussed earlier in this text, stating its lightness or darkness in forms of gray on a scale where white is zero and black is one hundred: "Of these two bunches of red grapes, the bunch on the left is a little darker." And when we refer to a color's *saturation* (or *intensity*) we are declaring its brilliance or lack of it. Some colors are vivid, others are not: That light grayish-yellow blouse is "quiet," but that red-orange one really "screams."

WARM AND COOL COLOR

A fourth characteristic of any color exists partly in the context of other colors, and has to do with a color's *temperature*, that is, its warm or cool nature relative to other colors. There is universal agreement that yellow, orange, and red are inherently warm colors, and that green, blue, and purple are inherently cool ones. But most other colors, especially *tints* (when white is added to a color), *shades* (when black is added to a color), and mixtures of various colors do appear warm or cool according to the temperature of surrounding colors. For example, a lavender flower among blue ones will seem warm, but among yellow and orange flowers, cool. Even among like colors, there are differences of temperature. You can see this at your local paint-supply store by comparing some seven or eight red chips to see which is the warmest one and which, the coolest. Likewise, green, blue, or orange chips, or color chips of any other hue will show a range of temperatures. Under most circumstances warm colors appear to advance and cool ones, to recede. This phenomenon can play an important modelling, atmospheric, and compositional role in drawing what you see.

ANALYZING OBSERVED COLORS

> ***The capital of painting is color, and the capital of drawing is line. The important visual element of value moves freely between these two realms.***

To more accurately match a subject's various colors you need to judge them according to the four color qualities noted above. If, for example, you set out to match the color of a manila envelope, you might begin by asking, "Is the envelope's color warm or cool?" Having noted that it is warm, you should then decide whether it is closest to yellow, orange, or red. Of course, yellow is the obvious choice. Next, determine whether it is a yellow nearer to green or to orange, and add that color. Then, recalling the value scale, select the color's value—twenty degrees? Forty? Adding white, black, or some other color should provide the needed value.

However, adding black to a color is often not the best way to produce a color's shaded version. Try instead to add the color's *complementary* hue. In the case of our envelope, adding a very small amount of purple to your yellowish mixture will both darken and dull the resulting color in a way that may give a better result than will the addition of black. Lastly, decide if the envelope's color is intense, moderately so, or dull, and adjust your mixture to reflect that choice. Each of these inquiries will bring you closer to mixing the needed color.

SOME OF THE ROLES OF COLOR

With rare exceptions, color in drawing plays a supporting, and not a starring role. Although there is no clearly defined border between drawing and painting, it seems reasonable to claim that any work in color that would make almost no visual sense if reproduced in black and white is probably better categorized as a painting. Likewise, it could be claimed that any *monochromatic* work (a work in one color only), and done primarily in line, is likely to be understood as a drawing. Although some exceptions to these two groupings can surely be cited, and despite the impossibility of tracing a fixed boundary between the great realms of drawing and painting, at least their respective "capitals" can be identified. The capital of painting is color, and the capital of drawing is line. The important visual element of value moves freely between these two realms.

> ***When listening to the blues we know the music isn't saying that everything is in the pink.***

But the supporting role of color in drawing can be profound, adding meanings that are not available to drawings in black and white. Its most straightforward role is to identify the hues of objects and areas: "this green apple sports a reddish blush on one side." Color can increase the impression of volumetric and spatial clarity. A black and white tonal drawing of several oranges and plums arranged on a light blue drape can be beautiful, even though the colors are represented by values. But in color, the warm and varied colors of the fruit seen against the receding nature of the cool drape would increase the spatial depth, the nearness of the fruit, and the drape's role in setting them off with color, as well as value contrasts. Something of this can be seen in Demuth's *Plums* (Plate 1). A black and white version (Figure 6.1) shows only the dark tone of the plums, which now appear somewhat less evident among the other dark tones, giving all the drawing's values a more pronounced two-dimensional activity. But in color, the plums produce an advancing purple arc that places the foliage further back, creating a sense of airy spatial depth that is largely lost in black and white, as is the warm-toned sunny atmosphere.

Color is a powerful agent of composition, creating associations, contrasts, and areas of emphasis impossible in black and white drawing. This is easily seen by comparing Figure 6.2 with Plate 2. Here, two identical images take our eyes along different pathways because of the introduction of colors in Plate 2. In Figure 6.2, we are directed mainly by value; in Plate 2, by color. Notice how, in Plate 2, dissimilar shapes associate by similarities of color.

In most paintings, colors play an active role throughout the work, covering all (or at least much) of the surface. In drawing, colors may often be few and sparingly

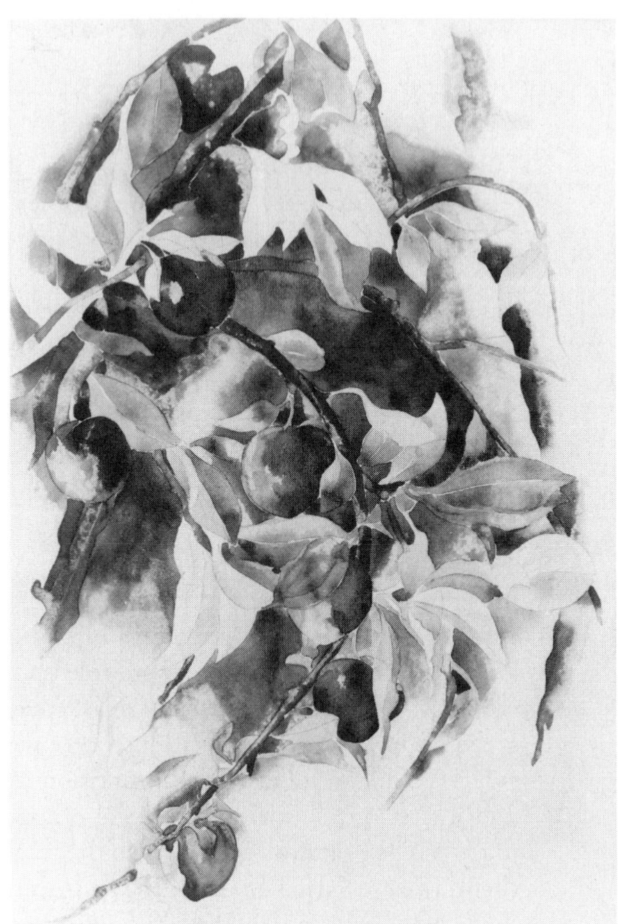

Figure 6.1 (A black and white version of) Charles Demuth (1883–1953), *Plums*, 1925. Watercolor and graphite on wove paper mounted on board, $18\frac{1}{8} \times 12$ inches. 1934.5, museum purchase. *Source:* © Addison Gallery of American Art, Phillips Academy, Andover, Massachusetts. All Rights Reserved.

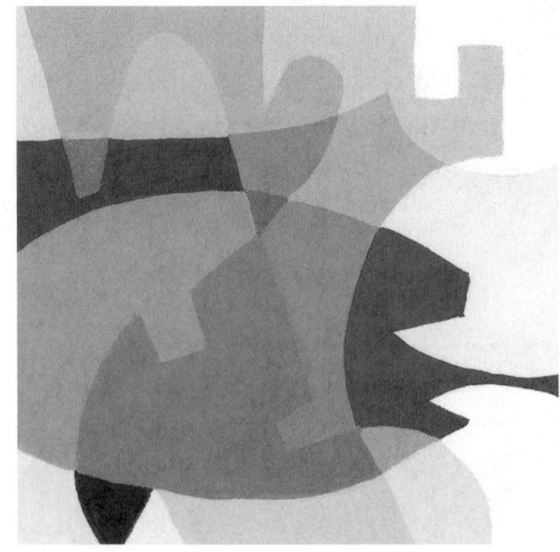

Figure 6.2

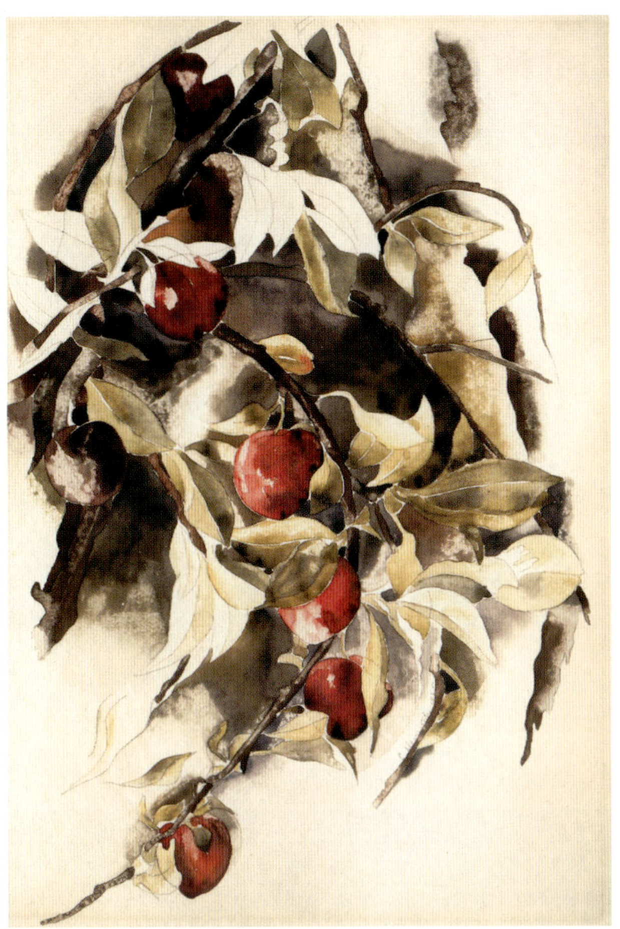

Plate 1 Charles Demuth (1883-1953), *Plums*, 1925. Watercolor and graphite on wove paper, mounted on board, 18 1/8 x 12 inches (1934.5). Museum purchase.

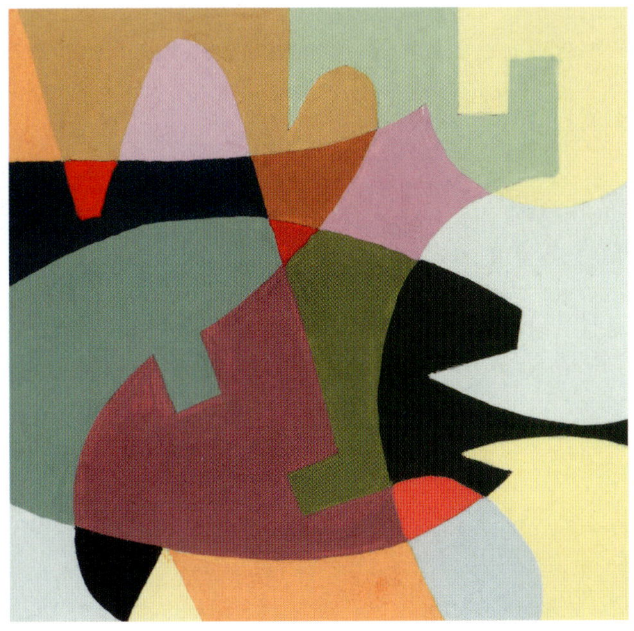

Plate 2 Color creates associations, contrasts, and areas of emphasis impossible in black and white works. Compare with Figure 6.2.

Plate 3 Jean-Louis Forian (French, 1852-1931), *Figure Studies*. Pen and watercolor, 31 x 19.9 cm. (K-20538). Photograph © National Gallery in Prague, 2004.

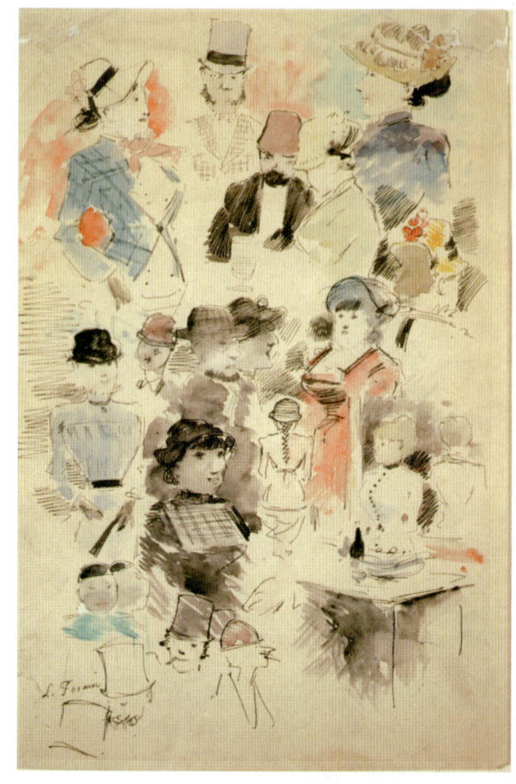

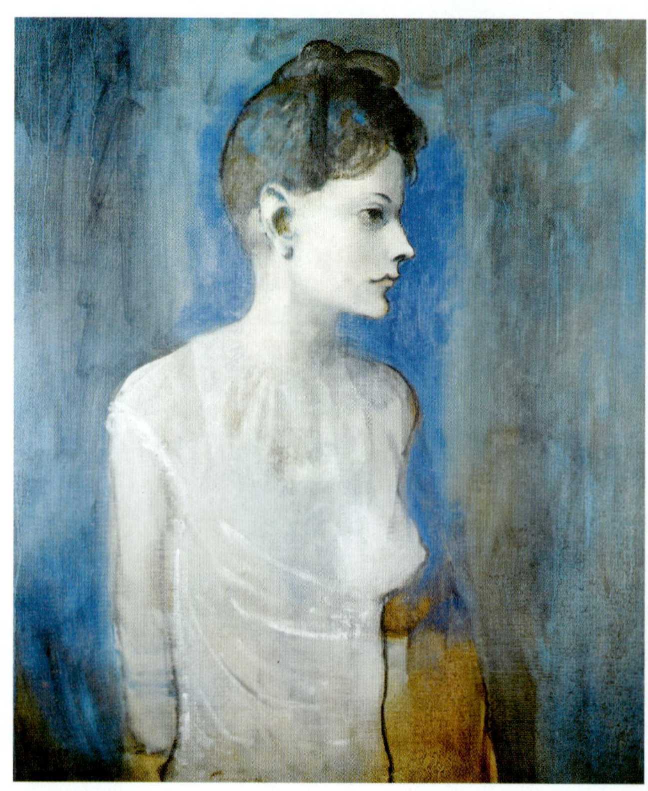

Plate 4 Pablo Picasso (1881-1973), *Girl in a Chemise,* 1905. (ART 15451). Photograph © Tate Gallery, London/Art Resource, NY. © 2005 Estate of Pablo Picasso/Artists Rights Society (ARS), New York.

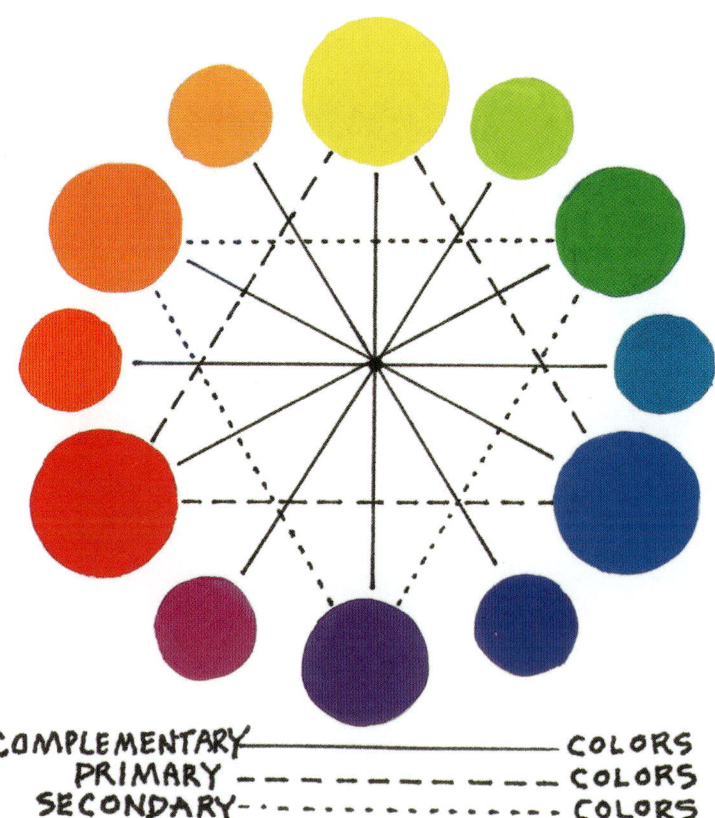

Plate 5 The twelve basic colors of the color wheel.

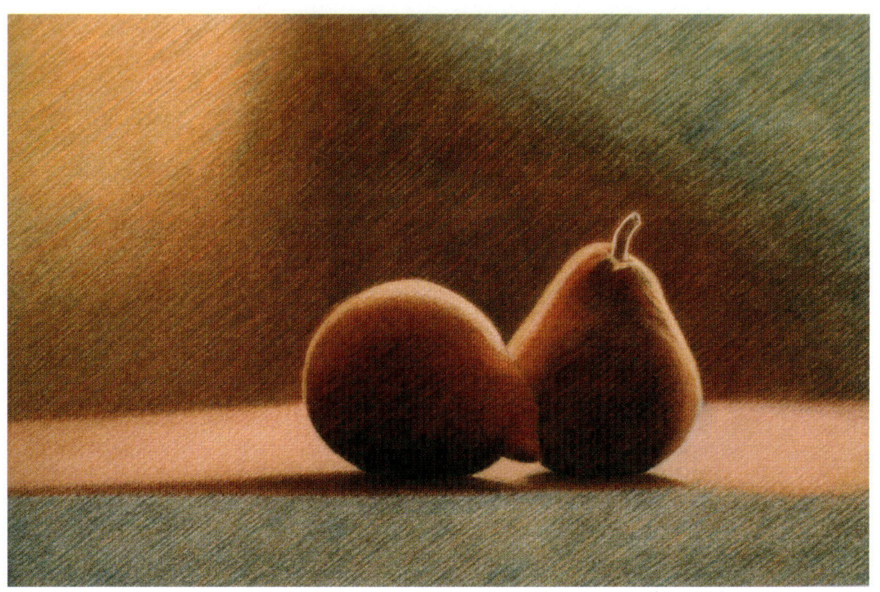

Plate 6 Martha Alf, *Two Pears # 3* (for Michael Blankfort), 1982. Pastel pencil on paper, 12 x 18 inches (31 x 46 cm). Collection of Elinor and Rubin Turner, Beverly Hills, CA. Courtesy of the artist and Newspace Gallery, Los Angeles, CA.

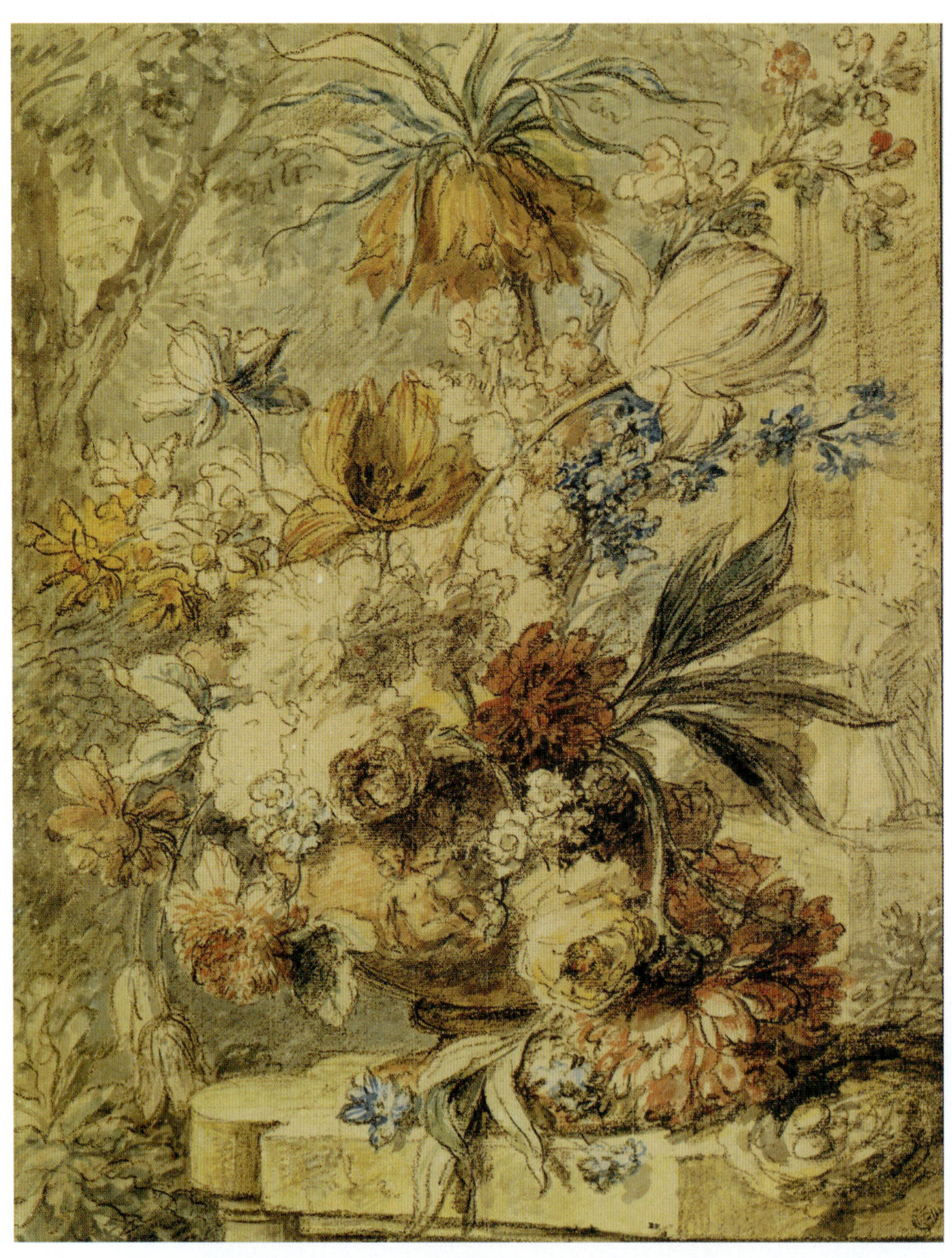

Plate 7 Jan van Huysum (1682-1749), *Vase of Flowers*, drawing. 47.5 x 35.6 cm. (INV 22669). Paris, France. Photograph © Reunion des Musées Nationaux/Art Resource, NY.

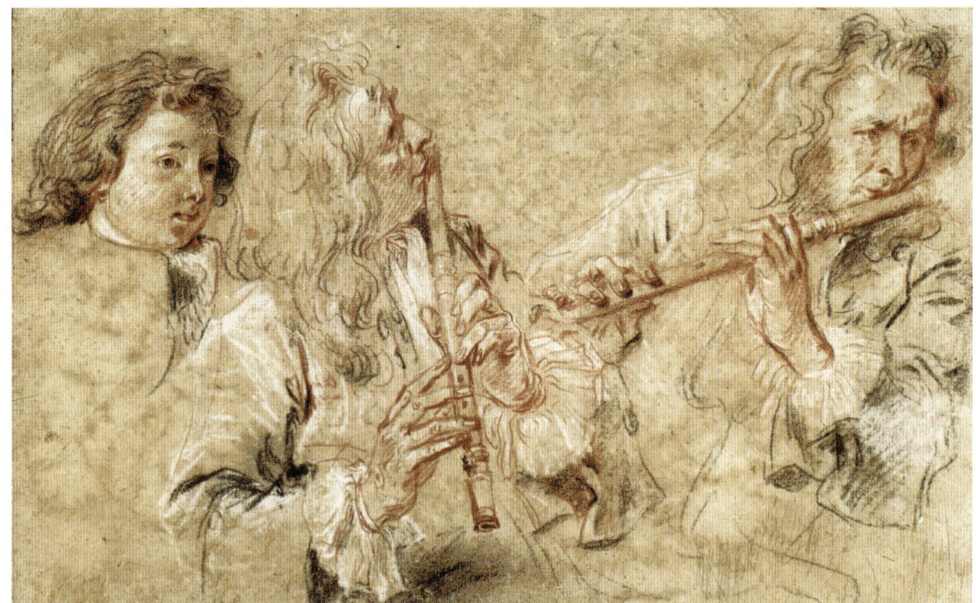

Plate 8 Jean Antoine Watteau (French, 1684-1721), *Two Studies of a Flutist and a Study of the Head of a Boy*, about 1716-1719. Red, black, and white chalk on buff-colored paper, 8 7/16 x 13 13/16 inches (21.4 x 33.5 cm). Courtesy of the J. Paul Getty Museum, Los Angeles, CA.

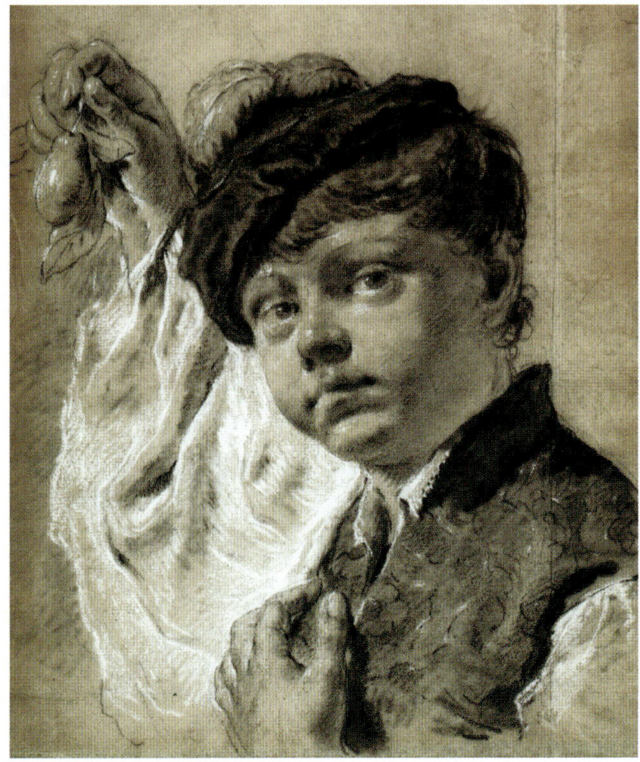

Plate 9 Giovanni Battista Piazzetta (Italian, 1682-1754), *A Boy Holding a Pear* (Giacomo Piazetta?), about 1740. Black and white chalk on blue-gray paper (two joined sheets), 15 7/16 x 12 3/16 inches (39.2 x 31 cm). Courtesy of the J. Paul Getty Museum, Los Angeles, CA.

Plate 10 Nathan Goldstein, *Seated Figure*. 7 x 10 inches. Sepia ink. Collection of the artist.

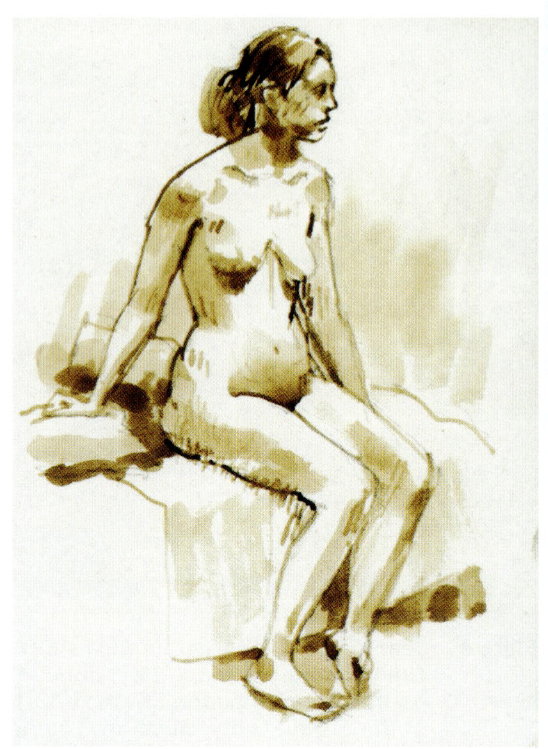

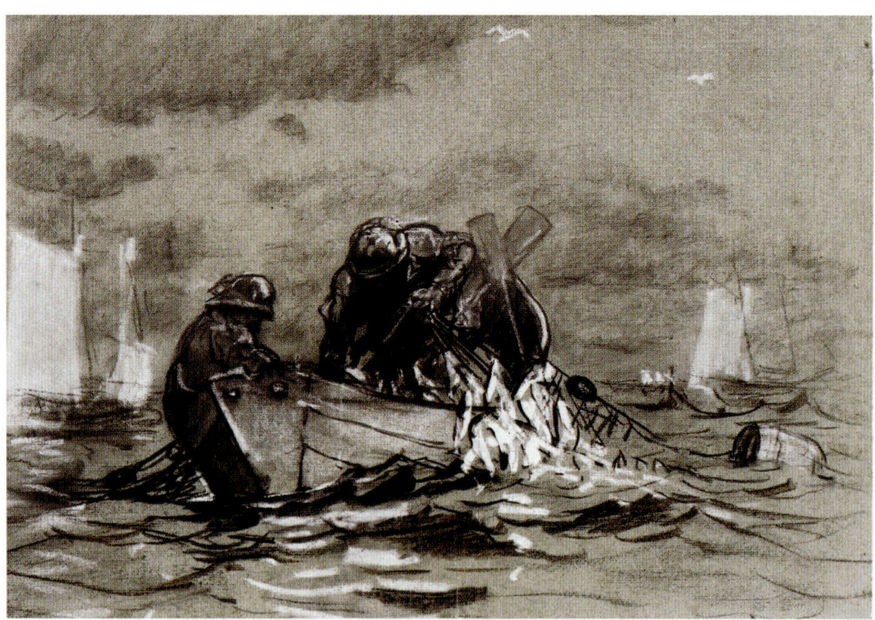

Plate 11 Winslow Homer (American, 1836-1910), *The Herring Net (*or *Banks Fisherman)*, 1884. Black, brown, and white chalk, brush and white gouache on green laid paper, 16 5/8 x 20 9/16 inches (42.3 x 52.3 cm). Cooper-Hewitt, National Design Museum, Smithsonian Institution, Washinton, D.C. Gift of Charles W. Gould (1916-15-2). Photograph: Matt Flynn.

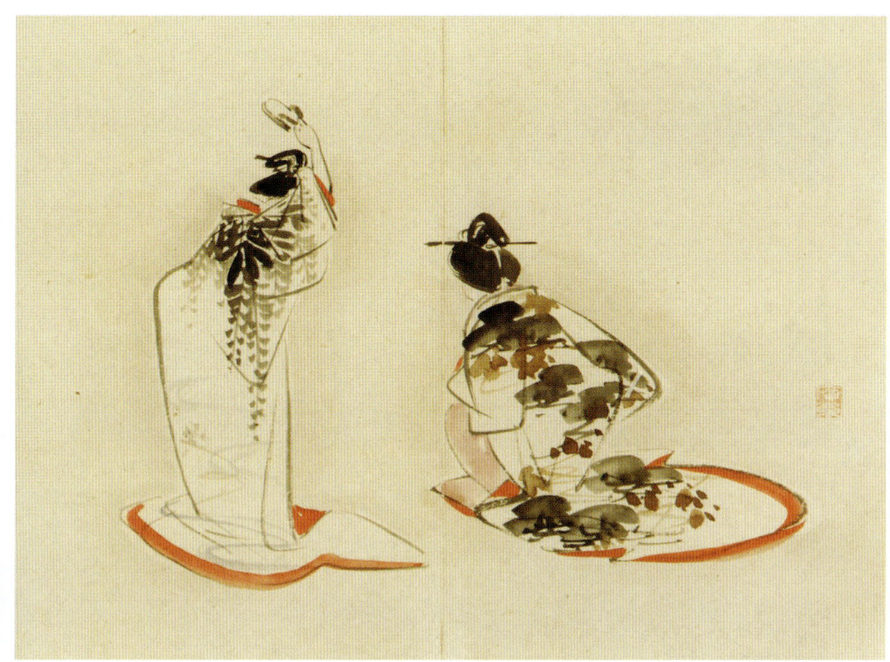

Plate 12 Utagawa Hiroshige (Japanese, 1797-1858), *Two Women Playing.* Color and ink on paper, 27.8 x 16.8 x 3.8 cm. Japanese, Edo Period (1615-1868). Freer Gallery of Art, and Arthur M. Sackler Galley/ Smithsonian Institution, Washington, D.C. Gift of Charles Lang Freer (F1904.357) (sec61).

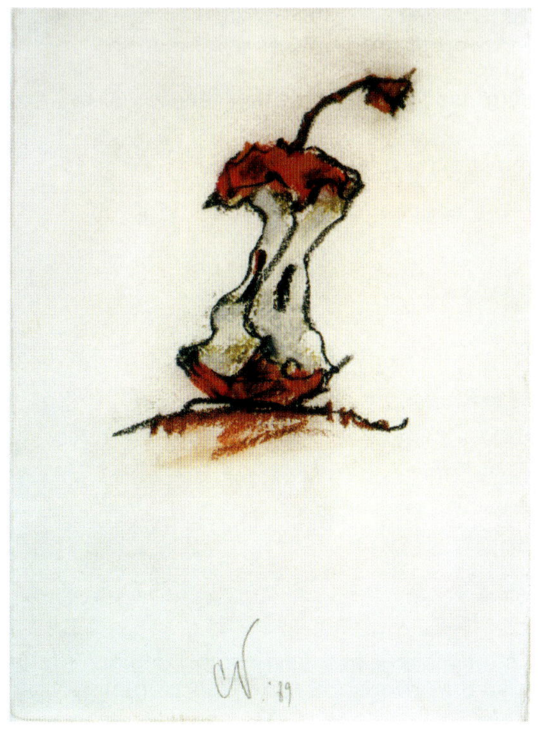

Plate 13 Claes Oldenburg and Coosje van Bruggen, *Apple Core*, 1989. Charcoal and pastel, 12 7/8 x 9 1/8 inches (32.7 x 23.2 cm). Private Collection. © Claes Oldenburg and Coosje van Bruggen.

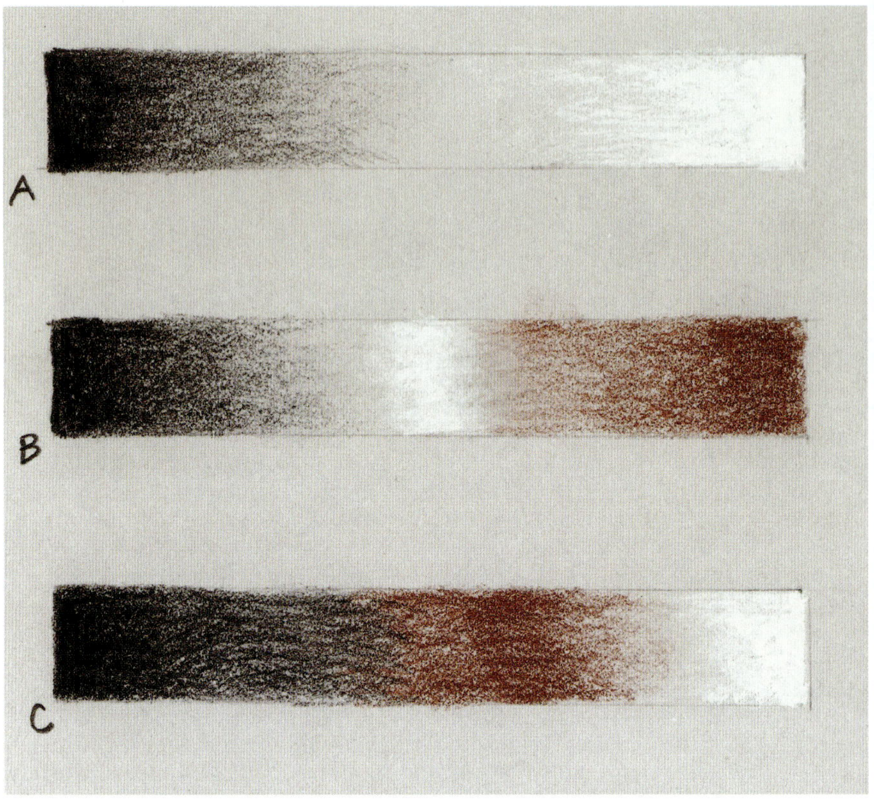

Plate 14 **A:** Value scale incorporating the tone of the background as a value on the way from black to white.
B: The tone of the background used only as a value in the presence of a third color.
C: The third color being used as a color rather than a value.

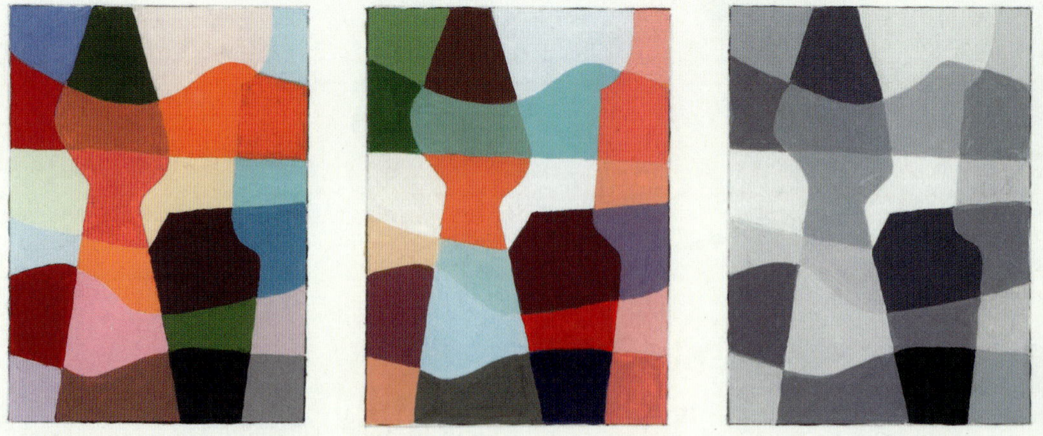

Plate 15 Note the different visual similarities and differences in the two color versions of the same arrangement of shapes, and that all three versions show approximately matching values of the shapes.

used, occupying only a portion of the drawing's surface, as in Forain's *Figure Studies* (Plate 3), where small washes of flat color enliven the page as they move our eye around on it. Note how both the red and the green shapes of color alternate between functioning as background and figure forms.

Color is also a powerful agent of expression, and its influence on mood is well known. All of Picasso's Blue Period works express the pensive melancholy that blue is capable of invoking (Plate 4). So strong is the connection between color and feeling that we've come to associate colors with moods. When listening to the blues we know the music isn't saying that everything is in the pink. We may be red with rage or gray with exhaustion, but never black with envy or in a green mood.

THE COLOR WHEEL

A useful tool in bringing some order to the great range of observable hues is the twelve-member color wheel (Plate 5). By arranging the colors of the spectrum with yellow at the top, the hues to the left and right of yellow grow darker in value as they descend to violet, at the bottom of the wheel. Additionally, this arrangement shows the hues to one side of yellow growing warmer as they descend, and the hues to the other side of yellow growing cooler.

The color wheel is based on the premise that there are three *primary* colors: red, yellow, and blue, and that among all other colors each of these three hues is least like the other two. That is, these three colors are the most dissimilar ones we can conceive of. Further, none of these three colors can be produced by mixtures of any other colors, whereas, at least in theory, all other colors can be produced by various mixtures among the primaries, plus black and white. As noted earlier, adding white to a color produces a *tint* of that color, and adding black, a *shade*. For example, pink is a tint of red, and brown, a shade of yellow.

The three primaries form a triangle on the color wheel. Roughly equal mixtures between any two primaries form a second triangle. Thus, yellow and red produce orange, yellow and blue produce green, and red and blue produce violet (or purple). These three hues are called *secondary* colors. One characteristic of the secondary colors is that they always hint at their "parentage." Mixtures between any adjacent primary and secondary colors produce the color wheel's *tertiary* colors, of which there are six possible combinations. Their names are always determined by their "ingredients," as in yellow-orange or blue-green. Like the numerals of a clock, these twelve hues complete the color wheel.

Viewing the color wheel gives us a better understanding of how colors gradually change in value and temperature, and helps us to imagine how other crossovers on the color wheel can produce still other colors. Among the possible crossovers are those directly opposite on the color wheel, for example, orange and blue, yellow and purple, and red and green. Such opposing hues are called *complementary* colors. Roughly equal mixtures between complementary colors will result in variously warm or cool, grayed or *neutral* colors. Notice that such complementary mixtures are always made of one warm and one cool color. Roughly equal mixtures between hues that are near neighbors on the color wheel will produce less grayed results.

Unequal mixtures of complementary colors will produce more or less muted versions of the dominant color. If, for example, a very small amount of green is added to red, the resulting color will be a less intense red. Any hue on the color wheel, when placed alongside its complementary, will bring both colors to their fullest intensity. The term *simultaneous contrast* refers to the brilliant effects of such a meeting of complementary hues.

In objectively drawing what you see it is seldom that all or most of a subject's colors are brilliant members of the color wheel. Except for plumage, fruits and vegetables, flowers, sunsets, the colors of some fabrics, and a few other subjects, most of the colors around us are tints, shades, and mixtures of the twelve hues of the color wheel, plus black and white. For the most part these more muted colors have no names.

It is important to recognize that using color to draw what you see still requires you to regard the values of the things you see. Even changing some of the hues in an observed subject is less of a departure from what is before you than changing their values. For example, if you are making a colored drawing of a landscape, it may be expressively useful to alter the color of the foliage, houses, sky, and the like. As long as you keep fairly close to the values in the subject before you, you can maintain the way light falls on the landscape, explaining the structure and position in space of its various parts, and the landscape's overall atmosphere. But disregarding the subject's values when using color can easily confuse you about light's behavior and may weaken the drawing's clarity of structure, space, and atmosphere. Color does not replace value, it gives values their observed or desired colors. In Alf's *Two Pears No. 3* (Plate 6), the artist has plainly altered the color of the pears and of the cast shadows, but not their values. By doing so she is able to transform the subject in a dramatic way while benefiting from the clarity of form and space that value provides.

Many artists employ color to enhance a drawing's impact by using some of the devices of painting. Often, such colors are laid on in a more or less flat manner, with the tonal modelling of forms and the drawing's lights and shadows expressed by an ink or chalk line, as in Plate 3, and Van Huysum's *Vase of Flowers* (Plate 7).

One manner of using color in drawing dates back over two hundred years and allows the artist to suggest the presence of more color than is actually used. In this mode, the drawing is composed of only a few colors such as black, white, and an earth-red chalk such as terra cotta, and is drawn on a warm- or cool-toned paper. By variously mixed hatchings of these colors on a colored paper, a variety of colors can be suggested, as in Plate 8. Note especially the use of color in the boy's head, and how the artist uses the paper's tone as a value in the modelling of the forms throughout the drawing. In France this technique was called "au trois crayon." But there are many variations on using limited color on a colored surface, sometimes employing more colors or using a strongly toned paper such as a brilliant red or green. Sometimes the color is restricted even further to black and white on a toned surface, as in Piazzetta's *A Boy Holding a Pear* (Plate 9), or even a single color on a white sheet, as in Plate 10 (Goldstein's *Seated Figure*).

Color in drawing is occasionally intense and plentiful. But when this is the case the color impact is almost always matched or overtaken by strong linear or tonal drawing, as Plates 1, 4, 6, and 7 show. Whether color in a particular work is muted or strong, or is sparsely or generously used is of course a matter of its function as well as of expressive necessity. For Watteau, Piazzetta, and Goldstein (Plates 8, 9, and 10), color does set a mood, but is primarily used to establish volume and space with greater clarity and impact. For Demuth, Forain, and Van Huysum (Plates 1, 3, and 7), color's role is more compositional; it helps to balance the work and to move our eyes around the image. And for Picasso, Alf, and Homer (Plates 4, 6, and 11), color is mainly in the service of expression. Even when, as in Homer's strongly gestural drawing, color is represented only by the color of the paper (see also Plate 9), the hue selected can work to amplify a drawing's emotive meaning as the gray-green page in Homer's drawing emphasizes the scene's cold, damp, and isolated atmosphere.

In a very different mood, Hiroshige's *Two Women Playing* (Plate 12), benefits from the dark to light range of brown ink strokes, the flashes of bright red, and the cream colored page. These welcoming warm-toned colors amplify the energetic brushwork, adding to the playful nature of the women. To better appreciate color's expressive ability, try to imagine Homer's drawing in the colors of the Hiroshige work and vice versa.

Sometimes the same colors can serve images of a very different kind. In Oldenburg's amusing *Apple Core* (Plate 13), there is again the warm-toned page, the brown and red colors, and even a similar gestural handling of the marks that we find in Hiroshige's drawing. But then, a comparative playfulness and animation is at work in both drawings, and despite the difference in subject matter (and cultures), the similarities of gesture and movement led both artists to similar color choices.

When drawing on a colored surface with black and white chalk, crayon, or paint, or even when you add a third color such as an earth red, green, or brown, it is almost always best to avoid physically mixing the two or three colors being used. To do so ignores the benefits that the color of the surface can provide in achieving additional color variations. A better solution is to integrate the color of the page with the colors being used, as shown in Plate 14A. Notice how, in Plate 14A, the black hatchings at the left of the bar grow less dense as they move to the right, allowing the *value* of the paper to participate in producing the steady lightening of the bar's tone. Note that toward the middle of the bar it is the background color alone that establishes the needed value. Then, just to the right of that place on the bar, a subtle introduction of white, growing stronger as it moves further to the right, completes the gradual black to white value change in the bar. Of course, black and white hatching or blending alone can give the same tonal result, but then the color of the page is excluded, lending to the sense of its separation from the rest of the work.

When a third color is added, it is still best to avoid its being physically mixed with either the black or white colors because, again, the paper's color is excluded and remains a passive feature in the work. Basically, there are two ways of using black, white, and a third color. The third color can be used as a value, as in 14B, where it "takes over" when black, however lightly used, is simply too dark in value to continue making the gradually lighter tone of the bar. The third color in turn gives way to the tone of the paper, and when the paper's tone is too dark, white is gradually added to complete the range from black to white.

A second way uses the color only as a color. Note how the bar in 14C turns from gray to red. In actual practice, artists often shift from one mode to the other in the same drawing, as Watteau does in Plate 8. In modelling the boy's head, Watteau mainly uses the first mode by using white for the lightest portions, hatchings of white and the paper's color for the half-tone areas, and some black hatched into the darkest places, as on the boy's forehead and far side of the face. But note that he uses red to show the blush on the cheeks and the color of the lips, as well as using it for some of the modelling in the head. In using only red and white when drawing the hands, and black and white in drawing the jacket of the musician on the right, Watteau is again suggesting the color of these parts, as he does in the hair, where all three colors are used. Despite these variations in Watteau's use of the three colors, there is no place in the drawing where the artist has physically rubbed one color into another. Solid areas of color as well as hatchings may be placed adjacent to one another but are not actually blended as they might be in some ways of using pastel.

Drawing in Color Exercises

1. Using Plate 9 as a rough guide, draw on a warm or cool colored paper, any simple subject of your choice, using only black and white chalk or colored pencil. Use the paper's tone to establish needed values, as in Piazzetta's example, where the tone of the paper represents darker passages in the boy's sleeve, but lighter values in his head and hand. But do not blend the black and white tones to produce gray tones, as this disregards the purpose of the toned paper. Instead, by applying the chalk or colored pencil in various linear hatchlings, allow the tone of the paper to optically mix with black to produce tones lighter than black, and with white, to produce tones darker than white.
2. Using Plate 8 as a rough guide, draw on a warm or cool colored paper, any simple subject of your choice, using chalks or colored pencils of black, any warm or cool earth color, and white. Note that Watteau uses these three colors to suggest some of his subject's colors, as in the warm-toned hands, heads, and instruments of the musicians, and in their cool-toned coats. In the example, the tone of the paper (as in Plate 9) continues to provide a variety of light and dark tones by optically mixing with the colors used. Note that the three colors are virtually never blended to produce still other colors and tones, but these colors enlist the color and value of the paper for these purposes.
3. Using Plate 6 as a rough guide, begin a simple still life by applying colors in large flat shapes that represent all the forms, interspaces, and background areas. These colors can be applied either by wet or dry media. Next, using hatchings of black or a dark-toned dry medium, develop all the needed tones and surface structures.
4. Using Plate 7 as a rough guide, begin a still life or landscape drawing on a light-toned sheet by first drawing the subject in a loose and linear manner, being mindful of your subject's larger gestural pattern. This can be done with either a wet medium, or a dry one such as graphite or crayon. Next, using watercolor lay in all the needed colors, working from the lighter to the darker colors. These colors needn't cover all of a form or an area, but may allow some of the toned sheet to show. Then, returning to a more linear drawing treatment, develop the subject further, suggesting light and shadow, more delineated contours and textures. Further use of watercolor may be required at this stage. Continue alternating layers of linear drawing and watercolor painting as needed, but avoid overworking parts. Try for something like the fresh and spontaneous handling seen in Plate 7.

The decision to use color, and deciding the roles it is to play in your drawings will, of course, be determined by your creative purposes. That the majority of drawings have been and continue to be monochromatic (usually black and white) testifies to the expressive power of line and value alone. However, many outstanding exponents of drawing, from the Renaissance to the present, have occasionally turned to color for results that monochromatic images cannot produce. But, as noted earlier, in such works color almost always plays a supporting, and not a dominant role. However, nearly dominant roles do occur, as Plates 1, 4, and 6 demonstrate. Yet, even when the colors used are few, as in Plates 9, 10, and 11, they can expand what the act of drawing can embrace. Drawing with color should be explored to see how (or if) it is suitable in helping you to better capture and communicate what is important in the things you wish to draw.

Earlier it was noted that color is a powerful compositional element. You will meet this element again, in the next chapter, where we turn to consider how (and why) compositional considerations can give your drawings greater clarity and meaning.

Things to Think About

1. When trying to match a color, what four aspects of that color do you need to consider in order to succeed?
2. Would you regard a drawing made with warm and cool grays to be a work in color?
3. If paintings can be done in black and white, and drawings in color, and if paintings can be made with linear tools like oil-crayon sticks, and drawings with paint, at what point would you consider a work to be a painting and not a drawing?
4. What do the secondary colors "reveal" that the primary colors cannot?
5. Generally, warm colors advance and cool colors, recede. When viewing, on a light gray wall, a 2-inch square of the color made by a mixture of equal parts of orange and white placed next to a 2-inch square of an intense green, which color would advance?
6. When drawing in color, are the values of your various colors as important as the values used when drawing monochromatically? Are color values more important? Somewhat less important?

Critique Considerations

1. When drawing with a wet medium, do some of the colors appear muddy—as variations of brown and gray? It may be that some colors were placed adjacent to each other (or painted into each another)

when wet, causing them to run together. This can result from an anxiety about having to manage strong and varied colors. In that case, making the colors very muted is safer because you can more easily judge their values. But bringing such works closer to a monochromatic state is a return to more familiar conditions. Playing it safe by using muted colors will, however, stand in the way of using color's ability to define, organize, and express.

2. Do some of your drawings in color seem "loud," even garish? It may be that you need to step back from time to time as a work progresses, to see what the overall effect of the colors are achieving. Strident color is often the result of using a great many colors, or very intense colors, or both. It may also show that you need to consider the value of colors more.
3. If the forms in your colored works seem unclear about their location in space and about their structure, you should make use of color's warm and cool properties to help clarify both conditions.
4. Does the color in your drawings seem added on or arbitrary? It sometimes helps to begin a work with color applied broadly, and then turn to the drawing aspects of the work in a manner that is compatible with the color.

7

Composition in Drawing

WHAT IS COMPOSITION?

> ***...a successful composition always reinforces the artists's expressive meanings.***

Every successful representational drawing is an interpretation of the subject's appearance, organized in a manner that effectively communicates intended meanings to the viewer. It is also, and importantly, an arrangement of the marks that make up the drawing's imagery. Good drawing has as much to do with order and arrangement as with all the matters discussed in the previous chapters.

To quote Webster's dictionary, composition is ". . . a definite pattern of organization." A successful composition is one in which the lines, shapes, values, volumes, textures, spatial conditions, and (when present) colors are arranged in a pattern that is both *balanced and unified on the page*.

What constitutes balance and unity will be more fully discussed later, but here it will be helpful to understand balance as a state of equilibrium among the parts of a drawing, not unlike the balancing between the two sides of a seesaw. An unbalanced drawing produces tensions that intrude on our comprehension of a drawing's purposes. The term *unity* describes a visual state of interdependence and belonging among all of a drawing's parts and of the marks that form them. An absence of unity always points to one or more isolated parts or to some visual disagreement that prevents the joining of a work's parts into an integrated whole, into a state of "oneness."

Additionally, a successful composition always reinforces the artist's expressive meanings. Some of these meanings have to do with defining what the subject looks like, but some have to do with the artist's feelings about certain properties in the subject, that is, with the subject's emotive potential. In fact, a good composition may be said to begin as an expressive necessity.

THE VISUAL ELEMENTS

Yet another condition of well-composed drawings is their evident vitality and spirit. Good drawings are not dead records of what was seen, but are imbued with various energies that give life to the drawing. These energies emerge from (and between) relationships among the visual elements of line, value, shape, texture, volume, color, and space. All successful drawings are the result of how the visual elements relate to form a drawing's depictive, organizational, and expressive nature. As Figure 7.1 demonstrates, visual elements do attract and repel each other, do suggest moving actions, and do form patterns. The emergence of these energies, movements, and patterns are given conditions in the act of drawing, no matter what the style or purpose. They are inherent to image-making and must therefore be organized in the service of what it is you want your drawing to say. Indifference to their presence only means that their random behavior will work against your purposes.

For example, you may intend a particular place in a drawing to be a focal point—a center of attention—but it may be robbed of its importance by stronger visual events elsewhere in the drawing, such as bold contrasts of values or strong directional movements. These may attract the viewer's eye more than does your intended focal point. Such competing relationships, intruding on your intentions, and possibly on the drawing's compositional balance and unity (see "Compositional Structure," in this chapter), must be adjusted in ways that enable you to keep an emphasis where you want it. This more subterranean, or abstract, life of the visual elements—and their organization in your drawing to give it cohesion and expressive clarity—is often referred to as a visual work's *dynamics*.

To compose a drawing then, is to devise a pattern of dynamics that succeeds in communicating your meanings to the viewer. It succeeds as a system of expressive order.

All the previous chapters emphasized one aspect of drawing: how to better interpret the things you encounter, in a more or less objective way. They concentrated

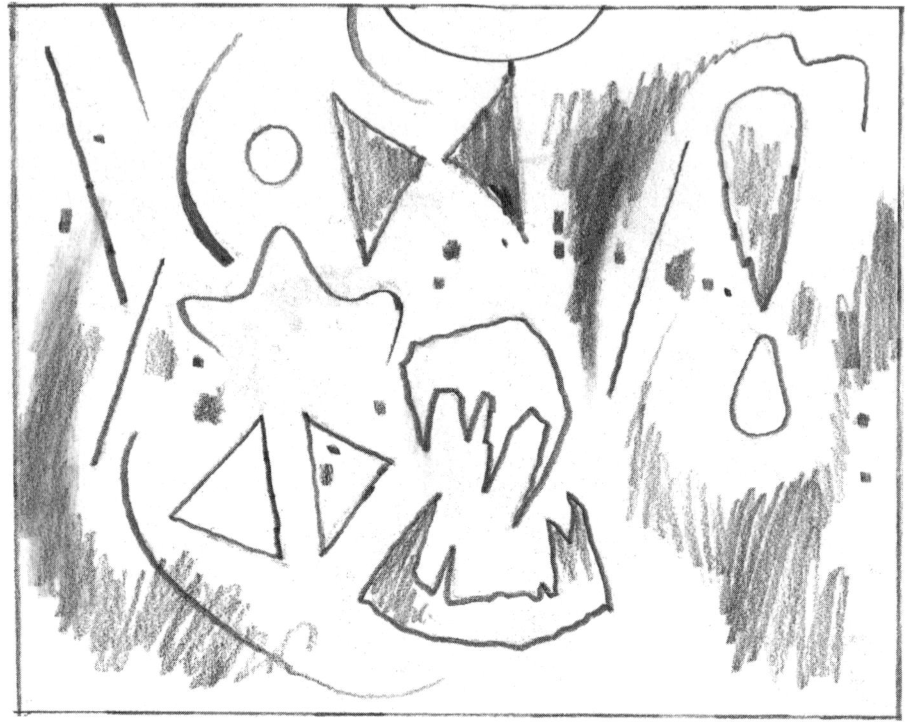

Figure 7.1

mainly on depictive matters, on a drawing's narrative *content*. Those chapters concentrated on relationships that, for the most part, can be measured. Here, we will concentrate on relationships of another kind: the underlying relationships (and energies) in a drawing that give it character and meaning. That is, we will focus on a drawing's dynamic *form*. To better understand how the visual elements relate and interact, let's begin with a brief discussion that both explores and reviews each element's general nature.

> ***Lines, even short ones, by their nature, are directional. They are ... always going somewhere.***

Line

Line is the most versatile and pervasive element in drawing. It is an efficient and direct means of establishing shape, showing overlap, and defining contours. In hatchings it produces values, and it is rich in its calligraphic, textural, and expressive

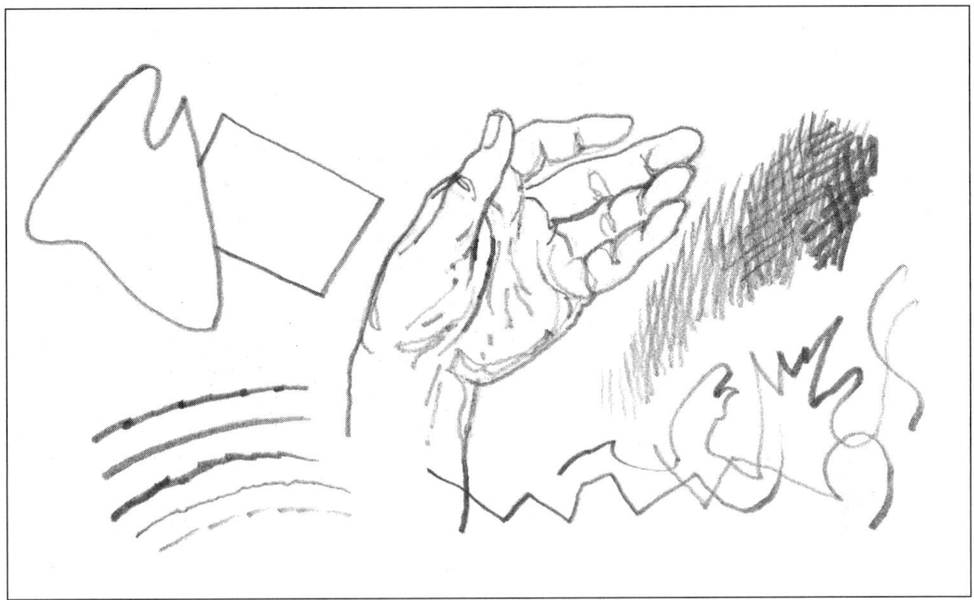

Figure 7.2

range (Figure 7.2). Lines in drawing are virtually limitless in their variety, as Figure 7.3 suggests. Note how some lines are related by some characteristics (such as width or value) and contrasted by others.

In addition to actual lines, we also sense "lines" when parts of our subject are in some kind of straight or curved orientation, as in the alignment of tables

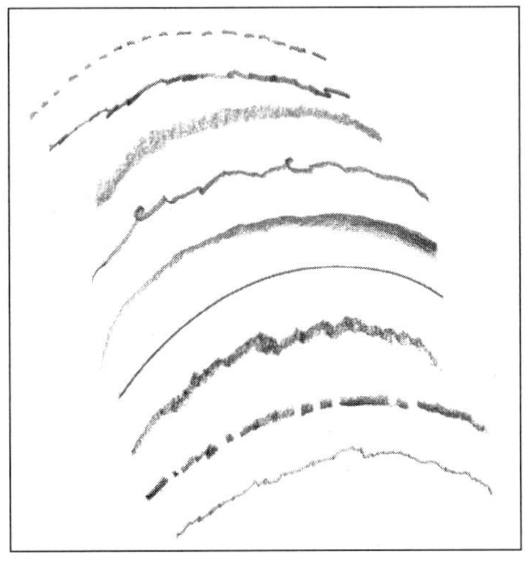

Figure 7.3

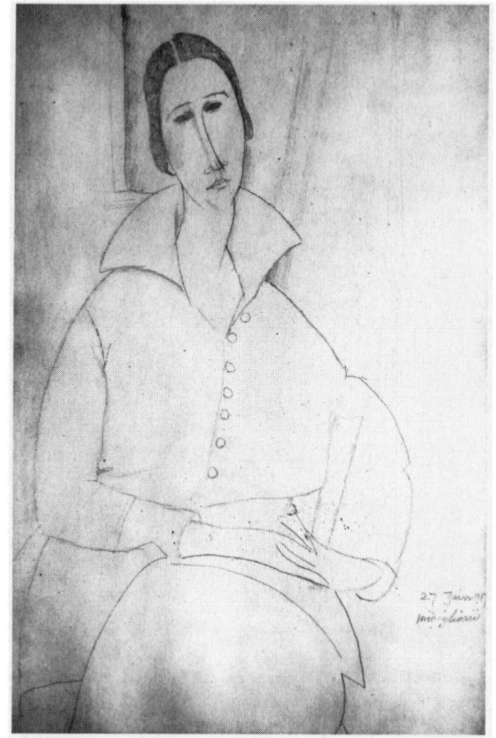

Figure 7.4 Amadeo Modigliani (French, 1884–1920), *Portrait of Mme. Zborowska*. Crayon, pencil, $19\frac{3}{8} \times 12\frac{1}{2}$ inches. 32.240. *Source:* Museum of Art, Rhode Island School of Design. Gift of Miss Edith Wetmore.

or trees (see "Seeing Alignments," Chapter One). We speak of cars or people "lining up," and of the bottom of, say, a framed mirror on the wall being "in a line with" the top of a nearby chair. Such alignments, by carrying the eye along their path, create moving actions that weave a drawing's parts together while adding expressive meanings. For example, the stately elegance of the woman in Modigliani's drawing (Figure 7.4) is strengthened by alignments that add to the graceful nature of her forms. There is the alignment of the buttons of her blouse that runs into the fold of the dress at the bottom, and into the right side of the window's frame at the top. Also, there is the curved alignment of the shoulders and upper arms, echoed in the collar, and the "bridge" formed by the lower arms and hands—just to name a few. These sweeping, rhythmic movements add to the artist's interpretation of his sitter's gentle grandeur. As this example shows, implied "lines," easy to overlook, are powerful compositional agents.

In drawing, lines as lines, edges, or alignments are everywhere, and are always active. Lines, even short ones, by their nature, are directional. They are always on the move, fast or slow, straight or serpentine, they are always going somewhere.

And, if we include alignments of other elements, such as shapes and masses (see Figure 7.1), it is evident that directed linear motions of some sort are always central to a drawing's dynamic life.

Value

As we have seen, values are produced by deposits of a dry medium such as chalk, pencil, charcoal, or crayon, or of a wet medium such as ink, watercolor, oil paint, and other fluid materials. Changes in value are the only means for showing how light, striking forms, explains their surface structure, and only through value can we show the local tones of our subject's parts, that is, the inherent lightness or darkness of the things we draw. Effects of illumination must, of course, rely on value. Unless values are too fused or faint to offer some kind of boundary we see them as shapes of tone. When such variously toned shapes are arranged to suggest a form's surface structure, the impression of volume and space is produced (Figure 7.5).

Value, then, can be a property of shape, volume, texture, color, and space. Value is also an effective means of showing both two- and three-dimensional space (Figure 7.6), and is therefore an important compositional tool for establishing order on a drawing's picture-plane and in its spatial field of depth. Values can make dissimilar parts of a drawing relate, and similar ones contrast, as Figure 7.7 shows. As an expressive tool, value is a powerful player, amplifying a drawing's mood by the way it is used (Figure 7.8).

Figure 7.5

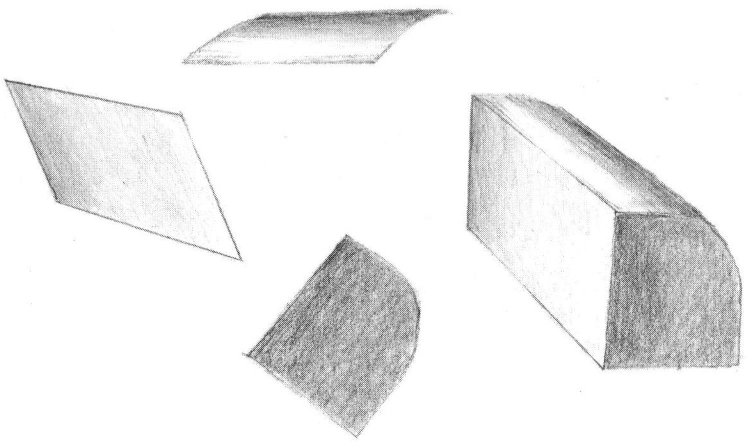

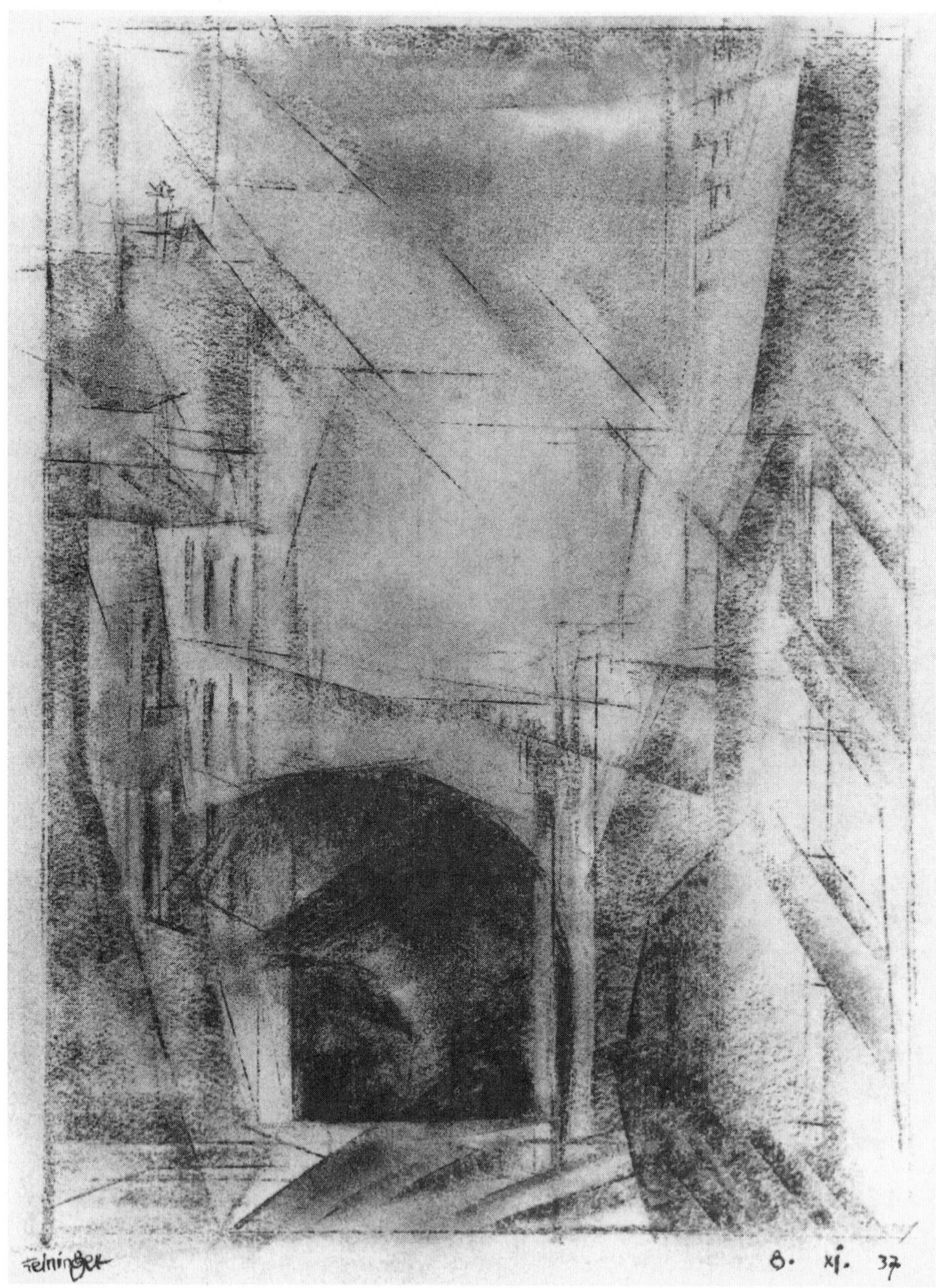

Figure 7.6 Lyonel Feininger (American, 1871–1956). *Bridge with Underpath between Buildings, Manhattan*, 1937. Charcoal on paper, $12\frac{3}{8} \times 9\frac{1}{2}$ inches. *Source:* Arkansas Arts Center Foundation Purchase: Barrett Hamilton Acquisition Fund, 1981. (1982.032.001). © 2005 Artists Rights Society (ARS), New York/VG Bild Kunst, Bonn.

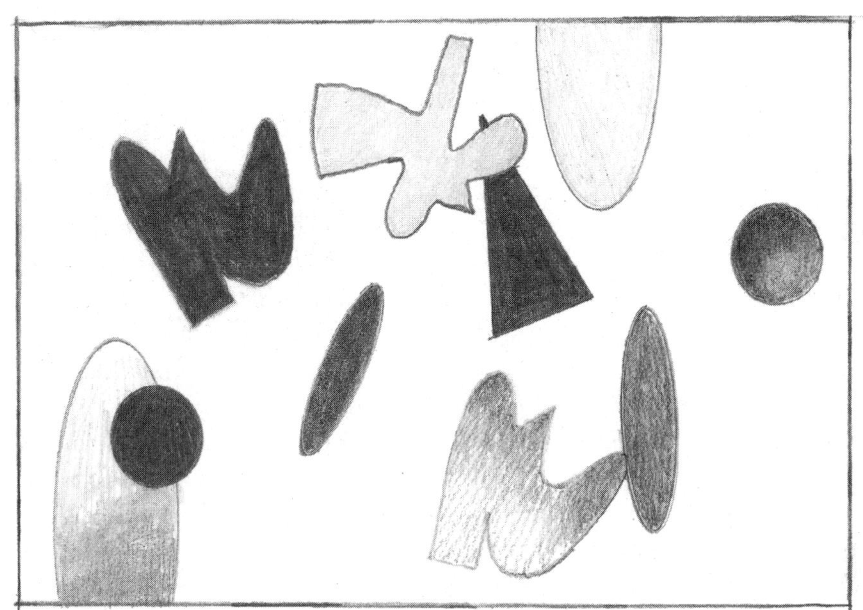

Figure 7.7

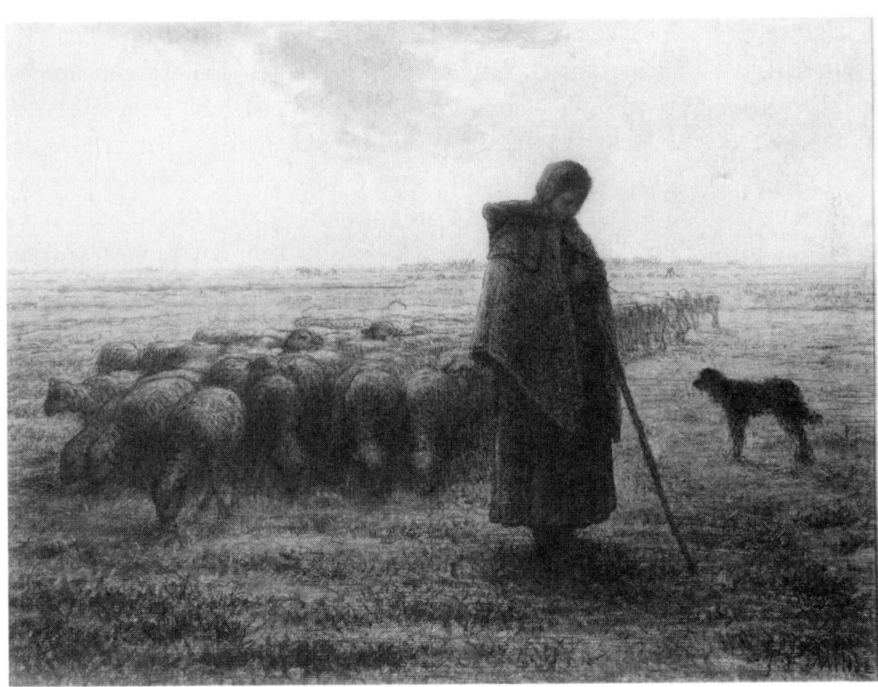

Figure 7.8 Jean-François Millet (French, 1814–1875). *Shepherdess and Her Flock*, 1862–1863. Charcoal and pastel, 36.4 × 47.5 cm ($14\frac{5}{16} \times 18\frac{11}{16}$ inches). Courtesy of the J. Paul Getty Museum, Los Angeles.

Shape

Virtually all values, planes, volumes, and interspaces have shape, have some more or less enclosed, two-dimensional configuration. As such, shapes in drawing can be said to subdivide the larger shape of the page, board, or canvas. Most beginning students find it difficult at first to hold in mind the duel truths about the things they are drawing: that they show us both two- and three-dimensional features. Used to seeing their world in terms of volumes in a spatial field, and usually wanting to emphasize these properties in their drawings, they tend not to consider the importance of seeing the actual silhouettes that *all* volumes and spaces possess. Both positive and negative shapes, by their configurations and groupings, establish patterns, directions, and suggestions of movement on the picture plane that have important compositional consequences. And, as we have seen, when accurately drawn shapes get together, they suggest volumes in space (see Figures 4.2 and 7.5). Shapes can be geometric or organic in character. They can be textured, can change value within their boundaries, or be unvaried in tone (Figure 7.9A). Shapes can be closed or open. Closed shapes are those entirely bounded by line, composed of value, or the result of positive shapes enclosing an area (Figures 7.9B and 7.10). Open shapes are those showing breaks in their linear or tonal enclosures that allow the eye to move freely through them (Figures 7.9C and 7.11). And, as Figure 7.12 demonstrates, shapes can also possess expressive meanings, as when some shapes appear action-filled or aggressive and others, stable or passive. As Figure 7.7 shows, shapes will relate or contrast according to their sizes, shape characteristics, directional orientation, proximity, and value. Although some shapes represent planes whose main function is to construct a subject's surface structures, these "plane shapes" are still part of a drawing's picture plane design and should be regarded in that way.

Figure 7.9

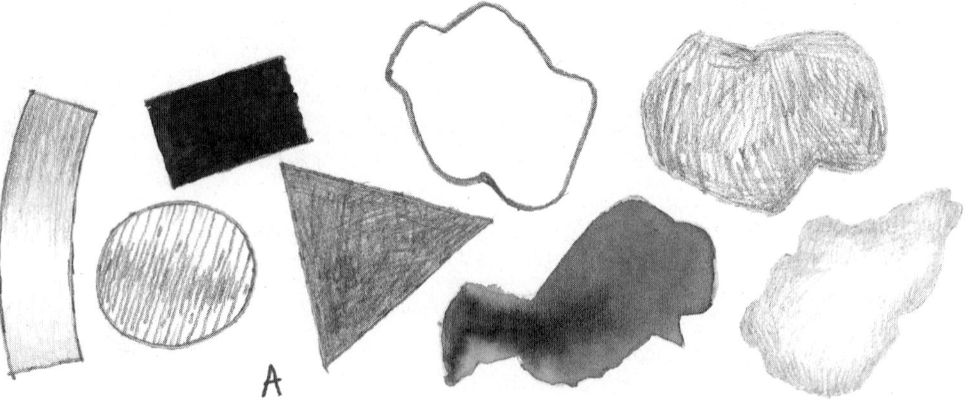

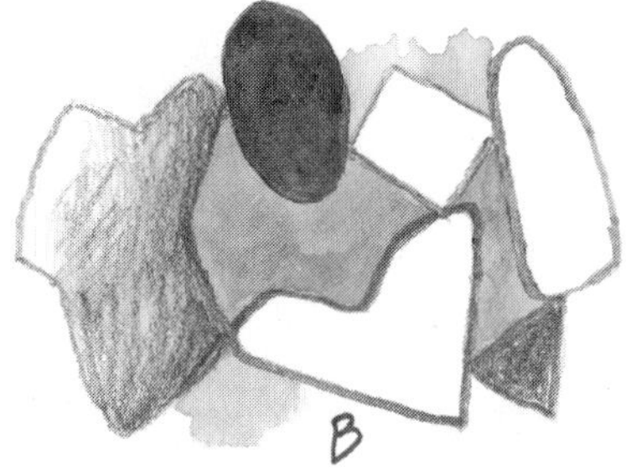

Figure 7.9

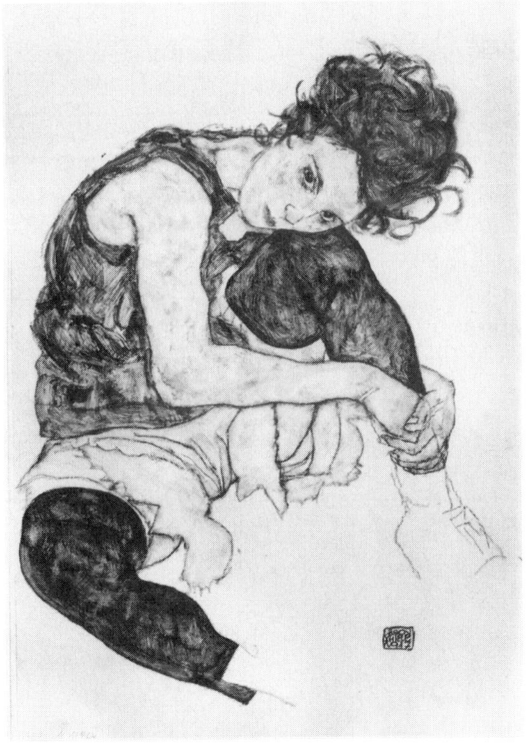

Figure 7.10 Egon Schiele (Austrian, 1890–1918), *Portrait of a Young Woman*, 1912. Oil sketch, 18 × 24 cm. (K-17864).
Source: Photograph © National Gallery in Prague 2004.

For example, in Matisse's *Reflections in the Mirror* (Figure 7.13), the horseshoelike shape of the woman's hair is seen again in an inverted, light–toned version that constructs the woman's abdomen. Again, the reflection's dark, inverted L-shape along the figure's torso is repeated in a larger version running from the figure's right lower arm down to her left foot. Other light and dark shapes, representing the planes of the mirror, the woman's limbs, the bookcase, some picture frames and the like, bear a similarity in

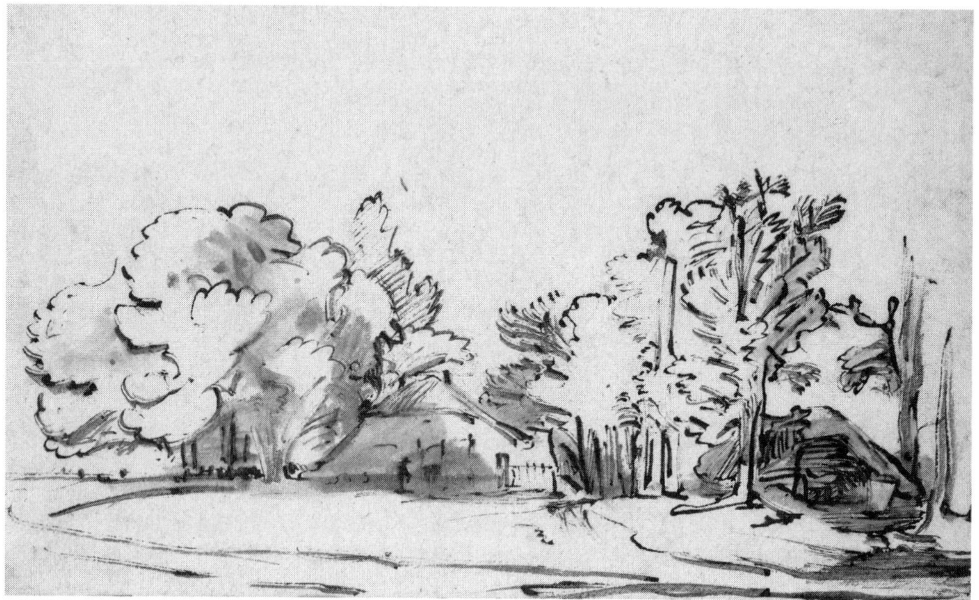

Figure 7.11 Rembrandt van Rijn (Dutch, 1606–1669), *Cottages Beneath High Trees*, ca. 1657–1658. Pen and brush with bistre, wash, on paper, 19.5 × 31 cm. (Inv. KdZ 2694)
Source: Photo: Joerg P. Anders. Photograph © Bildarchiv Preussischer Kulturbesitz/Art Resource, NY.

being vertically oriented or variations on the L-shape. Note, too, how the distribution of light and dark shapes help to animate and unify the drawing. Shape is an ever-present element in drawing. In fact, when you begin a drawing, the size and shape of your page is the first shape judgement you have made—one that will influence many

Figure 7.12

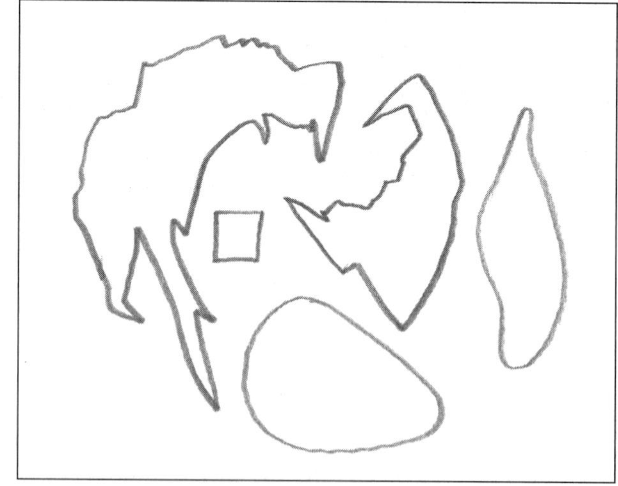

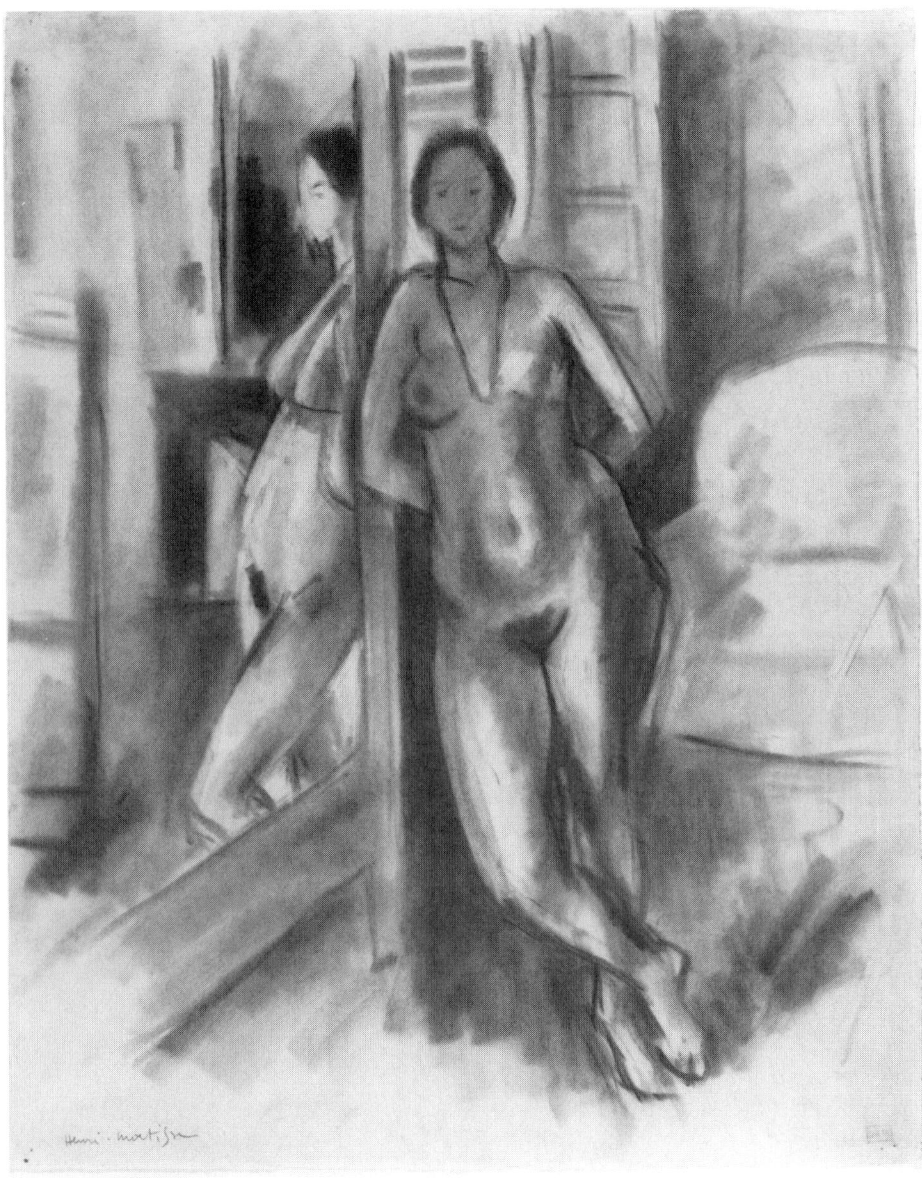

Figure 7.13 Henri Matisse (Le Cateau-Cambresis) (now Le Cateau, Picardy)(1869–Nice, 1954), *Reflection in the Mirror*. Charcoal on paper, $20\frac{1}{6} \times 16$ inches (51×40.6 cm.)
Source: Metropolitan Museum of Art, Robert Lehman Collection, 1975 (1975.1.669).

of your subsequent judgements as the drawing proceeds. Seeing the shape-actuality of planes, values, or interspaces remains one of the most important drawing skills, whether to clarify volume and space or to help establish a drawing's composition.

Texture

Artists regard the term *texture* in two ways. First, there is the texture inherent in a particular medium such as the rough and grainy look of charcoal, the slightly metallic look of graphite, the staccato of small pen strokes, or the stains and splashes of ink washes. Second, there are those recognizable textures that many artists create in their drawings, textures such as stone, silk, wood, and hair. In both cases the smooth or rough texture of the drawing surface influences the textural character of the medium and the imagery.

An example of the former is Figure 7.14, where the rapid sweep of the brush (showing the surface to be fairly smooth), tells of planes, shapes of tone, a light source, and the artist's pleasure in the look and feel of this fluid medium's texture. Note how the brush alone draws the left foot, and that a gray tone leaves the confines of the torso to suggest a cast shadow. Figure 7.15 is an example of the latter.

Figure 7.14 Marianna Pineda, *Crouching Woman, Right Arm Raised, Rear View*, brown and beige paper prepared with pink wash, 1986. Reproduced courtesy of the Boston Public Library, Print Department, by permission of the heirs of the artist.

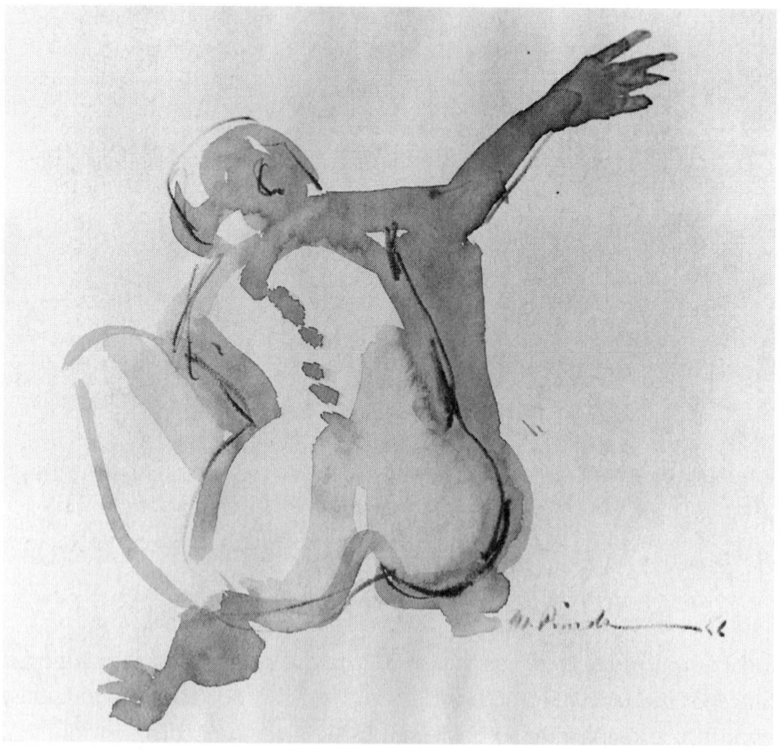

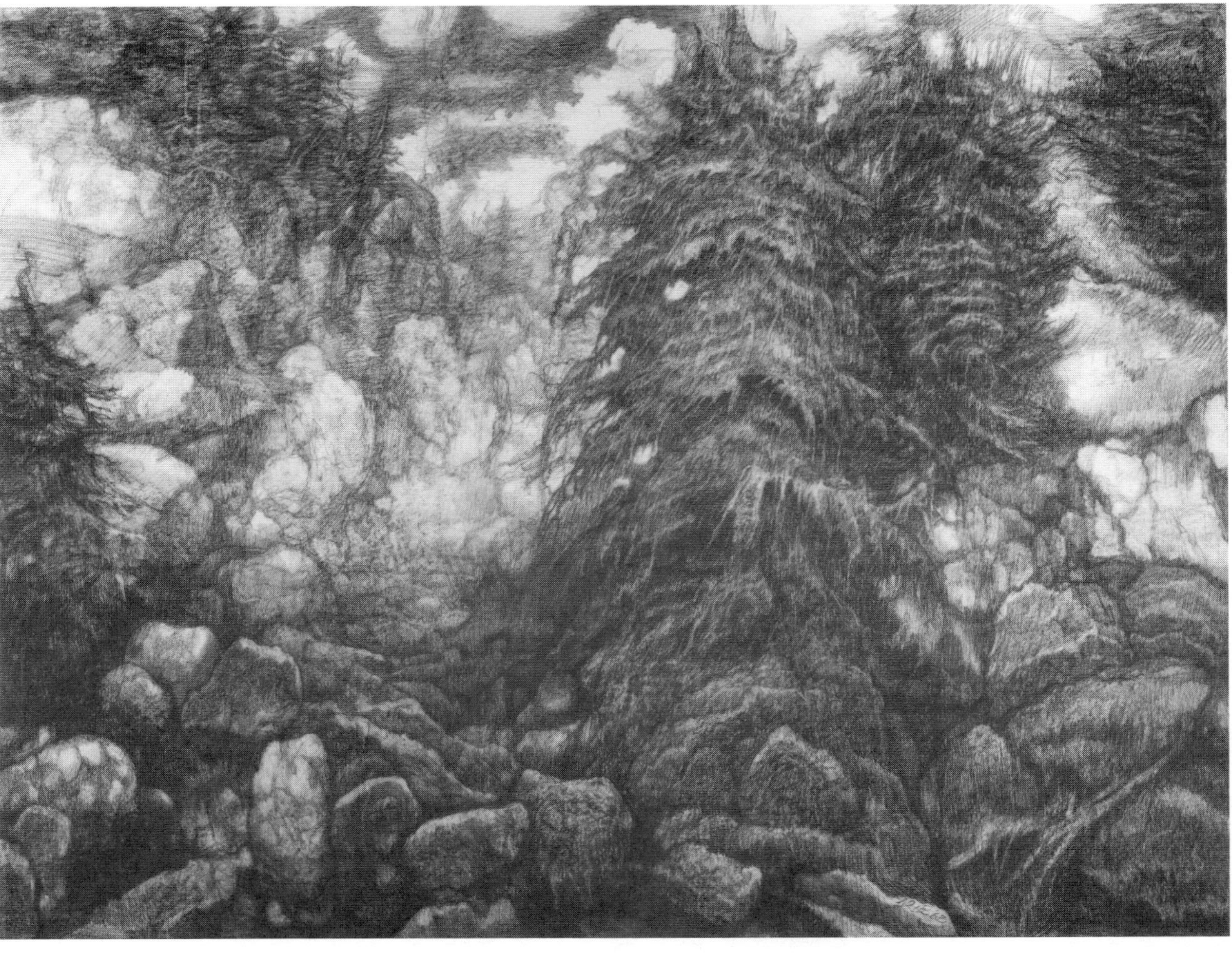

Figure 7.15 Hyman Bloom (American, 1913–), *Landscape #12*. 1963. Charcoal on cream paper. Image: 114.3 × 149.9 cm (45 × 59 inches). Other (Frame): 195.6 × 147.3 cm. (77 × 58 inches). *Source:* Photograph © 2004 Museum of Fine Arts, Boston. Gift of Emanuel L. Josephs in memory of Esta M. Josephs (1978.310.)

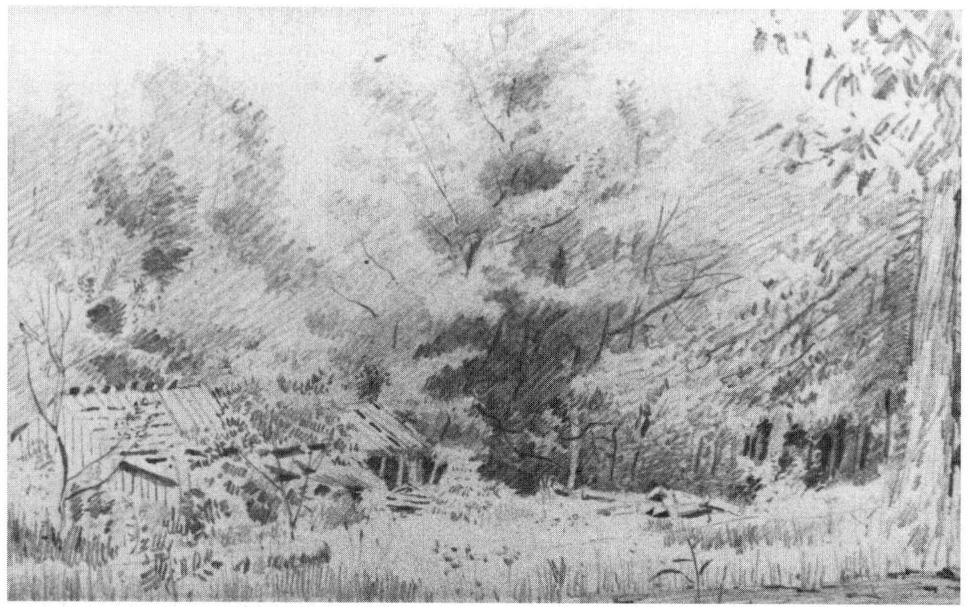

Figure 7.16 Louis Michel Eilshemius, *Old Saw Mill.* Drawing in pencil on white paper, $4\frac{1}{2} \times 6\frac{3}{4}$ inches. *Source:* Mead Art Museum, Amherst College. Gift of Mr. Roy R. Neuberger. (AC1959.156)

Although the rugged texture of charcoal is still evident, the artist is able to suggest the textures of rocks, branches, and leaves. Often, as here, artists will be responsive to both kinds of texture. Figure 7.16 also shows a sensitivity to both kinds of texture: to the fresh and subtle textures that graphite can give, and to the texture of leaf clusters, grasses, and tree bark. Sometimes it seems that experiencing a subject's texture is among the artist's most attracting motives. In Bohlen's drawing of an eider duck, a gentle handling of the soft feathers reflects the bird's fragile and graceful nature (Figure 7.17).

Texture can also exist in certain patterns or groupings. For example, a plaid or paisley shirt, a brick wall or a shingled roof, a leaf-laden tree, or a crowded stadium—all these possess a density of shapes or forms that, in drawing, are often suggested by "shorthand" marks that stand as symbols for the density of things being represented (Figure 7.18). Such texture-filled or "busy" passages of a drawing, contrasting with "emptier" passages, produce various shape or area groupings that have compositional significance.

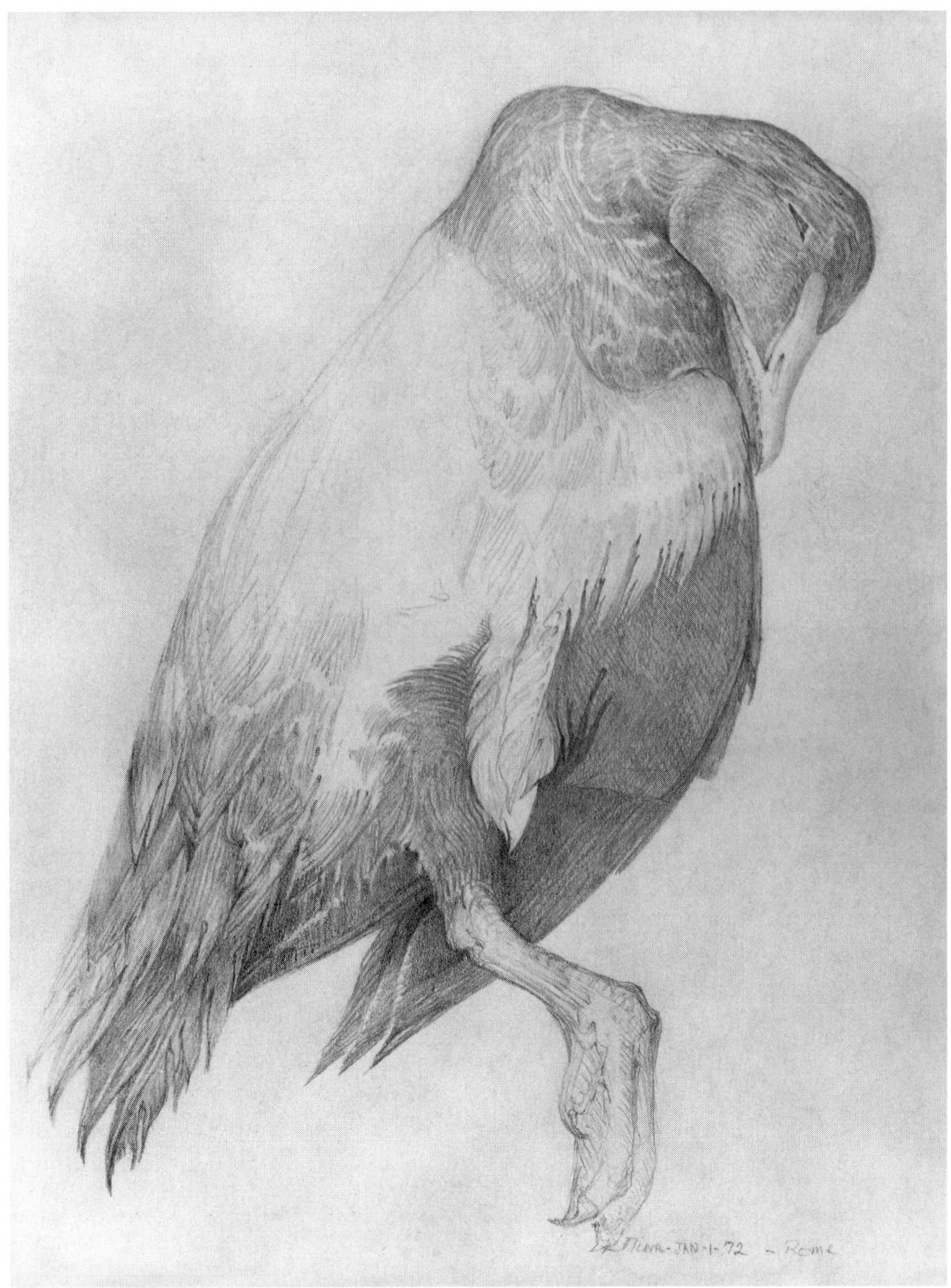

Figure 7.17 Nina Bohlen, *Study of an Eider Duck*. Graphite, 12 × 9 inches. Courtesy of the artist.

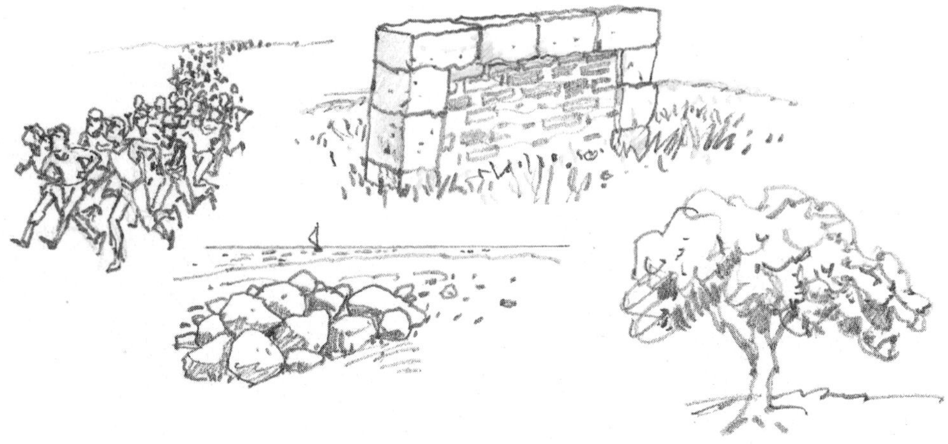

Figure 7.18

Volume and Space

Solid masses and their interspaces are also visual elements, and their arrangement in the spatial field is an important compositional consideration. Volumes either connect or contrast by scale, shape, structure, value, direction, texture, location, color (where present in a drawing), and weight. That is, we tend to see even unlike large forms as alike in their size; other forms, large or small, are seen as alike in their shape or structural character or in their common dark or light tone. We tend to note the common axial direction, even in differing forms, when headed (more or less) on the same path, and we see them in contrast to forms going in other directions. And we'll see volumes as connected or contrasting according to their similarity or differences of texture. We'll see even differing forms, when grouped together, as sharing a bond by their close proximity, and as opposed to other forms, which are further away. In colored drawings, we'll connect cool-colored forms and see them as contrasting with warm-colored ones, and we'll connect volumes such as boulders or boats as being heavy, in contrast to the lightness of clouds or sails.

Interspaces, too, connect in many of the ways noted above. In line drawings, the areas between and around solid masses also show direction, shape, and scale. In tonal or colored drawings they may show value, texture, or color. Good drawings rarely show such areas as altogether passive, as merely "left" by the demands of volume. Instead, the artist incorporates their shapes, values, and so forth into the grand strategy of a drawing's composition, occasionally altering forms in some way to

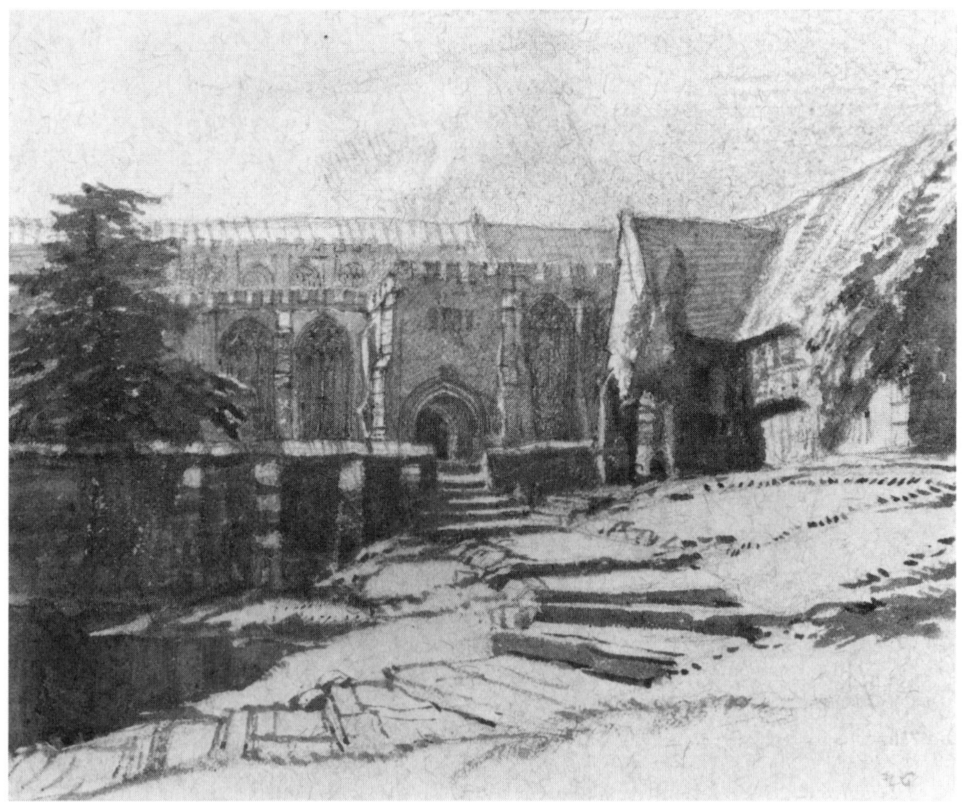

Figure 7.19 Frederick Landseer Maur Griggs (English, 1876–1938). *Sellenger, Church, and Church House*, 1917. Indian ink wash over graphite pencil on paper. Sheet: 14.1 × 16.8 cm ($5\frac{9}{16} \times 6\frac{5}{8}$ inches). *Source:* Photograph © 2004 Museum of Fine Arts, Boston. William A. Sargent Fund (47.1315)

better activate the compositional role of negative areas. Sometimes, a drawing's main compositional strategy has to do with the experience of space, as in Figure 7.19, where we are led up a gently curved, rising slope of worn steps and into the church.

The matter of suggesting a form's weight, sometimes overlooked, is an important representational as well as compositional issue in drawing. A possibly apocryphal comment attributed to the French artist Edgar Degas is that he had grown weary of walking through the Louvre, looking at paintings . . . "of knights in paper armor under lead clouds." Achieving the feel of a form's weight in a drawing has at least as much to do with "becoming" the form, that is, with experiencing its weight, as with seeing its structure. Identifying with the things you draw effects the way you show them. A feather requires a different touch than does a hammer.

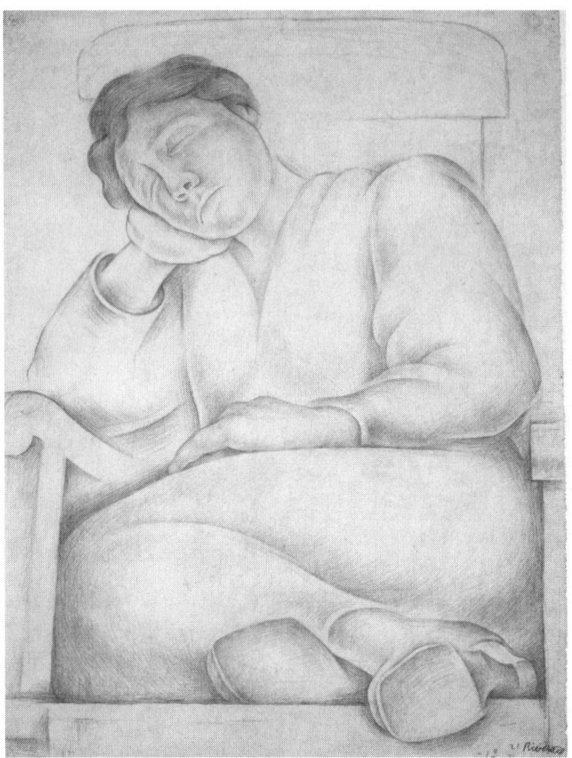

Figure 7.20 Diego Rivera (Guanajuato, Mexico 1886–1957, Mexico City). *Study of a Sleeping Woman*, 1921. Black crayon on off-white laid paper (62.7 cm. × 46.9 cm.). (1965.436) Courtesy of the Fogg Art Museum, Harvard University Art Museums. Bequest of Meta and Paul J. Sachs. Photo Credit: David Matthews. © 2004 President and Fellows of Harvard College.

The distribution of volumes in drawing has strong compositional consequences. Two-dimensionally, an imbalance in a drawing's picture plane is likely if it is loaded down with weighty forms far to one side or the other, upsetting the drawing's equilibrium in the same way a seesaw will tilt down on the side bearing the most weight.

Arranging masses within the three-dimensional "stage" of a drawing's spatial field of depth also plays an important role in establishing compositional order. Sometimes, as in Figure 7.20, the field of depth is quite shallow. Yet note how Rivera balances the forward thrust of the armrest on the drawing's left with the woman's shoe, on the right. The artist takes us into the spatial field in a series of steps: the advancing shoe, the lower leg, the upper leg, the woman's left arm, and

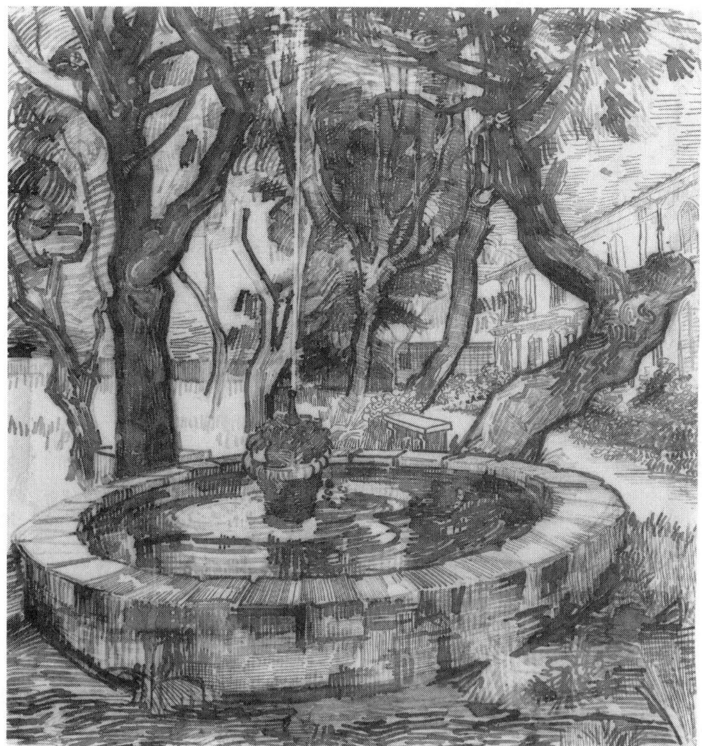

Figure 7.21 Vincent Van Gogh (1853–1890), *The Fountain in the Garden of St. Paul's Hospital at Saint-Remy.* Black chalk, pen, reed pen & China ink on paper, 45 × 48 cm. *Source:* Amsterdam, Van Gogh Museum (Vincent van Gogh Foundation).

her torso. The head gains importance by coming forward, over the figure's "staircase," and by its weight, in need of support by the woman's right arm, which starts another series of steps going back into the spatial field. Note, too, how the distribution of these weighty volumes across the picture plane provides the drawing's seesaw equilibrium, referred to above.

Sensitivity to the arrangements of forms in a spatial field is often evident in drawings showing a deeper spatial cavity, especially when the drawing is carried out to the limits of the page, as in Figures 7.19 and Figure 7.21. However, in the case of preparatory studies, especially of the figure, or of objects or places an artist wishes to explore visually, such compositional matters are often dealt with in a rudimentary way. But even then the configuration of the image is usually balanced on the page. Very often, these studies do not extend to the boundaries of the page (see Figure 7.10), and may show little or no background, as in Figure 7.22.

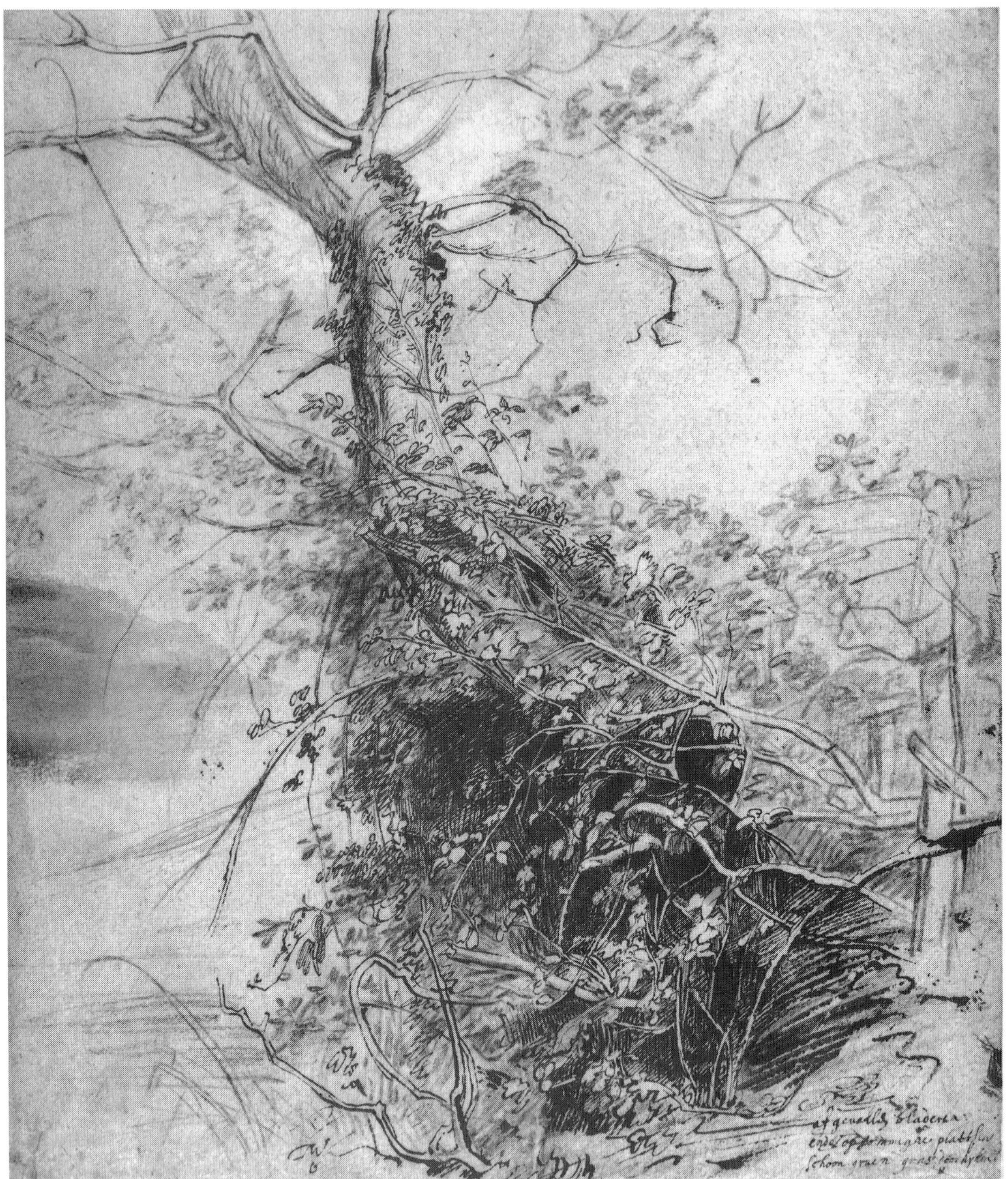

Figure 7.22 Peter Paul Rubens (1577–1640), *Tree with Brambles.* *Source:* The Devonshire Collection, Chatsworth. Reproduced by permission of the Duke of Devonshire and the Chatsworth Settlement Trustees. Photograph: Photographic Survey, Courtauld Institute of Art.

Color

A color's hue, value, intensity, and temperature are critical to composition and expression. A wrong note of color, whether it is off in value, brilliance, temperature, or hue can intrude on a drawing's balance and unity, as well as on its expression. It can isolate a part, rob the part of needed clarity or emphasis, or call too much attention to it.

How the values of parts relate in black and white and how colors cause these parts to form new connections and contrasts can be seen in Plate 15. Note that the values in the two color versions are the same as those in the black and white version. As this illustration shows, color's compositional role in forming relational ties is both versatile and powerful. Along with its role in clarifying volume and space, and in amplifying a drawing's expressive meanings, color is one of the most potent (and challenging) of the visual elements.

COMPOSITIONAL STRUCTURE

> ***In art, imbalance and disunity always intrude on both dynamic and depictive meanings.***

Having examined the visual elements for at least some of their compositional functions, you may have a better appreciation for the fact that the lines and tones you draw—and the shapes, textures, volumes, colors, and spaces they in turn create—have two "lives" in drawing. They exist as a depiction (whether of a representational, abstract, or nonobjective kind), and as an emotive dynamic system, that is, as an expressive order. They are both the *what* and the *how* of every drawing. It is through the mutually reinforcing effects of these two functions of the marks that your drawings will come alive.

All good drawings show some balanced and unified resolution among the elements—some cohesive and harmonious union of a drawing's content and form. For this to happen, artists must be sensitive to the relational play and the visual energies generated between the elements, for every line and tone drawn releases visual energy of some kind and relates with other lines and tones in some way.

Consider balance and unity. Earlier, we described balance as the result of an arrangement among the elements that achieve a state of equilibrium. For this balanced state to occur, every directional thrust must be countered, every weight, counterweighted, and every element engaged with a number of other like and unlike elements in various kinds of interdependent activity. A well-balanced drawing reveals a self-governing cycle of visual activity. These interacting activities also help, through their bonds of association and interdependence, to give a drawing that sense of oneness, or unity. Because an image cannot be unified if it is unbalanced, nor balanced if it is not unified, these two qualities cannot be fully disentangled. But their resolution in a drawing is vital because without balance and unity a work's intended expression is seriously diminished. In art, imbalance and disunity always intrude on both dynamic and depictive meanings.

These compositional states, however, do not come about only from the union of similarities. In fact, where everything in a drawing is overbearingly connected or too much alike, the results will be dull. There is no variety of visual activities. A chessboard, for example, is certainly balanced and unified, but visually humdrum. Along with relationships based on similarities is the stimulating action of contrasts. In drawings where balance and unity are achieved despite daring contrasts, visual actions may skirt imbalance and disunity only to arrive at a sense of order and oneness that is all the more satisfying for the inventive risks taken. Good compositions always show an engaging variety among their parts.

Of course, contrasts, in the end, must belong to the whole of the drawing in some way. For example, in Rodin's *Standing Nude* (Figure 7.23), the scribbled handling of the figure's drape is in strong contrast with the liquid treatment of the figure itself. But closer inspection reveals that the shape of the drape's lower portion is an inverted "copy" of the shape of the woman's legs. Additionally, this portion of the drape, along with the upper, more lightly drawn portion, acts as do parentheses, which, by their position, texture, and airiness emphasize the figure's supple and weighty forms. Visual relationships, then, not only join parts of a drawing together, but by placing some parts in opposition to others, create groupings, patterns, and variety.

Additionally, in well-composed drawings the relationships show a hierarchy of visual importance. That is, the artist emphasizes one or two kinds of visual activity, relying on them to carry the main responsibility for forming the drawing's expressive order. Other kinds of relationships will then serve lesser but still important roles, such as providing variety to the image or creating various depictive or dynamic effects not otherwise possible. For example, in Figure 7.24, the "starburst" of limbs and adjacent forms and tones, as well as a page-enveloping cross, made up of the two figures, the bench, and the pillar, are two major visual themes. The periodic appearance of black lines, hatchings, and gentle washes of tone, and an overall encircling pattern, are minor themes.

Were it not for a hierarchy of such relational activities, every visual theme in a drawing would be clamoring for attention, to the detriment of balance and unity, and to the drawing's expressive purpose. It is the hierarchy of these visual themes that give a drawing its main dynamic character.

To better appreciate how visual relationships and themes at work in our drawings may achieve a balanced and unified state, we must first examine briefly some

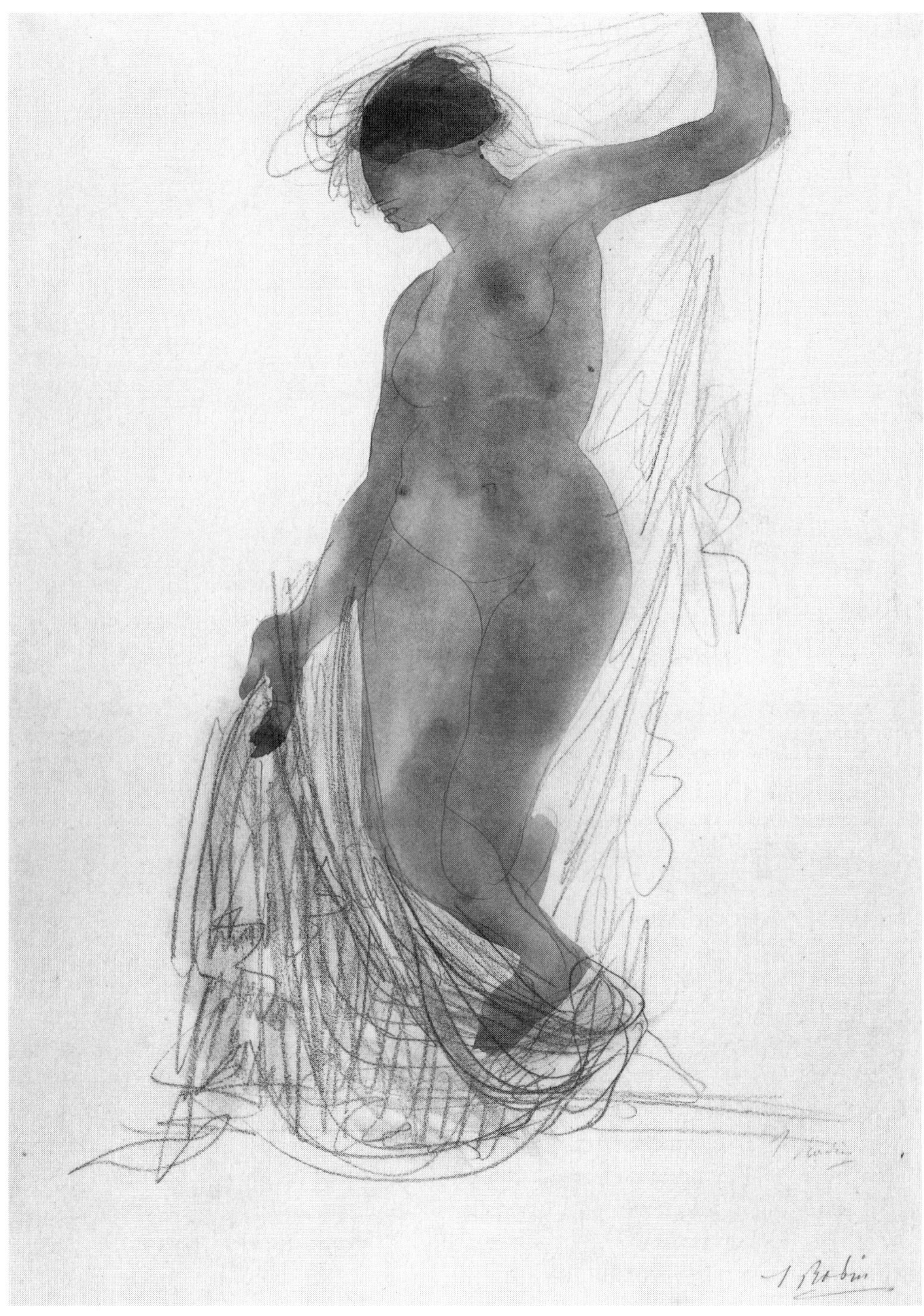

Figure 7.23 Auguste Rodin (French, 1840–1917), *Standing Nude with Draperies*, c. 1900–05. Watercolor and graphite on ivory wove paper, 44.5 × 31.5 cm. *Source:* Alfred Stieglitz Collection (1949.900). Reproduction, The Art Institute of Chicago.

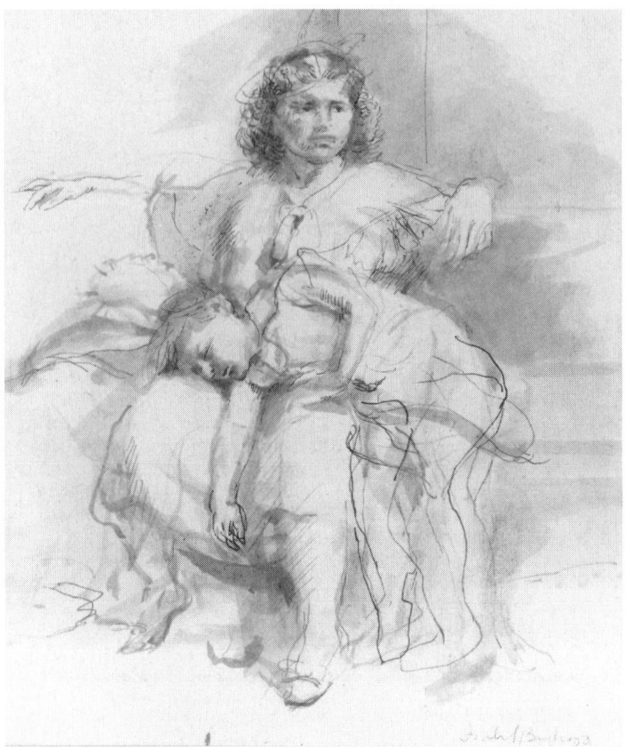

Figure 7.24 Isabel Bishop (1902–1988), *Waiting*, 1935. Ink on paper, $7\frac{1}{8} \times 6$ inches. (18.1×15.2 cm.). Private Collection. Courtesy DC Moore Gallery, NYC. Photograph Copyright © 1997, Whitney Museum of American Art, New York. Purchase 36.31.

general categories of visual relationships. These categories are really more convenient than defensible, because any attempt to clarify visual relationships invariably fails to account for some phenomena too ineffable or illusive to be articulated. However, discussing those that can be described may help to apprehend those that cannot. As we examine the following kinds of relational play among the elements, remember that the term *element* refers to any visual notation—from a line, a smudge of tone, or a shape—to a surface plane, a texture, or a volume.

All elements engage in several relationships at the same time. A single line may be relating simultaneously with several other lines, planes, alignments, or volumes in connections and contrasts that will carry its kinship with them far across the pictorial field. The relational possibilities based on similarities and contrasts among the elements are limitless. In the best drawings, their dynamic activities are capable of endless interactions.

Most visual relationships generate energies that suggest movement or a striving for movement. A sensitivity to implications of movement, or to any kind of motion, weight, or change, is not only at the heart of what guides the artist toward compositional balance and unity, it is also a matter of vital concern to each of us as we live our lives from day to day. We instinctively react to real or imminent motion or change because such activity may spell either danger or opportunity. (Is that crouching animal about to leap this way? Is the child's hand moving toward mine?) So deeply engrained is this response that even the illusion of motion or change in a drawing holds our attention. In artists, this sensitivity is highly developed. Their functional "survival" eye, merging with their relational eye, helps them to see even subtle inferences of action. We respond to implications of movement with interests that have deep roots in our psyches.

Differing degrees of action can be sensed through the artist's *handling*, that is, through the the vigorous, deliberate, or other manner by which the drawing's marks are made. In Figure 7.25, some lines move quickly, as do those in the woman's right

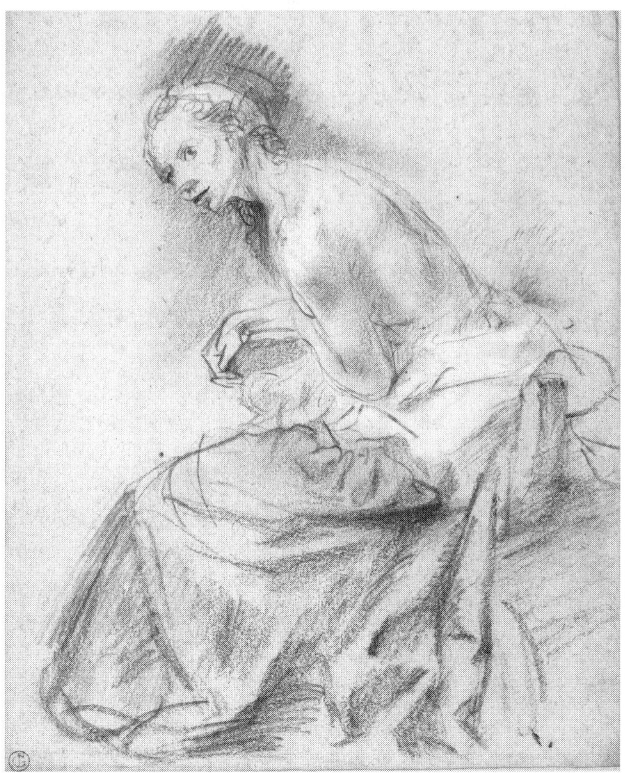

Figure 7.25 Rembrandt Harmenszoon van Rijn (Dutch, 1606–1669). *Study for the Figure of Susanna*, 1647. Black and white chalk, 20.3 × 16.4 cm. (inv. KdZ 5264) *Source:* Photo: Joerg P. Anders. Photograph © Bildarchiv Preussischer Kulturbesitz/Art Resource, NY.

hand, and, here and there, in her skirt. Other lines, such as those of the left arm's contour and along the figure's torso, move more slowly. Likewise, compare the "speed" of the broadly noted tones of the skirt with the more delicate application of tones on the woman's left arm and back. Shapes, too, convey their particular energy according to their configuration. The oval, for example, suggests a leisurely motion, but the wedge always races after its own point.

Many visual energies are generated between like elements. Consciously or not, we tend to compare lines with other lines, shapes with other shapes, and so on. The more there are of such elements showing moving energies of various kinds, the stronger are the actions produced. For example, in Figure 7.25, note the more energetic feel of the woman's skirt, as many fast moving hatched lines and gestural contours animate that form. They take on even more force when we contrast them with the more precise line drawing of the upper body. A similar situation exists among the values, which also show more animated energy in the skirt than in the upper body.

Of course, other energy-producing relationships occur between unlike elements. A figure's leg, a calligraphic line, and a wash of dark tone might all relate if the artist were to emphasize their common S-shaped movement. The tilt of the woman's arm in Figure 7.25, repeated by the tilt of the lower torso and the line (seen through the skirt) that reveals the woman's lower leg all gain strength by their common direction.

Some kinds of relational energy, such as visual weight, physical weight, or tension (to be discussed) suggest that movement is imminent or inevitable rather than occurring. But the visual elements of line, shape, value, volume, and color and the dynamics of direction, rhythm, and handling create the strongest kinds of moving actions.

Direction

> ***If a few directed actions could be regarded as a rhythmic breeze, twenty or thirty of them is a windstorm.***

We sense a directed action when one or more like or unlike elements move on a straight or curved path toward an intended point on or beyond the picture plane, or move forward or backward in a spatial field of depth. The use of many long lines, edges, or alignments make for stronger motion than will fewer, shorter ones. The same holds true for shapes (whether as planes or interspaces), and for values and volumes: the more there are of them, the larger they are in the drawing's format, and the longer their centerlines—the more forceful will be their directional movement in the composition.

Only shapes, values, or volumes of a circular or squarelike configuration, or whose form does not plainly show a long axis, are more or less free of directed movement, except as they join up with other elements to align in a directed action of some kind—for example, the pearls in a necklace that form a sweeping arc. Blurred elements move faster than focused ones, and the directed force of any element can be slowed or checked altogether by other elements that intersect or overlap part of it.

Drawings may show little or no textural activity, value, or even volume. Their imagery may be sparse or dense. But no drawing is conceivable without some directed movement. Every mark (and the shapes, tones, and volumes they depict) releases a directed energy of some kind and the artist's task is to govern these energies in ways that will organize the image and have it communicate the artist's intended meanings.

Rhythm

A directed movement, a texture, the size and character of a shape, or a degree of tonal change, when these are recurrent in a work, are some of the ways that produce rhythm, an intensifier of direction. Rhythm is most easily observed in the repetition of similarly directed movements among lines, shapes, planes, or volumes. If a few directed actions could be regarded as a rhythmic breeze, twenty or thirty of them is a windstorm. The hatched lines in a structural drawing or the tree branches and rolling hills in a landscape drawing—these and many other rhythmic occurrences add to a drawing's vitality and power.

Handling

As noted earlier, the artist's handling, the forceful, delicate, or other manner of mark-making has organizational and expressive meaning. The stylistic and idiosyncratic accents and cadences of lines, tones, and shapes, appearing everywhere in a drawing, will provide at least some degree of unity. Handling can be thought of as a kind of handwriting. And like your handwriting, the deliberate, playful, or boisterous nature of the handling is an insight to the artist's sense of order and temperament.

Partly a matter of neuromuscular coordination and partly a matter of emotional and creative disposition, the artist's handling produces a kind of visual meter that sets up a certain pace among the elements that affects the way we read the resulting image. Handling is always influenced by the medium and the tools used in drawing. These materials not only affect the nature of the marks made, but, because each medium has its particular traits and limits, they even influence the kinds of observations that artists make. You would not draw a tree or a waterfall using pen and ink in the same way you would draw those subjects using charcoal.

Some artists do change the handling in one part of a drawing from the handling in another part, but when they do, the change is usually gradual or integrated in the composition. Both of these tactics are employed in Figure 7.26, where the more spontaneous and generalized treatment of the background is seen in the first two heads on the left in the foreground. Even the third head shows some surviving, sketchy handling. Note that despite the more tonal and fully developed forms in the foreground, the artist retains a few white shapes, to integrate these with the many sparkling whites of the background, and that the domes in the background echo the rounded hats in the foreground.

Although handling is something to think about and examine in the works of other artists, it is best left to emerge in a more natural way in your drawings.

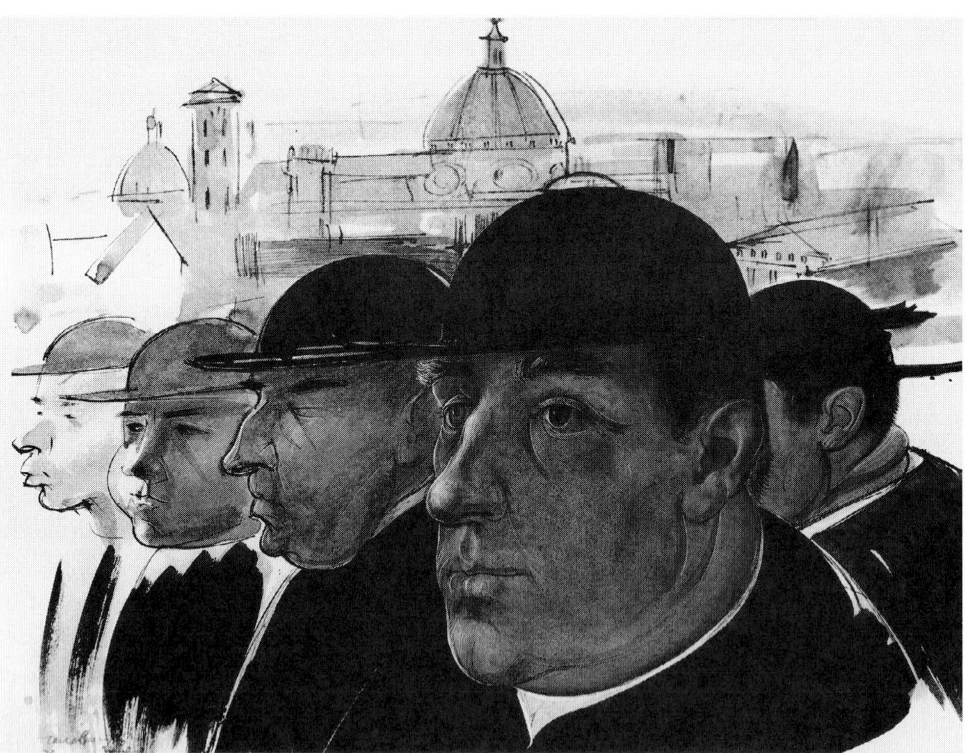

Figure 7.26 Ture Bengtz, *Priests, Florence*, pen and wash, ca. 1961. Courtesy of the Boston Public Library, Print Department.

You should concentrate on analyzing and identifying with the subject before you, rather than to try for adopted effects. As with your handwriting, which developed the manner needed to accommodate your temperament and motor control without your thinking about it, handling is best formed as a natural response to these same conditions.

Proximity

Like or unlike elements will relate according to their position on the picture plane or within a field of depth (Figures 7.27 and 7.19). Notice how, in Griggs's drawing, the dark, conical shape of the tree on the far left relates with the similarly shaped and toned forms on the right side.

Elements will also relate by being in clusters if the elements surrounding them are plainly different (Figures 7.28 and 4.27). Of course, we understand the parts making up Moreau's sleeping child to belong together, but our concentration on the child is intensified by the "simpler" and larger elements that encircle her. In fact, at the only place where the surrounding lines, shapes, and tones grow smaller (where the bedding comes up against the child), it is less clear where the child ends and the bedding begins. For seasoned artists, matters having to do with the location or the density of the elements are not random occurrences but important compositional considerations.

Figure 7.27

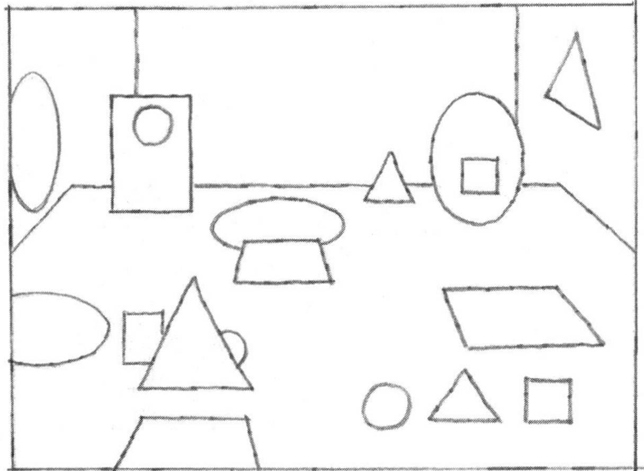

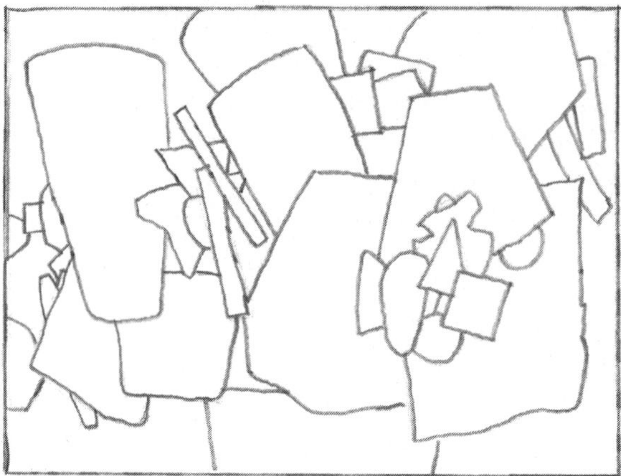

Figure 7.28

Visual and Physical Weight

The term *visual weight* refers to an element's ability to attract our attention by its directed action (usually on the picture plane), by its eye-appeal (usually due to its contrasting scale, value, or shape with other elements in the work), or by both. Physical weight, as we saw, has to do with our prior knowledge regarding the actual weight of forms. We know that rocks are heavy and feathers light, and that has compositional meaning as we try to balance a drawing's parts.

Some directional and eye-appealing aspects of visual weight are demonstrated in Figure 7.29. Here, the darker shapes "call" to us more insistently because of their directional movement and their contrast with neighboring shapes. In doing so, they take on a role in balancing the drawing. For example, in Figure 7.29, the dark cluster of forms in the lower left attracts our attention by its collective dark tone and by its diagonal orientation, which starts us on the road to the mountain's pinnacle. And this visual weight is important to the drawing's balance, which would otherwise be too heavy on the right side. Note, too, that while the physical weight of the mountain presses downward, its visual weight takes us upward as we experience the last turn of a picture-enveloping, reversed letter S, that begins in the drawing's lower left corner and proceeds up the ramp to the mountain. Unlike physical weight, which always presses downward, visual weight, although it often does press downward, can be exerted in any direction.

Be it a line, shape, mass, or texture, all the elements possess some degree of visual weight, that is, some degree of eye-appeal that has compositional significance.

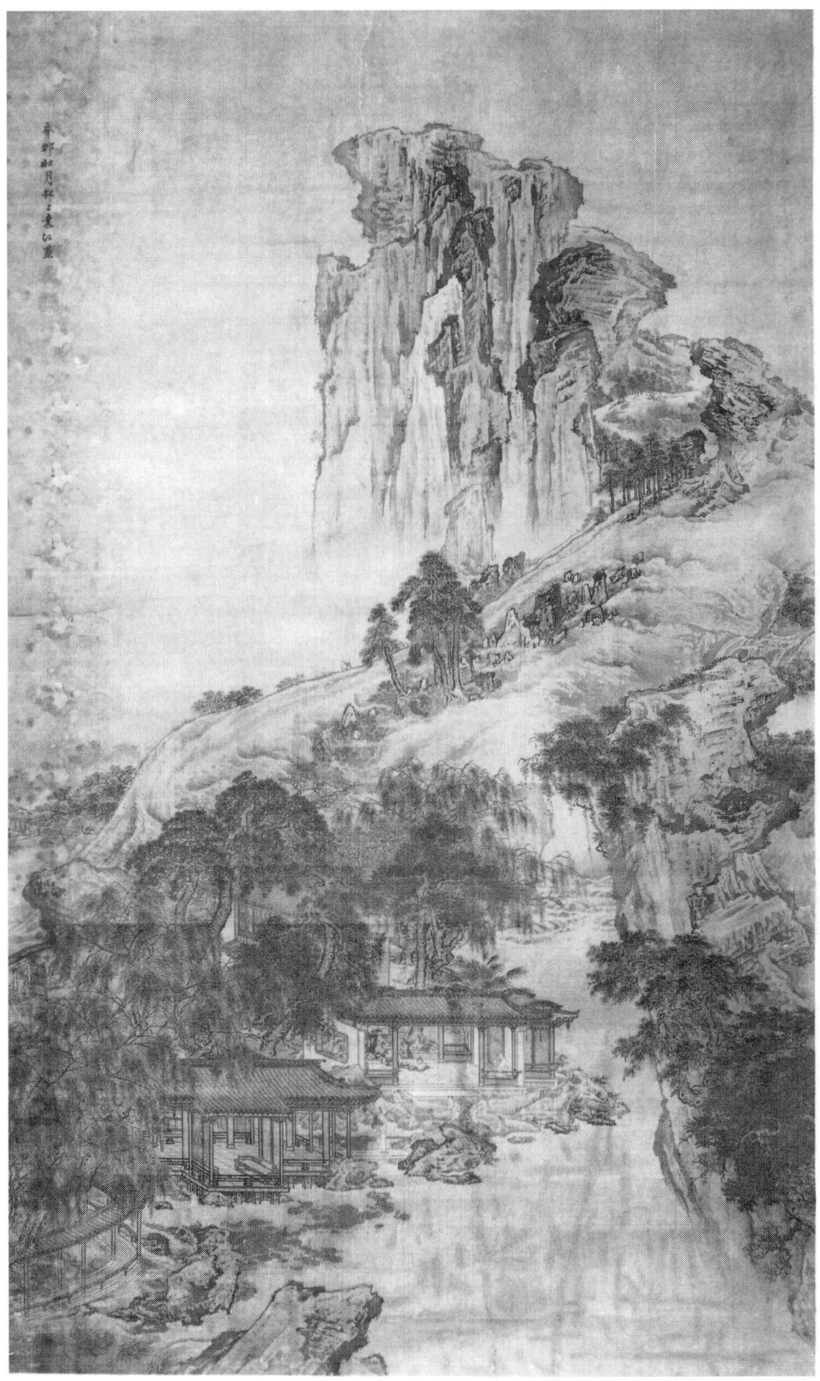

Figure 7.29 Yuan Jiang (Chinese, Qing, 18th century), *Landscape*. Object Place: China. Hanging scroll; ink and color on silk, 233.4 × 137.3 cm ($91\frac{7}{8} \times 54\frac{1}{16}$ inches).
Source: Photograph © 2004 Museum of Fine Arts, Boston. Gift of Edward Jackon Holmes (29.1156).

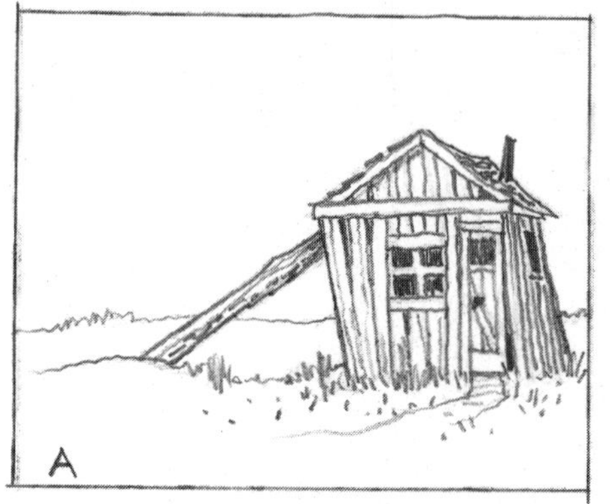

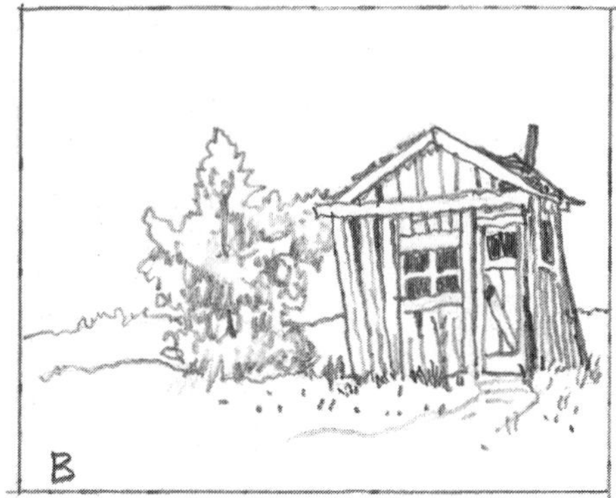

Figure 7.30

But because representational drawing has to do with a more or less objective account of what is actually seen, it is often the case that many of the things we see possess both physical and visual weight and need to be brought into balance. In representational drawing, our understanding of a part's small or great weight, rigidity, or pliancy, and it's living or inert nature, is both a challenge and an opportunity for expression often dismissed by some abstract approaches to drawing.

For example, we understand that the considerable weight of the old, left-leaning shack in Figure 7.30A can be held in check by the sturdy, right-leaning beam. The problem of the subject's physical weight has been solved. But the shack's visual weight plainly overtakes that of the beam, making the drawing too heavy on the right. If, to correct matters, we replace the beam with a large bush, the problem of the subject's visual weight is solved, but because a bush can't hold up a shack, the physical weight imbalance is back (Figure 7.30B). What to do? One solution is to show the bush behind the beam. Another is to show the beam as nearly black and to keep the values of the shack quite light in tone. There are other solutions (especially if color is being used). But however the problem is solved the completed drawing must achieve both physical and visual balance.

Both physical and visual weight can be increased or decreased, according to the nature of the elements adjacent to what is being changed in weight. For example, if, in Figure 7.30A, the value of the sky is made darker behind the beam, two things happen: the presence of a large dark tone on the drawing's left side increases visual weight on that side, and the contrast between the value of the sky and the beam is increased, adding to both the visual weight and physical weight on the left side.

Thiebaud, in Figure 7.31, integrates physical and visual weight in a way that gives the viewer two equally appealing "readings". No sooner do we see the volume

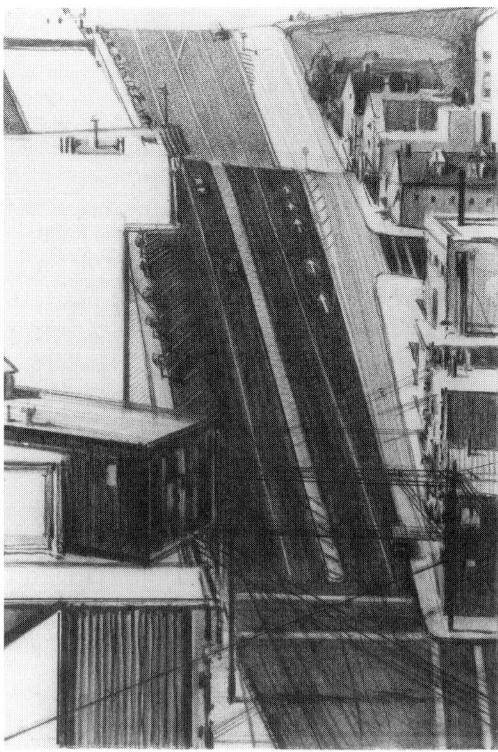

Figure 7.31 Wayne Thiebaud, *Down 18th Street (Potrero Hill)*, 1974. Charcoal on paper, $22\frac{3}{8} \times 14\frac{7}{8}$ inches. Photo courtesy of the Allan Stone Gallery, New York City.

and space of the buildings and the rising road than our attention is called to the angular shapes tones and of textures that subdivide the page. These readings continue to alternate, giving us the feeling that we are looking down on this urban scene one moment and the feeling of the speedy and impersonal city scene that such harsh shapes and angles suggest.

Because visual and physical weight are always given conditions in the things we see, their balanced and unified resolution in any drawing is a challenge that must be met and resolved. Mere accuracy does not address the expressive order that is possible and necessary when a subject made of real mass and existing in real space enters the two-dimensional realm of the page.

Tension

As used here, the term *tension* defines the sense of elements or parts of a single element striving to join, clash with, or repel each other—or striving to alter their location or shape. When two or more elements or parts of the same element are so arranged as to almost touch, we feel them striving to complete the union, as in

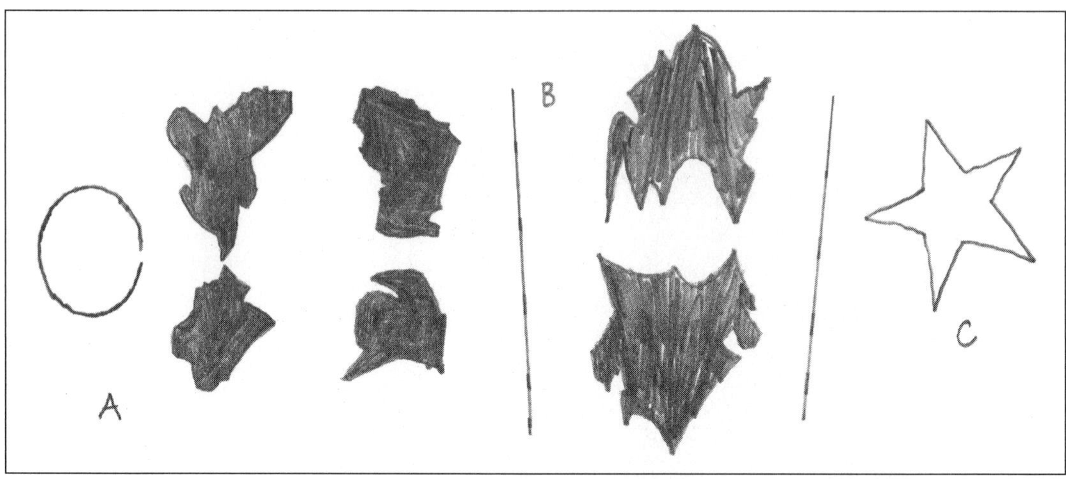

Figure 7.32

Figure 7.32A. Here, two of the four toned shapes seem to want to join together, as do the ends of the C-shaped line. But when elements confront each other in roughly equal force, they sometimes appear to challenge each other for dominance, as in the "standoff" between the two closely placed shapes and the two shapes on the right side in Figure 7.32A. But elements can also appear to repulse each other, to strive for more space between them, as in Figure 7.32B. Similarly, the five or six triangles of a star shape strive to pull away from their common center, each moving in the direction it points to, while their common center holds them together (Figure 7.32C).

The elements engaged in a tensional situation of any kind suggest a charged field of energy between them; they seem aware of each other. It is as if such lines, shapes, textures, values, or volumes contend with each other for supremacy or for a better resolution of the energies existing between them. Figure 7.33 illustrates a few tensional situations. In drawing A, some aggressive lines threaten a passive shape. Their closeness creates a tension called *closure*, a state in which elements, while not actually touching, are so close that they are seen as touching or as needing to touch. Seeing such an arrangement we wish for them to meet or to have more space between them, but find this degree of closeness creates ambiguity and visual tension.

Yet, closure sometimes adds attention and clarity to a passage. In Figure 7.34, the contour of the woman's left side stops just short of its meeting with the right upper arm, allowing the arm to more freely pass ahead of the torso. But it is our response to the closure phenomenon that tells us the contour line will continue. Similarly, a few of the lines of the seat stop to allow the right leg to move convincingly

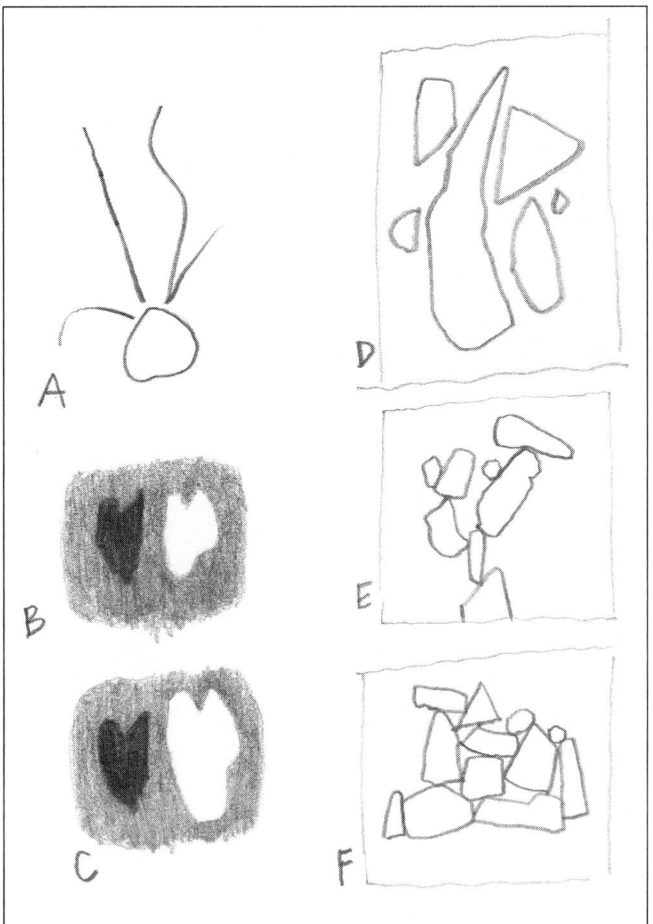

Figure 7.33

more forward. Interestingly, Matisse originally drew the mirror image of the model as touching the model herself, at the shoulder. But note that he erased some lines to allow the figure's forms to come ahead of those in the mirror, but he left enough space to avoid the feeling of closure. In other areas Matisse lets lines move through forms, again to avoid closure.

Some artists favor high tension images. In drawing B of Figure 7.33 there is a high degree of tension between the white and black shapes, played out upon the more passive shape of gray. Tonally, the white and black shape are opposites, the gray background favors neither one, the shapes are about the same in size, and they are somewhat similar in configuration. They appear to be sparring for advantage, or about to move in some way to end the impasse. In drawing C there has been a

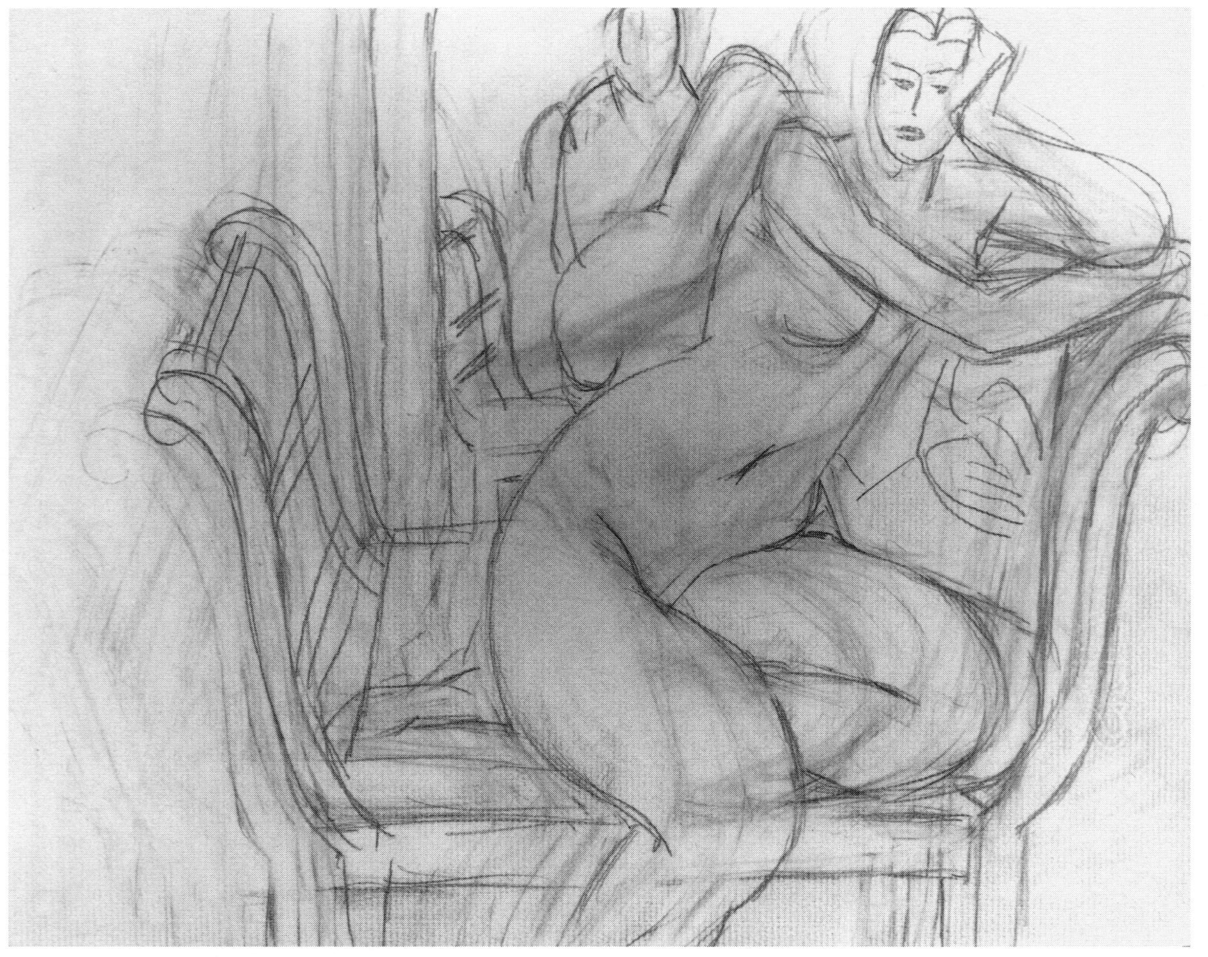

Figure 7.34 Henri Matisse (French, 1869–1954), *Artist and Model Before a Mirror.* Pencil on paper, $9\frac{3}{4} \times 12\frac{3}{4}$ inches. *Source:* Arkansas Arts Center Foundation Purchase: Fred W. Allsopp Memorial Acquisition Fund, 1984. (1984.018.001) © 2005 succession H. Mastisse, Paris/Artists Rights Society (ARS), New York.

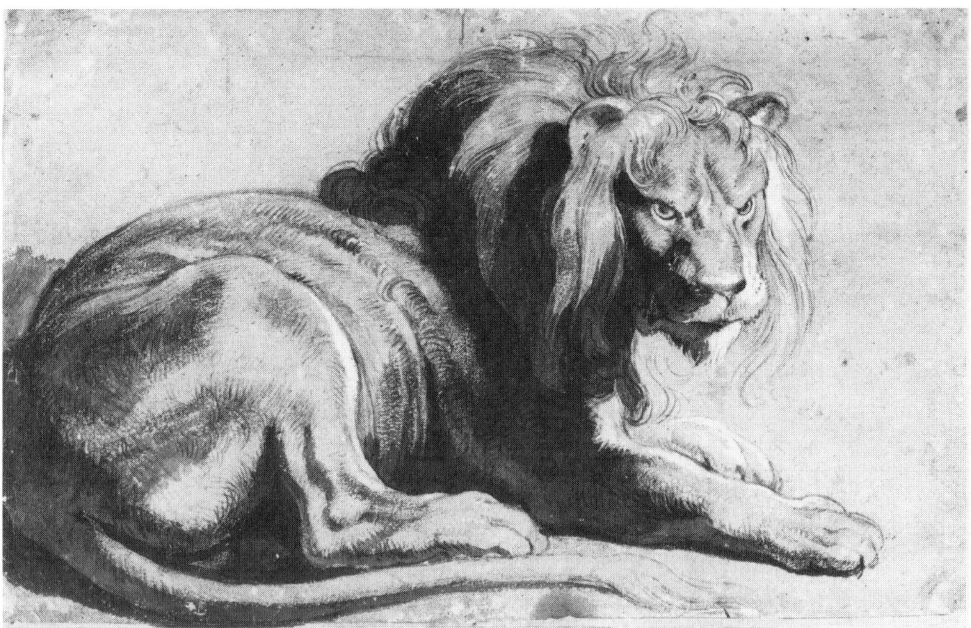

Figure 7.35 Peter Paul Rubens (Flemish, 1577–1640), *Study of a Lion*. *Source:* © Copyright The British Museum.

change, making the white shape dominant, and there is a lessening of tension. Similar strong tensional behavior of tonal shapes is seen in Rubens's *Study of a Lion* (Figure 7.35). Here, light and dark shapes (as in the mane) make deep penetrations into each other's "territory," animating what might have been a more placid drawing, with powerful thrusts and tensions that echo the nature of the animal itself.

Drawing D of Figure 7.33 shows that elements can also express a striving to repel each other, or at least to avoid combat. This is seen in Figure 7.34, where the armrests (including the one in the mirror image) "stand aside" to allow the S-shaped curve of the model to dominate. Only at the far right side do the figure's arms and the armrest join to create a large pattern that reaches from the model's right shoulder to her left knee. Again, in Figure 7.35, we feel the lion's rear leg stops to "allow" the right foreleg to come forward in a more dramatic manner. Rubens achieves this in two ways: first, by entrapping the rear leg in dark-toned shapes that are in a tensional confrontation with the lightly drawn leg, slowing down its directed movement; and, second, by speeding up the moving energy of the right foreleg with a rush of dark tones that begin in the lion's mane and run along the leg, urging it forward.

Artists use tensions to animate and compose their imagery. But however daring such confrontations are, they must find some eventual union and balance. In drawing E of Figure 7.33 the several shapes that compose the drawing are balanced

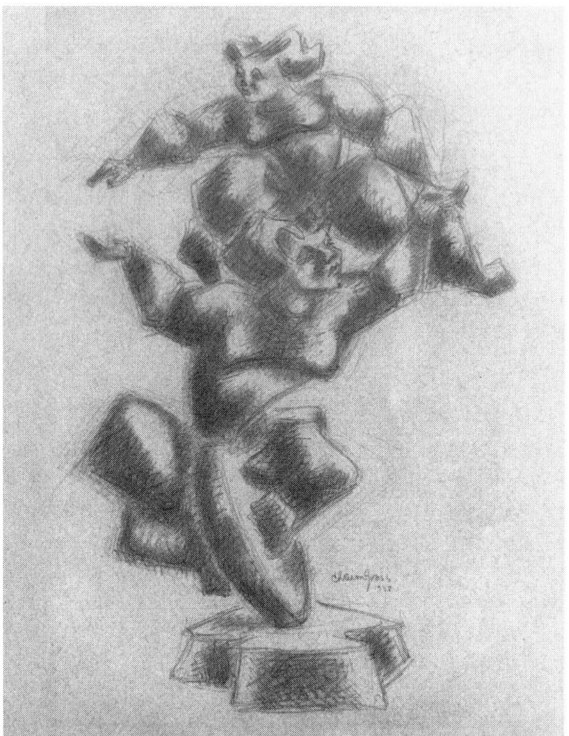

Figure 7.36 Chiam Gross (1904–1991), *The Unicyclist*, 1938. Graphite on paper, $24\frac{13}{16} \times 17\frac{3}{8}$ inches (63 × 44.1 cm.). *Source:* Collection of Whitney Museum of American Art, New York. Gift of Mr. and Mrs. Benjamin Weiss (78.36).

but arranged in a way that creates considerable tension—we wonder if they will "hold." But some artists find such high-tension images desirable, as in Figure 7.35, or in Feininger's charcoal drawing (Figure 7.6). Other artists favor less tension-filled images, as in drawing F of Figure 7.33, or Figure 7.34.

Gross's The *Unicyclist* (Figure 7.36) shows something of the "balancing act" found in drawings E. Note that you need a little time to experience the tension-filled standoffs and tilts in order to find the drawing's overall balance and unity. Note, too, that in doing so you are responding to both visual and physical weight conditions in the drawing.

In considering the relational dynamics that animate and organize your drawings, it is important to recognize that your creative, expressive eye and your intellectual, analytical eye must join forces. Choice, feeling, judgment, and intuition all need to negotiate a drawing's final form and content. In the best drawings, we sense the artist's awareness of the "two lives" that visual works embody—the "what" and the "how."

Some Compositional Exercises

1. Using Figures 7.6 and 7.13 as rough guides, compose a drawing that relies on alignments and distributions of both line and value to achieve balance and unity.
2. As in Plates 6 and 11, where color and value are used to create a mood, make a drawing in any color media in which these two visual elements are the dominant means for establishing the composition.
3. Using Figure 7.22 as a rough guide, make an out-of-doors drawing that stops short of the boundaries of the page but is balanced on the page. As in Rubens's drawing, where a strong center of attention gradually trials off into the page, your drawing should likewise have a dense, compressed area that "releases" moving energies into the page.
4. Compose a drawing in which balance is achieved by countering physical weight with visual weight.
5. Compose a drawing that integrates shape-dominated areas with areas in which volumes dominate, as in Figures 5.10 and 7.26.
6. With Figures 7.10 and 7.11 as general guides, compose a drawing in which line and shape are dominant but strongly suggest volume and space.

Things to Think About

1. What are some of the ways by which a visual weight may counter a physical weight?
2. Can a drawing of a single object such as a green pepper or a shoe be compositionally successful if it is the only form on the page? If it can, how would you go about it? If not, why not?
3. How important is the two-dimensional composition of the forms in a highly realistic drawing?
4. What is meant by the *what* and the *how* of drawing?
5. Why are various kinds of contrasting visual activities desirable in drawing?
6. Can you give some examples of visual tensions?
7. How do the terms *direction* and *rhythm* differ?
8. How may *handling* contribute to a drawing's unity?

Critique Considerations

1. Do some of your drawings appear to be heavily weighted to one side of the page? If so, is it the result of physical weight, visual weight, or both? If it is physical weight, consider locating your subject's parts on

the page where there will be a better distribution of weight to the left and right of an imagined vertical centerline. If it is visual weight, check to see if it results from the alignment of parts, from a common value among a group of parts, from a strong directed motion, or from one or more strong contrasts. If both kinds of weight are at fault, you need to anticipate their behavior at the outset of a drawing and plan a composition that avoids both problems. It may also mean that your concentration is exclusively on a drawing's depiction, with little or no regard for the dynamic energies inherent in the depiction. You may be concentrating too much on the "what" and not enough on the "how" in your drawings.

2. Do some of your drawings seem unbalanced because of powerful diagonal movements? Consider that the diagonal arrangement of parts in a square or rectangular format will always generate very strong directed thrusts. Such diagonal movements will be even stronger if they run from one corner to another. Diagonal movements are often required in a work, but need to be cancelled out by some counter movements to regain equilibrium. That can be achieved by value, texture, and color (where present), or by linking up diagonal thrusts with movements running in other directions that turn diagonals back onto the picture plane.

3. Do some of your drawings seem too crowded for the format? Is there a feeling of compression—even of claustrophobia? This is sometimes due to the absence of "rest areas" among or around the drawing's forms. That is, areas of more open space that keep the image from looking as if it were packed into a container too small to accommodate it. This is a more common occurrence in drawings of the figure or of the head.

4. In your landscape drawings, is the shallow or deep space between the foreground and background clearly defined? If the middleground is unclear about its depth, its surface-structure, or the volumes in it, this will be detrimental to the drawing's composition because of an inconsistency in the way form and space is expressed and because the design of the forms in space will be uncertain.

8

Seeing with the Mind's Eye

DRAWING FROM IMAGINATION

Up to now this book has emphasized the options, challenges, and general drawing processes that come into play when artists draw, in a more or less objective way, the subjects actually before them. We considered the need for measurement, gesture, structural analysis, and perspective, to name some of the concepts and procedures important to creating drawings that strongly reflect the properties of an observed subject. In this chapter, however, we will explore the important matter of drawing subjects that you recall or imagine. What is changed when we draw what is not directly before us?

It may come as a surprise to some readers to know that drawing a subject from memory or imagination calls on virtually the same skills and procedures as when drawing "from life." Again, matters of measurement, gesture, perspective, and the rest of the material dealt with so far are at the heart of the drawing process. But how are these matters applied when no subject is present? In fact, *there is always a subject present.* Only now it appears on the screen of your imagination. Whether you are recalling or inventing people, places, or things, or whether you are "seeing" them in a realistic or more subjective way, there is at least a generalized image of the subject in your mind's eye. This image is often poorly lit, a little out of focus, and not very steady, but it is there. How to transfer it to the drawing surface is the subject of this chapter.

When a subject is actually in front of you, it significantly determines the drawing's theme and details. It is the stimulus to which you react. Of course, we always bring feelings and ideas to our drawings, which have little to do with the subject and which make our interpretation unique, but it is the subject, in all its substantial presence, that starts and influences the process. However, when the subject is on the murky screen of your imagination, it offers more in the way of generalities than specifics, and it is all too prone to change its forms or arrangement as you "watch." This requires you to be insistent and disciplined about keeping the image steadier in your mind's eye. And the more strongly you feel the expressive necessity for making the drawing, the steadier and clearer the imagined subject becomes, as does the compositional strategy for bringing the drawing into being. But speedily roughing in the envisioned subject's general form characteristics, its essential arrangement, and the spirit of its moving energies, that is, its *gesture* is even more important now then when a subject is actually present.

In fact, one of the key skills in drawing what you see in your mind's eye is the ability to take in the entire subject and set it down in gestural terms, as Rembrandt does in Figure 8.1. By establishing the composition's main sweep and grouping of the figures, as well as some general information that will help in drawing the figures, Rembrandt has securely fixed on the page most of the vital characteristics of the image in his mind.

It is often the case that your stored knowledge about the forms that you are imagining falls short of what you would like to include in a drawing. Unlike the generous supply of facts and details in subjects placed before you, the image in your mind's eye is always limited to your prior visual experiences. You cannot draw any form from imagination that you know only in a general way or not at all. For example, try drawing from your imagination an elephant seal or a monarch butterfly. But, because we can all call to mind a number of geometric volumes, it would be fairly easy to imagine and draw a block or a cylinder, shown from a number of different views, including quite foreshortened ones. However, changing the block into a bookcase or a cabin, and the cylinder into a layer cake or a leg makes it more difficult to show such forms in different positions because of their various structural features and details.

To draw these more complex forms your memory must have "on file" what their surface structures and details look like, and how they might appear from various angles. Very few of us can call up such information from our store of recollections. Even so, there is often a temptation to push the drawing forward based on such information as we do have. But that risks overusing our few remembered form solutions until they become cliches.

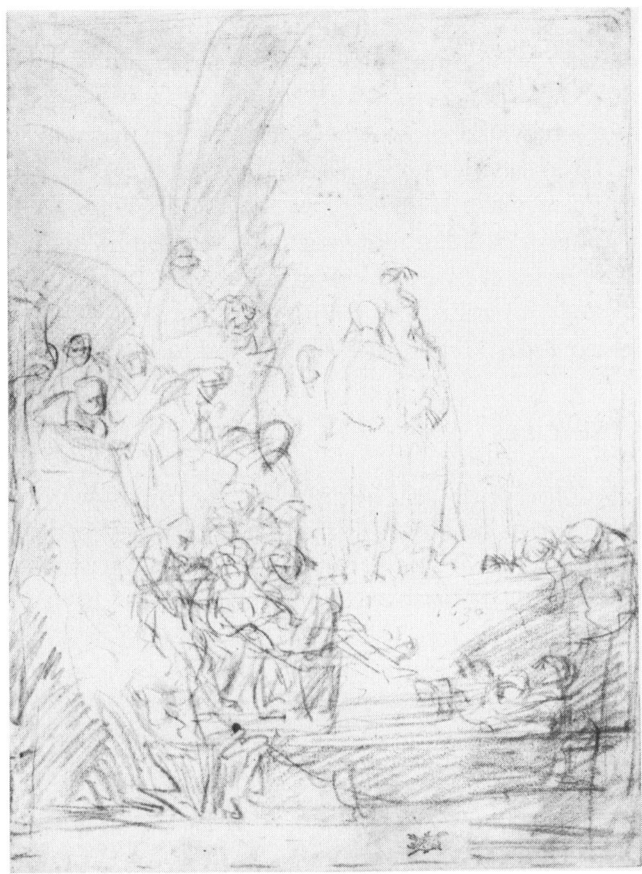

Figure 8.1 Rembrandt Van Rijn (Dutch, 1606–1669), *The Entombment of Christ.* 1630. Red chalk, heightened with white, 203 × 280 mm. *Source:* © Copyright The British Museum.

Improving the Ability to Draw the Forms in Our Mind's Eye

Our limited supply of stored knowledge about the structure of the forms that we choose to draw can't begin to match the rich variety that nature always provides. Furniture, fire engines, people, cats (and virtually everything else) all possess limitless variations of shape and structure, of which we can recall only a few.

To broaden your range of form options you need to research the imagined subjects you mean to draw. If the subject *is* to be cats, make many drawings of them from observation. Look at animal anatomy books. Study some sculptures of cats, and of tigers and leopards, too. Get to know your subject's form and nature better.

If your subject is to be something that doesn't actually exist, say, angels or dragons, find drawings, paintings, and sculptures of angels or dragons. Study the construction of bird wings or lizards. Look at works from all cultures and periods that have some bearing on your subject. Make some preparatory drawings that show your subject from several views. Doing so may pose questions and problems you'll want answers to before you begin to make your more declarative drawings: "Do I know enough about the way folds in clothing move over a figure?" or "What perspective issues apply if I show a worm's eye view of an angel or a dragon?" Some of these preparatory drawings should be made from paintings, sculptures, and the like, and some from your (now) expanded "repertoire" of facts and form solutions.

Some Envisioned Image Exercises

1. A good way to develop your skill at drawing the forms in your mind's eye is to start with forms about as simple as the block and the cylinder, modestly changing their appearance, until they grow more complex, as in Figure 8.2. In doing so, you may want to review the

Figure 8.2

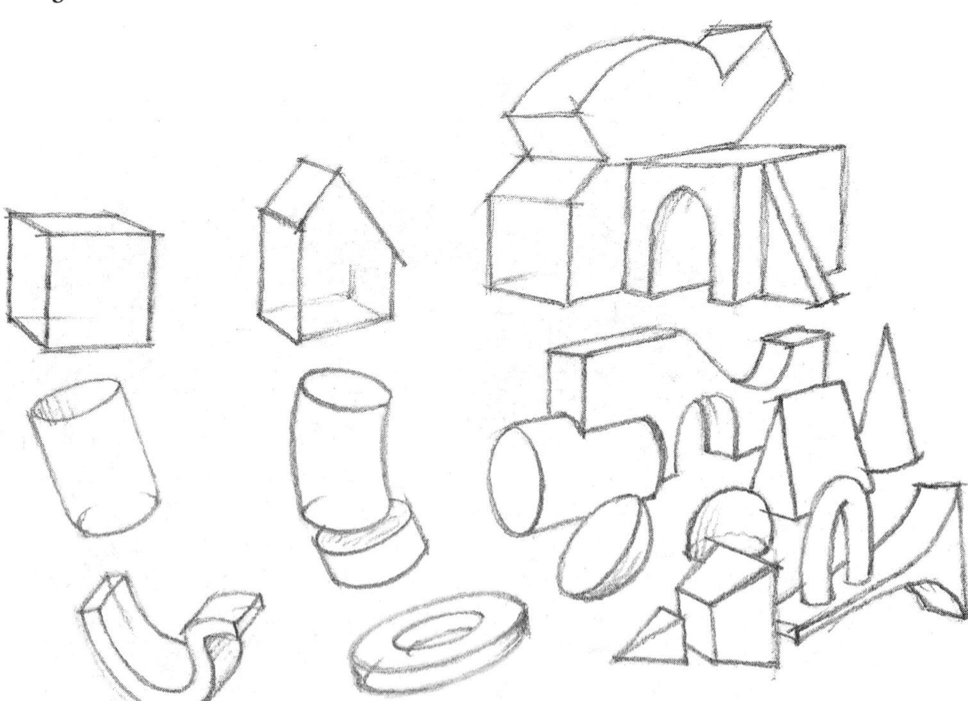

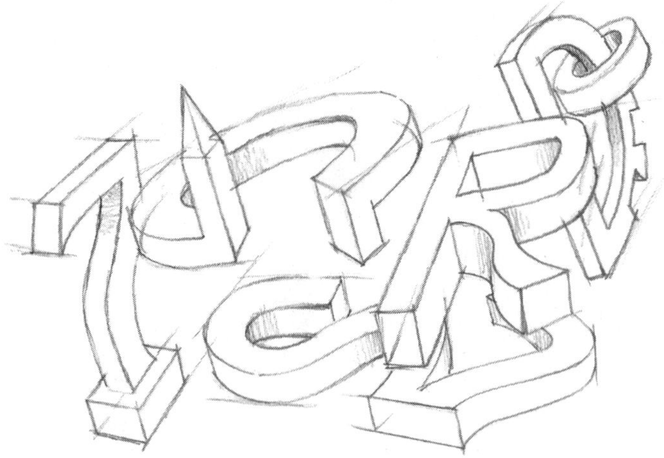

Figure 8.3

sections on perspective and structure in Chapter Four. With no subject in front of you to reveal its perspective and basic structural nature, you need to apply both these concepts to the view of the form that you are drawing, in order to show it more nearly as you imagined it.

2. A second category of relatively simple forms we are all familiar with is numbers and letters. Selecting several numbers or letters and drawing them in different positions, and making some of them more complex, as in Figure 8.3, will help you to "see" and control forms that appear on the screen of your imagination. That such forms hold the potential for serious creative activity is seen in Figure 8.4, where the artist, having selected a light source, dramatically illuminates these flowing letters.
3. Another exercise for developing your ability to create envisioned images is to use as your subject a photograph of something that interests you, and draw it as it might look from a somewhat different view. For example, your photograph may show a front view of a seated figure, positioned more or less at your eye-level. Your drawing may then show what the subject would look like from a worm's eye-view, from a view somewhat to the left or right of the photograph's front view, or from a view looking down on the subject. Of course, perspective will play an important part in figuring out what you would see from these different angles. But so too will your ability to see a form in one position and, in your mind's eye, turn it to another one. Piranesi's vision of an ancient port (Figure 8.5), complex as it is, comes down to an arrangement of

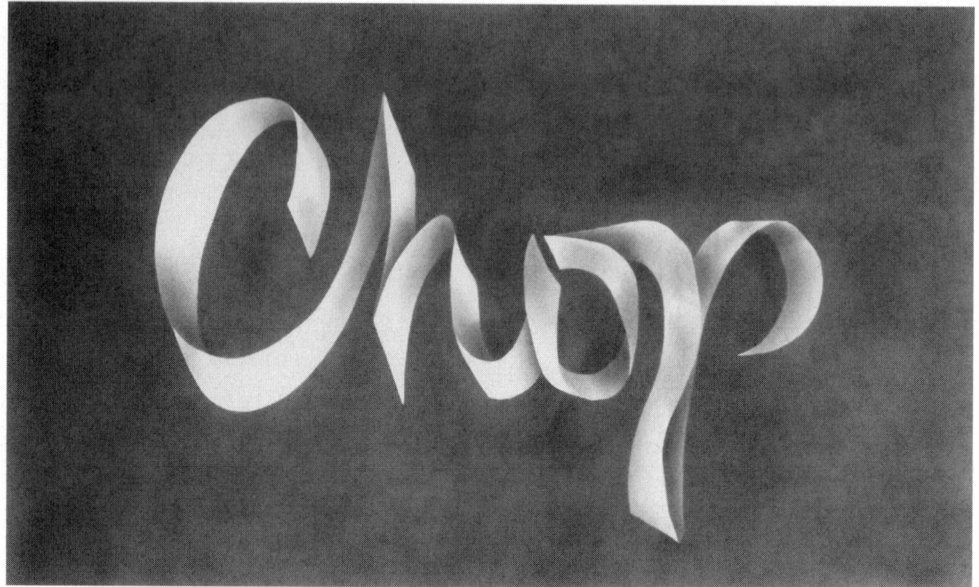

Figure 8.4 Edward Ruscha (American, born 1937). *Chop*, 1967. Graphite/paper, $13\frac{1}{4} \times 21\frac{7}{8}$ inches. *Source:* Collection of the Modern Art Museum of Fort Worth. Gift of the Junior League of Fort Worth.

forms that are basically blocks, pyramids, and cylinders, turned in various ways. Remembering that all forms can be reduced to simpler, more geometric ones helps to reposition them, as your imagination requires (Figure 8.6).

Sometimes, too, an imaginative work is stimulated by an existing work or a photograph, and altered according to the artist's purposes, as in Figure 8.7, where the artist probably started by studying a likeness of Queen Victoria and let his imagination carry him further. But note that the insects would almost certainly have been studied from nature before or during the drawing's development.

The ability to invent simple geometric forms and to expand upon them, as in Figures 8.2, 8.3, and 8.6, is the mainstay in bringing to the page the forms you envision, in terms that viewers will comprehend. This is so even when the forms created show purposeful distortions, exaggerations, and omissions. Although an observed subject may have stimulated the artist, Braque's *Musical Forms* (Figure 8.8), shows planes and forms that are fragmented, simplified, and reshaped in ways that reflect the artist's imagination. But it is the artist's understanding of the basic volumetric nature of these forms that enable him to restate the subject, in this case,

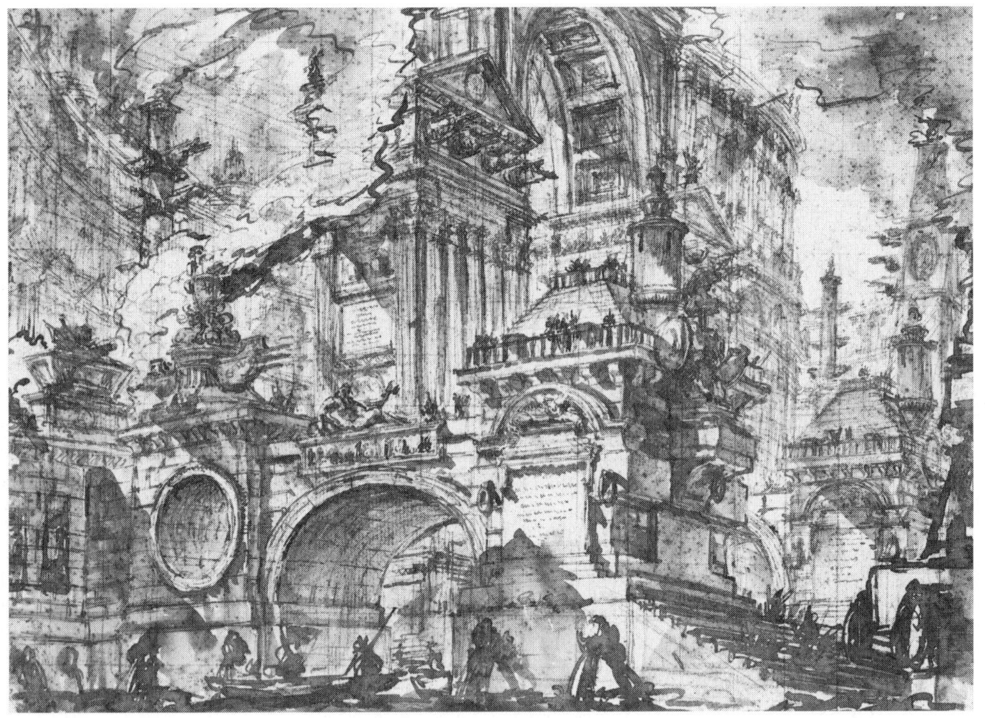

Figure 8.5 Giovanni Battista Piranesi (Italian, 1720–1778). *An Ancient Port*, 1749–1750. Red and black chalk and brown and reddish wash, squared in black chalk. Courtesy of the J. Paul Getty Museum, Los Angeles.

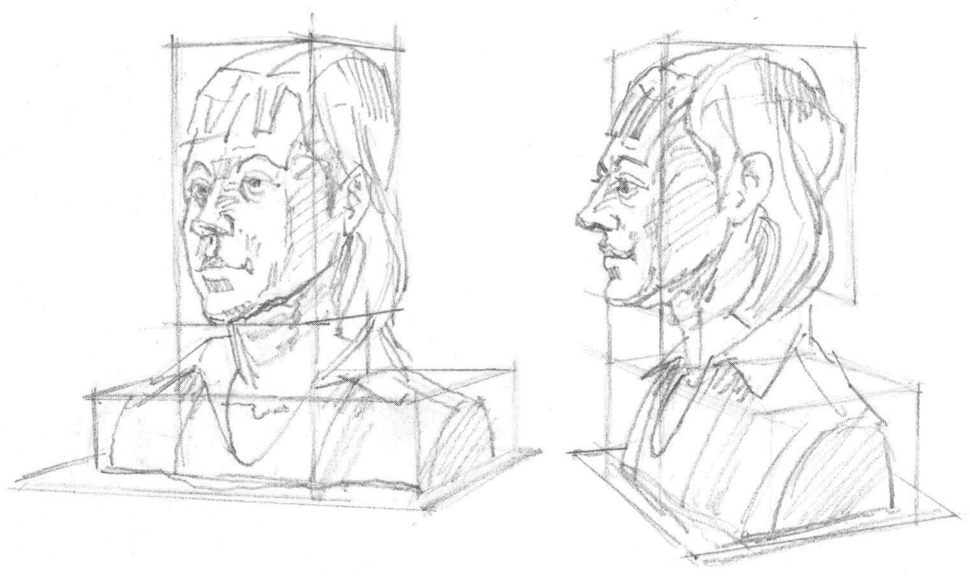

Figure 8.6

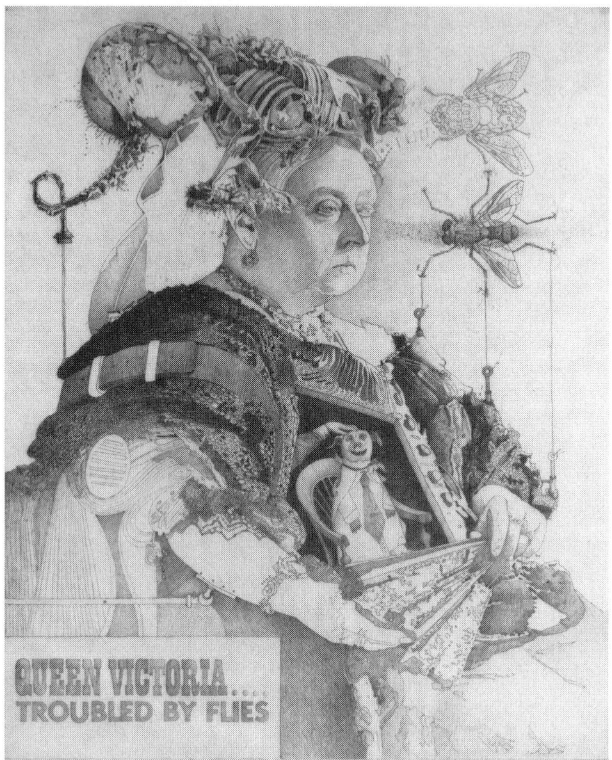

Figure 8.7 Dennis Corrigan, *Queen Victoria Troubled by Flies*, 1972. Cronaflex, 13 × $10\frac{1}{2}$ inches (33 × 27 cm.) Courtesy of the artist.

according to the tenets of Cubism, which, among other things, favor interpenetrating forms, ambiguous spatial effects, and an emphasis on shape and texture.

For some artists the stimulus to draw can be almost entirely provided by an envisioned arrangement of unrecognizable forms, as in Figure 8.9. Although there are a few vague references to human form, it appears to be the roller-coaster arrangement of these forms (many of them close to pure geometric solids) that holds the artist's attention. The motive for the expressive meaning in Gorky's drawing is found more in the moving action of the forms than in their identity.

That the action in a subject's arrangement can hold more importance than its subject does, whether imagined or observed, is seen in Diebenkorn's *Still Life/ Cigarette Butts* (Figure 8.10). Although probably drawn in the presence of the subject, Diebenkorn, like Gorky, is more attracted to the moving actions of the subject's components than to their identity. Against a background of dark and light-toned rectangles the artist sets off a picture-enveloping whirlpool of objects that carries some

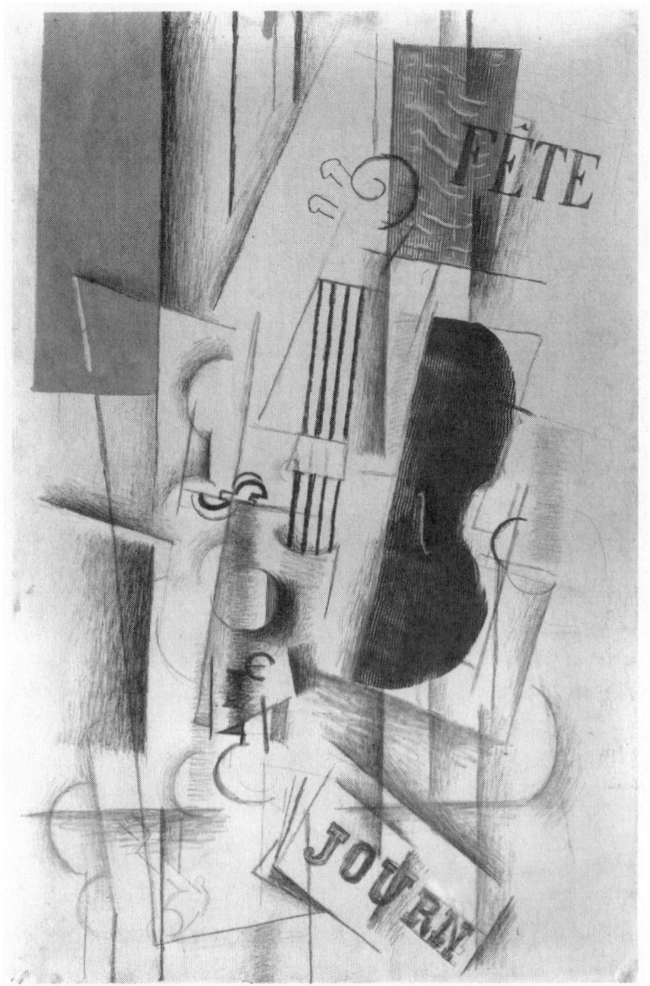

Figure 8.8 Georges Braque (French, 1882–1963). *Violin and Newspaper*, c. 1912–13. Graphite, coal, and oil on canvas, 36 × 23$\frac{1}{2}$ inches (91.5 × 59.7 cm.). *Source:* Philadelphia Museum of Art: The Louise and Walter Arensberg Collection, 1950. © 2005 Artists Rights Society (ARS), New York/ADAGP, Paris.

of these large rectangles along with it. A second theme consists of small circles (dishes, eyeglasses, cups) that create a kind of beat—of pulsations—as they, too, are caught up in the revolving movement. The artist's imagination has transformed some studio paraphernalia into an appealing compositional and expressive event.

Earlier it was noted that the skills and processes of drawing a subject from your imagination are similar to those of drawing an observed subject. Artists activate

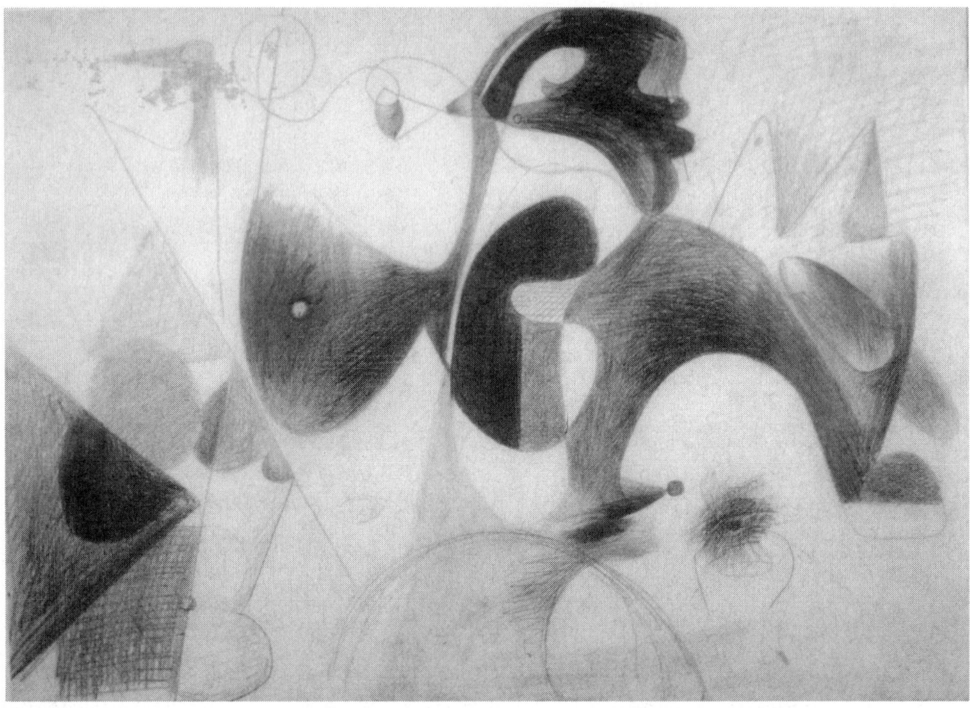

Figure 8.9 Arshile Gorky (American, b. Armenia 1904–1948). *Untitled*, 1930. Pencil on paper, 19 × 25 inches. Courtesy Stephens, Inc. © 2005 Estate of Arshile Gorky/Artists Rights Society (ARS), New York.

> ***The better you are able to analyze and take command of the forms you want . . . the less dependent you will be on the "raw material" of what observed subjects offer.***

both kinds of imagery by directed energies, tensions, visual and physical weight, handling, and the rest. And, as the envisioned drawings in this chapter and the observed drawings throughout this book demonstrate, they all try to present the image in a compositionally integrated and balanced state. To do less is to lessen a drawing's visual and expressive clarity.

The main thrust of this book has been to explore the challenges, options, and tactics of drawing in an objective mode with the subject physically present. But examining how to proceed when the subject is in the mind's eye also supports the book's theme in an important way. The more you are able to invent forms that show their structural condition clearly, the less likely you will be to unselectively record

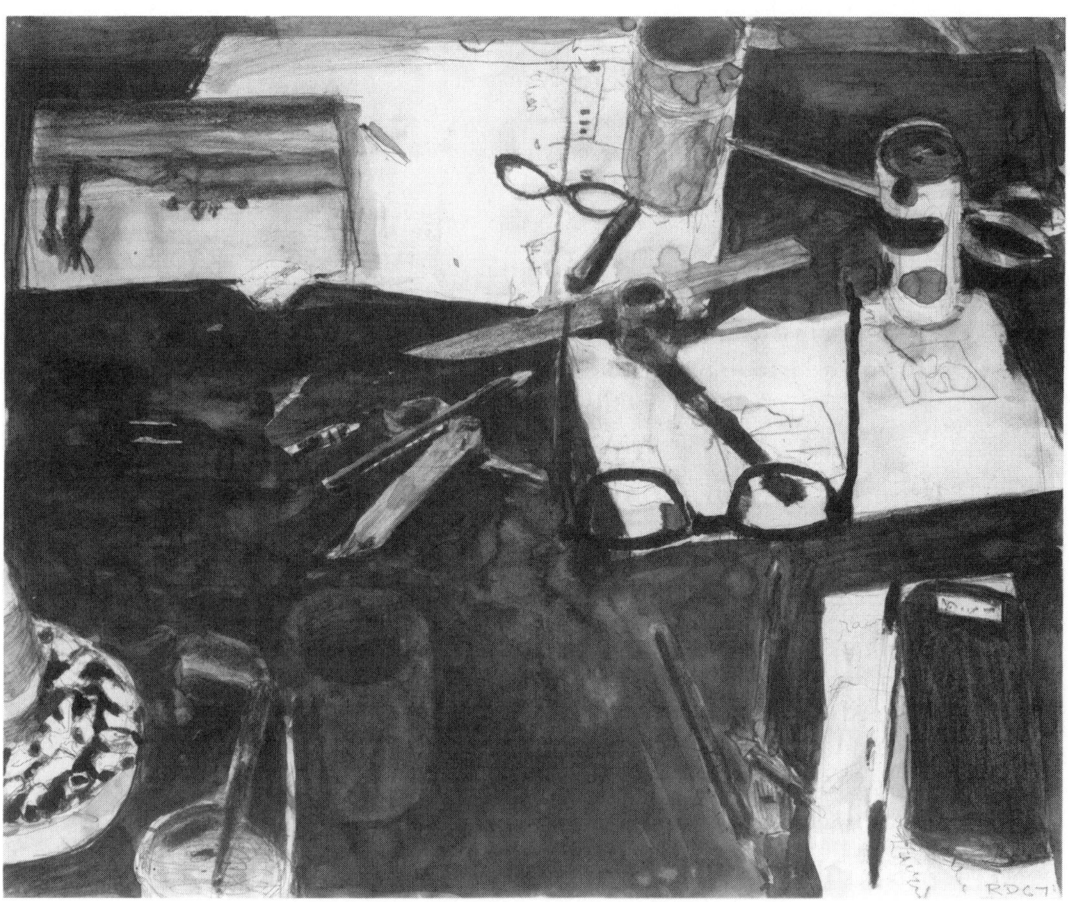

Figure 8.10 Richard Diebenkorn (American, 1972–1993), *Still Life: Cigarette Butts and Glasses*, 1967. Ink, conte crayon, charcoal, and ball point pen on wove paper, $13\frac{15}{16} \times 16\frac{3}{4}$ inches. *Source:* National Gallery of Art, Washington, D.C. Gift of Mr. And Mrs. Richard Diebenkor, in Honor of the 50th Anniversary of the National Gallery of Art. Image © 2004 Board of Trustees, National Gallery of Art, Washington.

unimportant surface details and unhelpful accidental effects of lighting on a subject before you. The better you are able to analyze and take command of the forms you want, and draw them in the way you want them to appear, the less dependent you will be on the "raw material" of what observed subjects offer. To draw what is before you in a compelling way is not usually a process of unselectively copying a subject's surfaces and details as you find them. It is allowing your informed inquiries, choices, purposes, and feelings to form images that live.

Things to Think About

1. What determines how clearly you will see the images on the screen of your imagination?
2. What might you need to research if you wanted to make a drawing of an early, prehistoric "missing link" to modern humans?
3. What might you need to research if you wanted to make a drawing of melting shoes and hats?
4. Can you envision a three-quarter front view of a male head, simplified into planes and geometric forms? Can you then draw what you "see" in your mind's eye?
5. If you were to draw the interior of a room you can recall (even vaguely), how would you go about establishing the view and the drawing's composition?

Critique Considerations

1. Do your envisioned drawings lack the volumetric and spatial clarity of your drawings made from observation? If so, it usually means you need to make more preparatory sketches that investigate the structural essentials of the desired forms *and* of the field of space they occupy. It also helps to check the perspective of the forms to more clearly establish their positions in space as well as their relative sizes (see "Blocking and Perspective Fundamentals," Chapter Four).
2. Are the forms in your envisioned (tonal) drawings illuminated by the same source? Does the light seem to strike from several sources? Is the light helpful in explaining the forms' surface structure? It is useful to come to a decision about the lighting before you begin the drawing.
3. Do the forms of your envisioned subjects seem stiff or lacking in rhythmic or gestural underpinnings? Too often, drawings made from imagination are begun by bypassing a gestural phase altogether and fixing instead on the rendering of parts in a sequential manner, a procedure that invites rigidity, errors in proportion, and an absence of unity in the resulting image. Try to begin an envisioned drawing by first searching for the large moving actions, as in Figure 8.1.

9

The Materials of Drawing

The tools and materials with which we draw play an active role in our drawing that influences the images we make. Each tool, medium, and surface has its own character, strengths, and limitations, and these traits combine in various ways to affect not only the way our drawings appear but also the way we see our subject.

For example, if you make three drawings of the same subject, using pen and ink for the first, charcoal for the second, and brush and ink for the third, the drawings will differ according to the strengths and limitations of each medium. With pen and ink you may find the subject's contour and calligraphic possibilities appealing, but its textures and tones less so. But, using charcoal, the subject's textures and tones may be the very things that attract your interest. And, with brush and ink, it may be the subject's planes and the light falling on them that you will want to emphasize (Figure 9.1). All of these conditions exist in the subject, but the medium plays a part in deciding which of them you will bring to our attention in a drawing.

The following is a survey of the most frequently used drawing media, tools, surfaces, and materials, with suggestions on how they may be used to better serve your creative needs. A word of caution: some media and materials contain toxic ingredients. You need to carefully read the manufacturer's cautionary labels

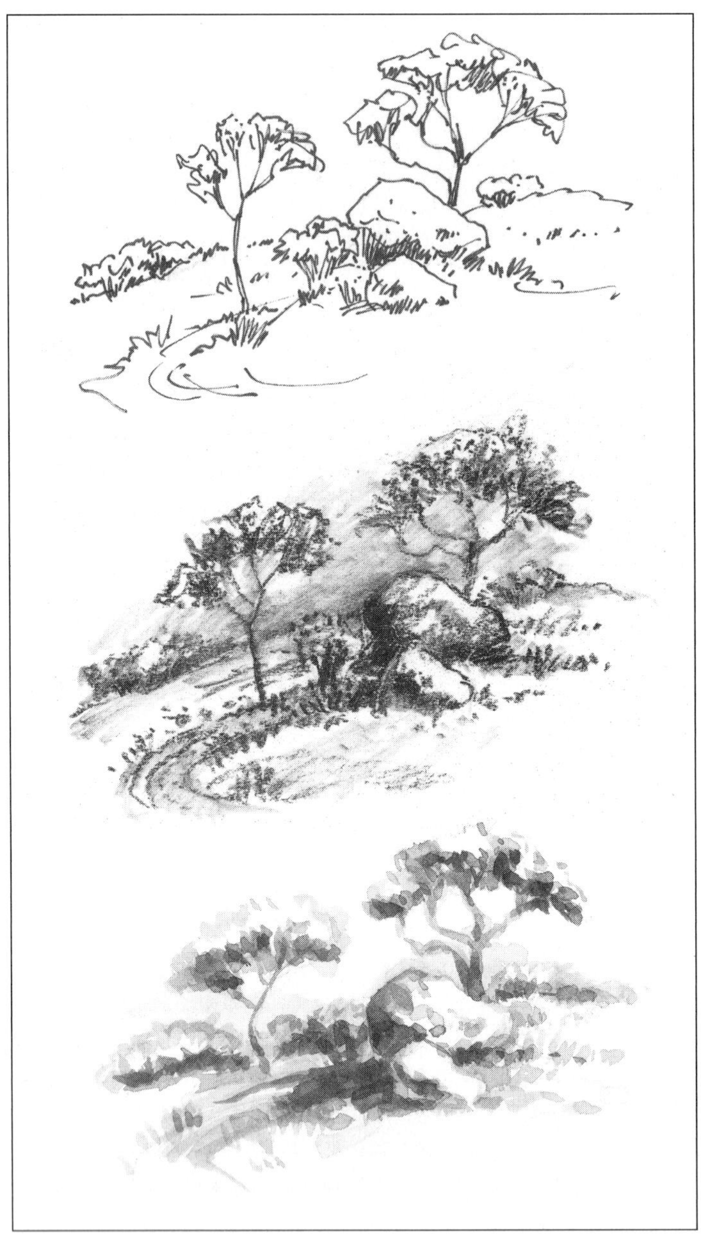

Figure 9.1

regarding the materials used in paints and solvents: follow all directions, work in well-ventilated rooms, and avoid ingesting anything by inhalation or through open cuts.*

*For additional information on health and safety practices, see Monona Rossol, *The Artist's Complete Health and Safety Guide*, 2d ed. (New York: Allworth Press, 1994).

DRY MEDIA

The term *dry*, as used here, defines all those abrasive media such as chalks, pencils, and crayons that are applied by rubbing across a roughened surface, filing away minute particles that lodge among the hills and valleys of the drawing surface.

Vine Charcoal

Among the oldest media known, vine charcoal remains one of the most versatile and popular mediums in use by students and professionals alike. Usually made from 6-inch lengths of willow, beech, vine, or basswood twigs, and varying in thickness from $\frac{1}{4}$ inch to $\frac{1}{2}$ inch, vine charcoal is simply carbonized wood. It is usually available in three or four degrees of hardness, from "very soft" to "hard." Vine charcoal's versatility in producing delicate or strong visual effects make it a desirable medium, especially as it contains no adhesive agent, or *binder*, which makes erasures difficult, and can be easily dusted away. But for this reason completed vine charcoal drawings must be sprayed with a protective layer of *workable fixative*, a weak solution of shellac or lacquer that holds the charcoal particles to the drawing surface.

Fixative is available in aerosol spray cans or in bottles. In bottle form it can be applied by a hand held mouth blower, available in most well-stocked art supply stores. Workable fixative not only isolates the charcoal particles already drawn, it also enables the user to add additional layers of vine charcoal (or some other media) to a drawing.

Although vine charcoal's rugged character and ease of application make it more suited to drawings of a bold and spontaneous nature than to works of delicacy and precision, it has a long history of use in the art academies of the West for just such extended "academic" tonal studies. Vine charcoal is applied either by close hatchings or by turning a short length of charcoal on its side to produce broad strokes (Figure 9.2).

Vine charcoal can be blended with a rolled up paper stomp called a tortillon, available at most art supply stores. It can also be blended by using a small piece of cloth, chamois, or even facial tissue. The kneaded eraser (see "Erasers," this chapter) is also useful for such operations and, if shaped to a point, can be used for picking out small, light tones or lines.

Charcoal holders enable the user to draw at a greater distance from a work and to utilize small fragments of charcoal. Charcoal powder, available in most art supply stores can be easily made by pulverizing vine charcoal, and is applied by rubbing on with a tortillon, chamois, or cloth. Charcoal sticks can be sharpened to a point with a fine-grained sandpaper.

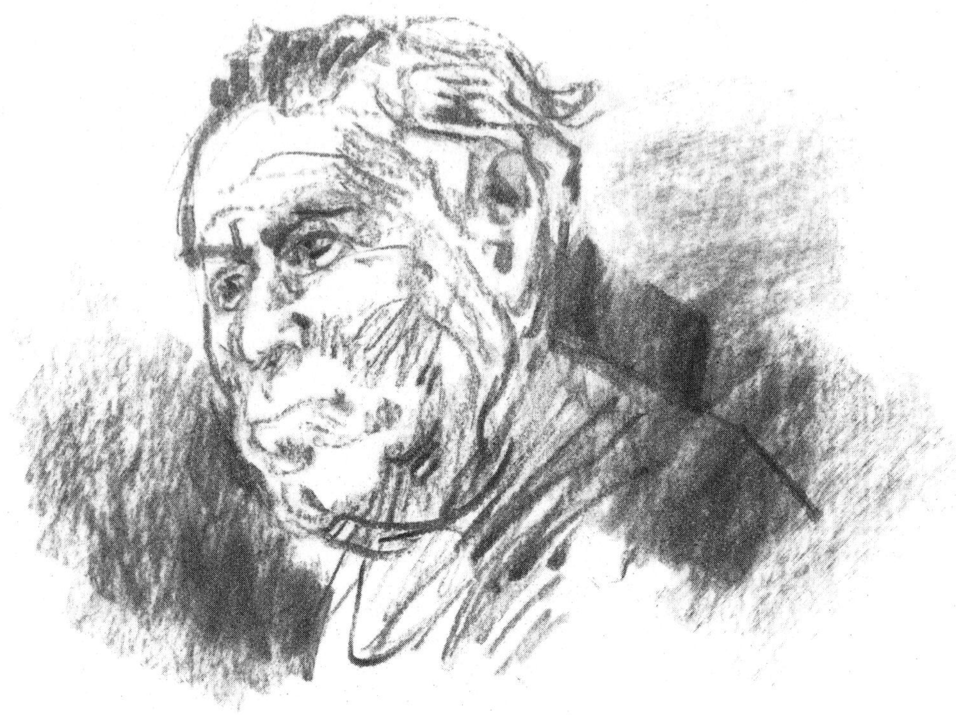

Figure 9.2

Vine charcoal takes well to any drawing surface with at least a moderate grain or "tooth," but adheres poorly to smooth surfaces. It is compatible with all members of the charcoal or chalk families and is often used in combination with other dry or wet mediums. Because it is easily brushed away or fixed, vine charcoal has been used for centuries to make the preliminary drawings that underlie many paintings.

Compressed Charcoal

Made of pulverized carbon (charcoal) and a binding agent, compressed charcoal produces an even wider range of values than vine charcoal, and is less easily erased or blended. It is available in either round or square-sided sticks and in pencil form in several degrees of hardness.

Compressed charcoal is ideal for gesture drawing and for drawings of a large and bold kind, and is often used for its great tonal range and rugged line quality. However, extended studies in this medium, especially in pencil form, are not uncommon.

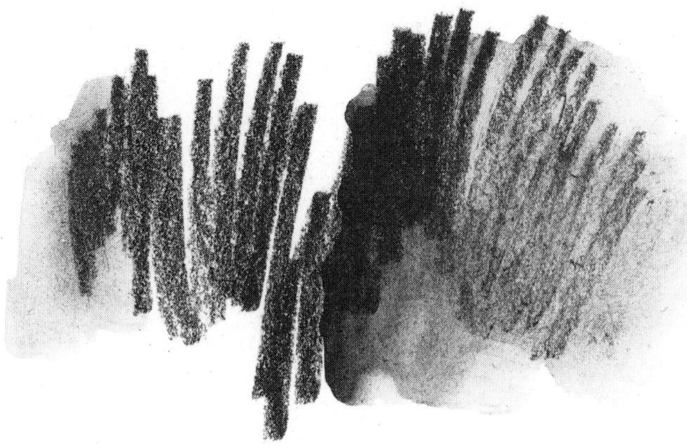

Figure 9.3

Compressed charcoal intermixes well with vine charcoal and other types of chalks and is sometimes used over wet mediums. Being somewhat soluble, it can be brushed over with water, or other fluids to produce various textural effects (Figure 9.3).

Graphite

> ***Despite graphite's versatility and ease of erasure, its freshness . . . that is, its pleasant texture and look of spontaneity . . . is fragile and easily lost.***

Erroneously called a "lead" pencil because of the use in antiquity of various metallic styluses, of which lead and lead alloy metals were very popular, graphite pencils are among the most favored drawing mediums for art students and artists alike. Graphite pencils come in a range of some twenty degrees of hardness. The hardest pencils range from the moderately hard 1H to the extremely hard 9H. The latter is capable of only thin gray lines. The soft pencils range from the moderately soft 1B to the velvety soft and dark 8B. Graphite pencils designated H, F, and HB are of subtly differing degrees of hardness that fall between the H and B categories.

Graphite sticks and blocks are manufactured in far fewer degrees of hardness, and mainly in the softer designations. Of these, 2B, 4B, and 6B are the most readily found in art stores. Graphite powder, sometimes available, is easily made by pulverizing "leads" or sticks of graphite of the desired degree. Some artists use

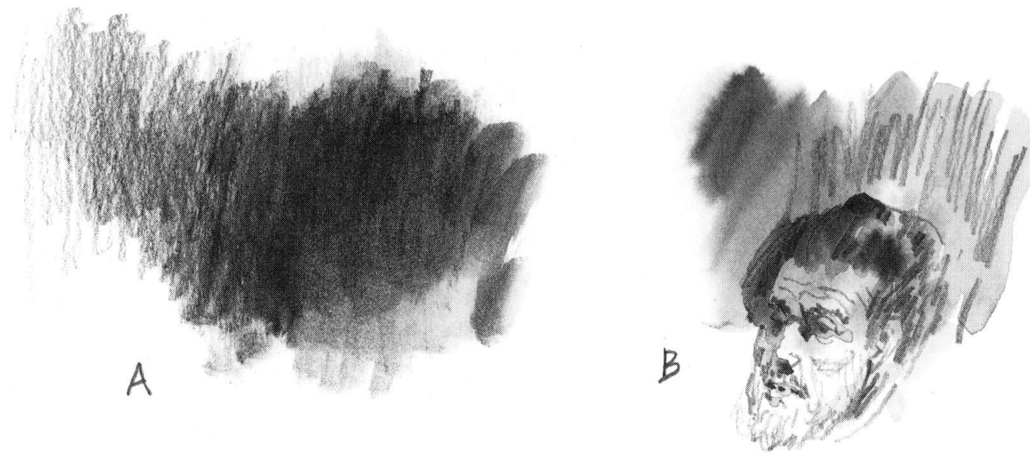

Figure 9.4

turpentine, mineral spirits, or rubbing alcohol as solvents for graphite, which imparts a metallic character to this medium (Figure 9.4A). Thin graphite leads in a variety of hard and soft degrees are available for use in mechanical writing pencils, as are thicker leads, for use in specially designed artist's lead holders.

Despite graphite's versatility and ease of erasure, its freshness—that is, its pleasant texture and look of spontaneity—is fragile and easily lost. Extensive blending, erasing, smudging and reworking causes graphite drawings to take on a shiny and worn look. Seasoned artists seldom employ such reworking of the surface, preferring instead the texture and freshness of massed lines and broad strokes. Graphite is sometimes used in mixed media combinations, including those that employ fluid media such as ink, watercolor, or oil (Figure 9.4B).

Chalks, Pastels, and Crayons

The term *chalk* has come to be freely applied to a variety of dry drawing media that includes compressed charcoal, pastel, and conte crayon. Among artists, the term generally refers to any of the black, brown, or reddish drawing media made of dry pigment and nonfatty binders, or to the natural chalks used by earlier artists. The term *pastel* defines chalks containing high-grade and usually permanent pigments that are manufactured in an extensive range of pure hues and in several shades and tints of each hue.

Pastels are made in cylindrical or square-sided sticks or in pencil form. Their soft, rich texture and spectrumlike color intensity give them a painterly look and brilliance when applied in layers of densely placed strokes. Pastel pencils are harder than their stick counterparts and are often used in smaller works or when a high degree of exactitude is desired.

Pastels cannot be mixed in the manner of paint but must be optically "mixed" by hatchings and layers of color that collectively produce the desired hue, value, and intensity. Therefore, a minimum set should include some forty or fifty sticks selected from the over 600 hues, tints, and shades available. Unlike some fluid media, pastel does not undergo any color change after it is applied. If pastel works are protected by framing under glass they can remain unchanged indefinitely.

Another medium, sitting astride the categories of pastel and crayon is conte crayon. While similar to pastel, it possesses a slightly greasy texture. A longstanding favorite among artists, conte crayon is highly regarded for its versatility. Its effects range from the most delicate to the boldest of strokes and tones, making it an excellent tool for quick, rugged drawings as well as for more refined and precise studies.

Black conte crayons come in three degrees of hardness: HB (hard), B (medium), and 2B (soft). There are also four variations of the earth-red color known as sanguine, a dark brown tone called bistre, and a number of other colors, including white. Conte crayon pencils are also available. Like compressed charcoal, conte crayon is difficult to erase, although light lines and tones yield to vigorous rubbing with a firm drawing eraser. When brushed over with water or turpentine, the strokes dissolve readily, producing strongly toned washes.

Another kind of colored drawing stick, using a waxy or oil based binder is the oil pastel stick. Craypas, Pentel, and Grumbacher are a few brand names. The term *pastel* can be confusing here, as this crayonlike medium cannot be mixed with true pastel. Available in a wide range of colors, these oil sticks readily dissolve in turpentine or mineral spirits to produce tints, color mixtures, and washes. More nearly a painting than a drawing medium, these soft-textured oil sticks are excellent for works of a bold or sketchy nature, but are less suited to sustained or precise techniques.

The wax-based media available for drawing range from the familiar crayons of childhood to more sophisticated and often light-fast materials in both pencil and stick form. Drawings made with any of the wax-based media do not require protection by applying fixative. This being so, they are well suited for sketchbook drawing. But like works in pastel or chalk, they cannot be cleaned and should be properly stored or framed.

Several brands of colored wax-based pencils, such as Derwent, Faber Castell, Prismacolor, and Verithin, offer pencils in a wide range of colors. Some manufacturers market a watercolor version of such pencils that enable the user to produce tints and washes by adding water to the colored pencil strokes.

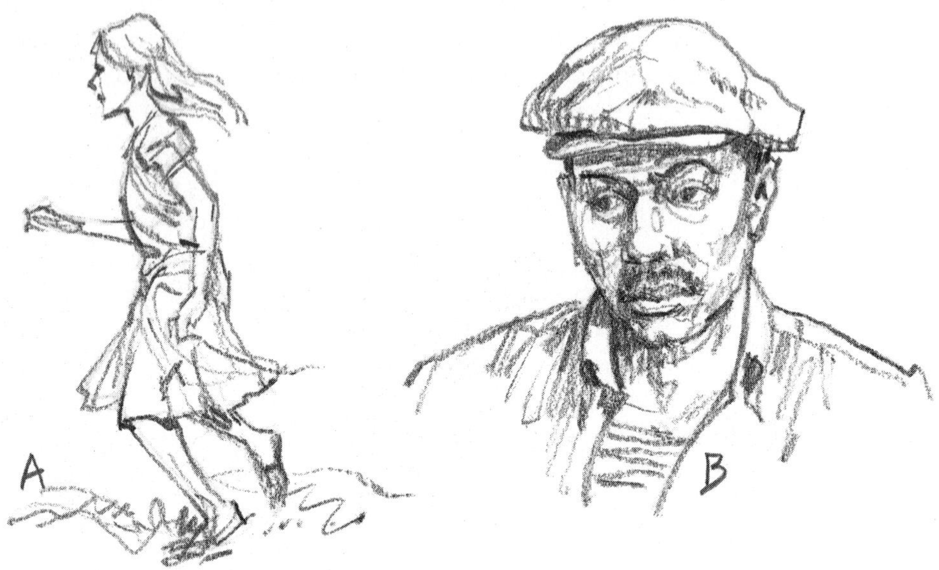

Figure 9.5

Being wax-based, such pencils or sticks seem to glide across the surface with less resistance than any other dry medium, often giving a more calligraphic richness and fluency to spontaneous drawings (Figure 9.5A), and a special elegance to more fully realized ones (Figure 9.5B). Although complete erasures of bold strokes are impossible, very light lines and tones can be almost entirely erased, and working from light tones to darker ones is a wise tactic for such media.

One group of fatty-based materials developed for use in the graphic process of lithography has always been popular among many artists. Black lithography crayons and pencils come in several degrees of hardness, but are as a group more greasy and handle more broadly than other wax-based media. A black, wax-based lithography ink called tusche is also available. All are soluble in turpentine or mineral spirits.

WET MEDIA

The terms *wet* or *fluid*, as used here, define all paints and inks requiring a solvent such as water, turpentine, or mineral spirits to be used, and tools such as pens or brushes, to be applied to a surface. The effort required to apply lines and tones with any of the fluid media is far less than when using dry media, which, as we have seen, produce marks by the friction of abrasive action. The relative absence of resistance when applying wet media is sometimes a problem for the beginner, who may find it difficult to control the easy flow and immediacy of the pen or brush. While chalks and pencils may need to be urged on toward an energetic handling, pens and brushes may need to be restrained from "runaway behavior."

Inks

All inks are a combination of liquid or dry pigment, a binding agent that holds the pigment in suspension, and water. Water-soluble inks use a water-soluble binder such as animal-skin glue, and waterproof inks use a binder such as shellac, which does not dissolve in water. *India ink*, a long-standing favorite among artists, is a dense and waterproof black ink that produces the deepest black tones, but cannot be used in fountain pens, where its density and drying properties are serious drawbacks. However, a number of black inks recently developed provide about the same deep blacks, but have the advantage of being usable in fountain pens. Even so, the fountain pens must be periodically cleaned and the ink prevented from drying.

Inks are available in a wide range of permanent and impermanent colors, including white. Users should check a manufacturer's catalog to see whether a particular ink is light-fast or not. Some brands of ink, such as Pelikan, offer a variety of permanent colored inks. The several colored inks used in ballpoint and fiber point pens are light-fast, but are usually available only in cartridge replacements, not in bottles.

One of the oldest inks is the Oriental *sumi* ink, made of carbon, a water-soluble binder, and water, and shaped into blocks. When the ink block is rubbed on a slate inkstone containing a small amount of water, either an ink paste or ink liquid is produced, depending on the ratio of ink to water.* Today, sumi ink is also available in paste or liquid form. It is a deep black ink that produces excellent washes of tone when diluted with water.

Earlier drawing inks, such as *sepia*, a rich brown ink, originally made of the inky substance from the sacs of cuttlefish, and *bistre*, a yellow-brown ink once made of fireplace soot, are now artificially made. Some artists mix various colored inks together to achieve colors of ink otherwise unavailable.

Most inks, and especially permanent ones, because of solids and some binders, will form dried ink deposits on pen points and brushes. On pen points, also called nibs, these deposits should be carefully scraped away from time to time, using a penknife, or by immersing the nibs in commercially prepared pen-cleaning solutions. For brushes, prevention is preferable to treatment, and at the end of a drawing session, brushes must be thoroughly washed with soap and warm water.

*To make a similar black ink, see, James Watrous, *The Craft of Old Master Drawings* (Madison: University of Wisconsin Press, 1957), p. 86. This excellent book also provides readers with formulas for making chalks and crayons, as well as other inks.

Other Wet Media

Although every fluid medium, including oil paint, has been used for drawing, more typically artists have turned to water-based media such as tempera, gouache, acrylic, and watercolor. Of these, watercolor has been and continues to be the most popular. Watercolor washes often underlie drawings developed further by dry media such as graphite or charcoal. It is best applied with soft-hair brushes to any heavyweight paper with a moderate to rough tooth. Because of watercolor's transparent nature it is generally used by working from the lighter to the darker values.

All other water-based media should also be applied to a heavyweight surface with either soft-hair brushes or with the stiffer, bristle brushes. Working from lighter to darker values is optional. With the exception of acrylic paints, the colors of all water-based media will darken slightly upon drying.

Gouache paint is an opaque medium, but can also be applied in transparent washes. It is sometimes combined with watercolor, especially when changes in color or value are required, or to paint light-toned details over darker watercolor washes. Some manufacturers offer an acrylic-based gouache that is extremely opaque but is less suited to dry brush painting, which is a method of applying thin layers of paint in a way that shows the tracks of individual brush hairs (Figure 9.6).

All water-based paints are intermixable, except for mixing ink and acrylic, which results in a wrinkled and beaded paint surface. In most mixed media using watercolor or ink, these media are usually used first, with other (often dry) media applied later in a work's development. This has to do with ink and watercolor being absorbed into the paper rather than sitting upon it and creating their own "terrain,"

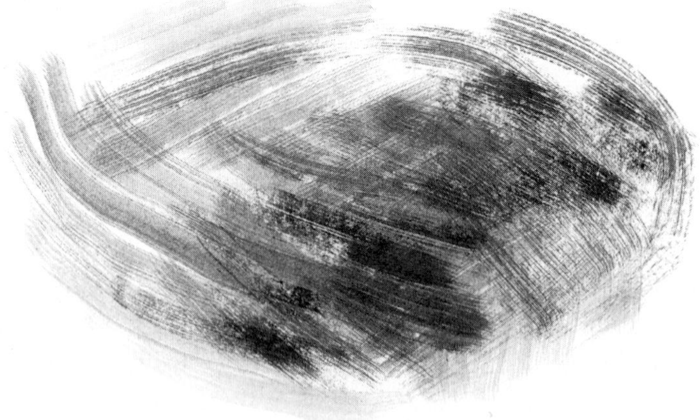

Figure 9.6

which makes it more difficult for other media to be applied in a controlled way. However, there are too many variables in such combinations to cite rules or procedures, and users must rely on trial and error to find those combinations (or treatments of a single medium) that best suit their interests.

Oil, tempera, and acrylic paints are less often used in drawing, perhaps because of the natural tendency to use these media in ways that produce pronounced impastos, that is, thick deposits of paint, a characteristic that many artists find foreign to most approaches to drawing. But these paints are all capable of interesting effects when used in thinner layers or for washes of color. Oil paint requires a surface that has been prepared to receive this medium. On paper, board, or canvas, a thin layer of acrylic gesso, or any of a number of other agents that isolate the surface from the deteriorating effects of oil is necessary.

PENS AND BRUSHES

The designation *pen and ink* is sometimes applied to drawings made with tools other than, or in addition to, the modern steel pen or the reed and quill pens used by the old (and some contemporary) masters. Any pointed tool can serve as a pen. A twig, the sharpened end of a brush handle, an eyedropper or cocktail stirrer, or indeed any object that can be dipped in ink to produce marks can be used for various linear and textural effects. Although the wide assortment of pens available today meets virtually every drawing need, it is instructive to explore these more unorthodox means of applying ink. Here, however, we will concentrate on the three basic types of pen: the traditional dip pen, the fountain pen, and the ballpoint and fiber point pen.

Today, the mainstay of dip pens is the steel pen point. Although examples of steel pen drawing date back to the Renaissance, it wasn't until the early 1800s, when their uniform manufacture ensured the availability of particular types and styles, that steel pens came into popular use. The wide selection available today ranges from flexible to rigid pens producing barely visible thin lines to those producing lines over $\frac{1}{4}$-inch wide. The many types of pen points and the individual needs of the user make it impossible to recommend specific ones. Most artists favor a flexible, rather than a rigid pen, which is capable of producing thin lines with little pressure, and broader lines with increased pressure (Figure 9.7).

On rough-grained paper the steel pen point is likely to make its own flat "road," thereby losing some of the tactile benefits of the interplay between the tool and the drawing surface, and it is more prone to spatter ink by becoming snagged on fibers of an uneven paper surface. However, on smooth papers, and when fine lines or close hatchings are required, the steel pen's free-flowing and incisive character exceeds those of the reed or quill pen.

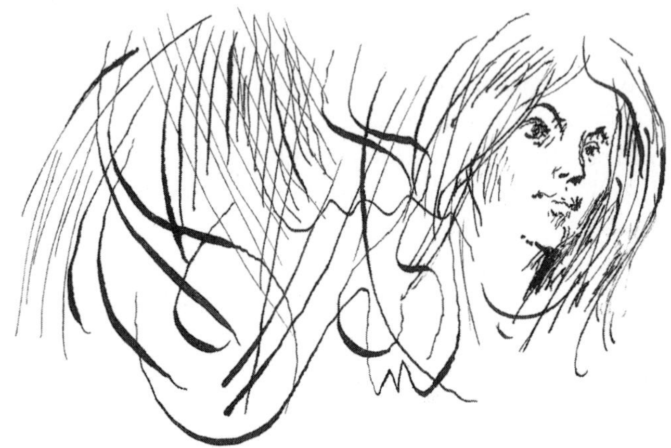

Figure 9.7

The reed pen is among the oldest drawing instruments used with ink. Found along some river banks and marshes, the hollow, tubular reeds are dried, cut to a comfortable length, and sharpened to a point at one or both ends. Bamboo reed pens are commonly available in art supply stores.

The reed's wood-like, absorbent point wears down quickly and needs to be re-sharpened often. Users soon learn to shape the point so it that best suits their needs. The reed pen differs from all other kinds in that some of the ink is taken up into its spongy walls through capillary action. Once the dipped pen has run dry, increased pressure forces out this "reserve" of ink in the form of light, chalklike lines (Figure 9.8).

The quill pen, made from the heavier pinion feathers of the goose, crow, or swan, requires very little pressure in use. The tubular, hornlike wall of the quill, being thinner and lighter than that of the reed, allows a finer and more flexible point to be cut. The quill pen responds to the slightest inflections of the hand and can produce both fine and broad lines by changes in the pressure of the stroke. Unlike the steel pen, both the reed and quill pens take well to rough-toothed papers. Not usually available in art supply stores, usable quills are sometimes found in novelty store or butcher shops.

Fountain Pens

There are two basic types of fountain pens. One features the traditional type of (usually) flexible nib that provides a variety of line widths. The other type is a tubular, styluslike nib that produces an unchanging line width. The latter pen, sometimes used for technical or mechanical drawing purposes, imparts an etching-like quality not easily attained by other kinds of pens. Both types of pens are usually designed to take

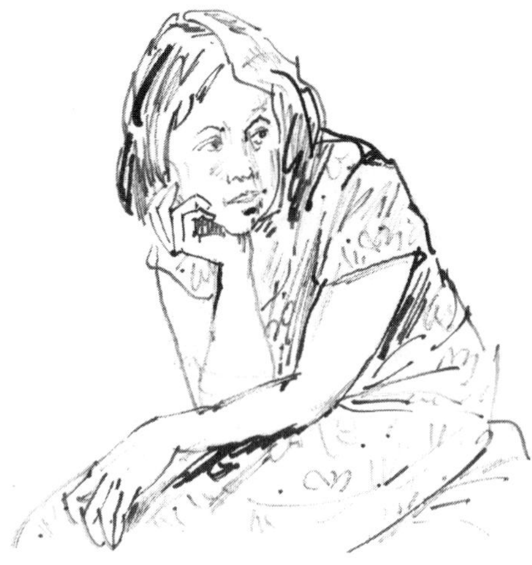

Figure 9.8

an assortment of threaded screw-on or clip on nibs, allowing the user to change nibs when necessary, a feature that greatly expands the use of these instruments.

Most fountain pens designed for artists' use require a water-soluble ink (see "Inks," this chapter). If these instruments are thoroughly washed every few weeks by flushing the ink chambers with warm, soapy water, followed by clear water, they are relatively trouble free and give good service. Although fountain pens designed to use the dense and waterproof India inks are available, the drying properties of this ink make such pens prone to clogging unless frequently used and cleaned. Two advantages of the fountain pen are the generous supply of ink it holds, and the ease with which it can be carried about. Its main disadvantage is the clogging that occurs when the pen is left filled and unused for long periods of time.

Ballpoint and Fiber Pens

These two types of pens are serviceable additions to the many drawing tools available to the artist. The limited line variation of both and, in the case of the ballpoint pen, the relatively weak tone of the black (or other colored) ink are regarded as disadvantages by some artists. Others welcome the almost invisible thiness of the (fine) ballpoint's lines that permit the user to gradually build up "clouds" of subtle cross-hatchings with a delicacy impossible to achieve with other types of pens. The effortless gliding of the ballpoint pen, especially on a smooth surface, tends to promote a flowing and rhythmic line use, and works well in executing intricate details.

The (usually nylon) fiber pens, even those claimed to produce very fine lines, cannot match the line delicacy of the ballpoint (or many other pens). This type of pen is better employed for quick sketches, where its bolder line and easy flow are advantageous traits. Fiber pens take well to many kinds of papers.

Brushes

There are two basic types of artist's brushes: the long-handle, stiff, coarse-hair bristle brush, generally made of hog bristle, but also made from somewhat less stiff nylon "hairs"; and the long or short-handle, soft-hair brush, made of sable, squirrel, camel, or other animal furs. Both types of brush come in several shapes, and each shape is available in a wide selection of sizes.

Bristle brushes are seldom used with watercolor or ink. They are at their best with oil paint, where the stiff bristles can hold, apply, and plow through thick, heavy paint. Although some artists use natural bristle brushes for acrylic painting, many prefer the nylon "bristle" brushes, which give good service with this medium.

There are several classifications of bristle and nylon brushes, determined by shape:

1. *Flats:* square-ended brushes, available in some eighteen to twenty sizes.
2. *Brights:* square-ended brushes, identical to flats except for being somewhat shorter in length, available in some eighteen to twenty sizes.
3. *Filberts:* slightly more full-bodied than flats or brights, and rounded at their end, available in twelve sizes.
4. *Rounds:* round bodies and pointed at the tip, available in twelve sizes.

Soft-haired brushes are available in the same shapes and sizes as bristle or nylon brushes, but they are usually referred to as round, flat, or oval brushes. Sizes commonly range from the tiny 000, used for minute details, to size 12, almost $\frac{1}{2}$-inch wide. Some manufacturers offer short-handle brushes in even larger sizes.

There are a few other shapes and types of brushes occasionally used in drawing. One is the *fan* brush, so-called because the brush hairs spread open, suggesting the shape of a fan. It is available in both bristle and soft-hair, and, while it is often used to delicately blend colors together, it can be put to other uses. Another type of brush, usually made of Siberian squirrel hair, and available in twelve or more sizes, is the *mop*, a term that reflects its very soft nature and capacity to hold ink or paint. In the larger sizes it is often used to lay in large washes of ink or paint. Oriental soft-hair brushes, sometimes called *bamboo brushes*, are excellent for producing a wide variety of strokes.

The most versatile and popular brush for most drawing and watercolor painting purposes is the round red sable. Its remarkable spring and maneuverability, and its ability to retain a sharp point over years of use when well cared for (see "Care of Brushes," this chapter) are legendary. Handmade of hair from the tail of the red sable, these rather expensive brushes are more economical and efficient in the long run. Less expensive brushes may not perform as well or last as long.

A serviceable runner-up to the genuine red sable brush is the synthetic "sable" brush, made in the same variety of styles and sizes. They too, have excellent spring and durability. Winsor & Newton's Sceptre brushes and Robert Simmons's white sable brushes are two of the several excellent brands of synthetic brushes available in most art supply stores.

Care of Brushes To keep your brushes in good condition, a few precautions must be observed. As soon as possible after use, wash them thoroughly with any household soap and warm water. Each brush should be washed until the lather shows no trace of color. Bristle brushes can be rotated in the palm of the hand to work the soap up higher in the bristles. The hairs of both bristle and soft-hair brushes should be squeezed to force the lather near the hair base forward toward the tip. After washing, shape the brush and allow it to dry completely before placing it in a closed storage container. If oil paint has been used, the brush should first be cleaned with turpentine or mineral spirits, followed by washing with soap and water. Many artists, as a safety precaution, prefer to wear disposable gloves for these operations.

Never allow paint or ink of any kind to dry on the brush. Doing so destroys the spring and shape of any brush, even if subsequent washing has removed as much paint or ink as possible. Avoid washing any brush in hot water, or allowing them to soak in warm water for an extended time. This will dissolve the glue or resin used to hold the brush hairs in place, causing them to loosen and fall out of the brush *ferrule*, the metal sleeve at the neck of the brush, into which the hairs are deeply set. Never leave brushes resting on their tips in the container that holds the water or, when using oil paint, the turpentine or other suitable solvent. Doing so will soon destroy the brush's shape. Soft-hair brushes are especially vulnerable to this kind of mistreatment.

Using a Brush and Wet Media

Although ink or watercolor is sometimes applied with the bristle brush, it is the soft-hair brush that is most frequently used. Some artists employ both kinds of brush in the same drawing to achieve various textural effects. Ink or paint is applied either full strength or diluted to various degrees with water or with an appropriate thinner. Typically, brush and ink or brush and watercolor drawings show fresh, spontaneous, and resolute characteristics, but extremely exact works are also possible in these versatile mediums. In fact, naturalist artists and medical illustrators often select brush and ink (or brush and watercolor) as their preferred medium. The point on a round sable brush, even a good-sized one, can produce a line even finer than is possible with the finest dip or fountain pen.

Brush drawing with either ink or watercolor works well on most surfaces, but it is best to avoid very absorbent or very smooth papers at first, as they create unnecessary obstacles for the beginner. A paper with a modest tooth and heavy enough not to buckle and ripple will serve best for most purposes (see "Papers," this chapter). Wet media shrink paper fibers, and thin papers will buckle and wrinkle to an extent that interferes with completing a work or getting it to lie flat.

Some artists will begin a brush drawing by first roughing in a sparse and schematic underdrawing in graphite, but care must be taken to restrict such an underdrawing to light, diagrammatic notations that indicate shape generalities which establish the location and scale of a subject's parts. An underdrawing that goes on to develop contours, details, and even values will seriously restrict the free and assertive use of the brush.

Bigger brushes are usually more beneficial to both conception and handling.

Some student brush drawings show an overcautious handling due to an overworked underdrawing. Or an overcautions drawing may be the result of unfamiliarity with the medium or using a brush that is too small. Bigger brushes are usually more beneficial to both conception and handling. A good guideline to follow is that if your brush feels comfortable for what you are drawing (or painting), it is probably too small. You are likely to find stronger, more economical and satisfying solutions if the brush you are using feels a little large for the task at hand.

PAPERS

A paper's physical composition, weight, absorbency, and surface texture always influence the development and "look" of a particular drawing. The way a medium or a drawing instrument takes to a paper not only determines how an artist proceeds with a work but may even affect the outcome.

The great number of types and weights of paper and their differing surface characteristics may make it difficult to decide what kinds of paper to use for various mediums and purposes. The following may help you to decide which papers to try.

Drawing papers are classified according to surface character and weight.

A paper's surface character is determined by its tooth (smooth, medium, rough) and its absorbency (very little, moderate, high); its weight is determined by the weight of 500 sheets, called a *ream*, and measuring approximately 20 by 28 inches. Newsprint, for example, the paper used in the publication of newspapers, is a 30- to 35-pound smooth-surfaced, highly absorbent paper. Some of the heavier papers, used primarily for watercolor or gouache painting, weigh up to 400 pounds per ream and are about as rigid as cardboard.

Most *permanent* drawing papers, that is, papers that will not deteriorate or turn yellow for a great many years, are made of linen or cotton rag pulp. These rag papers are durable and tough-surfaced, capable of withstanding repeated erasures and other kinds of rough handling. They are also among the most expensive papers. Other drawing papers, made of some combination of wood and rag pulp, treated by some preservatives, and of a more or less neutral pH (an absence of destructive acids) are usually permanent, fairly durable, and less expensive. The least permanent papers are made of wood pulp, untreated by any preservative agents, and are relatively inexpensive. These are the papers most commonly used by students for the many drawings generated by the study of art, from gesture drawings and throwaway experimental sketches to more finished works. The great number of drawings every student produces makes it nearly impossible to buy the more expensive papers. However, as your studies advance, and especially as you turn to works of a more extended and demanding kind, it is important to investigate some of the better papers. The differences in their response to your needs and their plainly superior surfaces and durability are soon apparent, and worth the difference in price.

Watercolor Papers

Heavyweight rag watercolor papers (suitable for all water-based media) are further classified into three types:

1. **Cold-pressed:** Of a moderate tooth and absorbency, this paper accepts all wet (or dry) media well. Its appealing surface makes it the most popular type of watercolor paper in use.
2. **Hot-pressed:** A hard-surfaced, smooth paper, often the paper of choice for some artists using watercolor or pen, brush, and ink. It is the least absorbent of the three types.
3. **Rough:** A moderately absorbent paper with a very pronounced tooth, it is the least suited to precise pen and ink drawing. It gives watercolor and ink washes a brilliance and sparkle less evident with the other surfaces.

These three papers are sold in single sheets, in blocks, and in rolls. In sheets, the most common size is 22 by 30 inches, although sheets as large as 40 by 60 inches are often available. In rolls, 60 inches by 10 yards is the usual size. Watercolor blocks come in sizes as small as 7 by 10 inches to 18 by 24 inches. The papers in blocks are glued on all four edges to flatten any buckling that may occur when water-based media are used. Papers lighter than 140 pounds will buckle even with a restricted use of water. Single sheets of a 200-pound weight or more will not buckle under most circumstances.

Other Papers

Newsprint: Inexpensive and impermanent, it is the mainstay in many art schools for quick drawings and other kinds of studies with all dry media except graphite, which produces faint, gray lines when using the harder leads. Of a light-toned, warm gray color, newsprint comes in both smooth and rough textures. Being lightweight and highly absorbent, it is unsuited to wet media. Newsprint paper begins to yellow within a few months and to deteriorate within a few years. Despite its limited life span, newsprint is ideal for the countless quick sketches, experiments, and preliminary studies you need to make but may not wish to keep.

Charcoal: A 60 to 70 pound paper of moderate absorbency, its pronounced tooth is designed to file away charcoal and pastel particles. Most charcoal papers contain some rag content, and the best grades are 100 percent rag. It is available in a variety of colors as well as white. It takes all dry media well but is too thin for use with fluid media.

Bond: A generic term for a number of white, moderately grained drawing papers. There are too many variations in their manufacture to cite consistent characteristics. As a rule, such general drawing papers take all dry media well but are too thin for wet media. Bond papers range from impermanent types to papers containing a substantial rag content. In weight they may be as light as 50 pounds or as much as 80 pounds.

Bristol and Vellum: Heavyweight papers, they are often made of wood pulp, but the best have an all-rag content. Sold in variously sized pads, these are serviceable papers for virtually all media. Of postcard weight, bristol and vellum papers are usually treated with preservatives and chemically whitened. Of the two, bristol has a smoother surface, ideal for pen and ink drawing. Vellum has a slightly grained surface that takes the softer dry media better than bristol. Tough and versatile, these papers give you good service for the money.

Tracing: A semitransparent, nonabsorbent, lightweight paper, it has a subtle tooth, much admired by many artists. Finished drawings done on tracing paper must be backed by a sheet of white or colored paper because of its transparency. This paper is also used to develop further a preliminary drawing placed beneath it, enabling the artist to see the preliminary work and make desired changes easily on the tracing paper overlay. This procedure, a commonplace among illustrators, should be used more often than it is by students, who could then more effectively and quickly adjust and develop anatomy, perspective, composition, and other matters in their drawing studies. The better tracing papers are permanent and some are of moderate weight.

There are, of course, many other types of paper suitable for drawing. Many of the printmaking papers used in the making of etchings and lithographs are frequently employed for drawing purposes. As a group, most are permanent and sturdy papers, have a moderate tooth, and are fairly to very absorbent, making them less suited to wet media. Oriental "rice" papers are even more absorbent than Western printmaking papers, but many are designed for use with sumi ink and brush in a technique that takes advantage of the delicate spread of ink washes that such papers afford. Even common kraft paper, the brown paper used for wrapping packages, provides a pleasant tooth and tone for some drawing purposes, and is fairly durable. Recently developed papers made of spun glass, plastic, and recycled paper products all serve various drawing interests and, like the more traditional papers described above, should be investigated.

ADDITIONAL DRAWING MATERIALS

Workable fixative, discussed earlier, is often necessary for the preservation of works done in most dry media, and the tortillon, is a useful tool in some drawing techniques. Here, brief reference to other standard tools and equipment will serve as a checklist for outfitting the art student's drawing kit.

Sketchbooks

Sometimes overlooked, the sketchbook is basic to an artist's research and development. As noted in the Preface, the sketchbook is a kind of private visual journal where experiments, ideas, observations, and both visual and written notations can be more privately collected for further use. It also serves as a portable studio, enabling you to explore and record subjects far from the studio and classroom. Sketchbooks are commonly available in sizes ranging from the tiny 4 by 6-inch book that can be easily carried about in your pocket, to books as large as 11 by 14 inches. Papers vary from those designed for dry media to those intended for watercolor painting. The most convenient (and popular) sketchbook sizes are $8\frac{1}{2}$ by 11 inches and 9 by 12 inches. Typically, sketchbook papers are of a moderate weight (between 40 and 80 pounds) and designed to accept any dry medium as well as pen, brush, and ink, although these papers are usually too lightweight for more than a slight treatment with washes of ink or other wet media.

Sometimes overlooked, the sketchbook is basic to an artist's research and development.

One convenient type of "sketchbook" enables the user to fill a pair of sturdy, spring-operated covers with any combination of papers cut to the size of the covers. Called *spring binders*, such paper holders are available in several sizes in some stationary stores. In addition to the advantage of a sketchbook you can fill with a variety of papers, the spring binder permits you to add and remove papers at will.

Erasers, often overused to adjust minor surface details at the expense of a drawing's freshness, are more than correcting tools—they are drawing instruments. Erasers can lighten or blend marks and produce various textures. When rubbed into dark-toned passages, they can create light or even white lines. The *kneaded eraser*, of a gray and pliant material, can be shaped to a point for picking out small light areas, or stretched to produce a large surface for removing or lightening large areas of graphite, charcoal, or pastel. Sometimes no rubbing is necessary with this eraser. It can simply be pressed onto an area you wish to make lighter and lifted up. It will carry away some of the pigment particles, producing a lighter tone. Repeating this procedure will lighten tones even further. An additional advantage of this useful tool is its soft composition, which will not damage a paper's surface. When the eraser's surface is soiled, it can be kneaded to produce a clean exterior. Among the most versatile erasers, it is especially well suited for use with vine charcoal, but is too pliant to entirely erase very dark marks in graphite or pastel.

These more "stubborn" marks require an eraser of a more dense and abrasive texture, such as the Pink Pearl eraser, similar to the eraser atop the common household pencil. The familiar Artgum eraser and the more recently developed vinyl erasers are also capable of removing graphite, compressed charcoal, and pastel.

Drawing boards in several sizes are available at art supply stores. Usually made of Masonite, all have clips for holding drawing sheets in place, and the larger boards have a cutout handle for easier carrying. Drawing boards can be easily made by cutting composition, Masonite, or plywood panels to the desired size, and then attaching the sheet with spring-operated clips.

When using a drawing board, place it as near to vertical as possible to reduce the likelihood of distortions in your drawing. When the drawing surface slopes away at a marked angle from your line of sight, every curve and angle drawn is seen in a slightly distorted way.

Ideally, drawing boards should be placed on an easel. In addition to seeing your drawing on a plane parallel with your subject, you are more likely to use your entire arm (and body) in the act of drawing, instead of the more pinched movements of the fingers that we associate with writing. Then, too, when drawing at an easel you are more likely to be positioned somewhat farther from your drawing, an important advantage in noting discrepancies in the work. Learning not to "crowd" your work is basic to good drawing, and drawing at an easel helps to develop this important discipline.

The purchase of a lightweight easel for drawing at home or out-of-doors need not be expensive. A simple metal or wooden sketching easel will do provided it is stable in construction and design. Tabletop easels are also available, and if space is a problem, many easels are designed to fold away into compact units.

No drawing kit would be complete without a mat knife or penknife for sharpening conte crayon, compressed charcoal, and pastel pencils. These materials often break in even the best pencil sharpeners. These knife-sharpened materials can be brought to a point by turning it on fine-grain sandpaper. Mat knives are also necessary for trimming paper and for cutting mats.

Finally, a pencil sharpener for graphite pencils; a roll of masking tape for attaching papers to boards or to create temporary borders for wash drawings; some brush and pencil containers made from empty coffee cans or plastic jars; a water container for use with fluid media; a small jar of white, opaque, water-based paint, for covering over unwanted lines or blots; a block of disposable palette sheets; and an art bin to store your materials in, will round out those basic items required for the study of drawing.

Glossary

Analytic (analyze, analysis): In drawing, to find in a subject facts pertaining to proportion, direction, shape, structure, organization, and dynamic phenomena.

Axis (axial, axes): The imaginary centerline of a volume; the centerline assumed to run in a volume's longest dimension is called the long axis; the centerline running at a right angle to the long axis is called the short axis.

Binder: The ingredient in a medium that holds the pigment particles in suspension (in wet media) or together (in dry media).

Calligraphy (calligraphic): Pertains to the character of drawn lines; most frequently applied to lines of an animated, often cursive nature.

Configuration: As used here, synonymous with silhouette; refers to a shape's two-dimensional nature.

Complementary colors: Colors located opposite one another on the color wheel; for example, red is the complement of green. Complementary colors always consist of one warm and one cool color.

Content: Pertaining to a drawing's narrative matter; the drawing's representational or storytelling aspects.

Contour: In drawing, the lines or edges that describe a form's shape with implications of mass.

Depiction (depict, depictive): Refers to a drawing's representational content; the act of producing a subject's objective appearance.

Direction (directional): The path the eye follows because of an alignment of elements on the picture plane or in a spatial field of depth, or because of a form's long axis.

Dynamics: In the visual arts, the sense of moving actions among elements and of tensions setting off energies and strivings for change, which figure prominently in a work's compositional and depictive nature.

Emotive: In drawing, to empathetically interpret a subject's dynamic and expressive potential; a drawing's capacity to convey the artist's feelings about the subject.

Experiential: As used here, the sensation of touching a subject's forms; of kinetic identity; to feelingly identify with a subject's character and dynamics.

Facets: (See *Planes*.)

Foreshortening (foreshortened): Defines a form's position in a spatial field where some of its surfaces are shortened in the direction of depth. All volumes show some surfaces shortened in this way, but the term is usually applied to forms or surfaces seen nearly on end.

Form: In the fine arts, this term usually refers to a work's overall visual nature, especially regarding the character of its dynamics. As used here, the term is also synonymous with volume, mass, and solid.

Geometric: Pertains to both shapes and volumes whose usually simple form structures are seldom seen in perfect form in nature, as for example, the circle, sphere, square, block, and cylinder. Artist understand geometric forms to underlie all the forms they see, as in the sphere that underlies an apple, or the wedge that underlies a foot.

Gesture (gestural): Refers to the basic arrangement of a subject's parts and to the directed actions sensed among them; a subject's underlying pattern of moving energies and essential form characteristics.

Grain: The surface texture or tooth of paper or other supports used for drawing.

Handling: As used here, pertaining to the nature of the artist's mark-making, from a deliberate and premeditated manner to an impulsive and urgent one.

Hatching (cross-hatching): A technique of modelling form and space in which ranks of parallel lines produce light or dark values depending on the density and width of such lines in a given area. In cross-hatching, such groups of parallel lines are drawn crossing over each other at different angles.

Hierarchy: As used here, the ranking of compositional themes in order of visual importance.

Intensity: In the visual arts, pertaining to a color's brilliance and saturation.

Intersection: As used here, pertains to the point at which two contours or edges meet.

Interspace: As used here, an enclosed area seen as background or as the part of a form adjacent to the part being drawn. For example, when drawing the shape of a doughnut, its hole is an interspace, but when drawing the shape of the hole, the doughnut is the intespace. The term also pertains to areas separating or surrounding forms. Used in this way, synonymous with the term *negative space*.

Light-fast: A color's ability to retain its hue, intensity, and value permanently.

Local tone: The actual value (or values) of a form or space; the inherent lightness or darkness of a form's parts aside from the effects of light upon it. For example, a canary is inherently light-toned, a raven, dark-toned.

Location: The proximity of forms or other elements to each other; the association of like or unlike elements according to their position on the picture plane or in a field of depth.

Mass: (See *Volume*.)

Medium (media): The dry or wet materials used by artists to produce drawings.

Model (modelling): In drawing, the process of creating the impression of volume and space by using value.

Monochromatic: Pertaining to the use of a single color in a drawing; any work executed in one color, but often showing variations of that color from light to dark values.

Negative space: (See *Interspace*.)

Optical: As used here, pertaining to what the eye actually perceives.

Organic: In the visual arts, pertaining to the shape and surface-structure of forms in nature, from an acorn to an elephant.

Physical weight: Refers to the actual weight of known objects.

Picture plane: The flat and bounded surface on which a visual work is executed. Artists consider the fact that a drawing's marks, existing on the surface of the support, are major compositional and expressive considerations, separate from the role of marks in creating the illusion of volume and spatial depth.

Planes (planar): In drawing, the flat or curved facets that define a form's surface-structure. For example, the six sides of a block are planes.

Positive shape: In the visual arts, an enclosed area representing the two-dimensional configuration of a volume.

Relate (relational): The act of seeing visual associations and contrasts among a subject's parts based on scale, value, direction, shape, structure, texture, location, and color.

Rhythm (rhythmic): In the visual arts, the recurrence of directed movements among a work's lines, values, shapes, colors, textures, or volumes.

Solvents: The thinning fluids used in wet media to thin paint or ink, to produce washes, or to clean painting utensils.

Space (spatial): In the visual arts, pertaining to intervals between boundaries and points on the picture plane (two-dimensional), and to areas possessing depth as well as length and breadth (three-dimensional).

Structural analysis: As used here, the investigation and interpretation of a form's surface-structure.

Surface-structure: Pertaining to the planes and turnings of a volume's surface.

Temperature: In the visual arts, pertaining to the warm or cool nature of colors.

Tension (tensional): Pertaining to elements or parts of a single element that appear to be striving to join, repel, or clash with each other, or to alter their location or shape. Elements engaged in a tensional confrontation suggest a charged field of energy between them. Often such elements seem to compete for supremacy.

Thinner: (See *Solvents.*)

Tooth: (See *Grain.*)

Two-dimensional: Pertaining to the visual conditions of the elements on the picture plane.

Three-dimensional: Pertaining to the visual conditions of volumes in a spatial field of depth.

Underdrawing: The initial sparse gestural or diagrammatic drawing notations intended as a guide to a drawing's subsequent development.

Visual weight: Pertaining to an element's or a form's power to attract the viewer's attention by eye appeal.

Volume: As used here, any three-dimensional form, regardless of identity, structure, or size: a green pea and a skyscraper are both volumes. Synonymous with the terms *mass* and *solid.*

Index

A

B

C

Index

I

J

K

L

M

N

O

Index

P

Q

R

S

T

U

V

W

Y